D1639541

# MODERN BUSINESS PRINCIPLES AND PRACTICE

*General Editors*

J. M. PARRISH, M.A. (Oxon.)

JOHN R. CROSSLAND, F.R.G.S.

ACTIVE SYMBOLS OF THE MODERN FACTORY

# MODERN BUSINESS
## PRINCIPLES AND PRACTICE

BUSINESS MANAGEMENT
ADVERTISING: SALESMANSHIP

*Advisory Editor*
SIR JOSIAH STAMP, G.C.B., D.Sc., LL.D., *Chairman of the London Midland & Scottish Railway, Director of the Bank of England.*

*Edited by*
STEPHEN CHAPMAN
M.A. (Cantab.)
*Barrister-at-Law*

ODHAMS PRESS LIMITED
LONG ACRE, LONDON, W.C.2

*Printed in Great Britain*

# INTRODUCTION

SIDE by side with the more spectacular and diverting branches of knowledge, this volume on Business may look a trifle drab. Indeed, you may keep this Sahara on the map of world wisdom for rare and reluctant fact-hunting only. Yet it has been planned both as a reference book and as a consecutive and logical survey of the entire field of industry, of the making, the buying and selling, the advertising, the transport, and the delivery of goods. Factory, shop and office, machinery and men, all have their place in this panorama.

The opening chapters deal with business in its broader and also in its personal aspects, the later with particular branches. Every chapter stands in its logical place; for modern business is like the moving assembly belt in a motor works; it has a continuous flow. First comes the planning of the business; next the erection of factory and plant; then the buying of the raw materials; their fabrication into finished goods; the costing of the job; the advertising and sale of the goods; their dispatch to Manchester or Mysore; the recording of the work and the sale of it at every stage; finally the striking of a balance, a profit or loss, on the transaction.

Every one of these processes may be performed eventually by one large concern in its central factory; or they may call on a score of factories and services and selling agencies situated in half-a-dozen counties or countries; or they may have been done by a small proprietor and a couple of assistants in a Lancashire shed. But before the transaction was completed most of the functions successfully described in the following chapters had been performed. Probably they were carried out more or less in the order in which these chapters follow one another.

By following the successive processes through, you will get a clear picture of the structure of modern business. You will see just where the interests of the various departments in a business may clash; yet how dependent each is on the efficiency of the others; how management secures the harmonious working of the all-too-intricate machine.

Incidentally you will be reading a serial romance by several hands, with a single hero, the business man, and two rabid villains, inefficiency and waste, who stalk sinister through the book from the first page to the last.

The reader will realise that not all the divisions of business offer an equal number of opportunities. One man with a couple of assistants may do all the buying for a firm employing fifty salesmen, and a thousand factory workers. Yet each has received treatment. The Editors have endeavoured to give a connected living picture of the organisation of commercial life, for a view of the whole is essential to the business man who would judge soundly on details. Each of the units in the pattern is seen through the eyes of one who spends his working hours in helping to arrange its elements in the best, the most efficient, form—or is analysed and explained by a specialist who is practised in presenting both the broad view and the essential detail.

### THE FAIR FIELD THAT COMMERCE OFFERS

In following the course of the business process, the reader may wonder just which branches offer the widest opportunity. From a recent inquiry, Dr. J. A. Bowie estimates that of the 18,250,000 people working for their living in this country, 3,000,000 are engaged in shop-keeping and merchanting, 1,500,000 in "personal services," 1,250,000 in transport, 1,250,000 in public utilities, like gas, electricity, and water services, 6,250,000 in productive industries.

For how many executives and managers are there openings to direct this vast army? Dr. Bowie believes that there are about one million suitable openings for the man or woman possessing a University degree in economics or commerce. The positions actually open probably amount to four per cent. in the year. There should, therefore, be openings for about 40,000 graduates a year. Yet the universities provide only a few hundred, and so the young men of ambition, but without a university degree, have probably something like 39,000 openings available to them. Every year business requires more trained executives, just as it requires more labour-saving machinery. It is hope that the present volume may fire many readers to train themselves for one of the executive positions in industry.

# CONTENTS

# THE NATURE AND SCOPE OF BUSINESS

*by STEPHEN CHAPMAN, M.A.(Cantab.), Barrister-at-Law.*

IN primitive times a man's existence depended solely on his own exertions. He tilled his land, and out of it he reaped the food to keep his body and soul together. He hunted in order to get his meat, and by a single operation provided himself with food to satisfy his physical cravings and with skin trousers to satisfy his psychological cravings. It may be that he garnered other things, too, in his forays; for example, a wife to help him with his tilling and to make his trousers more neatly than he could hope to do himself. In such a world there was no scope for the purely business man.

Times changed, however, and with advancing civilisation, particularly with the growth of city life, it became more difficult to satisfy even the simplest needs. Moreover, the needs themselves became more elaborate. It was therefore necessary to look elsewhere for the means to satisfy these needs, to turn to a neighbouring town which had perhaps more wine than it required for its own population, and ask if it could spare some. This meant giving something in return, and the one city had to produce something in excess of its own requirements in order to pay for goods bought from its neighbour. Naturally men began to specialise in this sort of thing, to make it their business to provide people with things they needed and did not possess, and to know where these things could be obtained. In short, men began to busy themselves about other peoples' affairs, and to realise what they needed more clearly than did the people they sought to serve. Thus arose the business man.

## BUSINESS EXISTS TO SATISFY HUMAN NEEDS

IN origin therefore the business man owed his existence to his ability to provide people with things which they needed and had not got. To-day it is exactly the same. Civilisation has developed, and conditions are far more complicated. Materials are collected from every corner of the world ; they pass through an enormous variety of industrial processes in order to be reduced to some practical form ; and by means of commerce the goods thus produced are conveyed all over the world into the homes of those who want them. But fundamentally, whether a strict severance is preserved, according to their various purposes, between industry on the one hand and commerce on the other, or whether the two are run together into a composite thing and called business, the basis is the same as it was in early times.

This basic principle is often expressed by saying that business aims at satisfying material needs. To some extent this is true in the strict sense of the words, but the word " material " needs further definition if this description is to be altogether true. A large part of business is concerned with providing the wherewithal to keep the body comfortable ; food to eat and wine to drink ; clothes which will keep it warm in winter without looking heavy and cumbersome and ugly, and clothes which will in summer be suitable to the warmer atmosphere ; furniture and frying-pans, shaving-cream and shooting-boots, emeralds and emery paper—things such as these provide material satisfaction in the sense that they are connected, immediately or remotely, with physical comfort and well-being.

It is somewhat different when it comes to buying a book. No one will question that, whatever may be said of writing books, publishing them is a business enterprise. The result is a material object which occupies room on a shelf, but the joy of reading is as far from a material pleasure as pleasure can be. Man cannot live on bread alone ; he has a spiritual nature which is every bit as imperious as his need of food. The business man recognises this, and produces books and gramophones and wireless sets accordingly.

### BUSINESS PROVIDES SERVICES AS WELL AS GOODS

NOR is it only material objects which the business man provides in order to satisfy these needs. When a person goes to a cinema, or takes out an insurance policy on his life, he receives nothing material in return for his money but a piece of paper. A cinema and an insurance company is none the less for that a business concern. What each of them provides cannot be classified as goods ; they are rather opportunities—an opportunity to see something which will give pleasure; an opportunity to save money and make provision for a wife and family after death. Generically such things can be termed services, and a very large amount of business enterprise is directed to supplying an enormous variety of such services. Hotels provide accommodation, railway companies provide means of getting from one place to another, shipping companies cater for health by means of holiday cruises—the examples are legion.

But health services are not provided by shipping companies alone. There are such people as doctors who have made human sickness their life's work, and have studied all the known means of preventing it from arising and of treating it when it has arisen. The doctor, too, like the shipping company, aims at satisfying a human need, and offers services for doing so. In his case the services are the experience he has gained from a thorough education in, and arduous application to, the study of the human body and its ways and its enemies. It often happens that a doctor can be of great assistance where a shipping company would be no use at all. Nor does he, any more than the shipping company, disdain payment for the services he renders. Nevertheless he is not a business man, and his work is called a profession, not a business.

### WHERE BUSINESS AND PROFESSION DIFFER

It is fruitful to analyse this distinction between a business and a profession a little more closely, because such an analysis throws further light on the nature of business. A doctor is an expert; he has studied one particular branch of human knowledge as deeply as his assiduity and his mental ability have allowed him. The business man, too, is an expert; he has specialised in one particular activity, which may be only one process among many that a particular article goes through, and he may be surprised and indignant if it is suggested that there is anything in connection with his subject which he does not know. It is not by terming either an expert that any proper distinction can be drawn. It is rather in the application of the expert knowledge that the true distinction lies.

The doctor's work is purely and essentially of a personal character. He comes into personal and intimate contact with his patient and uses the background of his expert knowledge in order to deal with the problems afforded by that patient's condition. He is interested in, and must apply himself for the moment solely to, the one particular instance to which his attention is drawn. He has no concern with things in a general way.

The business man on the other hand finds that his work is the direct opposite of this. The troubles of one particular individual do not concern him at all ; it is the mass of the population with which he has to deal. A human need begins to interest him only when he discovers that, so far from being confined to one particular instance, it is widespread and general. From that moment it enters into the realm of practical business ; it becomes a business proposition to find a means that will satisfy it. No business man would make buttons if there were only one person in the world who needed buttons, unless of course he needed them in fantastic numbers. A doctor will perform on one patient an operation which no doctor has ever performed before or is ever likely to perform again.

### PROFITS THAT JUSTIFY THE BUSINESS MAN'S EXISTENCE

It is then only when a need, be it material or be it spiritual, transcends the particular and attains the general that it comes within the scope of business at all. The reason for this is not far to seek ; it is purely and simply a matter of profits. The business man, like any other person, is anxious to eat and drink and satisfy his various other needs. Like any other person he can only do so in these days if he has money, and he seeks to earn his money by catering for the needs of other people and making a profit by doing so. The profit he earns is in fact the justification for his existence. If he finds it possible to make a profit out of what he is doing, that indicates to some extent that he is doing something worth while. If he is producing something which the general mass of people do not want, or will not buy at his price, he is being no use to anyone, least of all to himself, and he must turn his energies into more useful channels if he is to exist.

It may be that with good luck, coupled with good judgment, he finds that his profits are turning out favourably. Again that is to some extent an indication of his usefulness. Other people may also have done useful work, work maybe of far greater value than his, and have reaped nothing, or nothing comparable, in return. This, however, is no blame to the business man. He has chosen a job which will earn money from the public; that others cannot obtain such high payment in material form for their work is the inevitable, if distressing, concomitant of the work which they have chosen to do.

### BUSINESS CANNOT BE COMPARED WITH ART

It is profitable in this connection to consider for a moment the work of the artist, the classic example of work which seldom finds adequate material reward. To the artist it is the particular job in hand which is worth while; everything else is immaterial. What other people think or do, whether they appreciate his work or not, may arouse in him indignation and contempt; it cannot alter his fundamental attitude. All he can do is be true to himself. He has a soul and a conscience which to others is denied, and these he must follow wherever they lead him. Maybe he paints a picture and no one understands it, still less buys it. He continues to go as hungry as he was before, but he has fulfilled his mission in that he has regarded beauty as the supreme goal of his endeavour. His day will come.

It is good for the world that such beings exist; without them it would be a poor place indeed. It may be years, even centuries, before the true value of their work is realised, but when it is, the whole fabric of human thought and conduct may be altered. By comparison with their work business can be made to appear sordid and contemptible, a pandering to all the meaner instincts of humanity, blind to all the nobler values, intent only on reaping a handsome harvest of profits. Such a diatribe is not only unjust in the extreme, being based on a comparison which cannot fairly be drawn; it is also a dangerous boomerang for those who use it.

Every servant is worthy of his hire, the business man no less than the others. The public stipulates the quality it desires, and the business man sees that it gets it. It is his business to supply needs as they arise, and he must have the means to judge whether he is being of use in his service or whether he is not. His profits are his guide. It is unjust to compare him with an artist, who is the servant of no man, and never can be. It is humiliating for the whole of humanity when a great artist is left in hunger and poverty to die, but it affords no reason why a servant who is hired to do certain work, and does it well, should not be paid his wages.

### IS BUSINESS INHUMAN ?

AN association with profits is thus thrust upon business by circumstances beyond its control, and it is frequently inferred that of necessity this association carries contamination with it. It is said that business is fathered by ruthlessness out of unscrupulousness ; that in the efforts to drive a bargain the nature of the means adopted is entirely ignored, and dishonesty is connived at, provided the end is attained. It would be a ludicrous picture were it not so violent. The curious thing is that it should have ever commanded credence at all in a nation of shopkeepers.

It cannot be denied that there was a time when workers were brutally treated. In the early half of the nineteenth century labour was plentiful and cheap ; if one man failed to stand the pace, another could speedily be obtained. With heavy demands being made on the factories, and with a public that was relentless if it did not get what it wanted, the result was inevitable. Labour was driven at full pressure, and when it was worn out, as of course it soon was, it was simply cast aside. All human values were utterly ignored and human life was appallingly cheapened. Those days have passed away, although the traces they left behind have not by any means been effaced.

To-day things are very different. Labour is organised so powerfully that it commands an authoritative control of the situation. Public opinion is more sensitive, and has found expression in numberless Acts of Parliament designed to see that conditions are made as human for the workers as possible. Moreover, processes of manufacture are more complicated, and skilled labour is proportionately more valuable. The personnel of a business has thus acquired a new and profound importance. It has been realised that the best work is not obtained by sweating a worker ; to ensure his efficiency he must be well and carefully looked after. In short, personnel has attained the position of being regarded as the most valuable asset of a business.

### THE ILLUSION OF DISHONESTY IN BUSINESS

SIMILAR reasoning serves to dispel the illusion that business is dishonest. Competition is so intense that no business can afford to lose a good customer. But smartness and trickery, let alone dishonesty, as means of enticing a customer to buy have long since disappeared from the armory of business, if they ever existed there at all. Willy-nilly business cannot escape its destiny. It exists to serve the public, and by that canon alone can it be judged. Its reputation travels quickly and travels far, and dishonesty soon leads to loss of business. A customer who is disappointed, let alone deceived, takes his custom elsewhere, and probably carries others with him. No one nowadays is so dishonest as to pick his own pocket.

But it is perhaps by watching a person among his own associates that his moral standards are best observed. It is a test from which the business man emerges triumphant. In days of intense competition, when every business must either sink or swim, there is a grave temptation to use any means in order to win the public's favour. An opportunity may occur when this favour can be won at the cost of a little blood from a competitor, and it would be no cause for astonishment were such an opportunity taken. But the business man realises that, though it may be his chance to shed blood to-day, it may be his blood which will flow to-morrow.

### BUSINESS DEPENDS ON CONFIDENCE

It has long been the proud boast of the business man that his word is his bond. A vast amount of business is carried on by brokers of a variety of kinds; yet if reference is made to the reports of cases tried in the English Courts it will be found that there have been astonishingly few cases in which brokers have been concerned. Again, there are certain types of contracts which are enforceable at law only if they are in writing. Such contracts are made orally every day in every business in very large numbers, but it is a very rare thing for advantage to be taken of the legal technicalities. Business men realise that business could hardly be carried on at all if time had to be spent in putting such contracts into writing.

Business, in fact, is rooted on confidence. Once an element of suspicion is aroused, the speed which is so essential disappears, the machine begins to creak and jar, and the whole business world is thrown out of joint. In its own affairs each business must go its own way, and the ultimate criterion for everything has always been, "Does it pay?" The criterion which was successful at home was naturally tried abroad, and each individual business went out to meet its friends and rivals with the same idea in mind, so that it became enshrined as the supreme ethical standard of the business community.

# THE MANAGER AND HIS JOB

*by ROGER CHAPMAN, M.A. (Cantab.), Fellow of the Institute of Chartered Shipbrokers*

IT has been stated that a business man should have character, a capacity for organisation, willingness to accept responsibility, and an instinct for leadership. These qualities, useful to all business men, are essential for the business manager. We cannot, therefore, do better than divide his activities under these four heads, and deal with each one separately.

It is vitally important that a business manager should be above all things upright, honest, and fair. He should be an example to his staff and associates in this direction, and should always deal with others in business as he would expect them to deal with him. The character of a business or of an office will usually be determined by that of the manager, and all business men should aspire to have it said of them that their word is their bond. Character of this sort was the reason for the success of British business men in the building up of the present-day business world, and is rightly put first and foremost in the make-up of a good business man.

Every business depends very largely on organisation to increase efficiency and prevent waste. Good organisation, which results in departmentalising the work of the business, ensures that each employee is doing the work for which he or she is best suited, that each department is pulling its weight, and that the various separate units of the whole are co-operating effectively. Specialisation and delegation of authority are dependent on organisation, and these are the two main factors in the smooth running of the office machine.

Specialisation is necessary to ensure that each member of the office staff does the work for which he is best fitted, and that each one becomes a real expert at his particular work, which would not be possible if he were doing work of all sorts. Delegation of authority is absolutely vital if the business is to grow, as the amount of work one man can do is necessarily limited, and it is only by delegation that this can be increased

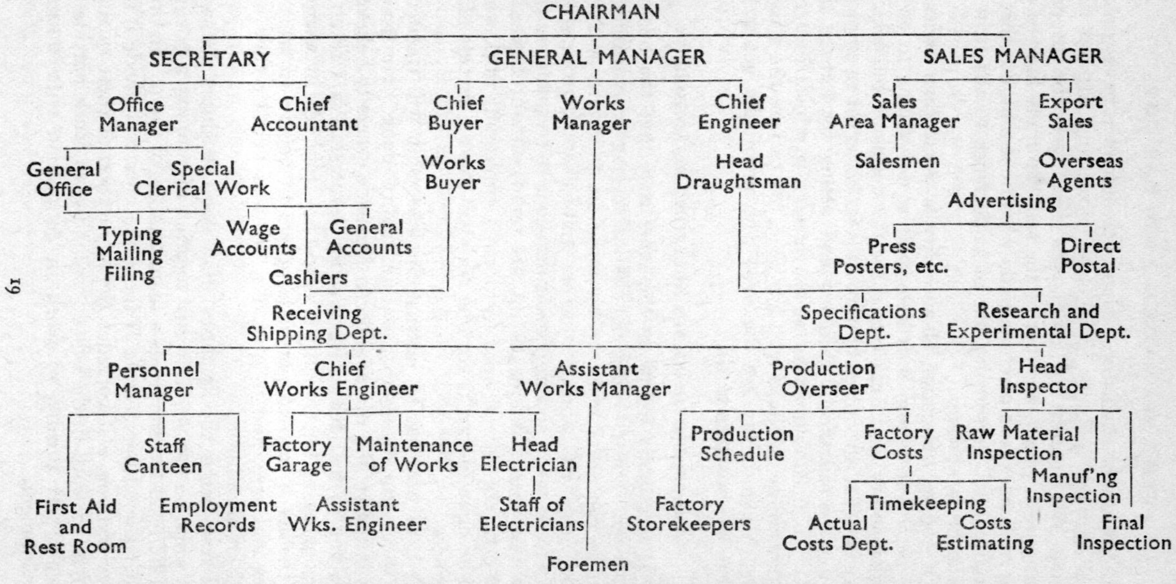

LINES OF CONTROL IN A TYPICAL MODERN MANUFACTURING BUSINESS

without loss of efficiency. Many business men have come to grief through inability to delegate work, and without delegation the interest of employees can never be properly maintained. Each member of the staff naturally likes to feel that he is not just a machine to do what he is told, but that his initiative and personality are of importance to the firm for which he is working.

Of course, delegation of authority is worse than useless if the person to whom it is delegated is not willing to accept responsibility, and unable to make the decisions and take the initiative that is required of him. It is far better for an employee to make a mistake by thinking and acting for himself than never to make a mistake at all through a refusal to accept responsibility. Those who are prepared to take the risks of accepting authority are the ones who eventually get to the top in the business world.

### MANAGEMENT INVOLVES ACCEPTING RESPONSIBILITY

IT is frequently found, in the same way, that the business manager himself does not like accepting responsibilities, that he can never make up his mind on important decisions, and is, in general, a procrastinator. In business there are always risks to be taken and important decisions to be made, and the business man who makes up his mind without hesitation, and does not put off until to-morrow unpleasant work which can be done to-day, is the one who will make a success of his business.

A man who has an instinct for leadership will frequently be successful owing to this one quality alone. He usually has initiative and drive, and can persuade others to believe in him and in his ideas. Instinct for leadership is a result of personality, and personality is a great key to success in business. It enables a man to persuade others to believe in what he does and says, and to give him business because they have faith in his abilities.

These being the qualities of a good business manager, the work he has to do in his vocation of running a business can be regarded simply as a manifestation of them. In order to get a good perspective of the subject we will divide it into three sections, and consider the application of these qualities —first, to work in the office ; secondly, to work outside the office ; and thirdly, to work in connection with business development.

## THE OFFICE: HUB OF THE BUSINESS MACHINE

THE management of a business in the office is the first task of any business man. The office has to be organised, staffed and maintained in such a way that it will run smoothly and efficiently, and with the minimum of day-to-day control. An office that will more or less run itself is a great boon to a business man, as it gives him time for thinking out new ideas, building up new business in different directions, or a larger business in the same line, visiting other people and places, and making personal contacts from a business point of view.

The office itself should be departmentalised in such a way that there is a more or less self-run department for dealing with each side of the business. For instance, in a shipping office there will be a general office and postal and telephone department, a chartering department, an accounts department, and a forwarding department, besides the manager's office, which undertakes a general supervision of the whole, and allocates to each its share of the work to be done.

The manager needs to be well aware of the work that each department is doing, but should not concern himself too particularly with the details, as these can be quite well left to the department, and only take up time that the manager can utilise better in other directions. A business man who interferes with the work of his subordinates prevents them from taking any real interest in their work, and is doing work himself which it is not his duty to do. The manager's task should be to direct and guide the machine, not to worry about what each part is doing; so long as it is being done efficiently, and so long as the machine as a whole is running smoothly, he had best leave it alone.

Each department, including the manager's office, requires to have filing systems suited to its particular needs, so that all letters and papers are quickly filed out of the way, and yet remain handy for reference if required. A business man can carry only a certain amount of knowledge in his head, and if he fills his brain with a lot of trifling detail there is no room left for matters of more importance. His filing system should be a second brain, with all the facts and figures essential to his business stored away in an easily accessible manner. Filing systems that are important for an ordinary office are a letter file dating back six years at least, files of invoices and receipts, quotation files with cross references as required, sales and order files, and others of various sorts.[1] These files help to keep the office organisation at the finger tips of the manager, so that any fact or figure requisite to his business can be obtained at a moment's notice. Most papers of more than a year old can be put away in a storeroom, where there will also be the stocks of new letter paper and printed forms of various sorts required by the particular business. In order to save waste and expense, it is necessary to know how much of these various stocks are required, and to ensure that, while there is always ample in stock, there is never more ordered than is reasonably necessary.

### SECOND SELF TO THE MANAGER: THE GOOD SECRETARY

It is usually necessary to have a typing department as well, where the typing work of all the departments can be done, in the case of a large business, though in smaller firms each department does its own typing and correspondence. The manager has his own typist or secretary, and a good secretary is a great asset, an *alter ego* who can enable a business man to do more work that he could ever do otherwise, by having things ready for him when he wants them, knowing where things are so that they can be got at a moment's notice, reminding him of letters to be written, meetings to be attended, work to be dealt with, things which he might forget in the rush and worry of a busy day. Many big business men become almost dependent on their secretaries, and are enabled to use their own abilities to the fullest capacity because of not having to deal with small matters of little importance, which the secretary does automatically without reference to the manager.

A business man's day in his office usually begins with a glance over all or most of the letters, which are then distributed to the appropriate departments. Certain letters he deals with himself, and dictates to his typist, or advises his secretary what answers should be sent. His next work is to see the various heads of departments, and discuss with them any points that have to be considered, and questions of policy that arise from time to time. A good business man will take the advice of his heads of departments to a great extent, as

[1] For further discussion of filing see "How Business Records are Kept" (p. 476).

they are experts in their particular lines, and have their fingers more closely on the pulse of their departments than the manager should ever have himself.

After these consultations he is more or less free, and can either continue in the office doing a certain amount of the regular office work himself, and considering particular aspects of the business which require his attention, or he may leave the office and go to see someone on business, either with a definite object in view, or in order to maintain regular personal contacts with the firms with whom he does or hopes to do business. If he is a factory-owner he may pay a visit to the works; if he is a shipowner he may go to see one of his vessels, or may visit the docks, either in a general way, or to see a vessel for which his firm is acting as agent. Once the office machinery has been started and is running smoothly, the manager is not really needed there, and his duty should be to work out new ideas for business, or for extending his present business; to travel round the country, or even round the world, creating and maintaining personal contacts, and getting the business into the office to be dealt with by the office machine that he has built up.

An efficiently organised office staff is a paramount necessity, as without it the manager cannot leave his office for any length of time, and therefore a capacity for organisation is a valuable business asset. In this way the manager has a good idea of the work each department is doing, and whether there is adequate co-operation to ensure that the work is being done with as much efficiency and as little waste as possible.[1]

## GATHERING THE FUEL FOR THE OFFICE MACHINE

THE office organisation and management deals with the business that comes into the office, and naturally with the average firm a good deal of business comes in automatically from regular clients and business relationships of long standing. Nevertheless the business coming in is in constant need of augmentation and alteration, and the work of business management outside the office is therefore very important; it is the work which supplies the fuel to keep the office machine going. This work can be done to some extent by letter-writing and telephone conversations, but needs to be supplemented by personal visits on the part of the manager.

[1] For further discussion of office organisation see "The Management of an Office" (p. 101).

Personal contacts are a vital factor in maintaining and increasing business, and time that is spent on personal calls on other business men is seldom wasted, although the results may not be immediately apparent. A manager on a personal visit can explain points connected with his client's business, can get to know exactly what his client requires, and can find out his point of view and explain his own point of view, in a way that would be impossible by letter-writing or telephone. It is only in this way that personality can be given adequate scope, and personality is one of the chief necessities in business management.

Where the particular business has a factory or workshop the manager should make regular calls to see what is going on, and to keep in close touch with all his employees. Many large and successful businesses have been built up to a great extent on close co-operation between manager and men, each understanding the other's point of view, and all working for the common good with real team spirit. The manager who makes regular tours of his works or branch offices, or visits the docks or ports with which he is concerned, if his work is in any way connected with shipping, will nearly always be found to have a better knowledge of his business than the manager who thinks he can conduct the whole of his work from his office desk. There is no better maxim for a business man than "See for yourself."

By regular outside work the business man meets new people and hears of new ideas and developments to an extent that would be impossible if he stayed at his desk the whole of the time. The qualities that go to make a successful business man can never be utilised to their fullest advantage in office work alone, and the manager who spends his whole day at his office desk is to a great extent wasting his time. Almost every business man could point to chance meetings outside the office which eventually led to valuable business.

Outside work is work that it is not easy to do. It is sometimes difficult to go and see some business man who may not want to be seen, who may be busy or bad-tempered, or who may have a complaint to make as a result of previous business. It is work that requires tact, courage, self-confidence, politeness, a nice manner, cheerfulness, and real integrity and honesty. It is easy to get into a lazy habit, to put off going to see some firm until to-morrow or next week, and to stay in the office doing internal office work that could quite easily be done later if not by someone else. But the work of visiting other firms is work that is absolutely necessary for business success, and it is chiefly in this way that a man of character can make his character felt in his business.

## HOW A BUSINESS IS BUILT UP

So far we have considered the work of business management in the case of a business that is already in existence, but an important part of the work to be done by the manager is concerned with building up a business at the commencement, developing that business from a small thing to one of importance and influence, and changing the character of the business where occasion arises, to meet new needs and changing conditions.

Naturally, the manager, when commencing his business, needs to consider at the start how much he is going to departmentalise it, and how much of the work he is going to keep directly in his own hands. He needs to remember that the more he departmentalises it the more expensive it will become to maintain, and the more business it will be necessary to obtain to make ends meet; if he keeps too much in his own hands he may confine himself too much to the office, and not be able to devote as much time as he should to outside work.

In the first place, it is usually well to have a separate accounts department. A good accounts department, keeping records of the incomings and the outgoings of the various sides of the business, and costs of each separate operation, is a very useful index of the extent of the business that is being done. A summary of the accounts position every week or every month enables the manager to have a very accurate idea of his position. Naturally, as the business grows, the accounts department should always be allowed to grow with it, and time that is spent by this department in dissecting costs, drawing up the results of different sides of the business, and generally putting its financial position in all its different aspects before the manager, is seldom wasted.

The various other departments should be created as required, a specialised department being organised to deal with any side of the firm's activities that is of sufficient importance to require full-time attention on the part of a department head and his staff. It is well for the manager to remember, however, that departmentalisation increases costs, and does not necessarily increase efficiency unless there is adequate co-ordination and co-operation between the various departments. For this reason control by the manager of all the departments, and a good knowledge of exactly what each is doing, is most important.

### ESTIMATING THE RESULTS OF THE PLAN

In building up or increasing a business it is very necessary to have an exact idea of what it is proposed to do, and also a careful estimate of the costs of the expansion and of the extra business that is likely to result from it. It is naturally to be expected that the results of business expansion will not be immediately apparent, and this costing estimate enables the manager to see if the cumulative results of his policy are in excess of his estimates, or not so good as he expected.

The manager must decide what new business he wishes to secure, what are his chances of being able to get it, and whether the office staff that he has is well qualified to deal with it. As a rule, it is well to try for business which can be dealt with more or less by the same office staff, and which is for this reason somewhat akin to the business that is already being done. This will avoid the necessity of having to increase the staff to any great extent, which would obviously greatly increase the office costs of the business.

For example, a firm might have the business of ship-brokers or ship's agents dealing with vessels at its own particular port. There are several ways in which expansion is possible in the same line of business without increasing the office costs to any extent, and so ensuring that any incomings from the expansion are nearly all profit. In the first place, the firm might try to get more agency work, but as there would presumably be other agents at the same port, this would be difficult to do without very strenuous competition. Secondly, the firm of shipbrokers might decide to buy a vessel of their own, and so become shipowners as well. The work could very easily be done, if they had the necessary capital, with the same office staff, and would perhaps give a better chance of making a good profit out of the business than agency work alone. Thirdly, they might decide to set up branch offices in other ports, but this would mean greatly increased staff, and would not really be increasing the business so much as creating new businesses in other places.

## THE MANAGER MUST CONTROL EXPANSION

It is always better that any expansion should be gradual, and that new staff should be engaged as a result of new business, rather than with the expectation of new business, unless a new line is being tried. Very often it will be found that new business can be dealt with, by a slight reorganisation or readjustment, with the same office staff, so that the office costs of the extra work gradually acquired in this way can be reckoned as almost nil. It is very important that the manager should have a more complete control of the office during development or expansion than when the business is running on a normal course. Points may arise at a moment's notice which require his urgent attention, and it is necessary that he should be fully conversant even with the detail work that is being done, so that he may be in a position to revise his ideas, if necessary, at any stage of the process.

It is very useful for him to have full figures kept of every side of the firm's work during these transition periods, and therefore an efficient accounts department is a great asset. Figures of incomings and of costs, particularly of any extra costs, and also of the increased business that is being done, should be carefully recorded and analysed, while comparisons with the previous year, and from week to week or month to month, showing how the business of the firm is reacting to the policy of the manager, should regularly be made. It is also useful to have graphs made from time to time of various aspects of the firm's activities, showing at a glance how things are progressing.

These figures and diagrams enable the manager to have an accurate and analytical idea of the position of the firm. He can decide from them what lines of business are worth continuing, what lines it may be better to stop, in which directions it might be worth while to consider development, and which particular branches of the business most urgently require his attention. They also enable him to see which departments are working well, and which may require more organisation or direction.

## STATISTICS WIDEN THE RANGE OF ONE MAN'S ACTIVITIES

The statistical side of business is a side that has been increasingly developed over recent years, and it is one of the chief reasons why businesses have been able to grow to such large proportions under a single manager. The various branches or departments of the business each prepare their statistical analyses at regular intervals, and from these the manager is able to keep his finger on the pulses of the business, and to have an accurate idea of the results of the work. His direction of the policy of the firm is dependent on the information he gets in this way, as much as on his estimate of the trend of outside factors. His heads of departments act as his lieutenants in the business, each running his own department with full delegation of authority, and taking his orders as to general policy from the manager. The work of directing the policy of the whole, and of seeing that all the various departments work together as a properly co-ordinated unit, with the maximum of efficiency and a reasonable minimum of cost is the manager's special province.

The financial side of business management is of great importance. Costing work, similar to that carried on in the production or transport or sale of goods, is necessary in order to see that the costs of any branch or department of the business do not exceed the direct or indirect returns from the work of that branch or department. It is important that the costs of each side of the work should be carefully balanced, and that careful analyses should be made of the work that is done. The work of the firm as a whole may be prejudiced if the costs of running the office are too high, while at the same time it is no good cutting down the costs at the expense of efficiency.

In considering the various items in the costs of the management of his firm the business man has to estimate whether each particular item is worth while, and whether expense could be saved by reorganisation in any direction, or by the introduction of any of the mechanical appliances now in regular use in many offices. For instance, the large banks have recently reorganised their work to a considerable extent by the introduction of automatic book-keeping machines, and any firm that has a large amount of invoicing, book-keeping, or accounting work will usually find a great saving in time and cost, as well as increased accuracy, by the use of such machines. By similar methods it is also possible to give more work to particular departments without having to increase the staff or the cost, so that new business can be taken on even though the return from it may be small.

### KEEPING A FINGER ON THE PULSE OF PROGRESS

REGULAR costing of the chief items of the work of the firm, and of the various branches and departments, ensures that any work that proves to be unprofitable can be stopped immediately, while business that turns out better than expected can be increased, even if it means increasing the costs in proportion. It also ensures that a branch or department which is not pulling its weight can be stopped or reorganised as necessary, so avoiding, or nipping in the bud, the heavy wastes of inefficiency.

It is always important that costs should be carefully set against receipts, as it is not worth while to continue doing business that is costing more than is received from it, except with any eye to future returns, and it is not easy for the manager to have an accurate idea of the position without regular information of this sort. Just as the manager should have a good idea of the work that each department is doing, so he should receive regular particulars of the cost of each department, in order that he can direct and control the business from a costing point of view.

### THE MANAGER A FIELD-MARSHAL IN THE BUSINESS BATTLE

THE business manager can to a certain extent be likened to a field-marshal on the field of battle. The field-marshal takes no actual part in the hand-to-hand fighting, but he knows where each unit is and what it is doing ; he receives regular reports from his lieutenants, straight from the field of battle, and from these reports he directs the action of the army as a whole, and eventually by his strategy wins the day.

So too the business manager ; he has extra knowledge and abilities which would be wasted in the daily routine work, while, as the amount of work he can do is limited, it is important that he should carefully select the most important duties of his business for himself, and delegate the balance to the greatest possible extent to his lieutenants. Those to whom he delegates in this way are possible future managers themselves, and therefore the extent to which they are prepared to accept responsibility in their work, and the way in which they carry out and control the work of their departments, is frequently the final deciding factor as to whether they are suitable for promotion to more responsible and more arduous duties.

## SUGGESTIONS FOR FURTHER READING

THE work of business management is work that is being carried on daily, with greater or less success, in large firms and small, all over the country. The foregoing discussion cannot profess to have dealt with the subject in its entirety, but it is hoped that it will arouse sufficient interest for readers to wish to study more detailed works on the subject. Those who wish to do so are advised to read *Office Organisation and Management*, by Lawrence R. Dicksee (Pitman); *Filing Systems*, by Edward A. Cope (Pitman), for the technical side of the subject. A book of a more general character is *Personal and Business Efficiency*, by C. A. Henderson (Pitman); while *Commercial Management*, by C. L. Bolling (Pitman), contains a very interesting outline of the whole subject. A useful plan is for the reader to get in touch with the secretary of the Management Library, 23 Bloomsbury Square, W.C.1. Membership of the library provides a means of keeping in touch with the latest publications, both in England and abroad, and of borrowing books which are expensive and not always available in ordinary libraries. The staff of the library also advises the diligent inquirer on further books to read.

# THE QUALITIES THAT MAKE A BUSINESS MAN

*by PATRICK McANALLY, B.A.(Oxon).*

A BOOK is not complete without a description of its hero. It is therefore necessary to attempt a characterisation of the business man. Most people will be ready to give an opinion : " A business man wears a black coat and striped trousers. He has a hearty manner. He knows how much you paid for every thing you possess, and could tell you where you could have bought it cheaper." This, it need hardly be said, is a caricature and a gross caricature. But, none the less, it has in it an element of truth. The type which occurs to the popular imagination is met from time to time, but what reason can there be for regarding it as the sole or the representative type ?

## THE NEED FOR ACCURACY IN BUSINESS

THE first notable quality in the business man is that he knows what he is talking about, because he deals with a number of simple wants. Writers, politicians, schoolmasters, and the like are in a different position, because the material they deal with is more abstract and elusive and calls for considerable discussion and analysis. But for the business man it is possible to do with much less argumentation, because, though frequently transient and always variable, the wants which he aims at meeting are simple and practical. If reference is made to a ton of pig-iron, or a mile of wire, or a yard of ribbon it is known what is meant, and much of the talk which is used in business is of this sort.

The advantage of knowing what you are talking about carries with it high responsibilities. Where every term that is used carries a precise and indisputable meaning, it is of tremendous importance to use the terms and interpret them with the most scrupulous accuracy. Every one knows that any enterprise must have an accounting system, and that in the use of it no casual mistakes are permissible. This is a very obvious example of the need for accuracy in business. Less obvious, but equally important, is the need for accuracy in attending to customers' instructions. These may be given in speech or writing, but in either case it is vital not to overlook small points, which may seem trivial to the seller but all-important to the buyer.

Another consequence of the fact that the wants which business supplies are simple is that mathematics can be used to a very large extent. In determining the qualities that make a business man, one cannot divide him up on a percentage basis. But in doing business one can, and must, constantly relate the various factors by means of arithmetic. By working out a balance-sheet it is possible to give a picture of the largest business concern at any moment, and to give it on the back of an envelope. It is the same with nearly all business problems. When the London and North-Eastern Railway introduced "camping" carriages for people to use on their summer holidays it was an interesting new experiment, and the question whether the price asked was favourable to the railway or to its clients was an intriguing one for the layman to set himself. The point is that the only hope of getting an answer was by working mathematically, and considering the precise quantities involved. The good business man must always be prepared to grasp his problems by treating them quantitatively.

### THINKING IN TERMS OF TIME

BESIDES quantity, the business man must appreciate time. Actions cannot be taken in complete isolation from each other. Before D does something it will be necessary for him to sound A to see whether he agrees, to instruct B to prepare some requisite information, and to inform C of what is about to happen; and all this chain of action must fit in with the desires of the ultimate consumer, which alter with considerable rapidity. This makes it vital to be able to visualise the various actions in their places in time. If this is not done, the requisite information may be lacking at an important juncture and the action contemplated will probably be unsuccessful.

A certain amount is said about the lightning decisions which business men have to take, and of the miraculous "hunches" which guide their footsteps. To work by inspiration is certainly a very romantic way of working, but it is almost equally certain that it is the wrong way for business men to work. The nature of their problems is such that they can nearly always be answered in terms of figures and facts, and if they are answered by "hunches," it usually means that too little attention has been given to the all-important elements of quantity and time. If the business man has given proper attention to them, he should be ready to make the most of each opportunity as it arises, and to look ahead as far as he need.

This first quality of knowing what he is talking about is one which the business man shares with many administrators. The next to be dealt with is one which he alone possesses. But it is so vital that he must have it whether he is proprietor of a winkle stall or of a world-wide corporation. It is that of being a merchant, or "entrepreneur," to use a technical term of economics. The world of business is a tissue of wants, and the merchant or entrepreneur type is the man who is so quick and confident in detecting these wants that he is prepared to utilise such property as he possesses in order to satisfy them. Plainly other men of affairs, such as the civil servant or the municipal employee, do not stand in serious need of this quality.

### KEEPING IN TOUCH WITH THE WORLD

If business men are to keep themselves constantly informed about the wants of the world at large, they must not keep themselves to themselves. It is essential that they should move about and see what is going on. There should be nothing of the recluse or the "grouch" about them. Examples of the way in which new wants occur are not difficult to think of. In the last few years, for instance, a new habit of going into the country has grown up, and been given the name of "hiking." The business men concerned should have noticed this when it began, and been on their toes to supply all that hikers might require. This new want came from the consumer end. Others originate when producers put striking new inventions on the market. Business men must be looking in both directions, and above all must never be caught asking the inane questions about everyday matters that are popularly supposed to be asked by judges.

To perceive wants as they arise is not enough by itself. It is also necessary to be able to demonstrate to other people how their wants may be satisfied. This faculty is required in dealing with colleagues, in buying, and most obviously in selling. Unless somebody can persuade somebody else that it will be to his advantage to do something or other, business simply comes to a standstill.

To be able to do all this is to be a merchant. The merchant

is a person who is always subject to scorn and abuse as a producer of nothing, but in fact he requires character and knowledge which entitle him to respect and credit. The knowledge required is mostly about merchandise. Selling seldom consists simply of moving goods from one place to another. The seller must know what goods are suitable for what purpose, so that he can guide purchasers in making their choice. He must also be able to suggest alternatives, if the goods asked for are not available, and decide whether the goods have been properly used if their durability is called in question. These, it has been said, are the qualities of the merchant. This does not mean that they must not be possessed in some degree by the production manager of a factory. Even to decide what sort of articles to try and produce with his machinery, the producer must be something of a merchant.

### THE BUSINESS MAN AT HIS BEST

THE exercise of the art of using exact knowledge of consumers' wants and exact knowledge of goods, in order to produce satisfaction, ought to breed honesty in the business man. If extravagant descriptions lead a customer to purchase something under false pretences, there is unlikely to be a second order. But, if the seller uses all his ability to provide precisely what is wanted, he makes goodwill for himself. This honesty and optimism that goes with it—the merchant's qualities—are attributes of the business man at his best.

The third main quality of the business man is ability to co-operate with large numbers of others. It is not a quality which he alone must possess, nor one which he must possess in every case. For instance the soldier and the civil servant must possess it, but the proprietor of the winkle stall need not, although he is a business man. But the nature of business is such that large numbers of people collaborating together can produce good results in most cases. This is because the things with which it concerns itself are relatively simple, and because business men know what they are talking about, and can split up the necessary tasks, and divide the labour among a large number of persons. If the subject matter of business were not fairly simple, it would constantly be necessary to make long explanations, and sub-division of labour would not be worth while.

It should not need emphasising that co-operation between one person and another is an activity into which it is possible to throw an almost unlimited amount of skill. People who are associated with each other in a concern at their worst occupy their time in avoiding every job which by hook or by crook they can put on to the shoulders of others. But at their best they undertake matters, and after devoting to them all the best effort that they themselves have to offer, they hand them on to others in the form most convenient for further handling. The man who can see what information his colleague will require, and how and when and where, is the good co-operator and also the one who will get most enjoyment out of co-operating. In fact, it is as necessary for business men to imagine themselves in the shoes of other people inside their own business as to see into the minds of customers who are outside it.

### RELIABILITY THAT SCORES OVER BRILLIANCE

THIS way of looking at business relations is probably particularly helpful for inferiors in considering their attitude to superiors. There are two legitimate ways in which inferiors may rise. One is by displaying intermittent flashes of brilliance, and the other is by showing consistent reliability. The latter is far the sounder. Inferiors probably ought to regard their superiors as overworked and harassed people, who want assistance which will be so reliable as to remove completely some of their worries from their minds. Brilliance alone will not do this, nor will mere plodding. What is wanted is steadiness in assisting the superior by relieving him of routine and dealing with new situations with initiative, if they arise.

The superior, for his part, must contrive not to be a harassed person. If he works several times as hard as any of his subordinates, he is probably wasting his own highly valuable capacities, and not making proper use of theirs. He must get out of his difficulties by thinking how to split up the work which he himself has performed, and give the easier portions to other people. This is not always free from difficulty, and undue multiplication of subordinates may only involve the superior in fresh trouble. But it is essential that he should give close attention to the way in which he delegates his responsibility.

This brings up the question of what makes a good leader. Those who explain wise action by miraculous " hunches," explain leadership by saying that one man is " a born leader of men," and that another is not. This is not helpful. Perhaps the first thing that ought to be said is that to lead people it is necessary to praise them or encourage them whenever they try, and administer the proverbial kick in the pants whenever they slack off. The second necessity is for the leader to back his words by actions, and never to ask for help from a subordinate in a matter which he will subsequently ignore or forget. In these two ways the leader can show his men that their best efforts are valued, and so spur them to try hard. To achieve this he must have eyes in the back of his head and a prodigious fund of energy.

### ENERGY THE PARENT OF INSPIRATION

By talking about energy we have got on to a new topic. Energy is not one among the other qualities. It is something without which none of them are of much value. This is a fact which does not apply exclusively to business. The old definition of genius as the "infinite capacity for taking pains" is trite, but well worth consideration in regard to all activities. Whether a man be an artist, or a statesman, or a business man, he is only half alive if he is not filled with energy and keenness for the work which he undertakes. If he is keen and energetic, the problems of his work will always be running in his head, and he will get new inspiration at the most unexpected moments.

Such an attitude may form the unifying element in a career by giving the business man an object to which to devote himself. Most human beings prefer to feel that they are being active, and taking control of the circumstances in which they find themselves, rather than being passive and drifting with the tide. They like also to look at something which they have accomplished, and relish to the full the sense of achievement, particularly if the world at large is ready to attribute some credit and prestige to such achievement. It may sound absurd to talk in these terms of business life, since it is supposed to be devoted to money-grubbing. One answer is that business men often want the sense of achievement that money brings more than the money itself. Another answer is that stranger things have been known. In fiction, if not in life, we have had Robin Hood and Raffles who derived a professional thrill from robbery, and valued it more than their ill-gotten gains.

If it is desirable that business men should devote themselves with energy and keenness to an object, in order to link their careers into coherent and successful wholes, it becomes necessary to describe the kind of object to which they should attach themselves.

The older idea was that they should make themselves complete masters of the ways of handling particular types of goods by apprenticing themselves at an early age to the trade in which they intended to live and die. It has already been stated that knowledge about his merchandise is of the very greatest importance to the business man, and probably for those who are going to work mostly at the production end, it is necessary to specialise on a particular kind of merchandise and not depart much from it.

### THE QUALITIES ON WHICH CAREERS ARE BUILT

But the knowledge of merchandise was only one part of what we call the merchant's qualities. The business man also needs knowledge of customers, a sense of quantity and time, and a faculty for co-operating. To utilise these qualities and build a career with them, it is not necessary to specialise in a particular type of merchandise. A man may set out to make himself second to none in supervising salesmen or in exercising financial control or in staff management, and move from one business to another although they are handling quite different merchandise. He may not even specialise as much as this, but simply devote himself wholeheartedly to the job of the moment and the exercise of the particular qualities in which he excels, regarding management as a distinct profession in which it is worth trying to attain success.

## WHERE TO READ MORE ABOUT THE BUSINESS MAN

Lists of the qualities that make a business man are very common. But they are apt to be trite and very much alike. More original and provocative work on the subject is harder to find. Graham Wallas does not deal much with business men, but probably his discussions of other professions are worth reading in this connection: they are to be found, for instance, in *The Great Society*, *Human Nature in Politics*, and *Our Social Heritage*. Novels about business men should also be helpful, if well written, and Sinclair Lewis's *Babbitt* is a classic on the subject.

# HOW TO CULTIVATE PERSONAL EFFICIENCY

*by* R. *SIMMAT, M.A., of the National Institute of Industrial Psychology. Author of " Personal Salesmanship," "Market Research," " The Principles and Practice of Marketing," etc.*

THE executives who can manage themselves and can also manage others are the key men in any organisation. Organisation requires nothing beyond a certain aptitude simply to give orders in business, but to inspire and stimulate those who are employed is an art. Some leaders are born to lead, others by diligent application have succeeded in acquiring the essentials. Industry cannot depend solely upon men with the rare gift of intuitive leadership. Leaders of the future must be trained ; they must also train themselves so that they can utilise the facts which the science of psychology is discovering about human nature, about the power of habits, the universality of primitive and acquired desires, and the dependence of reason upon both desire and habit. The industrial leader must learn to develop a balanced and controlled personality unruffled by conflict either in his environment or within his own structure of emotions. His personality must be constructive, ever seeking progress, knowledge, and experience as aids to assist his judgment.

Men to be managed must be understood. The differences between individuals are often very great. One man is lazy, another energetic, one is studious, another always seeking pleasure. Yet common to all men are certain factors. Man is born into the world with certain primitive tendencies to action known as instincts. The moulding of these into adult behaviour depends in the early stages of his existence upon what he learns from his parents, and later, on what he teaches himself. Few realise to what extent the habits they have acquired have made them what they are. The lower grades of factory and office workers are obviously dependent upon the habits or routine of the work that they have learnt.

It is not so obvious that habits are also important to the executive, since often little of his work is of a simple routine nature. But an executive has to be trained, he must acquire experience, and so during the period of his apprenticeship when he is working his way up the ladder he acquires habits of thought and action which, good or bad, form the background for his more mature years. During his early business career he may become tolerant or intolerant, lazy, or painstaking, modest or conceited, self-controlled or impulsive, honest or dishonest, and these habits once formed are difficult to change in later years. The aspiring young executive must take stock carefully of the habits he is developing and sternly eliminate any that are not going to be of assistance during his later business career.

### HABITS CREATED BY PRIMITIVE DESIRES

An individual's activity is composed of a complex composition of the many habits he has acquired in the expression of his original primitive needs. Whether his actions are good or bad, wise or unwise, does not in later years depend on the actual fundamental desires, but rather on the habits he has formed to satisfy them. It has been said that human nature is unchangeable. This is true to the extent that primitive desires are unchangeable, but the methods of giving expression to such desires can be changed by the development of habits. For example, the primitive desire to eat food is common to all, but, in some people, circumstances have developed the habit of eating frugally; in others, circumstances have developed the habit of eating wastefully.

Similarly, the primitive desire to rule is present in all, but in some it finds expression in family life, other men become despots in business, still others find satisfaction in the sensation of power resulting from scientific research. To understand and manage the heterogeneous mixture of impulses and desires in all the individuals comprising an organisation the executive must recognise and appreciate the differences between each individual. He must also recognise the power of action stimulated by example and experience.

Habits are formed like the path of a stream—by repeated action in one direction—often following a line of least resistance. Even if a habit is stopped for a short time, if the period of stoppage is not too long, it is simple to relapse into the old easy path of action. Once a habit has been formed it is difficult to break. Our line of action becomes set into a groove so to speak. It is thus important to get our actions into the right grooves—grooves that will be a help and not a hindrance to us.

## HABITS THAT FREE THE MIND FOR THOUGHT

Once a habit has been developed its practice hardly becomes conscious effort. This applies to both muscular and mental habits. If the executive's routine, his emotional attitudes, and his methods of thought are under the control of good habits, he is free to concentrate his mind upon the more important problems of his organisation, just as the skilled worker can attend to other matters while using his hands for the routine manipulation of his machine. As a new habit is developed and action becomes set in a groove the mind becomes more and more free from detail. As Professor William James once said, we should waste a great deal of time if we had to stop every morning to consider and decide which shoe or sock we put on first instead of letting habit function for us.

The state of an executive's development can be judged by the extent to which he has reduced the minor details of his business life to habit. The too conscientious executive and the one possessing insufficient confidence in his subordinates try to keep their minds on all the details of the work being carried on around them. The result is an unnecessary over-burdening of their own minds and inevitable inefficiency. The true criterion of the good executive might well be not how much he does but how little, that is to say, the extent to which he has reduced details to a routine, or delegated unimportant work to others, while preserving the function of full supervision for himself, and so leaving his own mind free to deliberate on the more important problems. If an executive becomes tired or suffers nervous prostration it is a sure sign that he is making conscious efforts in decision when the mental process should have been reduced to a habit.

Once habits begin to be formed they do not change without interference. Without guidance, no matter how much more effective any new mode of action may be, they cannot change. It is not wise to allow habits to develop in this way. It is leaving too much to chance. Habits should be regulated in the early days of their formation before they get too settled. Eliminate all unnecessary steps in the procedure of learning a habit. Select the best ways of doing things and make these into habits. They play too important a part in everyday life not to be chosen and developed with the greatest care. Once a routine has been decided set about developing it into a habit boldly, without hesitation ; be enthusiastic about it ; strengthen yourself against any temptation to slacken, carry it out as often as possible during the early stages, permit no exceptions, make sure you are doing it right, correct the smallest mistake before it becomes more serious. In the early stages the effort may be a hard one, but it will gradually become less and less so until the whole procedure becomes a routine.

### THE HABIT OF REMEMBERING THINGS

MEMORY is a form of habit. To remember is to recall some experience of the past. If an item of experience can be recalled when it is required, then it has become fixed in the memory. The experienced executive may be described as one who, first, has had experience of a vast number of situations and of making the decisions adequate to meet them, and secondly, is capable of recalling the experiences and previous decisions appropriate to making a decision to meet a present situation.

The more experiences an executive has had and the more ready his power of recalling them, the greater his value. He must know his organisation, his men, his machinery and his materials, and his knowledge must always be there ready for application. In business, experience should not be accumulated by chance. Every man has some experiences the value of which is not going to be great. There is a danger of extraneous experiences crowding out those that will be useful. Experiences and knowledge must be selected before being stored in the memory.

Whether a thing is remembered depends upon what are known as associations or meanings attached to the matter memorised. To strengthen these associations the material must be made interesting. It may be interesting in itself. If it is not, then one must continually think about it, and relate it to one's own needs and other interests. Then it will be remembered. Thinking, and not mere repetition, is the effective way to memorise. Think meanings and relations into things and you will remember them. Make everything you try to learn interesting to yourself. Try to recall it at intervals and put it into use at every opportunity. Don't try to remember too much or you may not remember anything clearly or usefully.

We only remember experiences to which we have attended. Attention is selective. Out of the mass of possible experiences surrounding us our attention selects some and makes them our own—of these some are remembered and some are not. If a new technique in window-dressing is of interest to us we stop to study it; if not, we pass on and forget about it; if we see a new type of office machine that might be of use to us, we pause to examine it, and so on. We can give an experience our attention either voluntarily or involuntarily, consciously or unconsciously. Experiences from without crowd in upon us; what is it that causes us to attend to some and ignore others? How can we train ourselves to attend to those which are the more important to us?

If something we want to attend to does not hold our attention, our mind wanders away to something else after a very short time. When we realise this we can make an effort to force our attention back again. Such efforts are tiring and often unprofitable. Change is one of the most important factors in holding our attention—so long as there is something new in an experience it is always easy to attend to it. Another important factor in determining the direction of attention is interest. It is easier to attend to things that interest us than to attend to those that do not.

### THE GIFT OF MAKING ROUTINE INTERESTING

MUCH executive work involves attending to matters that are neither novel nor in themselves of interest. However, this does not necessarily mean that the executive's attention should be strained. As with memory, attention can be trained by thought. If the executive thinks of the implications of matters which on the surface appear dull and uninteresting, he can make them of absorbing interest. For example, the checking of routine reports may, in itself, be very dull and boring; but, if they are checked with a full consciousness of their meanings in relation to the whole organisation, they can become intensely interesting. Thought will create meaning out of routine material—especially if it is both critical and constructive. There is nothing so lifeless that it cannot be enlivened and made interesting. In what other ways can it be done? What is wrong with the present method of doing it? How can it be done better? What would be the effect of any changes on the various people involved? By asking himself these questions the executive can create interest for himself; it will be less of an effort to attend, and also the work will be much more valuable. He can train himself to make things interesting.

In the modern business the division of attention by executive organisation is a most important factor in achieving efficiency. Each executive has certain functions to which his attention must be given and he is not expected to give it to any other. The executive must understand which items are of significance to him, but he must not only pay attention to the right things, he must comprehend their importance. To do this he must have knowledge and experience. It is his experience that enables him when attending to one item to know which to attend to next. He must both add to his present experience and compare it with other experiences before finally filing it away in the pigeon-holes of his memory for future recall.

The term personality is one that has always been difficult to define precisely. However, it is usually taken as meaning the sum total of an individual's capacity for reacting to his environment. If a man has a strong personality, it is usually meant that he is always capable of producing the right reaction to any set of circumstances. If he has a weak personality, he is incapable of adjusting himself appropriately to the external reality with which he is surrounded.

The human individual is not a completely organised and integrated being with a single will to act. The more he approaches this state of integration the more effective his personality. Every one is a mass of tendencies to act—many of them conflicting the one with the other. There are simple reactions to pleasure and pain into which consciousness rarely enters. There are instinctive needs and desires, many of them modified by environment and habit, and there are habits acquired during the years of mental development. Habits may become so strong that they approximate to instinctive impulses, as, for example, a craving for alcohol, the desire for coffee and a cigar after dinner, the tendency to go to the office by a certain route, and so on.

There is in the mind of the individual a continual conflict between this great mass of tendencies to reaction, and a controlling element dependent upon what the critical "ego" of the individual considers he "ought" to do. If the conflict between individual desires or between desires and the " ego " is so great that a single course of action is not possible, a psycho-pathological condition develops. The individual becomes mentally deranged. Even under normal conditions if the conflict between two desires is a lengthy one, mental fatigue is induced. The efficient personality is one in which the various desires, habits, and tendencies to action based on experience have been blended and synthesised into one harmoniously integrated behaviour pattern so that the possibility of conflict is reduced to a minimum.

### WHEN THE "EGO" TRIES TO ASSERT ITSELF

In business life the executive is always being called upon to make decisions. These are based on his experience. If his experience is inadequate, either his decision will be a bad one or the mental strain involved in obtaining the necessary knowledge at short notice will be very great. If his experience and knowledge have not been harmoniously synthesised, then conflict will ensue between the various items of experience. Possibly his background of experience may be such that any decision to act based on it may be considered by the executive's critical " ego " to be incompatible with his environment. There will then be a conflict between the " ego " and the instincts, desires, or the habits created by experience. Self-control will be necessary. Psychologists have realised that self-control by sheer force of will exacts a very great toll on the mental structure of the individual. Repression of impulses is dangerous and results in mental degeneration.

To understand and develop control of ourselves we must realise that we do not always do what we consciously intend to do. We may consciously determine to adopt a firm attitude towards a subordinate, but, if the habit of treating him as a familiar equal has been developed, this will be difficult to change. We are largely controlled by habit. Action usually results less from consideration of all circumstances and experience, than from these considerations failing to maintain a control of our actions.

The most important contribution our experience and knowledge make to our mental structure is the development of the habit of being able to judge conduct—our own and that of others. What we think is right and what we think is wrong is mainly a matter of habit based on experience and knowledge. If we are taught that to be dishonest is right, then our habits and conduct will tend in that direction. But because we are punished for dishonesty our habits have been developed to avoid it. Thus through punishment we acquire our early sense of what is right and wrong. In adult life our sense of right and wrong is also determined by what other people think or are likely to think of our actions, coupled with the degree to which we are influenced or can afford to be influenced by the opinions of others. Throughout our life we develop standards and habits of censoring behaviour, and these are the standards and the mechanism by which we control our own actions. In industrial life these habits are functioning almost continuously. Society, etiquette, and business relations impose further countless restrictions upon the executive. Almost all direct paths for satisfying his desires are forbidden in one way or another.

The forces restricting the satisfaction of desires are thus partly external, emanating from one's fellows and from social and economic laws, and partly internal according to one's own conception of what is the right and correct thing to do. The expert in business, the seasoned politician, the polished diplomat becomes adept at playing other personalities, the one against the other, so that the external factors do not hinder the fulfilment of his desires. If he is a real leader of men he will even play various personalities against each other so that they actually and as a group accept his rulings and assist him in the fulfilment of his desires.

### THWARTED DESIRES THAT FIND VENT IN BAD HUMOUR

UNDER abnormal circumstances such as extreme mental or muscular fatigue, bad bodily health, or when normal desires are controlled and repressed too severely, small matters that under ordinary circumstances would not be noticed cause disproportionate excitation. Thus many executives have their periods of acute "bad humour" when they are almost entirely unapproachable. Under such circumstances stimulations of any desire are cumulative, and each additional stimulus adds to the stored-up repressed impulses to action. Any small stimulus may cause the stored-up nervous energy to find expression in actions of unanticipated violence.

Such emotional "explosions" are bad both for the individual and for his business, but afterwards he feels much better and can think more normally. Time is a great power in relieving the situation. Different work, sleep, and recreation are a great help. There is much to be said for the old principle of counting ten before acting hastily. Time affords an opportunity for feelings and thoughts to arrange themselves in their correct perspective. Rest and recreation do more. They enable the mind to be refreshed, for the mental energy repressed in business hours to find another more healthy outlet. Every executive should have his hobby, his recreation, and other interests apart from his business work. In this way his mind is kept fresh, and nervous energy often repressed in the office finds another outlet. He preserves his balance and often his sanity.

On the other hand, individual development takes place largely as the result of conflict within the personality structure —provided a satisfactory solution of the conflict is found. It is a weak personality that shrinks from conflict. The strong man glories in it and advancing from conflict to conflict finds still greater strength. The strong personality does not fear to face realities, and in doing so becomes further developed and integrated. The great scientist glimpsing a new truth is stimulated with a desire to follow his facts to the bitter end, and his whole personality becomes integrated to achieve his great work.

The highly placed executive is confronted with apparently insuperable difficulties—opposition from colleagues, criticism from outside. His desire to overcome these obstacles is aroused in the fullest degree. His whole being is concentrated on the task. Events stimulate him still further. But throughout it all, provided he is sublimely confident in his experience and knowledge, the whole influence of his desire to succeed will be unifying and not disruptive. Without conflict, personality degenerates, and as long as an ultimate outlet is provided by success, the individual benefits from inner conflict.

### WHY EXECUTIVES HAVE NERVOUS BREAKDOWNS

If the result is failure and there is no outlet, mental disorder results. This is the explanation of many executives having nervous breakdowns ; but it is not, as is popularly supposed, the breakdown that has caused the failure—it is the failure to find the satisfactory outlet for the desire that has caused the breakdown. The nervous breakdown is the recognition within one's self of the failure. Confidence has been lost and the retreat of the personality sounded. If the executive refuses to have his confidence in himself shaken, if he repudiates the idea of failure and continues to concentrate on success, his personality must remain integrated and there can be no breakdown.

It is a commonplace in studying the psychology of childhood to encounter references to day-dreaming. Many of the desires of childhood cannot find fulfilment. If the child cannot obtain the toy he has set his heart on in reality, he finds his satisfaction in a dream world. He dreams of the toy. Many adults whose personalities are not strong enough to obtain for them the fulfilment of their desires, find refuge in a similar world of unreality. They refuse to recognise the painful facts of the reality that surrounds them and find their satisfaction in a system of unreality that they build up about themselves. The man occupying a humble position in the office tells his wife how important he is to the organisation. After some time he also tends to convince himself of his great importance. Such instances are very common. The process is an unconscious one and those concerned are often not even conscious of the incompatibility between the unreal world they have built up and the real world of facts. This process operates with every individual, but it is only when the inconsistency with the real world becomes too great, or the individual fails to appreciate the real orientation of his dream world, that he becomes abnormal.

### CLOAKING THE WRONG DESIRE IN CONVENTION

In normal business life a mental process known as rationalisation is very common. We have certain wishes and desires that escape the censorship of our habits and standards of conduct, because unconsciously we disguise them in conventional forms. This process of rationalisation is accelerated according to the strength of the illicit desire, and as our conscious control is impaired by fatigue, emotion, or external distraction. An executive may conceive an intense personal dislike for one of his staff. He will begin to look for faults in his work as an excuse to dismiss him. Then, when the man is finally dismissed, the executive will give as his reason the faults which in all probability never existed. The real reason which the executive would never admit even to himself might have been a trifling one. The offender may have dared to wear the same kind of suit as his superior!

Rationalisation is the sign of a weak personality refusing to recognise realities and preferring to exist in a self-created unreality. The weak man rationalises before he acts to convince himself that his course of conduct is right. After the act he again rationalises to spare himself the pain of admitting he has done wrong. The strong personality will have none of this. He does not shirk the effort of deciding a course of action. He seeks no excuses for his actions. He does not retreat into a world of unreality. He faces facts, meets them squarely, and abides by the consequences, because his desires have been analysed and criticised in the cold light of reason and his actions based on the standard of conduct he has set up. His actions are the expression of his whole personality in its healthy adjustment to reality.

It is easy for the weak executive to take the line of least resistance and begin a process of rationalisation to excuse and explain his conduct. Once the habit is formed its development is insidious. The executive seeking to develop his power of business leadership must train himself vigorously to face facts and not to shun them. Particularly is there a dangerous tendency to procrastinate and shun hard work or difficult decisions. Subordinates are quick to recognise these pretences and their respect is lost. The executive must be wary of both internal and external hypocrisy. It is easy to cloak many activities with a disguise of service or rightness. The wealthy business man, for instance, may make large donations to charity. In the course of introspection he may persuade himself he is doing so because of his interest in his fellows. The actual reason may be that he enjoys putting people under an obligation to him, or else he may wish to prove to the world at large how generous he is and receive praise accordingly.

We must not try to prove to ourselves that our actions are being done in a spirit of service when our real motives are entirely different. Let us be frank with ourselves and devote our attention to whether an act is right or wrong according to our standard of conduct, and not consider too deeply the manufacture of spurious motives as reasons for the act. Then our mental outlook will be healthier and our personality more in harmony with reality. The executive who faces facts in this way will be respected by others whether his acts are right or otherwise when judged by other standards. He may not be liked, he may even be hated, but the strength of his personality will be admired by all right-thinking men.

### HOW TO DEVELOP A HARMONIOUS PERSONALITY

The desires expressive of the bodily and mental structure of the individual once expressed are enduring. Re-education may blot them out but an everlasting impression remains within the personality. The basis for the solution of conflict is to seek the solution that is harmonious with, and best for, the entire personality. Be true to yourself. The process is one of integrating into a unified whole the confusion of conflicting impulses. This is not always easy. It means that desires must not be regarded singly. They must be compared with the personality structure and finally the solution must be transformed into action. The method of integration is that the elements of any one situation are analysed, considered in relation to the experiences of the personality structure, a solution is found, and finally this solution is given an expression in reality.

The analysis of the situation is complicated by the interjection of various desires, the real issue of which may be clouded by rationalisation. The desire for self-respect is often a potent factor influencing a decision. Individual vanity can easily dictate a wrong course of conduct. Personal feelings and relations may introduce other complications. To keep a man's mind healthy his self-respect must be nurtured. This applies both to executives and to their relations with their subordinates. No subordinate must be allowed to feel for a prolonged period that he is of little importance in the scheme of things. The man, be he executive or worker, who feels he is in a position not worthy of his ability, cannot develop a healthy mental outlook.

The primary craving for self-assertion and the respect of others is normal and, if judiciously stimulated, is a potent factor for achieving progress. Too much self-complacency is bad—but so is too little. The individual who is completely satisfied with himself is stagnant. It is critical dissatisfaction with existing conditions that is the driving force resulting in progress. Dissatisfaction is an unhealthy mental state. But once an outlet is provided it becomes a healthy natural urge, and achievement must result.

The problem of self-integration and self-development is then to provide a method of satisfying one's impulses of self-assertion and self-respect in such a way that the result will be in harmony and not in conflict with the other elements constituting the personality. In finding such a solution self-deception must be guarded against. There must be no self-pity or self-elevation. The deeper natural desires of the individual must be subordinated and synthesised and a healthy outlet found for them. They must be organised in their correct orientation to each other and their strength regulated in accordance with the circumstances of external reality. The control of these desires is not a simple problem of habit formation. Honest recognition of their implications will mean a great deal in achieving ultimate success.

The individual can with advantage take a normal and healthy interest in the gradual process of his self-development without incurring odium as an egoist. Once he has learnt to respect himself he will cease to be insistent in his demands for respect from others. His personality will begin to be integrated and adjusted to the demands of reality. His outlook upon life will be broadened and he will become more tolerant and understanding towards his fellows. He will be able to view the situations in business, and in life generally, more as a whole than as a series of isolated units. His interests will become less partial, personal bias and personal desire will be subordinate to what is right and what is wrong. As an executive his subordinates will be willing to let him represent them, and will willingly defer to his point of view. His personality will not clash with theirs but will adjust itself to them, and at the same time will be an instrument both for moulding and for stimulating their actions.

His personality must be such that subordinates will not repress their own wants and knowledge before it in an attitude of subservience. His personality will not rule through repression and control by force, but through leadership and getting the very best out of all with whom he comes into contact to help his leadership to be wise and effective. Society both in business and elsewhere is too complex for integrations to be contrived to include all its tangles, but the effectively developed personality will be more competent and ready to cope with difficult situations. Its powers, based on the trinity of experience, knowledge, and control, will give it strength to find an adequate solution, and in turn that solution will be stored away in the memory structure of the individual still further to strengthen the personality integration.

### FUTURE LEADERS OF INDUSTRY

NEW developments in industrial organisation, the rationalisation of production and distribution, the formation of the huge combines of to-day, have meant that new types of executive must be trained—men with the capacity to absorb facts, men with enormous breadth of outlook and the power effectively to decide the destinies of millions. It will be to these men that industry of the future will look with hope. Their knowledge will be obtained both from the universities and from the schools of practical experience, but on themselves alone will their self-realisation be dependent. The day of the individualist in industry is drawing to a close.

The executive of the future will find it necessary to live and direct his life not only within himself, but to integrate his personality and adjust it to act as an influence to inspire and stimulate those who are working for him to greater and more enthusiastic efforts. He must be a teacher as well as a ruler, a leader as well as a commander. He must possess the judgment to surround himself with men in whom he has confidence. He should not hesitate to delegate his work to them. He should keep his mind free from the burden of detail, and develop his personality so that conflict will give it greater strength. He must regulate his activities so that work will be balanced by leisure—so that his mental outlook will be continuously freshened to provide for any ordeal that may arise.

The young man with ambition to be such a leader in industry will have to plan his life for himself. During his childhood his parents should realise their responsibility and train him in habits of right thinking. When he reaches years of understanding his destiny is in his own hands. He must set his objective and integrate himself to its achievement. The discipline may be stern but he must not deviate from the path he has set for himself. Then when adequate experience and knowledge have been acquired, opportunity will present itself and he will be capable of grasping it and making the most of it.

## A GUIDE TO FURTHER READING

THOSE who are interested in the topics discussed in this section will find many good books to read. One of the most up-to-date and authoritative books on the new science of management is *Management of To-morrow* by L. Urwick (Nisbet). Another book in a similar vein is *The Philosophy of Management*, by O. Sheldon (Pitman). The most fascinating account of the integration of the personality is contained in *An Introduction to Social Psychology*, by W. McDougall (Methuen). For more general information the reader should refer to *The Principles of Psychology*, by W. James (Macmillan). A short volume on the importance of the personality in selling which is easily and quickly read is *Personal Salesmanship*, by R. Simmat (Pitman). Other extremely practical books are *Psychology in Business Relations*, by A. J. Snow (A. W. Shaw), *The Psychology of Management*, by L. M. Gilbreth (Sturgis & Walton), and *Industrial Leadership*, by H. L. Gantt (Yale University Press).

# HOW GOODS ARE PRODUCED : THE FACTORY

*by N. M. BALCHIN, B.A.(Cantab.)*

SOME years ago, when modern factory methods were beginning to attract attention in England, a humorous story was current concerning a certain factory in America. It was said that pigs were brought to the factory and driven in at one end of a huge machine, emerging at the other as sausages and Gladstone bags. In this story we have, humorously expressed, a statement of the functions of a factory. A factory may be a small shed or it may cover hundreds of acres. It may employ four men, it may employ ten thousand. But, fundamentally, it is a vast machine into which raw material in some form is fed, which carries out certain modifications to that material, and which finally produces a refined and " worked " product.

It is not easy to write in general terms of the process of production of goods, for the amount of refinement carried out in the factory varies tremendously. To take a simple example: it is comparatively easy to follow the process by which a maker of custard powder converts his raw material, cornflour, into his finished product. A modification has taken place—indeed a very important one, but there is an easily perceived similarity between the raw material and the finished article. When, however, a manufacturer takes the simple primary materials, wood and metal, and converts them into a product like a finished motor-car, it is clear that the process of manufacture has brought about an infinitely more complicated, more difficult, and more significant change. It is not too much to say that the degree of civilisation of a community as we understand it may be measured by the extent to which it can modify its raw materials by the manufacturing processes of the factory.

Despite these wide variations, however, there are certain activities which are common to all factories. The most important in order are: the receipt of raw material; the storage of the raw material; the process of modification of the raw material; the transport of goods through the factory during the process of manufacture ; the storage of the finished goods ; and the dispatch of the finished goods.

### A MAN AND A TYPEWRITER: A FACTORY IN MINIATURE

LET us imagine for a moment a factory in miniature—one man working a typewriter. He is working on a certain raw material—blank paper—to turn it into a certain finished product—typewritten sheets. What does he do ? He fetches a stock of blank sheets (receipt of raw material) ; he places these beside him on his left (storage of raw material) ; he places a sheet in the typewriter and types (process of modification of raw material) ; as he does so, the paper moves in the carriage of the machine (transport during manufacture) ; he removes the finished sheet and puts it on his right (storage of finished goods) ; he places the finished sheet in an envelope and posts it (dispatch of finished goods).

Here we have in miniature a reproduction of the whole process of manufacture. Multiply a thousandfold and we have a factory. And it is precisely by this multiplication of the individual worker that the factory has evolved. Before the days of factories we may assume that practically all work was done individually—one man carried out in sequence every process between the raw material and the finished article. In some industries craftsmanship of this sort exists to this day, but in the course of time it was found that better results were achieved by segregating the various processes, and arranging for one man to bring raw material for all, one to carry out one process and one another, and one to remove the goods they had made.

Upon this simple division of labour the modern manufacturing process is built, and to-day we have the large factory with its scores of specialists—men who, by devoting all their time to one small part of the work, achieve at that part a degree of proficiency impossible by the old method of one man carrying out the whole process. Here, then, is our definition complete—a modern factory is a place where a number of human beings are engaged in refining and modifying raw material, the community being so organised that the work of production and the responsibility for various processes is subdivided amongst its members.

If our definition that a factory is a vast machine holds good, it is clear that, in considering how goods are produced, two factors are concerned. First, *Equipment*, that is to say, the

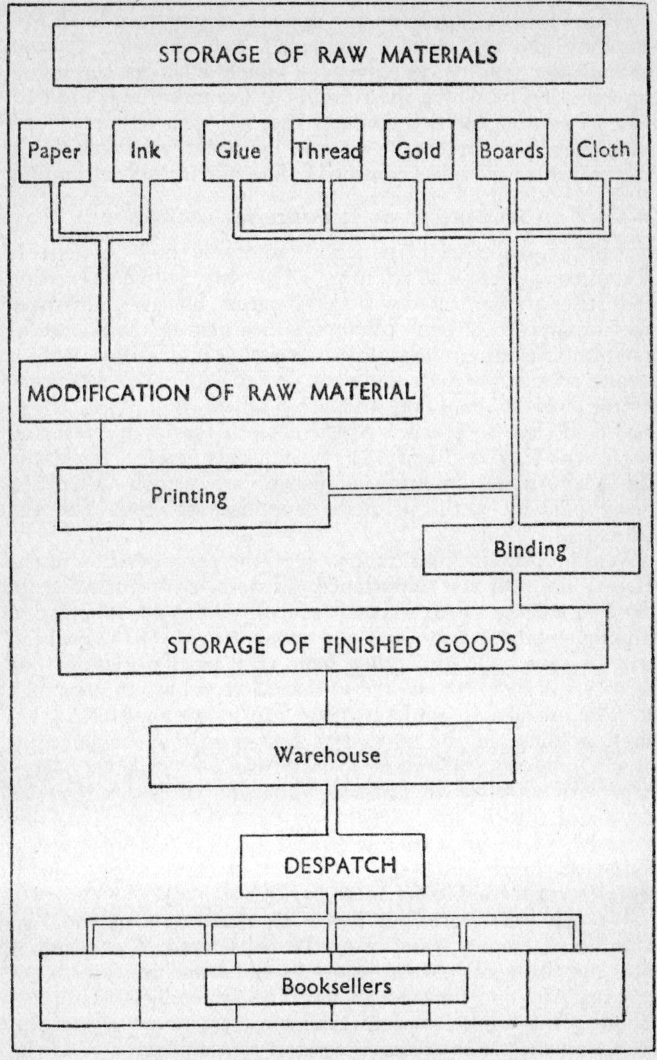


THE PROCESS OF MANUFACTURE

*An illustration from book printing and binding.*

machine itself—which for our purpose comprises the factory building and the plant it contains; and secondly, *Control*, that is the guiding intelligence—which includes the actual organisation by which the running of the machine is ordered. Let us assume for the moment that we wish to carry out a manufacturing process, and deal in order with the main factors which we must consider before our factory is running.

### HOW THE SITE OF THE FACTORY IS CHOSEN

THE general area in which a factory is built is actually often a matter of chance. The way in which certain industries are associated with certain areas, however, illustrates the importance of such matters as nearness to the source of raw material, the availability of suitable and skilled labour, and an adequate water supply and power. An obvious example is the whisky distilling industry, which is carried on in Scotland close to supplies of the essential grain and peat and where the Highland water is particularly suitable. Similarly, the heavy metal smelting industries are usually associated geographically with adequate supplies of coal for the furnaces.

Within a certain locality, however, the exact position of the factory site is of first importance. If we place our new factory close to a large town, we shall probably have no difficulty in finding suitable labour, and our transport costs to the railhead will be low. On the other hand, the ground rent of our factory will be infinitely higher than if we go into the country. It is a mistake to underestimate the importance of factors such as these in the successful and economic management of our concern. There is a classic instance of a very large firm with a factory in London which moved bodily into the depths of the country so as to be nearer the source of its raw material. One year later it moved back to London, having found it quite impossible to find suitable workers with which to staff the factory in an agricultural area.

We may, therefore, put down, as illustrative of the vast number of factors which must be considered in choosing a site, the likely cost of transport to and from the factory, of raw material and finished goods; the availability of suitable labour; the public services available (gas, water, electricity, etc.), and their cost; relative costs of rent and rates; and the goodwill or otherwise likely to accrue from association with a certain area. In most instances we shall probably find that

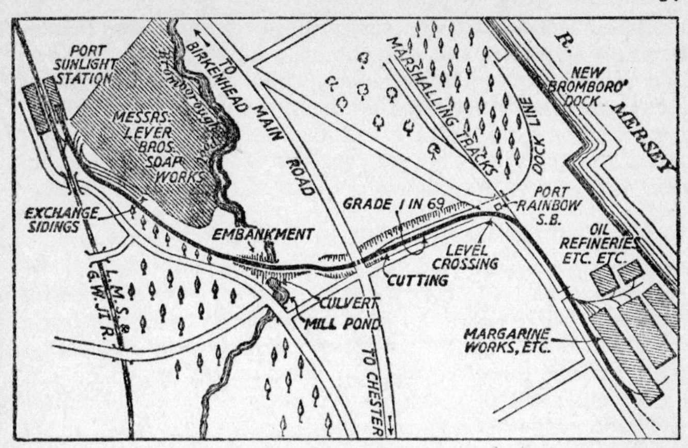


[*Railway* **Magazine.**

A SUITABLE FACTORY SITE

*A plan of Messrs. Lever Bros. Soap Works, showing their private railway line and the adjacent docks, water, and main road facilities for transport.*

to erect our factory in an area where other factories of a similar type already exist will lower our costs, as we shall be able to take advantages of the conveniences which they have been compelled to obtain.

### THE DESIGN OF THE FACTORY DEPENDS ON THE BUSINESS

It is hardly necessary to say that the whole design of our factory building must depend on the precise nature of the work to be done in it. It is a curious fact that this, platitudinous as it may sound, is still very frequently forgotten in factory design. All over the country are factories which, as architectural designs, are excellent. But they have been built entirely regardless of their purpose. The true art of the factory designer is to produce a strictly functional building ; that is to say, to visualise the processes going on, and to " build the factory round the job." It is extremely uneconomic to attempt to fit a process into an unsuitable building.

With this proviso, we may say that there are two main types of factory building. First, there is the *gravity type*, which consists of several storeys, and is designed to make use of the force of gravity to the greatest possible extent.

Broadly speaking, this type of factory operates on the principle that the raw material is taken to the top at the outset, and passes downwards through the building from process to process. Let us suppose that our raw material has to undergo five processes of approximately equal importance. Our factory might then consist of six storeys—the top for process one, the next for process two, and so on, leaving the ground floor for storage and dispatch. The gravity method is particularly useful where the cost of land is very high, or where the process concerns some such substance as flour, which can be transported from floor to floor by simply pouring it down gravity chutes. It is less useful where the article manufactured is in units which are so bulky or heavy that to bring them down is more difficult than to push them along on the level.

Secondly, there is the *one-floor type* of factory which, as its name suggests, is all on the ground level. Most of the typical, modern factories with their saw-toothed roofs are of the one-floor type. Here the principle is that the raw material enters at one end of the factory and moves through the sequences of processes at a constant level, emerging at the other end as the finished article. Factories of this type naturally take up more ground space, but they are comparatively cheap to build, and dispense with all problems of up and down transport.

It is not possible to make any real comparison between the advantages of these two types of factory buildings without reference to the processes concerned. On the whole, there is perhaps a slight balance in favour of the one-floor type, but the determining factor is often the amount of land available and its cost. On the new factory estates, where land is still reasonably cheap, the one-floor type predominates, but on valuable town sites the area needed for a one-floor factory makes its cost prohibitive.

## CHOOSING BETWEEN MEN AND MACHINES

HAVING selected our site and erected our factory, we now have to decide what plant we need and then buy it and install it. Here again one of the first factors we have to consider is cost. Whatever our processes may be, we are almost sure to be confronted with the problem of how far to mechanise our factory. There are few things that cannot be done mechanically nowadays if desired, and we are likely to be constantly faced by the problem: "Shall we do that job with the aid of a machine, or shall we employ men to do it?"

The answer is seldom simple. On the one hand the wages of ten men are greater than the running cost of a machine, the machine takes up less space, and probably does the job more quickly. But, on the other hand, the first cost of the machine may easily be several thousand pounds ; it may depreciate rapidly in value, and be obsolete in five years ; we may not have sufficient work to keep it going, so that it stands idle for half its time, steadily depreciating in value ; and it has not the unique advantage of the human being, that he can be utilised at any time for almost any job which has to be done.

In making our decision, then, we must be guided by one thing, and by one thing only—the answer to the question, " Is mechanisation likely to be a real economy, when all these factors have been taken into account ? " And in arriving at our answer, we must be influenced by the type of product at which we aim. There are still some processes in which the human workman can produce a higher quality article than the machine, and if we aim at a quality article with the intention of selling comparatively few in number, but of making a high profit on each one, it may pay us in the end to spend a little more on production cost to obtain the highest possible quality.

It stands to reason that Henry Ford, producing a car which is a marvel of value at its price, aiming, that is to say, at a low individual profit on each car but an output of thousands a year, will, broadly speaking, reap far more benefit from intensive mechanisation than a firm which produces far fewer cars, but which strives to make them the last word in luxury, and sells them at a much higher price. In short, The Ford Motor Company and Messrs. Rolls Royce are aiming at different markets, and their methods of production must vary accordingly.

In practice, the general answer to the question " to mechanise or not to mechanise " is likely to be provided by common sense and the accepted practice of the industry. But in an age of intensive competition, the clever mechanisation of a process, by lowering production cost, may provide a firm with just the advantage it needs to capture the market from its competitors. For this reason a word is necessary on the subject of buying plant. Except in very special circumstances we are likely to be confronted by an almost bewildering choice of machinery to do our work, and for every different make of machine the makers will certainly put forward the claim that it is the last word in efficiency.

We must, therefore, take great care over two things. First, machines, like human beings, do some types of work better than others. We must be careful to see that the machine selected is the best available for our particular job. If we wish to buy a machine for wrapping jelly cubes, we must see a demonstration machine actually do the job. We must not rest content with the fact that this machine wraps pieces of soap of approximately the same size at express speed. Nor must we forget the conditions under which the machine has to work. A machine which works beautifully under clear conditions may be a constant source of trouble if the atmosphere of our factory is unavoidably dusty. And a delicate, high-speed machine may shake itself to pieces if our floors are not firm.

Secondly, in estimating the cost of any machine, we must not allow it too long a life. We must be prepared to " write off " its first cost within a few years. The machine may be running perfectly ten years later. But by that time someone will assuredly have invented one more efficient, and, unless we are prepared ruthlessly to scrap our obsolete machine, however well it may be running, we shall find our production costs higher than those of our competitors. Every efficient factory makes careful provision for its machinery to be maintained in first-class condition. But the object of this maintenance should be to keep the machine in a condition to work at its fastest and best. It should not be to prolong its life after it is really obsolete.

### PROVIDING THE POWER TO RUN THE MACHINES

It is fair to assume that in these days our machinery will be run where possible by electricity. But we have still to decide whether we will generate our own power or obtain it from the general supply. Cost will almost certainly be the deciding factor. If we decide to generate our own supply we are faced with a choice between burning coal or oil fuel to drive our generators. This will again be largely a question of cost.

In the factory itself we have the choice between two methods of harnessing our electric power to our machines. We can have a large motor, driving a long shafting, and take our power from the shafting to our machines by belt; or we can equip each of our machines with its own small electric motor. Modern practice, speaking very broadly, favours the small unit motor. The cost is a little higher, but there is the big advantage that a motor breakdown affects one machine only, whereas with a general shafting, a motor breakdown may bring a whole shop to a standstill. It is only fair to say, however, that many of the largest and most up-to-date shops still obtain their power from a line shaft. Once again, the determining factor is the detailed nature of the work.

It has been demonstrated over and over again that good lighting plays a most important part in promoting efficiency. No one who has strained his eyes at fine work in a poor light can doubt that this physical factor is of first-class importance. A well-designed lighting system aims at providing the best possible illumination at the working point. It is not necessary to flood a complete workroom with a blaze of expensive light. But it is very necessary that the small areas where fine work is being done shall be adequately lighted.

Good lighting is not necessarily bright lighting. Indeed, care must be taken not to over-illuminate and so dazzle the worker's eyes with glare. The main necessities are the correct brightness of illumination and good shading, so as to throw the light on to the working point. It is often possible to economise on the total consumption of current, while improving the standard of lighting enormously, simply by taking care to concentrate the light where it is wanted. Standards of illumination have been worked out for practically every class of work, and the big firms of illuminating engineers offer free advice in the installation of the proper system for any species of factory.

### GOOD VENTILATION IS ESSENTIAL FOR EFFICIENCY

No one who has worked in a stuffy room can doubt that good ventilation is essential for efficiency. Ventilation must be designed, first, to keep the air pure and to extract dust, smoke, and fumes of all sorts; and secondly, to maintain a comfortable working temperature. In some factories, where the working temperature affects the material, complete systems of air-conditioning are installed, which maintain the air at a more or less constant level of temperature and humidity. Where such a plant is unnecessary, the air can be purified and kept moving by "blower" and "extractor" fans. It has been conclusively shown that the discomfort which we call

" stuffiness " is more a result of stagnant air than of too high a temperature, and even the most sultry room can be made tolerable if fans are used to promote air movement.

### EFFICIENCY ACHIEVED BY CAREFUL LAY-OUT

WE must now briefly consider the lay-out of our factory, that is to say, the actual arrangement of our departments within the walls, and of the machinery within departments. Few single factors can contribute more to the efficient running of a factory than a good and convenient lay-out; and since we have supposed that we have a new building, specially designed to accommodate our processes, it should not be difficult to obtain an excellent lay-out.

We have already said that before the factory is designed the actual sequence of processes and the relative position and size of departments should have been considered carefully, in order that the most suitable arrangement of accommodation can be made. Hence, when the factory is actually in existence, we should have little more to do than to move our machinery in. Nevertheless, it is worth while to consider the main principles on which the inside of our factory should be arranged.

Basically, there is only one very obvious axiom to be remembered, which is that the shortest distance between two points is the straight line joining them. Our lay-out must be such that the internal transport of goods in the process of manufacture is reduced to an absolute minimum. Ideally, we should have a single-floor factory, with raw material entering at one end, and moving in a straight line right through the factory, emerging at the other end as a finished article. Throughout the factory the end of one process should bring the goods to a point as close as possible to the beginning of the next, and so on.

In practice, it is hardly necessary to say, it is rarely possible to attain perfect, straight-line production of this kind. It may be that at one point the product has to be dried for several days in ovens, and it may not be possible to have the ovens in the middle of the production line. The goods must be carried away and brought back after drying. Alternatively, we may wish to produce several different articles, on which the processes are the same for the first few stages of manufacture, but which after that point require entirely different treatment.

We may even find that a process has to be repeated at

different stages in the production sequence, so that an article, after being treated by a machine as process three, may have to be brought back to the same machine again after process six. Unless we are very lucky, therefore, our final lay-out will almost certainly be a compromise—a compromise between the geometrical perfection of a straight line, and the necessary crossings of routes and retracements of steps which our processes demand.

### COST VERSUS SAVING OF TIME

LAY-OUT is an almost embarrassingly easy subject to discuss, because its principles are so childishly simple. On the other hand, it is a fiendishly difficult subject in practice, because the simple principles can so rarely be adhered to. It is an interesting and illuminating experiment to attempt to "lay out" some part of a private house—say a bathroom—with the object of saving oneself the maximum amount of trouble and time in the processes of bathing and shaving. In the first five minutes it will be found that the whole thing comes down to a matter of cost. Three steps can be saved if one is prepared to increase expenditure upon towels, two more if mirrors can be duplicated, and so on. Exactly the same situation always arises in laying out a factory.

Suppose for a moment we encounter one of the situations mentioned above, and that process three involves the use of a milling machine, which is also required for process seven. Now it is clear that we can do one of two things: either we can carry our work back to the milling machine used for process three, or we can buy another milling machine for process seven. The first violates our primary principle, since it involves the work doubling on its tracks; while the second enables us to keep the work moving in a straight line, but at the expense of providing another machine. Clearly we must ultimately be guided by what our common sense tells us is the greater disadvantage in cost and inconvenience.

We may very fairly sum up the solution of the lay-out problem, therefore, by saying that it consists of an application of simple geometric principles within the bounds of common sense. We can only adhere as closely as possible to our first principle, and, when circumstances arise which suggest that we can adhere to it no longer, consider carefully whether the saving of transport cost does or does not outweigh the cost of extra equipment.

Apart from the actual geographical position of departments and of machines within those departments, there are a number of subsidiary factors in the lay-out of a factory which are apt to be overlooked. In our enthusiasm to get the actual flow of production right we may tend to forget those persons and things which are not directly concerned with the producing process. There are such people as maintenance engineers and shop foremen, and such processes as inspection. There is a curious tradition that the maintenance engineers, actually most important and often rather expensive people, can be accommodated in any little corner which is not needed for anything else.

As a result, a mechanic takes from a machine a small gear wheel which needs a little filing, and solemnly carries it away to where his little hutch is situated, three storeys up, next to the stores. Small running repairs which would take two minutes if his shop were in the right place (that is, near the machines with which he has to deal) tend, as a result, to take half an hour. We also find the shop foreman given a little office next to a rivetting machine, with the result that conversation in his office can only be carried on by persons with well-developed lungs, who can shout down the noise of the machines. These are small points perhaps, and such difficulties are often not at all easy to avoid. But they illustrate the sort of thing which decreases efficiency, and which should not occur in the well-conceived lay-out.

## THE CONTROL BEHIND THE MACHINE

THE above is a brief description of the bare bones of a factory and its purely inanimate equipment ; the machine itself, to return to our original simile. We must now consider the nature of the guiding intelligence behind the machine. We have a building of a certain size, proportion and shape. In it we have certain machines arranged according to a definite plan. We have also by this time employed a large staff, men and women of a variety of qualifications to perform all the necessary kinds of work. It remains to describe the methods by which this collection of men, machines and buildings are welded into a producing unit and controlled.

The greatest essential in the control of our factory is that behind every process, every movement of material, and every piece of work done, there must be a definite plan, a plan which arranges beforehand what is to be done, co-ordinates individuals and departments in the doing of it, and, not stopping there, keeps a close watch to see that the agreed plan is adhered to. Let us consider for a moment a simple process of manufacture, and suppose that we are making kettles. We may have a department which makes the bodies of the kettles in various sizes and shapes, a department which makes lids, also in various designs, and a department which does the enamelling. We will also suppose that there is no central planning system at all, that the foremen of the various departments are left to exercise their own judgment as to what they will produce.

We can easily visualise a state of affairs in which the body-making department turns out thousands of large size bodies, the lid-making department thousands of small lids, and the enamelling department, in a wild spasm of enthusiasm, enamels them all blue. Meanwhile our sales department is crying aloud for supplies of medium size kettles enamelled brown. We have here a rather exaggerated picture of uncontrolled production. Our right hand does not know what our left hand is doing, because there is no co-ordinating plan of action.

The object of production planning is to provide this co-ordinating influence, and to ensure, in the above example, first, that all departments are engaged in the manufacture of the articles required either for orders, or to maintain stocks at an agreed level ; secondly, that the lids produced are of the right size to fit the bodies, and produced in the appropriate quantities ; thirdly, that the lids and bodies are produced at approximately the same rate, so that no large surplus of half-finished work is left lying about the factory ; and fourthly, that the enamelling department is not only instructed as to the colour to be applied, but is actually issued with the right enamel for the purpose.

### HOW THE PLAN IS SET IN MOTION

LET us now see exactly what the process of production planning involves, on the basis of our kettle factory. We have first of all to decide what we want to make. In some cases we may be making to order. The sales force sends us in an order for a certain number of kettles of a certain design, and we have to set to work and make them. Alternatively, we may aim at supplying orders from our stocks of finished kettles, in which case the work done in the factory will aim at ensuring that we always have enough of every type of kettle in stock to meet any order we are likely to get.

We naturally wish to keep our stocks as low as possible, because we do not wish to have our money locked up in stock. If we have twenty thousand pounds worth of kettles sitting on the shelves of our stockroom doing nothing, then we have twenty thousand pounds which for the moment is doing us no good, and earning us nothing. We must, therefore, decide beforehand what minimum stock we must carry, and every time any particular line reaches the minimum agreed, we shall set the factory to work to make more.

Suppose, therefore, that we decide that we need ten gross more kettles of a certain design, enamelled blue. Some time before we wish this work actually to begin, we shall issue a plan which says this order is coming along. We shall probably send a copy of this plan, first, to our storekeeper, who will get the raw material ready—the metal for the lids and bodies, and the enamel for the enamelling department ; secondly, to the foreman of each department, who will draw the necessary tools from the tool stores, get the blueprints from which he works, and get his machines ready for the job ; and thirdly, to the keeper of the finished work store, who will prepare space to receive the kettles when they have been made.

Of course the processes do not all happen together. It may be some days after the body-making department has begun the order before the bodies begin to reach the enamelling department, and some days later still before they finally reach the finished goods store. It is our job, therefore, not only to tell these various departments that the work is being put in hand, but to tell them as accurately as we can when it will reach them. To do this we have to know the productive capacity of our various departments for the line in question, and this involves knowing the likely output of every machine in the factory. This sounds impossibly difficult, but in fact there are factories manufacturing thousands of different lines where the production planning is so accurate that one can almost set a watch by the time at which machines change over from one job to another.

### WATCHING THE PLAN IN PROGRESS

It would, however, be a mistake to suppose that proper production control depends simply on careful forward planning, and on an accurate knowledge of the likely output of machines.

An equally essential feature is keeping a close watch to ensure that the plan is actually carried out. Although we may have the best staff and machinery in the world we can never be sure that something will not happen in the middle of the production process which will throw our whole time-table out. If a breakdown occurs in the body-making department, we shall find ourselves with our lids completed, but our enamelling department waiting for the arrival of more bodies before the order can be finished.

To guard against emergencies of this sort we may resort to a progress chart, a graphical record, kept by the planning department, of the actual progress of the order through the works. As each process is completed it is entered on the chart so that we may see at a glance precisely how far an order has gone at any given moment, and how its production is adhering to our original schedule. Supposing we find that a certain department has fallen behind the schedule, and that the order may not be completed to time for lack of the parts it makes. We must then inquire into the matter, and arrange for extra pressure to be exerted in this department to make up the lost ground, by putting more men on the job for a few hours, or by using an additional machine.

Broadly speaking, we may say that, in the average factory, the original plan demands a certain result in a certain time, and gives an idea of how that result may be obtained. Before the order is finally completed and safely lodged in store, the plan may need a number of modifications, but, provided the necessity for those is observed at the earliest possible moment and they are made without delay, the result is obtained within the time specified.

### TOO MUCH STOCK MEANS IDLE MONEY

It is uneconomical to carry larger stock than is absolutely necessary, as the stocks represent money locked up and lying idle, and this applies both to stocks of raw material and stocks of finished goods. But this desire to keep stocks to a minimum must, like every other principle, be applied on a common-sense basis. It may well be that we need keep a stock of raw material sufficient only to last us three weeks. On the other hand, we may be able to buy so much more cheaply if we buy in bulk, that it pays us to buy at a single purchase enough to last us six months or a year.

This problem arises constantly in regard to stocks of

finished goods. We may decide that if we keep what is normally a three weeks' stock of a certain line, no sudden demand is ever likely to find us unable to give delivery. But there is another very important factor to be considered. There is an economic minimum for a " batch," below which production cost tends to rise. To carry the point to absurdity, we may find that we have in stock one kettle less than the agreed minimum three weeks' stock. But it will clearly be absurd to manufacture one. We must make enough to make it worth while to issue tools, set up machines, and so on.

This question of length of " run " on a certain job is extremely important. In some types of work, it may easily take a day to set up a big machine to do certain work. It is clear, therefore, that our production planning must aim at giving our machines as long a run as possible once the expensive setting up has been done. We are thus confronted with a pretty problem; on the one hand, we must arrange long runs so as to keep our machines working for as great a proportion of their time as possible; on the other hand, we must not fill our stores with masses of finished goods which we shall not sell in five years.

The planner's dream is to work in a factory where only one line is made, of which the sales just keep pace with the rate at which it can be produced. His fate is usually to work in a factory where there are at least a thousand different lines, the demand for which fluctuates violently and incomprehensibly; he has no sooner had a machine set up to deal with one particular line, of which his stock is running low, than a rush order arrives for an entirely different line, which makes it necessary to pull the machine down again and turn it on to the new job.

### PRODUCTION TIME IS A TEST OF EFFICIENCY

It is the obvious desire of every factory to get its orders finished and away. Work in progress lying about the factory takes up space, and once again represents material, and therefore capital, lying idle. Theoretically, once a piece of material has entered the production process it should never stop. It should either be in the process of manufacture or going to the next process, and the production process should flow steadily onward like a stream. In practice, absolutely continuous movement of this kind is rarely possible, though it is approached in those factories where practically the whole process is carried out as the material moves along on a travelling band. It is usually a sign of bad production planning and bad co-ordination of processes if large quantities of half-finished work are scattered about the factory, piled on benches or on the floor.

In this connection it is interesting to compare the overall time taken to complete an order with the net working time during which work is being done on it. Even in reasonably efficient factories the comparison is usually surprising, and one is liable to find that an order which calls for the expenditure of ten working hours takes a fortnight to get through the factory.

In the absence of any organised system a department may " hoard " work which is ready to be removed, simply to ensure that when it has to be moved, the removal can be done " in one go." To illustrate what may happen if work is left about in this way, one can instance a certain factory in which a pile of half-finished work stayed in a department for weeks. Inquiry showed that it had been there as long as any one could remember. Presumably it was some order which had been begun, had reached a certain stage, and had then been completely forgotten.

This is an extreme example it is true, but it illustrates the way in which the overall production time can be needlessly increased by a casual attitude towards moving it on. With a proper system of planning and progressing, this cannot very well occur. The rate of progress of the work from department to department is arranged and closely supervised. A great deal can be done by encouraging workers, and particularly foremen, to regard any order as a sort of red-hot brick, something to be got rid of and out of the department as soon as the work which the department does on it is finished.

## MOVING THE GOODS FROM MACHINE TO MACHINE

THIS conveniently brings us to the consideration of internal transport, which is the system by which the goods are moved through the factory from machine to machine and department to department during the manufacturing process. Upon it depends to a great extent the factory's ability to get orders through all the processes in reasonable time, and it is almost entirely responsible for making the gap between overall time and net process time as small as possible.

If the total time in the factory is to be reduced to a minimum, every effort must be made to remove work from a machine or a department as soon after it is finished as possible. We may define the object of any system of internal transport as the supply of raw material and the removal of finished goods at such a rate that machines can be kept steadily supplied with work, while at the same time, the unnecessary piling up of raw material or finished work is avoided. The function of internal transport is similar to that of a Wimbledon ball boy, who must relieve the players of the trouble of fetching balls for themselves, while keeping the court clear of unwanted balls.

Every possible gradation in organisation of internal transport is to be found working smoothly in various factories. In one, the quickest, most economical, and most convenient method is for the actual worker to fetch his own raw material and carry away his own finished work. In another, certain workers spend half their time on the production process, and the other half in transporting work for their fellows. In a third there may be a centralised department which deals with nothing but the transport of goods about the factory; while in a fourth, internal transport is so highly mechanised that goods hardly need to be man-handled at all.

Efficiency in the transport of goods, as in every other piece of factory organisation, is not achieved by adopting the cheapest method nor by adopting the one that comes first to mind, nor even by adopting the most convenient. Maximum efficiency is nearly always a compromise between convenience and cost. In connection with mechanical handling of goods there is a great temptation to over-organise. It is universally admitted that it is desirable to cut out as much man-handling as possible. But the primary object of doing so is economy, and if, as some firms do, we install a thousand-pound mechanical handling device to save ourselves ten hours a year in men's time, we have probably made a poor bargain. The mechanical device may look prettier and more efficient, but in terms of men-hours, what it has saved us is negligible.

### INTERNAL TRANSPORT MUST BE EXACTLY TIMED

CLOSE attention to the problem of internal transport is an essential of good production planning. It is useless to produce a plan which dovetails the production time of department A with that of department B beautifully, unless we can be quite sure that the work from department A will actually arrive to schedule. This arrival to schedule is the responsibility of the transport department. The responsibility of department A finishes when it completes its own part of a job. The responsibility of department B begins only when the job arrives. The physical movement between A and B is the responsibility of transport. Transport must, therefore, like the producing departments, be given a definite schedule of work. It must be told what it has to move, when it has to move it, where it is to be found, and where it has to be taken. Those are the essential outlines of its work.

The detailed arrangements are a continuous quest for the cheapest, quickest, and most convenient method of accomplishing this schedule. The main bugbear to avoid is the "empty journey," that is to say, a situation in which a truck goes empty to point A, collects a load, takes it to point B, unloads, and returns empty to its starting point. Every time this happens the truck has made two useless journeys to one useful one. The situation is exactly as though the *Flying Scotsman* journeyed empty to York, picked up its passengers, took them to Edinburgh, and returned empty to London.

Our transport, in fact, must be so cleverly planned that an empty journey is a rare occurrence. And this involves a complicated system of routes so that every time a truck unloads, it can immediately pick up, on the spot, a fresh load to take to its next stopping place. Just how much time and thought may be necessary to perfect a system of this kind in a factory with a dozen different departments and scores of different lines can be readily imagined.

### MACHINES WHICH SPEED UP PRODUCTION

AN enormous number of devices for eliminating handling of goods are on the market and more are arriving every day. The subject is one on which scores of books have been written. Some of the mechanical aids, which are to be found in most up-to-date factories, may be mentioned in order to indicate the general principles on which such machines are made.

The endless belt conveyor, which consists of a long belt driven at a set speed by pulleys, is a popular device in modern mass production factories. By means of it, goods can be conveyed from point to point by simply putting them on the belt and allowing them to move on with it to the required point. The assembly lines of the great car factories, on which the complete car chassis moves steadily forward, and is worked on as it passes, is a development of this system. For certain processes the moving belt is ideal, and it is a great pity that the attractiveness of " keeping everything moving " has resulted in attempts to use this system for work to which it is entirely unsuited. Correctly used, a moving belt conveyor comes near to the ideal " flow " system of production already mentioned.

The roller conveyor is a rather simpler application of the same principle. Instead of a mechanically driven belt, there is an inclined runway of ball-bearing rollers. Goods placed at the top of the runway pass down it to a distant point under the influence of gravity. The roller conveyor is a great convenience in handling goods, and has the additional advantage that it can be made portable, so as to link up any two points desired.

The overhead gantry or grab is a useful device in handling heavy material. It consists of a sort of overhead crane, running on elevated rails, which can travel from end to end of a shop. If a large and heavy casting which would need the efforts of three or four men to lift it has to be taken from one end of a shop to the other, the gantry can be run on its rails to the casting, which is then picked up by it and carried to its destination and deposited.

Of all handling devices, however, one of the commonest and most useful is the jack truck. The jack truck consists of a truck with a frame which can be made to rise a few inches, like the jack of a car. Goods are stored on wooden platforms, which are raised off the ground on wooden legs. When it is desired to move the load on a platform, the jack truck is run beneath the platform and the jacking mechanism employed, so that platform and load are both raised bodily from the floor. The truck can then be pulled away to its destination, and platform and load lowered gently to the floor again. The great advantage of the jack truck, of course, is that it is not necessary to load goods on to the truck and unload them again at the destination. The effect is as though one had been able to pick up a piece of the floor and move it bodily without disturbing the goods standing on it.

#### WASTE THAT IS PREVENTED BY INSPECTION

ATTEMPTS to increase the speed of production of a facto y must never be made at the expense of quality or excessi cost. The process of refinement of a raw material, which i

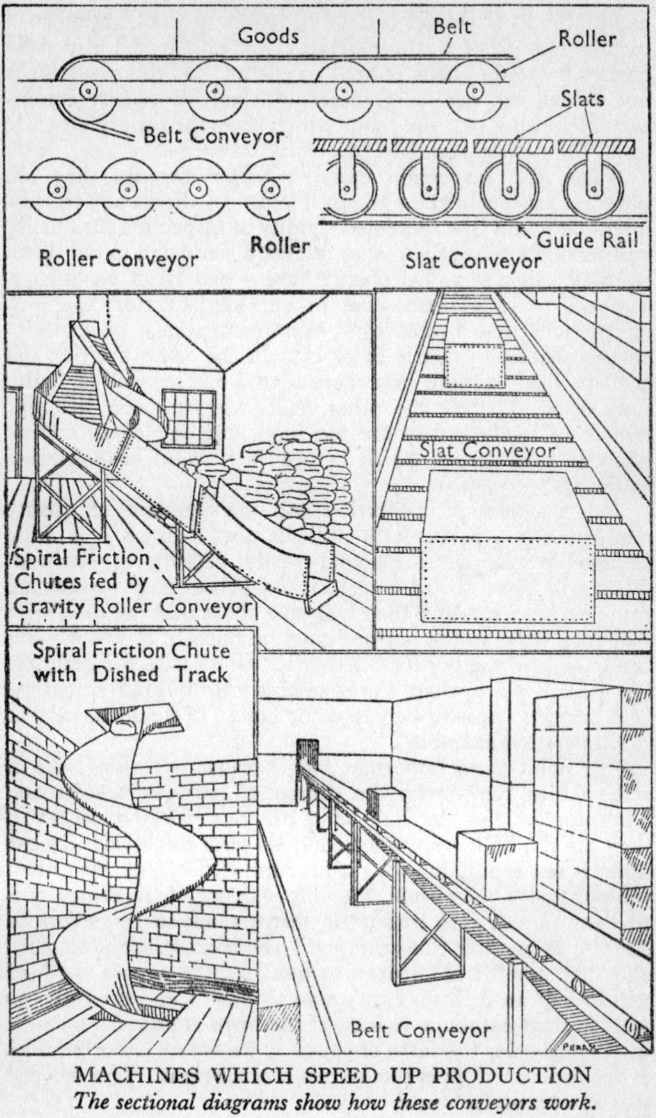

MACHINES WHICH SPEED UP PRODUCTION

*The sectional diagrams show how these conveyors work.*

manufacture, is almost certain to result in the creation of a certain amount of waste material. But in the well-organised factory a careful check is kept to ensure that this waste does not exceed the necessary minimum, and an equally careful check to ensure that the goods which leave the factory measure up to the desired standard of quality.

Waste and inspection come together because they are different aspects of the same problem. In almost any process it will be found that increased rigidity of inspection for quality will send the waste figures up, whilst a campaign to cut down the waste figures will probably have a bad effect on quality. Suppose for a moment that in our kettle factory we give instructions that a most rigid examination must be made to ensure that every kettle is of exactly the same height. We shall be likely to find that more kettles are rejected as faulty than usual. If, on the other hand, we complain that our figures of faulty kettles are too high, our employees will be likely to pass kettles which before they would have rejected as faulty.

This problem of inspection and the standard of quality demanded is a particularly difficult one, because it is quite impossible to give inspectors really definite instructions. They will know that the majority of kettles they inspect are quite satisfactory, and they will also know that the ones with half-inch holes in the bottom must be rejected as waste. But the trouble is the border-line cases. One kettle, for example, has a small place where the enamel is a little thin : otherwise it is perfect. Is it to be passed or not ? It would be easy to multiply such examples.

The point is an important one, because two things are at stake which may mean the difference between success and bankruptcy. On the one hand are our working costs ; if they are too high we cannot compete with our rivals. On the other is our reputation for quality, and if that goes, we cannot sell our goods. As usual, the only way out of the difficulty is to compromise ; to make the instructions to inspectors as definite as possible (for example, " the correct height for such and such a kettle is fourteen inches. You may pass anything within half an inch on either side of this "), and thereafter to trust to their common sense. If the work is one in which the inspection takes the form of gauging, we are on easier ground. If the article will pass the gauges it is all right. If it will not it is automatically waste.

### THE VALUE OF INSPECTION IN THE EARLY STAGES

In general we may find that it pays us to install inspection points at various stages in the process of manufacture rather than to leave all inspection until the job is completed. To take a simple example, let us suppose that we are working on a material which is liable to distortion, and that the process of manufacture takes six stages. Now, if it so happens that a certain piece of material becomes distorted during process one, and our only inspection point is at the end, then we shall go on and perform five more operations on a piece of material which must eventually be rejected. Whereas if there is an inspection point after process two, the faulty piece will be rejected then, and no more time will be wasted on it.

But factory waste is by no means solely a matter of spoiled pieces of work. Anything which can be lost, or wastefully cut, or misused, or broken, or blunted, can be a source of waste. Water, steam, power, light, packing materials, string, oil, raw material—all of them can be a fruitful source of costly waste. There are two very general remedies which can in particular prevent waste. The first is to keep a careful check on everything issued into the factory, and to compel the staff to account accurately for the materials it uses, and to make it responsible for the condition of the tools, etc., provided. The second is to enlist the whole personnel of the factory in the fight against waste by bringing to their attention its cost, the directions in which it is excessive, and specific means for avoiding it ; and by publishing the actual figures for the more important sources of waste, so as to keep in the mind of the worker the magnitude and progress of the fight.

### HOW STORES ARE ORGANISED

The normal factory is not only a place of production, but a place where raw materials and finished goods are stored. The organisation of storage is a most important phase of factory organisation. A good store is not just a dump, where things are kept without order, arrangement, or method. A good store has three main features : it must be easy to put things in ; it must be easy to see what the store contains ; and it must be easy to get things out.

To accomplish these ends, there are certain general principles which it is important to bear in mind. The store must be so arranged that there is plenty of gangway space in which to move goods, and the actual position of the goods on shelves or in bins must be such that they can be reached with reasonable ease. Far too many stores have corners which are accessible only to fearless Alpinists. For obvious reasons it will pay to keep the goods which are most frequently needed in the most accessible places, and in any event the relative positions of various goods must be determined on some definite plan, so that a worker fetching goods from store at least knows in what part they are likely to be.

Again, when goods are taken from store, they are usually being collected in definite assorted consignments. Is it possible to arrange the goods in store so that the collector of consignments may work methodically ? If they are arranged anyhow, a man collecting items from an order sheet will walk miles to and fro in the course of a day. If the store bins are arranged in the same order as the items on the sheet (or, alternatively, if the sheet is arranged in the same order as the bins !), he may collect a complete order in a single circuit of the store.

It is no reflection on the honesty of a staff if the stores are "out of bounds" except to strictly authorised persons, particularly if the stored material happens to be highly valuable. For the same reason, someone must check goods in and out of store with great care. It also greatly facilitates stock-taking if the bins themselves carry a visible record of the type and quantity of goods they contain. A "bin card" can easily be kept of such a kind that it can be altered every time goods are taken from the bin or put into it. Certain goods, moreover, are very rapidly ruined if they are not kept under suitable conditions of temperature, humidity, etc. If we are to avoid complaints from our customers our store must provide the right conditions.

Finally, it must be remembered that the stores are a very important part of the factory organisation, and the storekeeper must be kept informed of the demands likely to be made upon his space in exactly the same way that a foreman is told what demands are to be made on his machines. Far too often one finds that the first intimation the storekeeper receives that a consignment of goods is arriving, is their actual arrival on his doorstep. The result, of course, is that he has no chance of organising his work, and is forced to dump them in whatever space is available. Given proper notice, in the shape of a copy of the factory production plan, he has time to arrange for storage in a proper and convenient place.

### THE UNCEASING QUEST FOR IMPROVEMENT

LIKE every other worth-while occupation, the organisation of a factory is a job which has no end. It is better, says the proverb, to travel than to arrive, and with problems of organisation one has never arrived. But it is, nevertheless, highly important that we should keep on travelling; indeed, the greatest essential in a factory organisation is that however good it may be, an attitude of mind shall prevail which is always seeking for some new and better way of doing things.

In the well-organised factory, provision is made for this process of improvement. Improved methods and improved organisation are not the job of the management alone ; a busy factory manager, in fact, has often more than a full-time job in dealing with the immediate problems of setting and maintaining his schedules on the present methods. Every brain in the factory should be mobilised to tackle difficulties, and workers should be encouraged, by some sort of rewarded suggestion scheme, to put forward their ideas for improvements. Very often the man who works at a job, day in, day out, sees some opportunity for improvement which would never be noticed by any one not actively engaged in the work. It is extraordinary how many really useful ideas are actually forthcoming from a keen and efficient staff, if their co-operation is fully secured, and if they feel that their ideas are really welcomed.

### THE NECESSITY FOR A PAUSE TO THINK

FURTHERMORE, a certain amount of time should be allotted to the consideration of new and improved methods. One of the great dangers of a first-class and efficient organisation is that everything is so beautifully arranged, and everyone's time is so completely filled, that no one has time to think. The organisation gets to such a state that it resembles a cyclist grinding furiously along with head down, and working so hard that he completely misses a short cut to his destination.

For this reason it is desirable that some person or persons in the organisation should be relieved of the necessity of spending all their time on routine work, and should consider it an essential part of their job to experiment in search of improvements. Many firms, provided they are in a position to afford it, think nothing of sending their engineers all over the world to examine the plant used in other factories and other countries to see if any new discovery has evolved a machine which will simplify and cheapen their own work. The same principle applies equally to matters of organisation. New discoveries are constantly being made in the world of organisation, and not all useful schemes and ideas can be depended upon to come and knock at one's door. The progressive firm goes out and seeks them, experiments with them, and adapts them to its own use.

This aspect of organisation may be summed up shortly by saying that the efficient factory works out its organisation down to the minutest detail with great care, supervises its running with equal minuteness, and works incessantly towards the day when the whole structure can be joyfully scrapped, because something better has been found.

## SUGGESTIONS FOR FUTURE READING

BOOKS on factory methods and organisation are legion. The *Handbook of Business Administration*, edited by W. J. Donald, and *The Managements Handbook*, edited by Alford, are large scale reference books, dealing with most of the problems of organisation and management in great detail. Another standard book which has the rare advantage of being very readable is *Factory Organisation and Management*, by Davis. *Industrial Management*, by Robins and Folts, is an interesting " case book " of actual problems which have occurred in industry, and their solutions. It is particularly useful in that it cites specific instances rather than generalities. *The Meaning of Rationalisation* and *The Management of To-morrow*, two interesting books by Major L. Urwick, of the International Labour Office, deal with the significance of the modern movement in industry and the directions it is likely to take in the future.

# PSYCHOLOGY THAT MEASURES THE WORKER'S ABILITY

*by R. SIMMAT, M.A., of the National Institute of Industrial Psychology. Author of " Personal Salesmanship," " Market Research," " The Principles and Practice of Marketing," etc.*

THE benevolent industrial despot of the nineteenth century and of the earlier decade of the twentieth century, well-meaning and self-conscious of his good intentions, evolved a system of patronage to his employees which became known as " welfare work." The name was unfortunate. This system often was used by less benevolent industrialists with an eye to its advertising value. It was impressive to show visitors over oak-panelled staff libraries, spacious staff dining-rooms, and the elaborate offices of the welfare superintendent. Conscious of the patronage and even more conscious of the fact that their wage envelopes were still distressingly flat, workers became suspicious of the term " welfare work," even though in many instances management was making a genuine effort to ameliorate the conditions under which they performed their daily tasks. The term has fallen into disrepute, and the objectives which more far-seeing management really sought with welfare work are sought in a more subtle and more scientific way. Workers must be understood, not patronised.

Enlightened personnel administration recognises that if capital, or management, as the representative of capital, is to secure the maximum return from investment in labour—then, first, the right type of labour must be obtained for each job. There must be no more of the old system of indiscriminate hiring and then dismissal if the worker proved to be unsatisfactory. Secondly, workers once employed must be given working conditions under which they can give of their best—not badly ventilated, unhygienic sheds, nor elaborately wasteful and palatial factories, but just the kind of place most suitable for the work they are doing. Thirdly, the co-operation of the workers must be won by giving them security in their work, perhaps by means of a share in the profits of the business, by treating them with understanding, not with the sentimentality of the old welfare system.

Labour functions most efficiently when it is led, not driven, and the leader in industry to-day is more successful than the despot. The basis of all leadership is a sympathetic understanding of the nature of those who are being led. It follows, therefore, that a full knowledge of the mental make-up of the worker and the motives influencing his actions in his daily task, can alone enable us to use with best effect that most delicate and sensitive of all machines—the human individual.

### THE PROBLEM OF THE WORKER WHO FAILED

Some years ago an important problem confronting management was that of labour turnover. That is to say, management employed workers, and even went so far as to teach them certain phases of their trade—this more particularly in the case of young beginners : then, after time had been wasted and materials spoilt for periods of varying lengths, a comparatively high percentage of workers proved to be unsatisfactory, and either became dissatisfied and left of their own accord, or were dismissed.

Phrenology was the first attempt to allocate certain specific abilities which, when present in a person's mental equipment, ensured his success in a specific vocation, and, if absent, made it certain that he would prove a failure. But phrenology was based on a hypothetical correlation between the protuberances on the skull and the growth of the brain inside. Anatomists have unquestionably demonstrated that cerebral development does not necessarily correspond with the contours of the skull, and this rules out any value that may be attached to the phrenological technique as such.

Another method of judging character was the once popular one of physiognomy, which had as its support the contentions in Darwin's book, *The Expression of the Emotions*. Physiognomy based its claims on the supposition that the way individuals act and think is impressed after a time on their facial muscles and so becomes a fixed expression. This claim may have some reasonable basis, but the chief objection to this method, from the viewpoint of the executive who wishes to select staff, is that there is no foot-rule provided by which the temperament and ability of one individual can be compared with those of another.

It was a Frenchman, Alfred Binet, who in the early years of the twentieth century developed a technique to measure intelligence. He established that the average child of say

DEPARTMENT: Advertising NAME: Brown, J.

ENGAGED: 5/5/35 AGE: 24

CAPACITY: Copy & Ideas

COMMENCING SALARY: £—

PREVIOUS EXPERIENCE: 2 years Academy of Arts. 1 year Copywriter Blank & Co; good reference. 2 years Layout & Ideas, Green & Co. Salary £—; good reference; left on own account.

10/8/34 Produced good sales idea accepted by Smith & Co. for 12 months series. Good ideas for furniture advertising. Submitted "Roughs" that secured White & Co's a/c.

12/11/34 Salary increased to £—; appointed to "B" studio, second to Mr. Gray.

14/12/34 Gray reports good work but unpunctual in attendance. Inclined to resent admonition except by General Manager. Clever at Slogans; produced two accepted by Ready & Co. Gray suggests that Brown is type of man who might work better with less supervision.

5/1/35 Appointed to work on Ideas alone; responsible only to Mr. Drayson, Studio Manager.

A TYPICAL RATING CARD FOR EMPLOYEES

*Cards of this type serve as valuable guides for promotions* seven years could solve certain problems, and do simple tasks that the average child of six was not capable of. After many experiments on large groups of children of all ages, he evolved a system known as the Binet scale of intelligence tests. By means of this scale it was possible to test a child's native intelligence, and determine its relation to the intelligence level, the level being obtained by averaging the results of tests on large groups of children. These tests, which were not dependent on education or knowledge that the child had acquired, showed considerable differences between various children.

### A WAR-TIME DISCOVERY OF AN INVALUABLE TEST

THIS system of rating the intelligence levels of different individuals has been developed by Terman, Goddard, and others, but the real importance of the technique, as applied to the problem of selecting the right worker for a job was demonstrated on a large scale when America entered the Great War. The problem in the American Army was, with such a heterogeneous population, to know how to allocate recruits to various drafts—some for training as officers, others to be instructed as non-commissioned officers, and still others to be assigned to the labour corps. The solution was provided by the work of a large group of American psychologists, but the names of Yoakum, Yerkes, Woodworth, and Wells in particular, will always be associated with it.

The first foot-rule of mental ability devised by this group of psychologists was a series of tests known as the Army Alpha Tests. This consisted of tests in simple arithmetic and general knowledge, but also included tests of ability to solve abstract problems along much the same lines as the original Binet tests. There was, however, this big difference, that the Binet tests could only be given to one individual at a time and took over an hour to administer, while the Army Alpha Tests could be given to large groups of individuals in the space of about forty minutes. For those who could not read, a special series known as the Army Beta Tests was prepared. According to the score obtained in these tests, recruits to the Army were allocated to be trained as officers, or drafted as ordinary privates. Cases of low intelligence were either allocated to labour corps or rejected from the Army altogether.

The success of these measures in the American Army vindicated the procedure as being an accurate means of estimating the suitability of an individual for a particular type of work or training. The technique in the earlier stages was not perfected, but psychologists all over the world were stimulated to make a careful analysis of the requirements for particular kinds of work, and then to provide tests which could be utilised to measure the suitability of applicants.

It is not necessary to discuss in detail the many theories that have been advanced by psychologists in explanation and description of specific abilities in relation to the total make-up of an individual, but in the main these theories postulate the existence of two main factors operating to determine the in-individual's fitness for a particular type of work. First, there is the factor known as "general intelligence," which perhaps may best be defined as mental resilience, or ability to adjust one's self to one's environment. Alternatively, it may be defined as a capacity for solving abstract situations. Popularly, it may be conceived as the capacity of being able to look after one's self.

The second factor is known as "specific ability." By "specific ability" is meant the capacity to do a particular type of task; for example, the potential musician must be able to discriminate between different pitches and intensities of sound; the artist to appreciate the importance of various shapes and colours; the mechanical worker must have certain manipulative abilities, and so on.

### WORKERS WHO ARE TOO INTELLIGENT

RESEARCH has shown that vocations each require a certain level of general intelligence if the individual is to be efficient. These levels of intelligence differ according to the specific vocation. For example, the minimum grade of intelligence necessary for an individual to be a successful pneumatic drill operator is lower than that required to be a successful turner and fitter. It is not, of course, possible to state with precision the minimum grade of intelligence required for any and every task, but a comparative scale can be drawn up with a fair degree of accuracy.

Recent investigations have also tended to show that an individual can have too much intelligence for a particular task, and so become bored and an unsatisfactory worker. For example, if an individual possessing a high grade of intelligence is put on to work, such as operating a pneumatic drill, which requires only a low grade of intelligence, then his intelligence will not have adequate scope for expression, and he will become unsettled and leave for some other job as soon as the opportunity presents itself. It is therefore important to select workers for a particular task who possess not less than a minimum, and not more than a certain maximum, degree of intelligence that experiments have established as being necessary. The same applies to tests for specific abilities.

The procedure followed in developing tests, which will indicate an individual's fitness for a specific vocation may best be understood by a description of the work carried out by the writer when compiling a series of tests to be used for selecting the most suitable applicants for apprenticeship as turners and fitters. The first step was to investigate the nature of the work done by turners and fitters. This had then to be analysed into the possible abilities essential for success, such as judgment of spatial relations, steadiness of hand, and manual dexterity. A series of tests was then compiled which it was considered would provide a means of measuring these abilities.

These, together with a test for general intelligence, were given to groups of apprentices whose relative ability was known either by the foreman or through works records. The results of the tests given to these known groups were compared with their known ability, and where a test gave results showing correspondence with the known relative abilities of the group, it was assumed that this test would be useful in selecting future applicants. If the test results did not correspond or correlate with the known ability, it was eliminated from the series. When the final group of tests was arrived at, this was given to further larger groups of apprentices to determine maximum and minimum levels for each test, any score outside which would indicate the individual's unsuitability for that particular type of work.

When these standards had been arrived at for both general intelligence and specific ability, the battery of tests was ready for use in selecting applicants for apprenticeship. The progress of applicants selected in this way was subsequently followed up in staff records, and this follow-up established that, whereas under the old system of trial and error selection approximately 27 per cent. of those selected had been unsatisfactory, with the introduction of the system on the basis of psychological tests the proportion of unsatisfactory appointments was reduced to below 7 per cent.

ACCOUNTS DEPT. SMITH, J. M.

AGE ON ENGAGEMENT: 18

ENGAGED: 30/6/35 MARRIED/SINGLE

COMMENCING SALARY: £—

London Matric. Entered Billing Dept. 30/6/35. Strong, virile personality. Tall, speaks well. Member Amateur Debating Society. Good photographer, has keen ideas about pictorial display. Interested in photography for advertising, has had pictures accepted by Blank Ltd. Never written copy but has tried short stories. Has no other hobbies. Has lived in Bath area, knows district.

A TYPICAL PERSONNEL RECORD

*Records of this nature are often of great help in filling vacancies from the existing staff. J. M. Smith, whose record is given above, might do well in the advertising department, or as a representative in the Bath district.*

### HOW PSYCHOLOGICAL TESTS SHOULD BE USED

MANY large organisations in Great Britain now select their junior employees on the results of their performances in psychological tests, and, in general, firms using this method have reported substantial reductions in the number of unsuitable appointments. On the basis of years of experiment, standards for various types of work have been accurately determined. Most organisations supplement the psychological tests with other tests of educational standards. The applicant's scores in the various tests are carefully recorded, and when the question of promotion or transfer to another department arises, these are consulted and action taken accordingly.

The application of psychological tests to the selection of personnel has superficially appeared so simple and straightforward that many firms have been tempted to entrust their use to persons not specifically trained to carry out this type of work. There are many dangers in this practice, since important, though not immediately apparent, details of technique may not be observed by a person who is not trained in the methods of psychological testing. If the organisation is not sufficiently large to retain the services of a full-time psychologist, then the services of the National Institute of Industrial Psychology may be secured at a reasonable fee, either to develop a suitable series of selection tests, or to administer them and interpret the results.

## WHERE TO READ MORE ABOUT PSYCHOLOGICAL TESTS

COMPREHENSIVE details of mental tests and their use in selecting employees are contained in *Employment Psychology*, by H. Link (Macmillan), and *The Scientific Selection and Training of Workers for Industry and Commerce*, by Martin-Leake and Smith (Pitman). The relation of temperament to vocational fitness is described in *Talents and Temperaments*, by A. Macrae (Nisbet). The work of the National Institute of Industrial Psychology in the general application of psychology has been outlined in two volumes, *Industrial Psychology in Practice* and *Ten Years of Industrial Psychology*, both by Welch and Myers (Pitman).

# THE ART OF HANDLING MEN

*by PATRICK McANALLY, B.A.(Oxon)*

It is an axiom that it is very necessary for those who are in business to be able to co-operate. Most of the country's business at the present day is conducted by fairly large aggregations of people, and everybody who embarks on a business career must be prepared to spend his life rubbing shoulders with others. Such people cannot expect to work most of their time alone—each a law unto himself. If this description is true, it is reasonable to say that every business man is a personnel worker, and that all who have any supervisory duties are engaged in the management of personnel.

It is necessary to demonstrate here that the management of personnel is a distinguishable part of management in general. This fact has not long been recognised widely.

If there is no personnel department the work of selecting workers is likely to devolve upon foremen, who will use methods very much more rough and ready than those which can be used by a centralised department. In engaging workers as in most buying, a wide view of the market is of great assistance. The wages which are offered and accepted are determined largely by the usual operations of supply and demand, tempered by various agreements, customs, and regulations. The personnel department must survey all these factors.

It needs, first, something which will correspond with the trade directories used by the buyers of goods, something to tell it where it can expect to find workers. When a new works is being opened in a district in which the company has not operated before, some sort of regional labour survey may be needed. It is no use choosing a site with admirable railway and canal facilities if no workers will be available in the vicinity, or if they will come only if paid extravagantly high wages. Again, the class of workers available is important. Industrial skill grows up in a community with the passage of years, and it is usually worth while for this reason for a new branch of an old industry to settle near old branches, and for a new industry to settle near similar industries which have already established themselves and trained labour forces.

## HOW VACANCIES ARE FILLED

Once a plant is established, conditions will be better known and a labour survey will not be so necessary. All the same, means will have to be devised of getting in touch with new candidates for employment, as vacancies are bound to occur constantly. To some extent these may be filled from casual applicants for jobs. Other sources are the friends and relatives of people already employed in the company, and for temporary emergencies in some types of business, such as retailing, a list of female ex-employees who have left to get married is valuable. Labour exchanges are another source of supply with which the managers of personnel are bound to keep in touch.

None of these methods is quite appropriate for recruitment to higher executive posts. In so far as these are not filled by promotion inside a concern, it is the duty of the personnel department to keep an eye on likely men and women in other businesses, as workers of this sort tend not to spend the whole of their careers in the same place. Some of the larger companies draw recruits for executive posts from public schools and universities. If this is done, it is necessary for the businesses to keep themselves in touch with the academic institutions and to be sure that they understand the advantages and limitations of particular schools and universities. Such a recruiting policy is not likely to be a success if it is carried out by people like the dyed-in-the-wool Scottish railway official who asked a candidate : " An' why didn' ye tak' a commaircial course at Oxford ? " In taking on men and women straight from a university it is necessary to realise that they will require a certain time to learn their way about, before they can begin really to pull their weight.

In forming an idea of available sources of labour it is not always wise to confine attention to that which can be obtained at the moment. Sometimes changes will happen for which preparation ought to be made a year or two in advance. A particular trade may expand, so that as a result there is a great shortage of workers of a desired sort, or sometimes, though the demand remains constant, the supply may fall off ; for instance, there are trades for which most of the candidates are trained in schools provided by public authorities ; these schools may direct learners into channels which do not exactly suit the demands of industry, so that one kind of skill is a drug in the market while another is at a premium. If the personnel department is sufficiently wide awake to be aware of these fluctuations, it should not find difficulty in coping with them.

## HOW TO FIX THE REWARDS OF WORK

In determining the wages that are to be paid, the governing question will be what is being paid by other firms in the same trade or the same district. Unless the supply of labour is very large in proportion to the demand, it is necessary to offer terms which are not less attractive than those of competitors. Otherwise the quality of the labour force which it is possible to obtain will probably be very much inferior.

A second consideration, but one which perhaps should have more weight than it does, is the prevailing cost of living. To determine this is a somewhat difficult statistical problem. The " Rowntree Scale " and a scale prepared by the British Medical Association attempt to establish the minimum required for reasonably healthy living. Personnel managers need to be familiar with figures relating to this subject, both for the sake of ordinary humanity and in order to be sure that they can expect to be given efficient service by their more lowly-paid workers. They also need to know about changes in the value of money, so as to realise what amount of hardship will be involved, if it is considered necessary to introduce a percentage cut on all remuneration.

### A MISTAKEN VIEW ABOUT THE MONEY URGE

Money, it need hardly be said, is the main incentive in industry. It is often regarded as the only incentive, and the science of economics is often said to be based on this assumption. But to take such a view is in fact misleading. There arise occasions when the opportunity of earning more money does not encourage workers to increase their output in any degree, and some other incentive is required. Consequently it is of extreme importance to find the best way of applying the money incentive.

The most obvious and straightforward method is probably payment by time, so much per year or per week or per hour. The simplicity of this method has much to commend it, since it is always most desirable that employees should understand as fully as possible the system by which the amount of their earnings is calculated. But though a man may spend so many hours in a factory or shop, there is no knowing that he will occupy his time to the best purpose. To overcome this, payment by the piece is widely used, with the aim of allowing an individual to reap a reward for his more strenuous efforts.

The working of piece-rates involves more difficulties than are apparent at first sight. In the first place, the amount of output achieved does not depend in every case on the individual's own efforts, but on the co-operation of others who are responsible for routeing the work through the shop, maintaining an even flow, and seeing that the requisite tools are at hand and in good condition. It is very unfair that any one should take home a poor pay envelope just because, through the fault of others, he has had to spend time waiting for work.

In the second place, the setting of the rates is a hard and invidious task. Questions will always arise as to the length of time required for doing a given piece of work, and whether the rate is to be calculated on the results obtained by the best worker or those of the worst worker. Various systems, including the Bedaux system, which has achieved some notoriety, attempt to state absolutely the amount of effort which a human being can produce in the hour, and to relate all tasks to this. Their supporters are attempting something difficult and apt to provoke the hostility of workers, but probably their method brings accurate results.

### THE COMPLICATIONS OF REWARDING BY COMMISSION

In selling work, payment by results is achieved by giving a commission on sales, and for travellers representing wholesale firms there are further complications caused by the need for making just allowance for travelling expenses. Commission on sales may have unfortunate results. Wholesalers' travellers may be led by it to overstock the retailers on whom they call, so that the goods subsequently have to be heavily marked down, or taken back by the supplier. Retail shop assistants may be led to neglect customers who appear unlikely to spend much, and to be importunate to those who look more wealthy.

One way of avoiding some of these difficulties is to pay

the commission or the piece rate to groups of people instead of to individuals. If, for example, this practice is adopted in retailing, it may encourage the workers to treat all customers with equal civility, and allow those who are not the crack salesmen to earn good wages by performing important subsidiary functions such as stockkeeping and display, which would otherwise be neglected.

In dealing with money remuneration a final word is required about various irregular payments. These include bonuses for extra work of different kinds, and rewards for suggestions on how processes and methods might be improved. The establishment of a satisfactory channel for suggestions is often neglected. It should allow modest workers to submit their suggestions without too much publicity, and must give assurance that the management is prepared to give the suggestions serious attention, and act upon them, and distribute rewards with promptitude.

### THE RIGHT ATTITUDE TOWARDS PROMOTION

THE next consideration after money remuneration in the buying of labour is the possibility of promotion. What candidates for employment are usually most anxious to know is how fast they can get on, and whether high posts are filled by promotion from inside the firm or by the introduction of outsiders. There is one answer that the representative of the personnel management should always give to such questions. It is that the firm will always employ the best possible man obtainable for the money it is prepared to spend, no matter where he comes from. Very frequently the knowledge of the firm and its methods possessed by insiders will make them far more suitable for the higher posts than any outsider could be. The door should not, however, be barred to outsiders who may bring valuable new ideas, and save the firm they join from going to sleep.

Punishment and dismissal have also to be discussed in connection with the employment of labour, and unfortunately modern conditions have made them peculiarly unpleasant subjects. The possibility that they may lose their jobs is a sort of nightmare to most workers. At any time it would mean disturbance and trouble, but now it may mean dire poverty. Consequently, getting rid of employees may be a very distasteful task. The situation is aggravated where the difficulty of keeping them up to the mark in their work is most pronounced. Where production is being done on a moving assembly belt, or even where ordinary piece-rates are in force, it is difficult for workers to fall behind the required pace. But in selling and clerical work, where jobs are not so precisely defined, little slacknesses make their appearance very easily. The problem is then how to keep the workers up to the mark. Admonition by itself is not sufficiently serious, and dismissal is far too drastic for the worker who suffers it, and too unsettling for the others, who wonder if it will be their turn next. The imposition of fairly small fines is a suggested remedy, but perhaps it is inevitable that such trouble should occur as long as the unemployment situation remains in its present state.

## THE NEW EMPLOYEE: HOW HE SHOULD BE CHOSEN AND TRAINED

BEFORE any engagement is actually made, the applicant is interviewed by the Personnel Department. A short interview, besides revealing in a moment any surface qualities or defects in carriage and demeanour, also enables an experienced judge to form a very shrewd idea of the applicant's general character and ability. Account has always to be taken of excusable nervousness, but his mode of expressing himself, his appreciation of the point of the questions he is asked, his sense of humour, if present, and his modesty or its opposite, will provide at any rate the outline of his picture. The interview can also be supplemented by a variety of tests disposed to show his general intelligence and any special aptitude.

Even after engagements have been made, it may be necessary to give some training to the recruits before they take their places as regular workers. For production workers this will often consist merely of watching other workers perform tasks with which they have become familiar. It may also include some practice with models of machines or parts of machines. Training for selling work is perhaps more highly developed as a section of personnel management. It consists in the first place of a discussion of the technical nature of the goods to be sold, with a full description of the uses which they serve, and perhaps most important of all, of their faults and inferiorities when compared with other rival productions. The second part is designed to help the salesman or woman when actually face to face with the customer, and explains the arguments that are likely to be met and how they may be countered. The lesson often ends up with a "mock" sale, at which the members of the class take it in turns to be "prospect" and salesman; the members of the class then vote on what they consider to be the best performance put up by the salesman. These mock sales are sometimes very amusing to watch and to listen to, but it is a rather depressing thing to notice that often the salesman who has done best in the mock sale does not last long in actual selling. Staff training for sales people does not stop soon after they have been engaged. Even senior employees profit by meeting to discuss new difficulties and new ways of coping with old difficulties.

Employees who have been engaged and trained must not then be lost sight of. The personnel department will usually keep for each individual a dossier containing all facts likely to be of interest, if he is to be considered for promotion, transference, or dismissal. This sounds a simple idea. But in practice the obtaining of these facts is not at all easy. To give a character sketch of anybody is hard, and doubly hard when one is too busy to consider it as long as one would like to, and when the man's whole career may depend upon what one says. The personnel department must issue questionnaires for departmental heads to fill up, so that the questions are standardised and the duty of answering them cannot be avoided.

Such questionnaires will usually have down the left-hand side a list of qualities such as appearance, co-operativeness, initiative, accuracy; and to the right will be spaces for the departmental heads to mark the grade into which they think the individuals fall. This sort of system is probably as just as any that has been devised, but it is open to the objection that it is difficult to get consistent judgments from the same man at different times or from different men at the same time. These questionnaires may be supplemented by interviews between the individuals and the personnel department.

### DISCOVERING WHAT THE STAFF THINKS

SUCH are the means used by personnel departments to keep themselves informed about the characters and achievements of particular individuals in an organisation. The essential feature of them is the use of regular reports. It is also a duty of personnel departments to keep informed about what the mass of workers are thinking, and to provid machinery by which grievances which arise can be ventilated and eventually settled. This is best done by the institution o regular meetings between members of the management and o the working force. Representatives of the workers are ofte selected by ballot. For such meetings to be successful, it i essential that they should be fairly small and informal, s that the workers' representatives will not be afraid to say wha they think. The borderline between subjects which may b discussed at these meetings and subjects which may not i always likely to be vaguely drawn. The nominees of th workers are likely to make representations about wages an hours of labour, and also to assist the management to dea successfully with the varied problems which are discussed i the remaining part of this section.

## WORKING CONDITIONS THE BASIS OF EFFICIENCY

IT is necessary for the management of personnel to hav a really intimate knowledge of what it is like to b a worker in the business. Such knowledge will enabl waste of all kinds to be avoided by enabling and encouragin the workers to put more into their work, and by makin frequent changes of staff less necessary. Indeed the " rat of labour turnover " is to some extent an index of efficienc in personnel management. It is a figure which compares th average number on the staff with the average number o dismissals and resignations, as the rate of stock-turnove compares the average size of the stock with the sales.

### DANGER THAT LURKS IN EVERYDAY JOBS

THE first essential to good work is that the actual physica conditions in which it is done should be satisfactory To say that safety is highly desirable may seem hardl necessary. Yet managers of personnel must spend time i securing it, and must keep a watch on the number of accident which occur among their workers. The dangers of coal mining will probably be the first which present themselve to the lay mind. In addition there are dangers involve in working machines. For some dangers remedies and safe guards are specified, and factory inspectors pay periodica visits to see that they are not neglected. For others it i

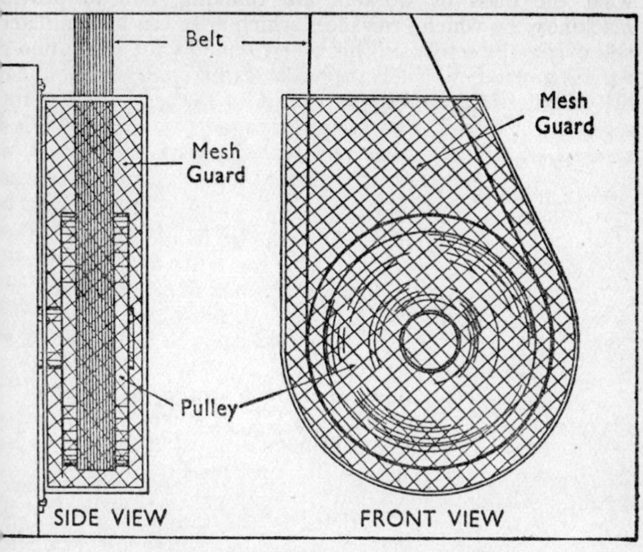


SAFEGUARDING THE WORKER

*A mesh guard used as protection from running shafting.*

necessary for the personnel department of the business in which they occur to design guards to protect the workers, or to invent other suitable precautions.

The main difficulty which is encountered, however, is not the invention of precautions but ensuring that when installed they are used. Intensive propaganda is often required to convince workers who have been safe ninety-nine times that the hundredth time they may suffer an accident.

After safety come such factors as good heating, lighting, and ventilation. In offices and shops it is often comparatively easy to ensure that the standards of physical comfort are reasonable, since these types of business can be carried on in ordinary rooms. But it will be realised that in manufacturing, more difficult problems arise ; when, for instance, foodstuffs are being cooked, or plastic materials moulded under great heat, or textiles manufactured in a place where air for ventilation might bring dust which would spoil the goods. The personnel management must make it its business to be aware of these difficulties and to reconcile them with some measure of comfort. To do this it will need to keep itself informed about the most recent developments in construction and engineering.

### COMFORT THAT ADDS TO THE VALUE OF OUTPUT

GIVEN good physical surroundings, the next step is to study the individual worker on the job. Is he regular in his output or irregular? Does he go home at the end of the day dead to the world, or with some life and vigour left in him? These are the chief symptoms of the presence or absence of an excess of fatigue and monotony. Literary people are apt to imagine that industry is little else but fatigue and monotony. To talk in this way is, of course, a mark of ignorance. Many operations are devoid of fatigue and monotony, and where they do exist they are really comprised of very complicated mental-physical states. It is only necessary to outline here some practical means by which they may be counteracted.

One fruitful cause of fatigue is the compulsion on the worker to use an unsuitable and uncomfortable posture. He may have to sit in a chair that is the wrong height or spend his time wheeling a barrow that is the wrong shape, or be given needless fatigue in many similar ways. A little thought will produce more satisfactory ways of doing the work. There are, for instance, chairs which may be adapted for all workers, whatever their build.

Allied with the question of posture is that of the motions through which the worker goes in doing his work. Generally speaking, if the path along which his hands move can be made smooth and curved, he will suffer less fatigue then if it is jerky. Elaborate "time and motion studies" have been undertaken, but a difficulty which they are apt to encounter is that the most suitable motion for one worker will by no means be the most suitable for all.

Besides posture and motion, the spells of work and rest which are in force in the factory make an important difference to the worker. The classic proof that longest hours do not give greatest output was given by experiments with munition workers during the war. It is also becoming known that output may be improved by carefully devised rest-pauses. These not only afford the worker physical rest, but break

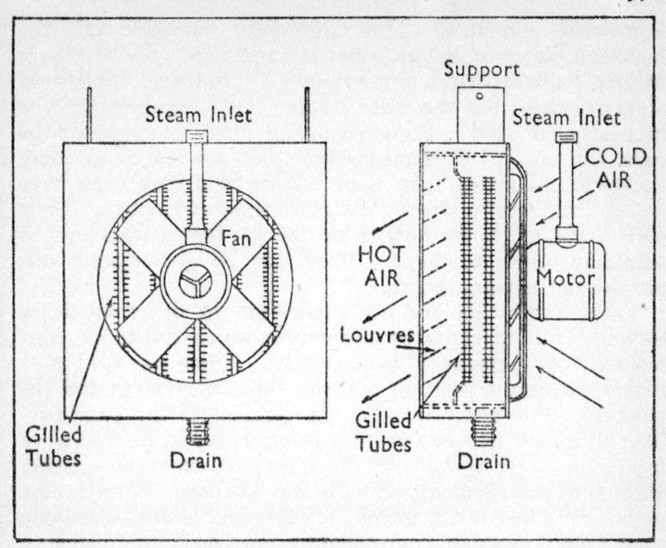


AN EXAMPLE OF MODERN HEATING AND VENTILATION

*Sections of an Air-Heating Unit which can be used as a ventilator only when the steam supply is cut off. It can be hung in a suitable position or let into an outside wall. Fresh air is drawn in by the fan, as indicated by the arrows, heated by high-pressure steam, and dispersed by the louvres which can be adjusted to deflect it in the desired direction.*

up the day, so that he does not feel that there is before him an endless amount of work on which he is making no appreciable progress.

Such are the principal ways of countering physical discomfort, fatigue, and monotony. We have purposely refrained from analysing fatigue and monotony, but it will be obvious that to mention them is to mention something not entirely physical. This opens up further problems with which personnel management has to deal.

## THE FOREMAN : A LINK BETWEEN WORKER AND EMPLOYER

For most men and women working in large organisations, a matter of day-to-day if not hour-to-hour concern is the disposition of " the boss," or, in other words, of their immediate superior. The immediate superior of the rank and file of most businesses is a foreman. Sometimes it will be a charge-hand, sometimes a "fore-lady," sometimes a shop-walker, but the word "foreman" describes the type in nearly all cases. Foremen are in many cases promoted from the ranks. This means that they are apt to be more energetic characters than their fellows, and may even have had to overwork to attain their more elevated position. They will very often know how to do the job better than how to stimulate others to do it. They may be conservative and narrow and self-important.

These characters are not mentioned in order to decry foremen, but to show up difficulties which are to be confronted by personnel management. Foremen are in a highly important position between the management and the workers. For many workers the foreman *is* the company. The company depends on the foremen for a great deal of leadership. He should not be identified exclusively either with the management or with the workers. How is the personnel department, using such foremen as are commonly to be found, to obtain from them the most useful performance of their duties ?

The answer probably is that it should try not to allow the foremen to be the overstrained links in the chains stretching from the chairman of the board to the rank and file of the workers. It should try in some way to make the highest and the lowest take a common interest in the enterprise. The same problem arises in nations and in armies, and the means of solving it are the use of flags, the cultivation of regimental reputations, and so forth. In Russia some attempt has been made to infuse by the same methods a nation-wide interest in industry, and factories and engineering products are treated with reverential pride. It is part of personnel management to surround everyday work with a similar glamour. Without real justice any attempt to do this will be the merest "eye-wash." But given justice, the deliberate cultivation of an X.Y.Z. & Co. spirit in dealing with customers, or of pride in the excellence of a product or speed of output, should help to weld the whole concern into one.

Some firms publish house journals which are designed to achieve this end. One expects on opening them to find very dull accounts of staff picnics and formal congratulations to promoted persons. These can hardly make much difference to the fundamental relations between management and workers. To be worth while, they might be several times more candid, and reveal matters now regarded as utterly secret. It is only by revealing its inner difficulties that national dailies make a nation live for its citizens. So to make a business live for its workers, a house journal should give an insight into the real strains and stresses which it is up against, so far as the conditions of competitive business permit.

### SHOULD WORKERS SHARE THE PROFITS?

To go to the full length of giving workers an interest in the business in which they work, is to institute a scheme of co-partnership or profit-sharing. Arguments rage and will continue to rage about who really produces the wealth which business brings into being, and who has the best claim to the profits which accrue. But it is easy enough to see certain important facts of the position.

At present workers get exceedingly little in comparison with the owners or capitalists and the managers. And, again, it is clear that in enterprises run on the usual joint stock company lines the relations between capital and labour are slight, and may easily appear unjust. The investor seldom comes near the enterprise, and may not enjoy a share of the ownership for more than a very short period at a time. The worker is on the spot six days a week, and does not leave and go elsewhere if he can help it. Yet the capitalist enjoys the profits and exercises control. A way of meeting all these difficulties at once is to distribute part of the profits to the workers.

There are various technical difficulties to be overcome. For instance, if the distribution comes too late after the efforts which have earned the profits, the causal connection between the two may be lost on the workers. But on the whole copartnership seems a promising way of giving workers a stake in their concern and making them feel that energy will redound to their own advantage, and slackness to their own loss.

The fact that shareholders pocket the profits was not the only grievance referred to. The other was that they nominally exercise control. It would seem logical to give workers a voice in the control, if they receive some of the profits. However, in practice this is apt to bring up unexpected difficulties, because the main decisions are of the kind that can be made much better by experts than by the man-in-the-street common sense of the ordinary worker. They should, in fact, be left to the higher executives. The ultimate purposes of a business are seldom in doubt ; it is their working out on which so much depends. Democratic forms are more suitable for giving a lead on what purposes should be adopted than on how to work them out. Probably, therefore, the most that either workers or shareholders should expect is to be given reasonably abundant information about what is being done, not to be asked what should be done, save in exceptional cases.

## SOME BOOKS ABOUT PERSONNEL MANAGEMENT

THOSE who wish to pursue this subject further should read *Personnel Administration*, by Yead and Metcalfe (McGraw Hill), a comprehensive American treatise which attempts to deal with all sides of the question. *Personnel Management*, by Scott, Clothier, and Mathewson, also gives a full and detailed account. *Human Problems of an Industrial Civilisation*, by Elton Mayo, faces the subject in its widest aspects and deals with it scientifically. The books of Whiting Williams also take a wide view, but are more personal and intimate : both *Full Up and Fed Up* and *Mainsprings of Men* can be recommended, but they are published in America and may be difficult to obtain from English libraries.

# THE MANAGEMENT OF AN OFFICE

*by CLIFFORD H. NURSE, A.L.A.A., A.C.I.S.*

It is quite obvious that to understand the management of anything the first requirement is a thorough knowledge of the thing it is proposed to manage, and this is particularly necessary in the case of such a complex piece of machinery as a modern office. The time has passed when it was thought that any one of average intelligence could be put in charge of the group of people known as "the office," which the management too often regarded as a necessary evil. The office is an important department in the life of any business, and the study of its proper management is likely to repay all those whose concern it is to have a business run as efficiently and economically as possible.

At the risk of offending the susceptibilities of those engaged purely on the buying and selling sides of a business, it can be stated with some justification that the office is in many respects the brain of a business organisation. It is the centre to which converges information from each part of the concern, as well as much useful knowledge from without its own four walls. Information about supplies and customers, purchases and sales, incomings and outgoings, and in fact about all the concerns of the place is stored in the office, and, like the brain when it works properly, is available for production and use whenever it is called upon.

Further, this storehouse of facts and figures is the main source of information upon which the executive takes action in the control of the affairs of the business. Whether the storehouse is sufficiently filled, and even more, whether it is filled in such a way that everything is accessible, may make all the difference between a well-conceived plan, the success of which is certain, and a plan which from its inception is doomed to disappointment.

It is the prime duty of an efficient office manager to see that his department is not only filled with information, but that it is so correlated and ordered that the facts required by the executive are available promptly, and can be given without the slightest doubt as to their accuracy. Results taken from office books which cannot be fully relied upon are of very doubtful value, whereas, when good office management has ensured that reports are reliable and can be acted upon without suspicion, it has often proved of inestimable service in indicating the correct course to be adopted.

In addition to these somewhat indirect means of being a real business asset, it will be shown that an efficient office is itself a money-making factor in business. By seeing that customers are freed from any annoyance through carelessness, and that payments to suppliers are made on the most advantageous terms, the office not only becomes a storehouse of knowledge, but also makes money for its company by acting accurately and alertly in its interests.

## THE THREE DEPARTMENTS OF AN OFFICE

THE management of an office can be considered conveniently in three fairly distinct provinces, for which the secretary, the office manager, and the accountant are responsible heads. The secretary is mentioned first as he is the first to appear in the formation of the company, and, by virtue of his position being recognised by law as well as by his immediate employers, he is properly regarded in most companies as one of the definitely senior officials. In very small offices the secretary combines with his statutory duties responsibility for the whole of the office staff, as well as for the preparation of accounts. When the office is of any size, however, it is of paramount importance to secure a proper and defined division of responsibility, and it will be found that it is quite easy to distinguish between respective functions.

Once the company is incorporated and has appointed its secretary, a manager will be needed to attend to its manifold office work. Keepers of bought and sales ledgers, clerks for the expense ledgers and all their relative subdivisions and dissections, clerks for invoices, orders, wages and salaries, and queries, as well as typists for correspondence and returns, will need proper supervision, and a manager will be required who knows all the duties of each member of the staff and will see that no overlapping occurs in the work that is produced.

The office manager having arranged for the production of figures which can be relied upon as arithmetically correct, the accountant is needed to correlate the results obtained, and to arrange for their proper presentation to the directors and to the shareholders in the form of the annual balance sheet. It is, of course, necessary for the accountant to work in close touch with the office manager if he is to obtain his figures in the most convenient form. His own staff will be relatively small, as he will be engaged largely on confidential work which it is not desirable to have in the same section as that of the general ledgers.

### THE SECRETARY A SERVANT OF THE LAW

THE company secretary must therefore be considered first. His responsibilities are very important as he is not only the servant of the board of directors, but he is also personally liable to fines and penalties under the Companies Act, 1929, if certain duties are not duly carried out. While directors are doubtless subject to even heavier penalties for contravention of the Act, the secretary will almost invariably be held to blame if any irregularity occurs, and knowledge of the Companies Act so far as it affects the statutory obligations of the company is therefore of the first importance to a secretary. He generally has the custody of the company's seal and is responsible for seeing that it is used only under proper conditions. He must see that the company's name is properly quoted on all notices, bills, cheques, etc., and particularly that at its registered office a plate is affixed clearly at the entrance to indicate that it is the registered office of the company whose full name appears thereon.

As legal servant to the board of directors, the secretary acts as intermediary between them on the one hand, and shareholders, customers, office staff, bankers, and the general public on the other. Although the office manager will communicate direct with customers on matters relating to accounts, the secretary will still be the official whose signature indicates that the communication represents the opinion of the ultimate executive authority, namely, the board of directors. His signature will therefore be required whenever the communication is desired to carry the impression of an official statement.

It will be obvious that the secretary of a large undertaking will be compelled to delegate a good deal of his work. The main responsibility for the good organisation of his department must, of course, fall upon the secretary himself. If the company is sufficiently large, one or more assistant secretaries will take charge of much of the routine office work, but they will be responsible to the secretary for the work.

Where this subdivision occurs, the secretary confines himself mainly to legal matters connected with the company, and to conducting the meetings of the board of directors. He acts unofficially as legal adviser to the board upon any cases of difficulty arising in connection with the company's business. In most cases he is regarded as an irreplaceable source of information and advice, not only by the board of directors, but also by its chairman, and the value to their decisions of the advice given by their secretary is often recognised by electing him to a seat on the board.

In the case of a company having branches or subsidiary companies at home and abroad, the assistant secretaries are often made responsible for one or more of these companies, leaving the principal to co-ordinate reports received from his subordinates, whom he trusts to furnish accurate and informative returns when required. Alternatively, assistant secretaries may be given responsibility for the conduct of the company's statutory work, correspondence, and legal and routine business.

The principal statutory work is the keeping of registers of mortgages and charges, and the annual list and summary, as well as the duties required by the Companies Act, 1929, in relation to the transfer and transmission of shares, register of members, issue of share certificates, etc. The latter is generally performed in the registrar's section under the supervision of a qualified registrar or transfer clerk, who is himself responsible to the secretary or his assistants. This section, of course, needs a staff of its own to deal with everything affecting the share capital of the company.

### THE WORK ENTAILED IN REGISTERING SHARES

THE principal books are the company's register of members and also a register of debenture holders in cases where a part of the company's capital requirements is obtained by the issue of debentures. The separate numbering of each share is the cause of the great amount of detailed work needed in the section, but debentures are now more frequently issued in the form of stock which, of course, can be transferred in any quantities, and the possession of the certificate alone indicates the nominal value of stock held.

It is obviously of paramount importance that this register of members is kept up to date, as it is often necessary to circularise members, and the register kept in this department is the record used for this purpose. On receipt of a transfer duly signed by the transferor and the transferee (with signatures witnessed), the transfer clerk must have the receipt of the prescribed transfer fee (usually 2s. 6d.) recorded, and satisfy himself that the certificate of the transferor is to hand, and that the transfer is correct in all respects for registration.

Methods differ widely in office routine, but it is usual for the transfer to be posted into a loose-leaf book which forms the permanent register of transfers. Having satisfied himself that the transfer is in order, a new certificate is prepared in favour of the transferee and passed to the secretary, who notes that certificates will be required to be sealed at the next meeting of the board of directors. In large companies it is usual for the full board of directors to authorise two or more of their number to constitute a sealing committee, who are thus empowered by authority of the board to act with the secretary in sealing new certificates, the issue of which is duly authorised by a board of directors' resolution.

The registrar's office likewise inspects and registers all probates received in respect of deceased shareholders, and if letters of request or any other authorisations are received for the transmissions of shares, arrangements are made for duly filing the documents and preparing new certificates in the same manner as in respect of transfers.

### THE HEAVY TASK OF PAYING DIVIDENDS

PREPARATION of dividend warrants is a heavy task on the registrar's department. This generally occurs twice a year in the case of companies making steady profits, and may necessitate temporary additional staff. Much is done to speed up this work by the use of addressing machines, several types of which are on the market. Most of these machines print from a stencil which can be prepared whenever a new member is admitted. The stencils are stored alphabetically in the same order as the register of members, so that whenever warrants are required they can be prepared immediately in the same order as the register.

By using " window " envelopes, the address on the warrant itself suffices, and these machines can easily print addresses at 2000 an hour without errors or omissions. Even with the introduction of up-to-date machinery, however, much clerical work is still necessary in checking the figures and in seeing that the totals paid agree with the calculations of the dividend due on the capital issued. Moreover, the banks generally like an initial of an authorised person, as well as the autographed signature of the company secretary, on each warrant to show that the warrant is *bona fide* and has been properly issued from the company's office.

The issue of additional capital likewise generally necessitates additional staff, as not only are share certificates required without delay, but it is also essential to check the amounts of brokerage payable, the amounts received on application, allotments, and calls, and the totals credited by the bank. It is not necessary to describe the work so done in any detail as it forms only a small part of the work of an office and is of a somewhat technical nature.

The correspondence section of the secretary's department is divided into two sections—the private and general. Letters are often opened in the first instance in the private section, which passes the general correspondence to a qualified correspondent for attention, while the more private matter is reserved for the secretary's personal attention. The secretary or his assistants deals with the private work of the board of directors, and the relative correspondence is dictated to and dealt with by the private secretary. All general matters are dealt with by a staff of stenographers under the control of the correspondent. Filing clerks are also necessary in this section.

The legal section is generally under the direct supervision of the secretary, except in large firms when there is sufficient work for the whole-time employment of a qualified barrister or solicitor. In practice the secretary frequently seeks the advice of the company's solicitors, but the directors invariably leave to his own judgment the desirability or necessity of taking outside opinion. The drafting of prospectus forms, for instance, is invariably done by a legal expert, but smaller questions relating to agreements of employment, Workmen's Compensation, and National Health Insurance, etc., can frequently be answered without recourse to expert opinion. The registration of the company's trade marks, patents, and designs is also frequently dealt with in this section.

### THE SECRETARY AS GUIDE AND COUNSELLOR

THE secretary has many other duties not easily definable. The departmental heads often desire to discuss with him questions of general organisation. He must be available to shareholders' special requests for interviews if friction is to be avoided; customers, whose accounts are too large to risk offending, sometimes feel that the secretary can do more than the office manager, and an interview is necessary, with its consequent inquiries and correspondence. It frequently happens, moreover, that the directors have a good deal of more or less personal work needing the attention of the secretary, which the latter cannot properly refuse.

This general work is additional to the clerical duties of furnishing necessary Income Tax returns and declaration; preparation for, and carrying through, the procedure at board meetings and shareholders' meetings; drafting agenda, minutes, resolutions, and sometimes drafting speeches to be delivered by the chairman. These manifold duties are not so easily delegated as the work of the general office, but they call for a high standard of efficiency in all his subordinates if the secretary is to retain the utmost confidence of his board.

He also renders all-important services to his board by advising on questions of finance. It is quite possible for profits to remain good, and for the balance sheet to show a considerable surplus of assets over liabilities, and yet for the business to find itself seriously embarrassed for the want of working capital. In other words, it may be solvent and yet unable to pay its way. This might be caused by insufficiency of available cash, or by overbuying and therefore carrying a stock which is too heavy for the business which is being done. Another frequent cause is that the firm is obliged to give a more extended credit than it receives. Whatever the cause, the board looks to the secretary, unless there is an independent financial adviser, to report on the position, and to suggest possible remedies as soon as future financial embarrassment becomes likely.

The rendering of monthly returns is the business of the accountant's department, but it should be noted here that their use is perhaps greatest in assisting the executive to avoid the above difficulties. The prompt and accurate information of the position contained in them enables effective steps to be taken, and forms an invaluable guide before a new enterprise involving special outlay is embarked upon, or before orders for additional plant and machinery are placed. These returns enable a careful survey to be made of the free capital which is available, and it is a useful practice to estimate as near as possible for some months in advance what the cash requirements are likely to be.

## THE MANIFOLD DUTIES OF THE OFFICE MANAGER

We can now turn to the field of activities supervised by the office manager, or, as he is still known very frequently, the "counting-house manager." His functions vary considerably with different companies, but in general he undertakes the management of all the office staff except those engaged on the more specialised work of the secretary and accountant. He therefore has to deal with the whole of the book-keeping relating to buying and selling, as well as with the proper regulation of factory accounts in manufacturing businesses. In some form or other the whole of the work that goes on in the business supplies data and records for his staff, and the mark of a good organiser is to ensure that this information is not only dealt with promptly, but that it is readily accessible and can be referred to with the least possible delay.

Perhaps in no department is it so easy to allow the work to become stereotyped as in the general office, and it is fatally easy to allow systems and methods to continue long after they have outgrown their usefulness. It frequently happens that the office is run in precisely the same manner for many years, and is only added to piecemeal as the work has grown. Increased sales have meant another clerk, extra help is needed for another section, juniors are promoted, and girls fresh from school are brought in to enlarge the present office. The tendency is thus for the office to increase in the number of its personnel, but to decrease correspondingly in efficiency. If, when trade increases, the whole organisation were examined without prejudice, and the management were persuaded to spend a little on equipment, it would very frequently result not only in a lowering of the wages costs which are a direct overhead charge against profits, but also in increased contentment of the staff.

### INVITING SUGGESTIONS FROM THE MAN ON THE JOB

It is often possible for improvements to be made without any cost at all, if the office workers are encouraged to make suggestions about the jobs they are doing every day of their lives. In the past, recruitment for the office staff has not always been from the best material because remuneration has been poor, and the idea of being a mere "pen pusher" is even less attractive than that of being a "counter jumper"! However, there are signs that by giving the office worker a greater degree of freedom, and by allowing him to make suggestions about his own job, a more alert type of worker is forthcoming.

It is certain that clerical workers will be encouraged to do more intelligent work if they understand how the job they are doing fits into the general system of things. The office manager will get the most willing co-operation if he is able to arrange the work in such a way that the workers feel a definite responsibility for their own particular portion of the general result. Even in the smallest concerns, where the clerical staff is limited to, say, half a dozen employees, care should be taken to see that each is responsible for certain parts of the work, and that responsibility should be his or hers alone. It is always inadvisable to allow similar duties to be done indiscriminately by whichever clerk happens to be disengaged.

Although it is necessary for each clerk to have a clearly defined job, it is generally also most desirable for another worker to be able to carry on in the event of some one being absent. When practicable it is a good plan to systematise the work, grading the various operations and paying according to their difficulty or importance. If this is done, it can generally be arranged for the junior to understudy the worker immediately above. In the absence on holiday or owing to illness of one worker, the understudy is then able to keep the other job going without special instructions.

In this connection it avoids any misunderstanding if definite duties are assigned to each worker. It is a useful practice to hand to each worker a typed list of the principal duties which he or she is expected to keep up to date, and for the prompt completion of which the worker will be held personally responsible, unless reference is first made to the senior clerk or office manager. If a copy of this table of duties is signed by the worker to show that the duties shown thereon have been undertaken, in the event of subsequent failure there is no room for a plea of ignorance or misunderstanding. Moreover, a series of signed tables as suggested constitute a very useful record of the work being done in the office, and, if additional work is needed, it is a convenient guide as to the point in the office on which the additional task can be fairly placed.

### MODERN METHODS OF HOUSING THE STAFF

THERE are also certain general requisites of the office itself if efficient management is to be practicable. In the provinces office accommodation is often better than in London, where space is so valuable. The tendency in London shops has been to secure additional selling space at the expense of office accommodation, and this has made efficiency difficult. Conditions have, however, tremendously improved, and some of the West End stores have office accommodation of which any one might be proud. Some of these companies have met the need for spacious premises and bright surroundings by allocating the whole of an upper floor for office and administrative staffs, while others have contrived to house the office staff adequately in a separate building. In the case of large undertakings, the demand for a light and airy office has thus been met, while lighting and heating arrangements are generally as hygienic as possible.

The desks should in general be so arranged that each employee can work undisturbed by his colleague. Windows ought to be large so that as much daylight as possible is obtained, and if the desks are arranged so that no worker either faces or is back to the windows, the maximum daylight will be secured. Another improvement in modern offices has been the replacement of the high desks and stools by lower desks and chairs having backs. Sloping desks are preferable to flat tables for ledger work, but they can be obtained for use with a comfortable chair, and this is one way in which the quality of the work as well as the health of the worker can be improved.

It might be useful at this stage to give a rough outline of the work that is being done day by day in the typical business organisation. The view of a modern office or " counting house " is somewhat bewildering—so many separate people doing their own job with no apparent relationship between them. It is necessary to get behind the mind of the office manager in order to appreciate how all these cogs in the wheel operate, and why each is necessary for the proper conduct of the business and the proper record of its affairs. The business of buying and selling requires similar books of account, whether it is a manufacturing concern, a wholesale house, or a retail shop. In general, the same course can be found in each type of business, subject to special adaptations to meet special needs.

In any business the buyer is commissioned by the management to make purchases on its behalf. In smaller concerns one buyer will do it exclusively, whereas in the larger stores each department has its own buyer, who is to a great extent responsible for the success of his individual department. In any case the prudent management will decide the financial course to be pursued, and will issue to its buyers instructions as to the amount to which they may commit the company. If the buyer exceeds the amount so allotted to him he will need to justify himself to the management, but as a general rule it is not the function of the office staff to check the total so expended.

### CHANCES OF DISCOUNT THAT MUST NOT BE LOST

Having passed the orders, invoices will arrive, and these will have to be recorded as commitments by the company. If the company have not made previous purchases from the suppliers, an inquiry should be made immediately as to the terms under which payment is expected. Prudent managements will always, in the absence of special conditions, arrange for sufficient credit to be available, so that the company can make all its payments under the best terms, and prompt cash terms should be negotiated whenever possible.

Opinions differ as to whether this is better performed by the buyer concerned in the purchase, or by the office manager. Here again it probably depends on the trade. In cases in which the buyer places a large contract at a special price, it may be better not to confuse bargaining on prices with cash discount, because the latter can be done later without jeopardising the agreed price. On the other hand, if a business is wanting orders (and is short of working capital), it is often possible for a buyer to negotiate very favourable cash terms before the order is placed.

It is probably preferable to work in this matter with the buyer concerned, and for the office manager to stipulate that the very best prompt cash terms are required, unless the buyer has already taken all practical steps in the matter. When the terms are agreed the bought ledger clerk should note them at the head of the ledger account, and it should be a very strict rule that the prompt terms are to be taken and utmost discount deducted, unless the office manager has agreed to another course of action.

When the invoice is received it is again a matter of arrangement whether it is entered in a journal before or after the receipt of the goods. In cases where invoices are large and not too numerous, it is probably better to enter them immediately in the invoice (or purchase) journal. In this case they are sent from the office to the receiving dock to be marked when the goods are received. The date of the receipt of the goods is noted in the invoice journal (or ledger), and the buyer approached for his initials or signature to the invoice signifying that it can be passed for payment. In cases, however, in which the large number of invoices make it more convenient for the goods to be received before they are entered into the books of account, arrangements will be made for them to be forwarded to the office immediately on receipt of the goods.

The ruling of a purchase journal varies with the type of business under consideration. In the case of a factory it is sometimes necessary only to classify purchases under two or three main headings, whereas in the case of a large store fifty or more departments will be involved. The journal is so arranged that the department to be charged receives the correct total, and in the bought ledger the fact is recorded that the company owes the amount shown in the account. It is usual for these journals to be ruled in a columnar form so that monthly totals of purchases are shown departmentally. The total of each invoice has to be taken from the purchase book and shown in the account in the bought ledger. If prompt cash terms are available, the clerk in charge of this ledger will see that a cheque is prepared immediately, so that the utmost discount is secured.

### THE PONDEROUS LEDGER A THING OF THE PAST

IT may be observed here that huge leather-bound ledgers have gone for ever. They have been superseded by loose-leaf ledgers, which are produced so that the maximum strength is obtained with the minimum of weight. The sheets are easily removable to reserve binders when required and it is usually due to poor management if the ledger clerk has not a compact book on which he can work comfortably, with the maximum accuracy and speed.

Although mechanical posting of ledgers has been freely adopted on customers' accounts, it has not been found quite so advantageous with bought ledgers. The varying terms of payment, and the need to scrutinise every account, continually demands so much individual attention, and necessitates a machine being idle for such considerable periods, that many managements consider a fully mechanised bought ledger department to be uneconomic.

In order to secure accuracy and ease of operation, there will be as many ledgers in the bought ledger section as the work justifies, each ledger clerk normally being responsible for her own ledger. If the purchase journal is dissected into the same number of separate sheets as there are ledgers, each ledger clerk will be responsible for the correct posting into her ledger of every item shown on the sheet ; the monthly total of the sheet is then used to check the accuracy of the posting during the month.

The cash is entered in the bought ledger from loose-leaf sheets, which are analysed into as many columns as there are ledgers. In this way each ledger in the section is capable of self-balancing, and it ought to be an invariable rule that every ledger is balanced (*i.e.* its arithmetic proved) every month. The following table illustrates the balance possible, inter-ledger transfers and special items being ignored for the sake of simplicity.

| | | |
|---|---|---|
| Total of accounts at beginning of month | | £1760 1 5 |
| Purchases during month (purchase journal total) . . . . . | | 7650 10 10 |
| Cash received from suppliers (per cash book) . . . . . | | 14 5 11 |
| | | £9424 18 2 |
| *Less*— | | |
| Cash payments during month (C.B.) . . | £5730 0 4 | |
| Discount received during month (C.B.) . . | 340 5 9 | |
| Purchases returned during month . . . | 150 1 11 | |
| | | 6220 8 0 |
| Balance (represented by list of outstanding accounts at end of month) | | £3204 10 2 |

On the selling side of the business the same principles apply, but more advantage can be obtained by mechanising the ledgers and other records. It is found that machines are more valuable for sales ledger work because the keeping of customers' accounts during the month is a purely mechanical operation, and does not need the constant scrutiny that is required of the bought ledger clerk in seeing that no prompt discounts are lost because of late payment.

A great contrast exists between the methods most suitable for manufacturing or wholesale concerns and those suitable to companies in the retail trade, because the latter have generally many times the number of accounts to handle. In the first place the former types of concerns make their sales to other companies, and the latter need an invoice on despatch of the merchandise. In the old days details of each consignment were entered into a sold journal by hand, and copied in detail on the invoice for despatch to the customer. The clerical work involved was prodigious.

To-day machines are almost universally used to type the invoice and day-book sheet in one operation (using a carbon between the paper). Not only does this give a better invoice, but a clearer permanent record is also obtained, and this record constitutes the sales journal for the purpose of posting to the sales ledger in the way already described. Machines exist to-day which, in addition to this, can be used to post the ledger accounts and statements in one operation. Again the old type of bound ledger has not only been discarded in favour of a loose-leaf book, but development has gone one step further in producing a card ledger, conveniently contained in trays. An export operator can post these cards quite quickly and obtain, not only much greater speed, but also greater accuracy than with the old hand-writing methods.

### ROBOT MATHEMATICIANS OF THE OFFICE

In the case of companies having a large retail trade the success of mechanical innovations is still more apparent: indeed it is difficult to visualise the chaos which would exist if nothing more speedy than the old pen methods had been nvented! In the retail trade the customer receives a "sales check," or "bill," when she does her shopping, and does not expect an invoice as the wholesale customer does. She does, however, expect a detailed account at the end of the month and, for the preparation of this, mechanical book-keeping machines, which copy the bill in its entirety into the customer's account, are invaluable. Before the bills from the shop are used by the ledger keepers, they are passed through a separate department which dissects them in order to summarise daily takings. Mechanical methods are essential to this department. All the duplicate copies of the bills issued in the shop the previous day are sorted, and totals first obtained of cash takings (to agree with the amount banked) and of sales for credit. These two main dissections are further re-sorted by machinery into departments, so that the daily departmental total of sales is obtained. The duplicate copies of sales for credit bills are sorted into ledger order (*e.g.* A–C may be one ledger, D–F another, G–J another, etc.). The aggregate of each ledger total is then agreed with the total sales for credit, before the duplicates are passed to the sales ledger department to be copied on the customers' accounts.

It will be seen that if each operator, as she posts her ledger, uses a machine which automatically registers a total of amounts posted, this total must agree with the pre-determined total obtained from the dissection department. The book-keeping machines are self-proving to the extent of giving, whenever required, the total figures which have been passed through. These totals must, of course, be checked by the operator before proceeding with other work. Furthermore, the machines automatically provide totals of cash posted, so that if the cash book is columnar, or any other device is used for obtaining a total to be posted into the ledger, the arithmetical accuracy of the work is self-checking. When the sales ledger has been posted for the month the total balances on each ledger can be checked with the totals passing through the book-keeping machine in a similar manner to the bought ledger balance referred to above.

These machines are so consistently reliable that, if an efficient operator is engaged, and each total is properly controlled, the accuracy of a big section of the work is proved automatically. Nor are they justified only because of their accuracy, but also because of the speed with which results are obtained. As monthly statements are prepared at the same time as the accounts, the accounts are ready for dispatch to the customer immediately the posting is complete.

### WHY BILLS MUST BE SENT IN PROMPTLY

One frequent cause of a shortage of working capital is extended credit given to customers owing to lateness in rendering monthly accounts. It does not apply so much in the case of companies where discount is an inducement to pay promptly, but it is of vital importance in the retail trade for accounts to be rendered at the earliest possible date in the month following the sale of the goods. It is probably true of many private consumers that they pay monthly accounts in the order in which they are received, and firms who send their accounts later are likely to be overlooked entirely until funds permit payment at a later date, possibly the following month. There is, therefore, a real reason for the officer manager to take all steps possible to secure the prompt sending of his sales ledger statements.

Usually members of his staff will despatch monthly statements, with the exception of accounts the payment of which is overdue ; these are normally passed to the officer manager or other official for attention. Correspondence and restriction of further credit may be necessary but the further steps, if any, which ought to be taken to enforce payment will depend upon the individual case.

The account may be passed o the firm's solicitors with instructions to issue a writ for its collection, or it may be passed to one of the mercantile agencies which specialise in debt collection, as well as in affording information regarding the status of firms. It will, of course, be understood that discretion has to be exercised in resorting to these measures, and the effect of such steps upon the goodwill of the firm is always considered. Goodwill is such a valuable asset, and is so difficult to build up, that nothing should be done to injure it.

### THE CASH BOOK AND ITS COMPLEMENTS

Mention must now be made of the other books for which the office manager is responsible, the most important of which is the cash book. In larger companies this book is generally very greatly subdivided, the main cash book containing totals only of the detailed items shown in subsidiary cash books.

When book-keeping machines are used it is usual for books to be almost entirely dispensed with. The total cash received by post, together with cash received in the shop or warehouse during the day, is obtained by adding together the figures shown on the duplicate copies of receipts which have been prepared. The total of these receipts must, of course, agree with the cash actually received and banked, and a carbon copy is retained for record purposes. Each receipt is sorted into its appropriate ledger, and, by means of a fresh dissection, the total obtained is divided into the number of ledgers in use. Each operator must then post each receipt to the correct accounts, and the machine automatically checks the total so posted.

Separate loose-leaf books are used for bought ledger accounts and for expense items so that the figures can be used simultaneously in the various sections of the office. All these cash books have the usual columns to record discounts received and allowed. Generally the total of these discounts is regarded as a normal item of the profit and loss account, the discount received being a direct offset to other expenses. In some firms, however, it is thought that discount earned in this way affects the departmental profits, and it is dissected so as to give credit to the department concerned. In whichever way it is treated, it is obviously an important item, and care should be taken to make it as large as possible.

When a large number of items are entered, it is necessary to make a weekly reconciliation of the balance shown in the cash book with that which appears in the bank pass book. In practice the balance shown in the company's cash book will never agree with its pass book balance because cheques will have been paid in which have not been cleared by the bank, and cheques which have been dispatched and entered in the cash book will not have been presented by the payees' banker. A specimen reconciliation statement is shown below:

| | | |
|---|---|---|
| Bank balance as per pass book . . | | £950 10 0 |
| ADD cheques paid in but not cleared— | | |
| P. Adams . . | £39 0 0 | |
| O. Burns . . | 40 10 0 | 79 10 0 |
| | | £1030 0 0 |
| DEDUCT cheques paid out but not presented— | | |
| Smith & Son . | £70 7 0 | |
| G. Thomas & Co. . | 120 1; 0 | 191 0 0 |
| Bank balance per cash book . . | | £839 0 0 |

There remains the "petty cash" book required for record of receipts and payments of office cash. It is necessary to give this book attention, as any irregularity in the office cash is easily overlooked, and yet, if neglected, would reflect seriously upon the efficiency of the office management. The method almost invariably adopted is to keep the petty cash book on an "imprest" basis. The principle of this method is that all outside receipts are banked, the book only being ruled to show the amount received through the principal cashier from the banking account.

As an example, let us assume that the petty cashier is supplied with a round sum of money, say £100. Out of this he makes payments during the day—carriage, postage stamps, odd wages, cash repayments to customers, etc. At the end of the day he submits a statement to the chief cashier of the total payments he has made (we will assume the above items amounted to £75, 3s. 10d.). He receives from the chief cashier a cheque for £75, 3s. 10d., which, when cashed, will restore his balance to the original £100. The amount of £75, 3s. 10d. is entered in the cash book concerned in the same way as any other cheque. In this way, although the petty cash book is not used for posting items direct to the ledger, it is systematically supervised because it is inspected by the chief cashier every time a cheque is required. It is further possible to check the cashier, if desired, at any time of the day, because the cash in hand, together with receipts or other vouchers for amounts paid out must invariably amount to £100.

The senior cashier's position is obviously one of some responsibility. Whenever the amount of cash is large enough to justify it, there ought to be two separate appointments, a receiving cashier and a paying cashier, the former being responsible for paying into the bank all receipts (he will usually have authority to endorse cheques for payment into the bank), and the latter only paying out cash on the imprest basis just described. This division of functions very much lessens the possibility of fraud, and provides a far more satisfactory check on money transactions at any particular moment.

## THE JOURNAL: "FATHER" TO ALL THE LEDGERS

No attempted record of books to be found in an office would be complete without reference to the journal, which theoretically can be used for every transaction, and in practice is always used when for some reason the other prime books of account are unsuitable. Before the system of double-entry book-keeping was originated, the day book or journal was the only book in use containing a record of everything that happened. With the greater complexity and subdivision of office work with the consequent subdivision of the office, it became the practice to use the journal only for transferring items from one ledger to another. It is a hard-and-fast rule that nothing must on any account be entered in the ledger which does not first appear in the journal, cash book, bought or sales books, or another of the subsidiary books. Being capable of almost any kind of entry, the journal may be regarded as " father " to them all.

An important section of the office is that responsible for payment of weekly wages to the staff. This department is sometimes supervised by the chief cashier and sometimes by the office manager, but in any case real efficiency is required if money is not to be lost and if the staff are to be contented. It ought to be a rule that no wages are paid unless the required authority is received from the executive official responsible for the engagement. In the case of factories, those on time rates are paid according to the number of hours worked, as shown on records received from the self-recording clocks and countersigned by the foreman, or from other sources. Payment is made to piece-workers in accordance with the amounts shown by the foreman of the room in which the worker has been placed, the onus of the correctness of the amount resting upon the foreman, countersigned by a responsible official designated for the duty.

When weekly wages are payable, the pay section of the office generally pays the amount shown on the agreement or other authority supplied by the engaging official. Whatever means are employed, it is essential that nothing is paid out unless the necessary authority is available, the nature of the authority required naturally depending entirely upon the special circumstances existing. The National Health and Unemployment Insurance cards are generally kept in this section, and the person responsible is required to see that stamps are properly affixed after the correct deduction has been made from the employee's remuneration before cash is paid out. In most companies it will be found that the employees will often be changed or transferred to other departments so that it is necessary for the pay section to keep a pen record of all such movements. Alterations take place so frequently that it is generally found impracticable to make great use of machinery in this section.

### HOW TO DEAL WITH INCOMING LETTERS

IN both the secretary's and office manager's sections, arrangements for dealing promptly with correspondence are, of course, most important, and in large organisations definite rules are laid down as to which officials are responsible for signing letters, etc. It is usual to engage a staff on early morning duty to sort and classify all incoming correspondence before the arrival of the general office staff. The office manager will generally delegate some one to superintend the opening and sorting of letters on his behalf. A staff of sufficient intelligence is necessary to ensure that letters which are obviously of a private nature are forwarded to the addressee unopened, while the remainder are taken from the envelopes and placed in separate trays for the attention of the department concerned.

In this connection it is most important to arrange properly for dealing with incoming cheques or postal orders. One safeguard which has been found useful is to make it a rule that the amount of all cheques or cash is marked clearly in blue pencil on the incoming letter. The cash is then separated from the rest of the correspondence, but before it is banked, the total of it is agreed with the total obtained from adding the figures shown in individual letters from which receipts are prepared. This ensures that the dealing with cash passes through more than one pair of hands, and if the general rule, that all cash ought to be handled or checked by as many people as possible, is observed, the chance of loss by theft is greatly reduced.

It is usual for the correspondence to be passed direct to the appropriate official, as directors or general managers will generally have sufficient faith in responsible heads of sections to leave them a free hand to answer correspondence connected with their departments. In some companies the institution of a special correspondence section is advisable. This consists of a number of shorthand-typists, each of whom mainly takes the dictation from one or other of the departments, but all of whom are in general available whenever need arises. The success of a separate section for this work depends entirely upon circumstances. Where each department has sufficient work to justify the employment of a separate secretarial staff, it is probably preferable to arrange staff accordingly.

Closely linked to correspondence is the art of filing, the importance of which can hardly be exaggerated. The time that is spent in searching for missing papers or letters, and the annoyance caused by the loss of some information will very quickly more than equal the cost of the installation of an adequate filing system. The number of filing systems on the market is considerable, but the first requisite is naturally that the system must be easily adapted to the business using it. Simplicity is also a great advantage, as it is obviously desirable to be able to employ the less expensive clerks to keep files in order, and this presupposes that the system is easily understood. It is further desirable that whatever system is installed should be capable of expansion, so that the present filing equipment does not become inadequate as the business grows.

Most filing systems can be classified as either on a horizontal or vertical principle. In the former case the papers are placed in drawers which, since they are supplied with tabs or labels, immediately show the contents. The vertical principle, which is perhaps more popular to-day, is for the letters or papers to be placed in small folders or files and placed upright in the drawers of a cabinet. Generally a separate folder for each correspondent or subject is used, unless they are sufficiently unimportant to find a place in a miscellaneous section. It will generally be found that a separate filing system is required for each department of the business (*e.g.* selling departments, sales ledger accounts, bought ledger accounts, staff records, secretary's department).[1]

## A MACHINE FOR NEARLY EVERY JOB

MECHANICAL devices have been found more and more essential to the efficient running of a modern office. Whereas a few years ago the typewriter alone was found, to-day there is not only a much improved and comparatively noiseless machine for letter-writing, but also a machine for almost every operation of a routine character. The typewriter is almost too well known to need mention, and the ease with which typescript is read compared with manuscript, and the number of carbon copies which can be taken from one operation, make its use practically essential.

[1] For further discussion of filing see "How Business Records are Kept" (p. 476).

[*Thomas Edison Ltd.*

AN OFFICE TIME-SAVER

*The Dictating Machine records the spoken word.*

In nearly every large business a private telephone exchange is to be found. Its operation is entrusted to an expert, whose duty it is to direct incoming messages to the right department and to inter-connect the various internal departments. Office managers will invariably have a telephone on their desks (the hand microphone being most popular), by means of which they can converse not only with any one in their office, but also with correspondents residing at a distance. It is obvious that internal telephone communication means an enormous saving of time to the executive, and in any large organisation it is to-day absolutely essential for the proper administration of affairs.

In addition to telephonic communication, it is usual for the manager to be connected by an electric bell, or " buzzer," to the room in which his assistant or private secretary works. If a simple code of signals is adopted, *e.g.* one ring for Mr.

[*Thomas Edison Ltd.*

AN OFFICE TIME-SAVER

*The typist " listens-in " and types from the recorded message.*

Smith, and two rings for a typist, it serves as a perfectly satisfactory indication as to whom the manager requires to go to his room.

Book-keeping machines have already been referred to in connection with the proper equipment of an up-to-date sales ledger section. Calculating machines capable of all kinds of speedy additions, subtraction, multiplication, and division are now on the market in great variety. In large retail organisations adding machines or cash registers are indispensable in checking cash takings, while they are also essential in securing daily sales figures classified under the various departments concerned.

In thousands of offices the Comptometer is found invaluable, for it adds, multiplies, subtracts, and divides money, weights, and numbers with the greatest celerity. It is a non-listing machine, fitted with a control key which provides certain mechanised safeguards in order to secure accuracy. Of list machines perhaps the type made by the Burroughs Company are most popular, while the Dalton and Sundstrand are most useful machines and differ from other adding machines in that they are operated by ten keys only. Whatever machine is employed it must be viewed from the point of view of the operator. The employment of skilled operators is essential, because it is probably true that success depends 90 per cent. upon the operator and 10 per cent. upon the machine.

Where a large amount of correspondence is required, the dictating machine is found a great asset. Letters, instructions, memoranda, etc., can be dictated to this instrument at any speed, thus dispensing entirely with the services of the shorthand clerk. A record of what is dictated is made on a disc (similar to the discs of old-fashioned phonographs). By means of headphones the typist can hear the record of what has been said, and does her work direct from the machine. That the dictating machine is of invaluable service is shown by its increasing popularity.

In the postage department mechanical stamping machines are largely used. By these machines the "frank" value and postmark date is printed on the envelope, and meters on the machine record the cumulative value of postage used. Machines of this type frequently "frank" over two hundred envelopes per minute.

## THE ACCOUNTANT: HOW FIGURES LIGHT UP THE SITUATION

We must now look briefly at the section for which the accountant is responsible. His business is not only to see that proper accounts of the business are kept, but also to see that the manager is supplied with regular information to enable him to keep a watchful eye upon economical production and administration. His accounts should be kept in such a way that the figures readily show what advice ought to be tendered on the financial aspect when any important step is being considered.

The chief accountant, therefore, not only prepares figures for the presentation of the annual balance sheet, but makes his returns illuminate the cost of production, administration, transit, and other services, so that the financial adviser or manager is able to see at a glance when undue expenditure is taking place.

### FIGURES THAT PICTURE FUTURE PROGRESS

WHEREAS it was once customary for firms to trade for a whole year without knowing with any certainty the results of their trading, it is now usual to require monthly or quarterly approximate accounts to show profit expectations and general tendencies of trade. By the aid of daily cash returns and weekly statistical sales records, a very fair picture of what is happening can be obtained, and the efficiency of the accountant and his department will be the measure of accuracy and promptness with which these periodical figures are prepared.

It will be evident that to obtain good results the accountant must work very often in close conjunction with the office manager. While the office manager produces records of sales and purchases with the corresponding debtors and creditors, the large number of figures dealing with expenses and records of total sales or purchases will ultimately be used by the accountant, and he should arrange periodical checks on the accuracy of the accounts produced.

Although periodical returns are a very important production of his office, the accountant will never lose sight of the final accounts which will invariably be checked by an independent firm of auditors. In this connection he will deal exclusively with all auditor's requirements, and his office will require to be so constituted that vouchers for all payments, and all other information likely to be required by the auditors, is readily available.

In practice, auditors often do a great deal of routine check work during the year, and leave the accountant to produce a final profit and loss account and balance sheet before they check the final figures. The responsibility for producing lists of balances, extracted from ledgers to back up the balance sheet figure of the total amount due to or owing by the company, rests with him and he therefore depends largely upon an efficient office for the accurate production of the information desired.

In addition to the figures of purchases, sales, expenses, etc., with which his department will deal, the accountant has the custody of the private ledger in which are recorded all transactions of a confidential nature, such as loans to or from directors or partners, and records in detail of balance sheet items not found in the general ledgers, such as cost of land and buildings, plant, machinery and equipment, share capital accounts, etc. In short, the details of items appearing in the printed accounts of a balance sheet which are frequently published in the press, and are familiar to every general reader, will be found in the department controlled by the accountant to the company.

Although this department will have the use of the mechanical aids which have been mentioned, the work is of a more individual nature and obviously no machine can be of much use in preparing the intricate annual figures with which larger organisations have to deal. For this reason the accountant's department will conform less to type, and it is not possible to suggest definite principles upon which its management should be based.

In general terms the accountant co-operates with the secretary in producing prompt and accurate records, which will enable the management to take prompt and effective action when necessary, but he relies to a great extent upon equal co-operation from the office manager to secure such efficient methods of producing statistics and analytical figures that the results will exactly balance with similar figures and fit as cogs in a perfectly going machine. If the office manager attends to its smooth running, the accountant takes the finished products from various sections, co-relates them and makes the figures so self-evident that the health of the whole organisation can be properly estimated ; when this is not satisfactory the figures ought to indicate fairly accurately a diagnosis upon which action can be taken.

## WHERE TO READ ABOUT OFFICE MANAGEMENT

THERE are many books on office management designed for examination purposes, but there is a curious dearth of books which are of practical use in an office. The secretary, being largely concerned with legal problems, relies mainly on a work such as Gore-Brown's *Handbook on Joint Stock Companies*, a comprehensive work of 916 pages which has run through many editions. A smaller book, though very complete and absolutely reliable is *The Secretary's Manual on the Law and Practice of Joint Stock Companies*, by Judge Haydon, K.C., and the late Sir Gilbert Garnsey,

K.B.E., F.C.A. A very useful book also is *Secretarial Practice*, the official manual of the Chartered Institute of Secretaries.

On the office manager's side Spicer and Pegler's *Practical Bookkeeping and Commercial Knowledge* (Pitman) can be recommended. In addition to an introduction to accountancy it contains notes on office organisation and control, insurance, banking and commercial terminology. *The 20th Century Business Book* also contains useful sections on office organisation and modern office appliances, with illustrations. *Office Organisation and Management*, by Lawrence R. Dicksee (Pitman), can also be recommended. For the accountant's work, reference should be made to any standard work on accountancy, such as *Advanced Accounts*, by R. N. Carter, M.Com., F.C.A., or *Bookkeeping and Accounts*, by L. C. Cropper, F.C.A.

# CORRESPONDENCE IN BUSINESS

*by ARTHUR F. DOGGETT, B.A.(Cantab.)*

No matter what branch of business a man enters, the ability to express himself clearly on paper stands him in good stead. In fact, it is, perhaps, not too much to say that this is the chief, if not the only standard by which a junior's capabilities can be judged in many of the great organisations of to-day. Modern business does not call for the flights of imagination that the master of literature achieves, but rather for the lucid expression of hard facts as they are found.

So far as the actual putting down of words on paper is concerned, business correspondence can be divided into two main fields—report-writing for internal use, and letter-writing to persons outside the firm. Each of these calls for a different style, but they have the common necessity of clarity of expression as their keynote, and this is the object which must always be kept in view. Report-writing is generally the first type with which the tyro comes in contact, and for this reason it will be dealt with first.

It is not unusual for a newcomer to a firm to be given the task of investigating and reporting on the working of some particular branch of the firm's activities, partly so that his superiors can see what he is made of, and partly for the reason that, through making some definite investigations, he is able to learn far more, and in a much shorter time, than if he were merely left to " browse around " and pick up what he could. In a large retail shop, for instance, the central management may wish to obtain information and suggestions on the desirability, or otherwise, of extending their radius of delivery by van ; the dispatch manager will be able to give his opinion, but it is likely to be biased, and for this reason a layman is detailed to investigate and report generally on the cost of extending the radius of delivery by, say, three miles, and on the probable increase in business which such a step would produce.

### THE REPORT : A NEAT AND JUST ARRANGEMENT OF FACTS

In the course of his inquiries he will gather a mass of information, and his final object will be the presentation of all the *pros* and *cons* in their order of importance, and as clearly and concisely as possible. This is not an easy matter, and however much data may have been obtained, it is of little value to a busy superior unless it is presented in an orderly and intelligent fashion. This first report is all-important and may have a far-reaching effect on the writer's career, so it behoves him to use all possible care.

In drafting the report, it is a good plan to address it in the top right-hand corner of the paper directly to the person or persons for whom it is intended, *e.g.* :

Mr. H. R. Jenkinson
From Mr. D. R. Bourne.
10*th August*, 1935.

In the top left-hand corner will appear the word " Report." Then follows the heading which should be underlined and set out well in the middle of the page, thus :

<u>PROPOSED EXTENSION OF DISPATCH RADIUS</u>

THE report itself should then start with the period over which the investigation was made, and should go on to set out the information acquired in the order of its importance. In this case, it would be well to state as nearly as possible such facts as the number of known customers who would benefit from the extension, how many of the firm's competitors deliver in the proposed new area, whether or not there has been a request by a large number of present customers to warrant the extension, etc.

Having set out the *pros* as far as they can be ascertained, the report must give the *cons* equal, if not closer, attention. These will include the extent of extra capital outlay for extra vans, and of revenue expenditure on account of extra drivers and van men and an estimate of the increased cost of petrol, oil, tyres, and general upkeep. The report should close with any strong views for or against the proposal expressed by any knowledgeable person met with in the course of the investigation, and the writer's own views may be expressed briefly. It should then be signed and dated.

In some houses it is customary for reports or memoranda to have each paragraph numbered. This is an excellent practice as it enables a critic to refer quickly to any special point raised

5

in the report. It is even more helpful if, in addition to the numbering of the paragraphs, each group is given a sub-title, as, for instance, below.

Mr H. R. Jenkinson,
General Manager,
from Mr. D. R. Bourne,
*10th August*, 1935.

*Report.*

*Proposed Extension of Dispatch Radius*

1. During the period from 6th August to 9th August I investigated the desirability of extending our radius of dispatch from 5 to 8 miles, and in the course of my inquiries I interviewed, among others, the dispatch manager, the statistical manager, and the garage manager, and I have made a thorough tour of the proposed new area.

2. *Population.*—The population of the area to be covered by the extension is approximately 35,000, of whom about 3,000 are customers already on our books.

3. *Competitors' Deliveries.*—The following firms of note already deliver in the proposed new area every day: Messrs. Harrods, Selfridge, Gamage, while the Army and Navy Stores and Messrs. Whiteleys deliver three times a week on Mondays, Wednesdays, and Fridays. . . . and so on.

The probable extra expense incurred would be set out in the same way.

One of the prime objects of the report is to enable superior officials to make a decision. It is, therefore, necessary to be brief, but not at the expense of clarity or omission of important facts or opinions. If the superior has asked for definite information on specific points, so much the easier for the reporter. He should stick to those points and not drag in a lot of information which may or may not be of interest. But it often happens that he is purposely given a completely free hand with a view to testing his capabilities of observation and accuracy, and, in such a case, it behoves him to put forward every conceivable point which has an important bearing on the subject. His chief will at least know then that little has escaped him, and that he can be trusted on future occasions to be thorough.

### MAKING FIGURES SPEAK PLAINLY

WHATEVER he does, he must keep to the point and whenever possible back up his facts with figures, making sure that those figures are accurate. If, as is so often necessary, figures have to be extensively quoted, they should be arranged as far as possible in tabular form ; they are so much easier to follow. This is even more important if comparisons have to be drawn. An example of bad method is given below, while the table underneath it shows how the same thing should be done.

> "The Selling Staff Costs in the ironmongery department were 6·2 per cent. as compared with 5·9 per cent. last year. Packing and Delivery Costs, 3·1 per cent. against 2·85 per cent last year, and Complaints, 0·75 per cent. against 1·3 per cent. last year. The reasons for the increase in the first two items are increased selling space and wider delivery."

| | 1934. | 1933. | Remarks. |
|---|---|---|---|
| Selling Staff Costs . | 6·2% | 5·9% | 300 sq. ft. extra space. |
| Packing and Delivery Costs . . | 3·1% | 2·85% | Wider delivery. |
| Complaints . . | 0·75% | 1·3% | Very satisfactory. |

In the latter case the reader can instantly refer back to any point that strikes his notice, and information can be set down more briefly, all repetition of phrases like "as compared with" or "as against" being cut out. The method of tabulation is far less cumbersome all round than the setting out of facts and particularly figures in paragraphs, although one is apt to lose force in explanation by too much tabulation.

## THE ELEMENTS OF LETTER-WRITING

THE writing of letters calls for further qualities which are not so necessary in the case of memoranda and reports. For one thing, the writer of a memorandum is generally personally acquainted with the person for whom it is intended, and, for another, it is easier to "get down to brass tacks." In a letter, however, a certain amount of embellishment is necessary, and such elements as tact and tone come more into the picture.

The structure of a business letter can be divided into the following parts: the heading, or description and address of the firm issuing the letter; the date; the reference; the initials of the stenographer and dictator of the letter; the address of the person to whom it is to be sent; the salutation; the body of the letter; the complimentary closing; the signature of the writer. These would appear in the way shown below:

George Black & Co. Ltd.,<br>
Wholesale Stationers,<br>
25 Holborn,<br>
London, W.C.2.<br>
*25th August*, 1935.

Messrs. Paynter & Lewis Ltd.,<br>
34 Heath Street,<br>
Cambridge.

Ref. TGH/MC.

Dear Sirs,

*Your Reference JRP/AL*

..............................................
..............................................
..............................................
..............................................

Yours faithfully,<br>
George Black & Co. Ltd.,<br>
T. G. Harrison,<br>
Manager.

The heading to a letter, in addition to giving the name and address of the firm, often includes the firm's telephone number, telegraphic and cablegram addresses, and trade mark or slogan. This is, of course, all printed on the notepaper in bold type. The date consists of the day of the month, the month, and the year, and it is preferable to set it out in full as above, rather than to put 25/8/34. The reference is for simplification of filing, and it is discourteous not to quote a reference when answering a letter. The address must contain all the information necessary for the correct delivery of the letter, and it must also contain any titles or rank due to the addressee, such as: The Right Honourable the Lord...... of...... K.C.V.O., P.C.; The Very Reverend the Dean of ......; The Worshipful the Mayor of.......

It is impossible to lay down hard and fast rules dealing with the body or subject-matter of the letter. There are numerous text-books which set out regulations concerning grammar, punctuation, etc., but which fail to point out the practical value of confining as far as possible each letter to one subject. If it is necessary to refer to more than one subject, each should be given a definite sub-title, but, whenever possible, one subject only should be dealt with in each letter. This, of course, may not be practicable when answering a letter referring to different subjects, but it is well to beware of introducing more than one topic in writing an initial letter.

The language should be as simple as possible, and the short word always preferred to the long. What is to be gained, for instance, by saying: "The sales commenced to deteriorate during the last week in July" when the same could be conveyed by: "The sales began to fall off during the last week in July?" People are too apt to think that the use of long words, and particularly of long words with a Latin origin, shows education and breeding. In actual fact, to people of education and breeding it often denotes exactly the opposite, and frequently leads to confusion owing to use of a word conveying to the reader an entirely different meaning from that intended by the writer. This raises the subject of the choice and aptness of words. In reading a sentence through, the writer should ask himself the question: "Can this mean anything else?" If he comes to the conclusion that it can, he must try again. If, at the end of the letter, he feels that each sentence can convey only one possible meaning, he has crossed the worst river successfully.

All this does not mean that there are not long words which, if used judiciously, will save sentences of explanation. Nor does it mean that a string of sentences, which convey exactly the right meaning to the reader, necessarily mean that the letter is a good one. There is such a thing as tact! In the examples given later on, an attempt will be made to show the right and the wrong way, or, rather, a good way and a less good way, of dealing with circumstances arising in the course of this important subject.

The complimentary closing includes such words as "Yours faithfully," "Yours sincerely," etc., and their actual choice must depend upon the relationship existing between the writer and the receiver of the letter. The day of "gush" in letters is fast disappearing, and false compliments are fortunately far more rare than they used to be, although there is still plenty of room for improvement in this direction.

### HOW TO SOOTHE AND HOW TO COMPLAIN

THERE are very many different forms of letter used in every business, and the type of letter to be written is governed by the particular circumstances which make it necessary. A letter sent in answer to a customer's complaint that the blue curtain material she bought three months previously as unfadable had since turned pink, would naturally differ in form and wording from one dispatched to a firm of motor engineers asking the reason for the delay in repairs to a lorry which had been promised for a certain date.

Again, there is a great difference between a collecting letter and a selling letter. A collecting letter is an endeavour, in all likelihood not the first, to persuade a long-winded customer to part with the necessary cash to settle an outstanding account with, perhaps, a veiled hint, in the last extreme, that his cash is preferable to his custom. A selling letter is an attempt to win a new customer, or to induce an old one to make a more expensive purchase than he had originally intended to do.

Let us take first the lady's complaint about her blue curtain, and let us suppose that it was received on the morning of 24th August. An answer that leaves much to be desired is given below.

Manning, Grainger & Co. Ltd.,
101 Oxford Street, W.1,
31*st August*, 1935.

Mrs. V. R. Jones,
Mill House,
Sadford,
Berkshire.

Dear Madam,

We are in receipt of your letter of 23rd inst., and note your remarks. On looking up your order we find that the materials were supplied to you in February last, and we consider your request that we should replace them is most unreasonable under the circumstances.

Yours truly,
Manning, Grainger & Co. Ltd.,
N. Ellis,
Manager.

The first failure of this letter is that it is far from being a prompt reply. There is no excuse at all for laxity in this matter. If a lengthy and detailed investigation into a complaint is necessary, as is often the case, a communication should immediately be sent to the customer, courteously acknowledging the receipt of the complaint, and stating that it is receiving immediate attention and that an explanation will be forthcoming as soon as possible. This can be done, if necessary, on a form letter, but a personal reply would create a much better impression on the complainant and would make her feel that her case was receiving prime attention.

The whole wording of the letter is bald and crude. Even if a customer has (probably on purpose) given the wrong date of purchase, the error should be pointed out in the most tactful manner possible, and, unless some special circumstances decree otherwise, some attempt at least to meet her request should be made. The affair might be handled as follows:

Manning, Grainger & Co. Ltd.,
101 Oxford Street, W.1.,
*24th August*, 1935.

Mrs. R. V. Jones,
Mill House,
Sadford,
Berkshire.

Dear Madam,

We thank you for your letter of yesterday's date and note with regret that the curtain material we supplied you has faded. We will take the matter up immediately with the wholesalers, and, in the meantime, perhaps you will be good enough to forward, at our expense, a sample.

Rest assured that we will do our best to give you complete satisfaction in this matter within the next ten days.

We are,
Yours faithfully,
Manning, Grainger & Co. Ltd.,
N. Ellis,
Manager.

In the meantime the original order would be traced and found to be dated 20th February and not 20th May or thereabouts, as stated in the complaint. If the colours were guaranteed fast, no real notice would be taken of this error in dates, and no mention of it would be made in reply to the customer. But if the material were not guaranteed as fadeless, then it would be mentioned, as the manufacturers would probably deny liability. As soon as the sample was received from the customer an acknowledgment would be sent to her. When the complaint had been fully investigated, and found to be reasonably justifiable, the answer shown below would probably be sent.

Manning, Grainger & Co. Ltd.,
101 Oxford Street, W.1,
*6th September*, 1935.

Mrs. R. V. Jones,
Mill House,
Sadford,
Berkshire.

Dear Madam,

Further to our letter of 24th August, in reply to your complaint, we have now been able to investigate the matter thoroughly.

We forwarded your sample of the faded material to our suppliers, and we had to place ourselves in their hands as this particular line was, we regret to say, not guaranteed fadeless. They agreed entirely that it was a bad case of fading, but said that this was only the second complaint they had received.

We are happy to say that they are willing to make good, and that we shall shortly be sending to you, under separate cover, 15 yards of blue repp, and shall be glad to receive your acknowledgment of its safe arrival.

In closing may we add that we consider this to be generous treatment on the part of our suppliers, as it transpired from the records that the original material was supplied to you on 20th February last.

Trusting that we shall have further opportunity of serving you,

We remain,
Yours obediently,
Manning, Grainger & Co. Ltd.,
N. Ellis,
Manager.

In the case of the deliquent garage, the personal element does not apply to the same extent as in the instance just quoted, and, although nothing is lost by courtesy, a very much firmer note can be adopted. Here, the firm is in the position of complainant, and each day's delay is causing it more expense and loss of business. The letter shown below would probably be sent.

Hurlstone, Norman & Co. Ltd.,
55 Bond Street, W.1,
*2nd September*, 1935.

The Manager,
Car Repairs Ltd.,
12 Cauldron Street, W.C.3.

Dear Sir,

Morris Van PN 3243

Our garage manager has reported that the above van, which was sent to you for reboring, and which was promised to be ready by mid-day on Tuesday last, 28th August, has not yet been returned. He further states that two telephone calls have failed to produce a satisfactory explanation of the delay.

We would remind you that this is the second occasion upon which we have had to complain about delay in matters of this kind, and we must inform you that unless the van is delivered in full working order by noon on Wednesday next, 5th September, we shall have no course but to withdraw our custom completely—a step we are very loath to take.

We trust that you will give this matter your most urgent attention as under the present circumstances we are seriously inconvenienced.

Yours truly,
Hurlstone, Norman & Co. Ltd.,
T. G. Rose,
Managing Director.

This letter may appear at first sight to be unduly stiff, but it must be remembered that no attempt at an explanation was forthcoming from the motor engineers over the telephone. It is not an easy case to answer and excuses would be useless. What is wanted is an explanation and apology for the inconvenience caused. The reply might read:

Car Repairs Ltd.,
12 Cauldron Street, W.C.3,
*4th September*, 1935.

The Managing Director,
Hurlstone, Norman & Co. Ltd.,
55 Bond Street, W.1.

Dear Sir,

*Morris Van PN* 3243

I received your letter of the 2nd inst. on my return from holiday, and I hasten to proffer my apologies for the failure to complete the work to time, and for the inconvenience your firm has suffered through delay in repairs to the above van.

Exhaustive inquiries show, that when the engine was reassembled after reboring, it was found under test that there was a flaw in the cylinder block, which necessitated our sending the block to Electric Welders Ltd. for repairs. This, in addition to causing delay, will, I regret to say, add £1, 12s. 6d. to the total cost of the repairs, but you may be certain that the job is a good one, as Electric Welders Ltd. are recognised as being a first-rate firm.

The above remarks are not meant as an excuse—for the fact that you were not informed earlier of this unavoidable delay is inexcusable—but as an explanation of the facts. It appears further that your garage manager was unfortunate in both telephone calls. In the first instance our foreman was out on a testing job, while, in the second, he was on the sick list, and in neither case was there a mechanic available who was cognisant of the facts of your case.

I trust, therefore, that you will accept my humblest apologies and assurance that in future your orders will receive special attention.

By the time this letter reaches you, the van will be back in your service in complete running order.

I am,
Yours faithfully,
B. Smith,
Manager, Car Repairs Ltd.

It would, of course, have been possible for Mr. Smith to write a much more humble and obsequious letter, but, nowadays, it would not carry any more weight—rather the reverse.

### HOW TO WRITE A COLLECTING LETTER

The aim of collecting letters is to collect outstanding debts, and considerable judgment is needed in their use. The attitude of a debtor can soon be gauged by the response, or otherwise, he or she makes to the rendering of statements. Some people leave the payment of accounts till the latest possible date on principle, while others are perforce "long-winded." In either case, a courteous firmness should be observed.

In large firms the preliminary stages of debt collection are generally dealt with by means of form letters, couched in terms such as these :

> "We beg to remind you that we have as yet received no remittance in respect of your account amounting to £5 15s. 6d., a statement of which was rendered on 31st March last.
>
> As our accounts are upon a strict monthly basis we would ask you to be good enough to make an early settlement.
>
> Yours faithfully,
>
> ...................."

If this produces no result, a personal letter is sent, the contents of which depend upon what sort of customer one has to deal with. The stage of threatening would not yet have been reached, and an appeal for fairness would probably have the best effect. The following shows how this can be done :

Barnewall, Cresswell & Co. Ltd.,
13 Piccadilly, W.1,
*3rd June*, 1935.

Miss K. Smith,
14 Brandon Road,
Edgbaston.

Madam,

*Your Account*, £5, 15*s*. 6*d*.

This account is outstanding on our books and we fear that our statements rendered on 31st March and 30th April last, and our letter of 10th May, may perchance have escaped your notice.

The keenness of our prices and the value that we offer are made possible only through the prompt payment of accounts by customers, and, as we ourselves have to work on a strict monthly basis, we feel sure that you will take immediate steps to clear this small account, a copy of which is enclosed

We are, Madam,
Yours faithfully,
Barnewall, Cresswell & Co. Ltd.
R. L. Graham,
Credit Manager.

Should a result still not be forthcoming, it would be time to adopt more stringent measures, and proceedings can be hinted at :

Barnewall, Cresswell & Co. Ltd.,
13 Piccadilly, W.1,
*30th June*, 1935.

Miss K. Smith,
14 Brandon Road,
Edgbaston.

Madam,

*Your Account*, £5, 15s. 6d.

We are sorry to note that you have ignored our letters of 10th May and 3rd June.

We have already pointed out the fact that our business is conducted on a strict monthly cash basis, and as this dress for which payment is asked was supplied to you on 10th March last, we regret that we shall have no alternative but to place the matter in the hands of our solicitors unless a remittance in settlement is received within seven days from the date appearing at the head of this letter.

Yours faithfully,
Barnewall, Cresswell & Co. Ltd.,
R. L. Graham,
Credit Manager.

## EVERY LETTER SHOULD BE A SALESMAN

SELLING letters cover a very large area in the field of business correspondence, and opportunities are constantly occurring in commerce for the writer of a good letter of this type to prove his worth. Many laymen think that selling letters are confined to the circulars and importunate brochures that are sent out by the million by various firms up and down the country as a form of advertising. There is, however, a more subtle type of selling letter, addressed to the individual, in which the personal touch can be exploited. The most fruitful channel is, of course, the answer to a customers' inquiry. Here lies the golden opportunity of killing the bogy of the "take it or leave it" accusation so often brought against British selling methods, particularly abroad; but there are more ways of killing a cat than drowning it in milk, and a short pithy letter which sticks to the point, and yet which brings forward all the main features of the article to be sold, is far more likely to gain its object than a flowery flight of the imagination as to the possible uses to which the article might be put.

Inquiries on the part of a customer may merely require a plain, straightforward quotation in reply. They can often be dealt with by means of a form letter, but, whenever possible, a typewritten letter prepared specially for the customer in question should be sent. Every customer likes to feel that his or her order is receiving special attention, and the personal touch is more than half the battle in salesmanship. Of course, this cannot always be done in businesses of any size, but it is possible nowadays to have form letters printed by means of a duplicator which can be distinguished from typed script only by an expert eye. Abstract replies to inquiries can be dealt with by this means:

> "Your inquiry concerning discount has been passed to our Credit Manager, who will communicate with you direct."

The chief disadvantage of this kind of letter is that the customer's address has to be typewritten, and, no matter how carefully this is done, the type will differ from that appearing in the body of the letter. Another drawback is that, in more specific replies, blanks in the body of the letter have to be filled in by typewriter or in manuscript, and this does not look well. For example:

> "We regret that we are unable to supply from stock the . . . you ordered, but we are endeavouring to procure . . . especially for you, and will notify you later as to the date of dispatch.
>
> "We apologise for the delay, and we hope that you will not be seriously inconvenienced thereby."

In most business houses there is a series of form letters, each one being designed to meet a special circumstance, and, used judiciously, they save a great deal of valuable time. Each series has a number according to the subject it deals with, and a careful watch must be kept to see that the right letter is sent, as mistakes are easy to make.

It is perhaps not too much to say that every letter to a customer is a potential selling letter. In other words, a good letter creates an excellent impression on the receiver, who immediately thinks: "These people know what they are about." Conversely, a tactless, blunt reply to an inquiry has the opposite effect, and no firm in these days of acute competition can afford to be slipshod in this matter of correspondence.

### SNARES THAT LIE IN THE WRITTEN WORD

THERE are no rules of thumb to guide the style of a good letter, but the modern tendency is towards simplification. Short sentences and short words are generally more expressive than long sentences full of stops and cumbersome words. Few people realise that the written word often conveys a different meaning from the spoken word. In talking to a person one can use all kinds of facial expression and other gestures to add meaning to one's words, but in writing one is much more limited. It is, therefore, all the more important, not only to choose one's words with care, but to take pains with their arrangement. After writing a letter, it is a good plan to read it aloud, and it will often be found that expressions which look well on paper lose a great deal of their meaning when spoken.

Until one gets into the habit of arranging one's thoughts in an orderly fashion, it is best to jot down on a piece of rough paper the main points that one wishes to make, and then arrange them in a logical order. A clear sequence should always be aimed at, and a fresh paragraph allotted to each point it is desired to make. When answering letters, care must be taken to deal first, as far as possible, with the successive arguments set forth in the letter under reply. If there is anything else to be said outside the points raised in a correspondent's letter, it is better left until the end. By this means the ground is covered far more completely than if ideas are merely put down at random. Above all, direct questions must be dealt with specifically, as it is extremely rude to ignore them.

It is essential to see that all important verbal arrangements, whether made at a meeting between parties or over the telephone, are immediately confirmed in writing, while fresh in mind. There are two main reasons for the desirability of this practice, the first being that it minimises the element of misunderstanding, and, the second, that it makes a permanent record of an arrangement so that others who are concerned, and were not present, can see exactly what has taken place. This is especially necessary when more than one person is likely to be handling a case.

For instance, a house agent who has just let a flat to a client may wish, before having a formal agreement drawn up, to have confirmation of the terms. He would write a letter such as the following :

*26th July*, 1935.

Dear Sir,

29C *Harding Road, Hampstead, N.W.*3.

I have pleasure in confirming the arrangements made between us to-day in respect of the above flat.

You agreed to take over from Mrs. Sherleigh the unexpired portion of her lease which lapses on 29th September 1935, at a rental of £110 (one hundred and ten pounds), per annum exclusive of rates.

Vacant possession of the flat will be given on 31st August next, upon which date you become responsible for the rent, which will be payable quarterly in advance. It is understood that the first instalment will include an additional £9, 3s. 4d. (nine pounds, three shillings and fourpence) to cover the month of September, and that the first payment shall be made forthwith or upon the signing of the agreement to be drafted.

With regard to repairs, you will not be responsible to Mrs. Sherleigh's landlords for any repairing clauses set out in her agreement with them, but you agree to reimburse Mrs. Sherleigh for any internal damage done during your tenancy. A record of the condition of the flat will accompany this agreement.

I think this embodies the points we settled, and on having your approval I will have a proper agreement drafted forthwith.

Yours faithfully,

.....................

This gives the client the chance of disagreeing with the terms of the arrangement, or of adding to them if he desires to do so, and thus saves time when the agreement proper comes to be signed.

## AN INTERNAL POSTAL SERVICE AT WORK

THE routine of dealing with incoming mail is important in any large organisation. There is a great deal of sorting and arrangement to be done, so that when the working day begins, there shall be no delay. When the mail runs into thousands of letters each morning, a special staff of letter-openers is necessary. The firm will generally arrange with the Post Office authorities to collect the first batch of letters and parcels so as to make sure of starting in time. For this purpose a special person is detailed each morning. He will arrive some fifteen minutes before the letter-sorters, who in turn will sort the letters into convenient heaps before the rest of the correspondence staff come to work.

In sorting the letters, those addressed definitely to a person by name will be placed in one heap, and will be taken unopened to that person. The same applies to those addressed to the heads of departments, such as "The Accountant," "The Managing Director," or "The Secretary." Others addressed openly to the firm will be placed in another heap, and will be opened by means of an electrically operated, high-speed machine. They will then be divided amongst the correspondence staff to be examined and entered in books which will state the date of reception, addressee, name and address of sender, and a general note as to contents. When enclosures accompany a letter, they should be carefully pinned together. Cheques, postal orders, and stamps will be duly noted in a cash book set aside for the purpose. When the contents of the letters have been examined and noted, they will be placed in convenient bundles to be dispatched by the internal post to the person for whom they are intended, and on delivery, a signature will be obtained.

Sometimes the letter-opening staff is composed chiefly of ordinary shop assistants, who come early and receive overtime rates. Where a large mail order business is done, it is, of course, necessary to have a special staff to deal with this branch of the business, but they often deal with ordinary correspondence, in the preliminary stages as well. Ordinary correspondence, apart from mail orders, is dealt with in the respective departments to which it belongs by the executives of the business and their secretaries. When they have been dealt with, they must be carefully filed so that they can be found easily when required.

The outgoing letters are collected from the various offices throughout the house by the internal post boys, and are dispatched through the central correspondence office. It is worth pointing out here the value of good quality notepaper for external use. Nothing creates such a bad impression on clients or customers as a thin, cheap paper with a badly printed letter head, and it is a false economy.

With regard to enclosures with letters, many firms adopt the practice of having a small coloured stick-on label attached to the covering letter to denote that there are attachments. If this is not done, it is usual to type at the bottom of the last page of the covering letter after the signature the abbreviation "Encl." with the number of enclosures attached, *e.g.* "2 Encl." The object of this is to warn the letter-openers to be careful to keep all the papers together. On the enclosures themselves it will be well to have some method of identification, as once they become separated, it may be difficult to trace their origin.

## BOOKS ABOUT LETTER-WRITING

THERE are numerous books on the subject of Commercial Correspondence, some long and some short. In the former category one of the best is perhaps *The Principles and Practice of Commercial English*, by James Stephenson. It is published by Pitman. That and Grout's *Standard English*, also published by Pitman, will give a thorough grounding in grammar and correct writing, but they are rather stiff reading and, perhaps, not as modern in style as they might be. At the other end of the scale there is an excellent little book written by H. L. Carrad, called *Commercial Correspondence*, and published in 1931 by the Gregg Publishing Co. Ltd. It aims first and foremost at teaching plain, straightforward expression, and fights hard against the use of flowery commercial English as practised by our fathers.

*English for Secretarial Students*, by Walter Shancross, B.A., published by Pitman, is well worth reading, as is also *Commercial Correspondence and Commercial English* (Pitman), although the latter part of its title does not sound exactly in accordance with the remarks in the previous paregraph. In Volume III. of *The Twentieth Century Business Book* (Newnes) there is an excellent chapter on the subject of correspondence in business, with numerous practical examples.

# THE ART OF GOOD BUYING

*by R. J. W. STUBBINGS, B.Com.(Lond.),*
*Chartered Accountant*

MAN'S invention of money was not only of immense practical importance, but had profound psychological influences. When a primitive man had a spare axe and wanted a cooking pot, he had to find another who had a spare pot and needed an axe. It may have been difficult, but when such another was found and the exchange made, both parties were content because the exchange was regarded as of equal advantage to both. When man invented money the position altered. Money could be exchanged for anything else, and as a consequence the man who exchanged money for what he wanted was regarded in some ways as having got the worst of the bargain. It was considered to be more profitable to sell than to buy, and a seller was accounted a better business man than a buyer. The seller was regarded as something in the nature of a wolf and the buyer as a sheep. Even the common law of England evolved a principle *caveat emptor*, " let the buyer beware," which indicated the necessity for the buyer to be on his guard when concluding a bargain with the supposedly more powerfully placed seller.

This difference in attitude preserved by business men towards buyers as distinct from sellers is modified to a certain extent by the commercial era in which they live. From about 1844 to 1897 a " buyer's " market prevailed, which meant that throughout the world the supply of goods was being carried out more efficiently than their distribution, and that sellers were, in consequence, expending more energy than ever to persuade buyers to buy. The era was one of declining prices, sharpening competition, and narrowing margins of profit. From then until 1921 a " seller's " market prevailed, with conditions exactly opposite—rising consumption, buyers trying to procure the available goods, soaring prices. A " buyer's " market then set in again, and the buyer was once more courted and besieged by importunate sellers.

In a properly organised commercial community the buyer performs a function as valuable as that of the seller, and it must not be thought that there is any logical justification for a divergence in the psychological estimation of their importance. Psychology deals with man's behaviour as it is, not as it ought to be, and provides the key to much that would otherwise be puzzling in the relationship of buyer and seller.

## BUYING BECOMES A FULL-TIME JOB

WITH the coming of steam-driven machinery in the early days of the nineteenth century the size and scope of industry in this country expanded enormously. The one-man business began to lose ground as compared with the partnership, and later with the joint stock company. The controlling factor was the immense amount of capital needed to establish a factory—an amount which could usually only be assembled by a group of men. Later, however, it was found that there was a limit not only to what one man could do himself, but also to what he could successfully supervise in person, and one side of the business after another was turned over to a responsible subordinate.

The buying side of these pioneer businesses was one of the last to pass from the hands of one or more of the proprietors. The raw materials of manufacture were bought by the partners in person, because they were experts in the business and knew from practical experience what had to be produced from the materials. They gradually realised that their interference in the running of the factory, unless they were trained engineers, was a mistake, and that even the art of selling might be practised more efficiently by someone with natural aptitude, although not possessed of the partner's technical knowledge of the product. But for long, and even in many cases until to-day, the proprietor or a partner or the managing director purchased all the more costly supplies the firm required.

Raw materials for a manufacturing firm and merchandise for a wholesale firm represent the largest single items of their expenditure in all but a very few businesses. It was, therefore, thought that the purchasing of these supplies should be in the hands of some one with a stake in the business and a lively sense of the responsibility he was undertaking. Gradually, however, it was realised that buying, like other functions in a big business, was a specialised job. If the managing director was going to buy pig-iron, coal and coke, and core-sand for the foundry of an ironworks, he was not going to have the time and energy left for considering and shaping the policy of the business.

## WHERE WHOLESALE AND RETAIL BUYING DIFFER

LIKE many other modern developments of business organisation, the specialisation of the buying in manufacturing and wholesale businesses became most marked in the United States. The specialist in buying for such businesses is a much more recent addition to the commercial world than specialist buyers for retail businesses. This contrast between the two types of buying is due largely to a fundamental difference in the service rendered. The buyer for a retail business, especially one dealing in seasonal or fashionable goods, can buy anything in the class of goods in which his firm deals which he thinks will sell advantageously. This requires a wide knowledge of the goods bought, and, in addition, a feeling for the trend of taste in an unorganised body of consumers. Obviously such buying calls for expert handling. The patent importance of a profound knowledge of the market in which the goods are to be sold has led to buying for a retail business often being placed in the hands of the chief salesman. This arrangement probably originated in drapery firms, but it has been applied by departmental stores to types of goods very different from fashionable and seasonal lines.

The organisation of buying for a wholesale and manufacturing business is very different. The purchase of raw materials and supplies for manufacture presents problems for the solution of which a salesman of the finished article may have no adequate training. Such purchasing involves at least an appreciation of engineering problems, of the percentage of waste involved in processing, and of many other questions which do not arise when the finished product is being sold. Even a firm which does not manufacture for itself rarely entrusts its purchasing to a sales manager. The selling department is, of course, consulted before purchases are made, but the actual buying is independently organised.

## WHY THE BUYER SHOULD WORK FROM THE FACTORY

BUYING for a retail business is more often decentralised than is the buying for a wholesale and manufacturing firm. All the more important drapery establishments in the North of England have purchasing agents in London; but, even where the buying department of a manufacturing firm is away from the factory, it is very often merely because the head offices are in a neighbouring town and the executive wishes the buying department to be situated in the same building for the sake of ease of control. The arrangement is usually of no advantage to the department, and purchasing organisations are often found in the factory, even though the head offices are situated elsewhere.

It is an advantage to have the purchasing organisation in the factory, because the requisitions, which form the starting-point of the buying department's cycle of operations, emanate from the factory. The management decides what and how much shall be manufactured, the planning department in the factory decides how much material of various kinds is required, and the buying department must see that suitable material is available when the factory is ready to commence production. The closest possible co-operation between the buying department and the factory being necessary, the logical arrangement is for them to be situated in the same place.

### PROBLEMS PECULIAR TO FACTORY OR SHOP

THE buyer for a retail business of any size is usually responsible for a much smaller range of materials than is the purchasing manager for a manufacturing business, Buying for a retail business is almost invariably organised departmentally, while the purchasing manager of a manufacturing business often buys plant and machinery, office supplies, lubricating oil, cotton waste, etc., in addition to the many items of raw materials needed directly for manufacture. This does not by any means indicate that the purchasing manager for a manufacturing business has a more difficult task than his opposite number in a retail business. He is not expected to have a profound technical knowledge of all the goods he purchases, and he must depend for advice and help on the heads of departments requisitioning the various materials.

The buyer for a department of a retail business may be only concerned with one line of goods, but he must depend entirely on his own judgment in purchasing that line. In addition, he must be able to deal with the large number of salesmen who wish to persuade him to buy " novelty " lines which may be failures, but on the other hand may, if rejected, be great successes in the hands of some rival. The purchasing manager for an engineering works, when interviewing a lathe-steel salesman, knows either that he wants to buy such steel, and which of roughly ten grades he needs, or that he is not requiring any and that he can use the interview to gain information for future use.

## THE PRINCIPLES OF GOOD BUYING

One of the greatest sources of waste in any industry is inefficient buying. Whether or not goods will sell well depends upon the price at which they sell as compared with their quality. Extensive advertising may boost the sales of an inferior article for a short time when sales are made to the general public, but specious propaganda will aid a manufacturing or wholesale business very little in selling a line if the selling price is too high as compared with its quality. The selling price consists, first, of the cost of the original goods as raw materials, and, secondly, of the cost of services, that is, wages, overheads, and profit. It is, of course, impossible to say what proportion of the selling price is represented by the cost of goods in each industry, because this varies very largely with the type of product. It would, however, be no exaggeration to say that on an average $33\frac{1}{3}$ per cent. of the selling price represents the cost of materials, the buying of which is the responsibility of the purchasing manager.

There is obviously great scope for an efficient purchasing manager to render immense service to his firm in buying items which represent such a large proportion of ultimate selling price. Nor does the advantage of efficient buying stop there. Absolute selling price is of less importance than price in relation to quality. A purchasing manager who invariably accepts the lowest tenders, as a principle, is running grave risks of irreparably damaging the reputation of his firm for the quality of its product. Not only is it better for a firm to sell 100 articles at 1s. than 150 at 6d., but it may in the long-run be better for it to sell 100 good articles at 1s. than 300 inferior articles at 6d., because the 100 buyers at 1s. will probably place repeat orders when they find the article is of good quality.

### HOW THE BUYER CAN SAVE MONEY FOR HIS FIRM

In addition to these obvious direct advantages of good buying there are various important gains which are not so apparent. The good buyer will find out the firms of suppliers on which he can depend to make prompt deliveries of carefully packed and examined goods, so that his factory will not be held up by lack of supplies. Certain expenses, such as rent, light, heat, insurance, depreciation, etc., are classed as overhead expenses and are incurred whether or not the factory is in production. Every delay occasioned by returning faulty supplies or by unpunctual deliveries adds to the ultimate cost of the goods produced, without in any way adding to their chance of selling.

Similarly, the choice of unsuitable or inferior tools, machines, or supplies for the factory may, without causing a complete breakdown, slow down production and unnecessarily increase costs. By constantly weighing the advantages of prompt delivery, and of certainty as to quality, against the lower price asked by suppliers not so sure to satisfy on these points, the purchasing manager can render his firm incalculable service. It is obviously wasteful to pay more for guaranteed delivery in three weeks, when supplies will not be required so soon. At the same time, the efficient purchasing manager will know what alternative sources of supply he can tap, in case his regular suppliers are able to deliver only half his requirements for a rush order within the prescribed three weeks.

### WHAT MAKES A GOOD BUYER

A SUCCESSFUL buyer must be a man of sound judgment both of men and of business. This implies a balanced outlook which will prevent him from being stampeded into hasty purchases on a rising market, or from being unduly influenced by the prejudices and narrower outlook of departmental managers. Good judgment of other men will enable him to detect the bluff of the salesman who invariably hints darkly of a coming rise in prices owing to "trouble in the works," or the supposed withdrawal of a line in the near future. Coupled with tact, which is a most important attribute of a purchasing manager, it will enable him to deal successfully with departmental heads. The latter usually consider the welfare of their own departments before that of the firm as a whole. At the same time, they are in possession of information of vital importance to the purchasing manager.

The purchasing manager cannot be expected to be in close touch with all the manufacturing processes in which the materials he is buying may be used. Some technical knowledge of all such materials is desirable, otherwise time will be continually wasted in referring to the departments using them. But, if the purchasing manager has been tactful in past dealings with heads of departments, he will be able to get a great deal of useful information and assistance only obtainable from a man specialising in the practical application of whatever the purchasing manager is buying.

Some firms arrange for periodic conferences between the purchasing manager and the heads of all departments for which he buys. At such meetings many of the minor irritations and misunderstandings certain to arise in the daily life of a big firm can be smoothed over, and it is useful for the departmental heads to hear of each other's troubles, even though they are not personally interested in the subject under discussion. These conferences provide the purchasing manager with an excellent opportunity to enlist the aid of all departments in saving the firm, as a whole, unnecessary expense. He can, for example, stress the importance of all requisitions bearing the latest date up to which the department can work without requiring the materials requisitioned. This may enable another requisition for the same material to be filled at the same purchase, thus obtaining better prices and transport rates for a bulk purchase than would have been possible if each requisition had been filled separately.

Initiative is a most important possession if a man is to be a successful buyer. It is not always possible for him to obtain the sanction of the board of management when an opportunity for making an advantageous purchase presents itself. Foresight may have told the buyer that this is the moment to buy; practical knowledge of the materials may tell him that the quality is exceptional, and his balanced judgment may assure him that he is not buying on the spur of the moment; but, if he has not got the initiative to conclude the bargain without first "mentioning it to Mr. So-and-So," then the advantage is easily lost.

### SUBTLE METHODS OF BRIBING THE BUYER

ONE of the most difficult tasks that confront a board of management when choosing a purchasing manager is the assessment of his moral integrity. No man on the staff is more open to the temptation of accepting bribes than he is. A considerable amount of bribery in the form of monetary gifts in return for favourable consideration of the firm's quotations does go on, but the more usual method is more subtle. Many salesmen spend a lot of time in establishing personal contact with the buyer whose orders they want. The latter may be quite proof against a bribe of money, but he may not see that the dinners and drinks to which the salesman treats him, or the tips for the "course" or the Stock Exchange which he gives him in the strictest confidence, are only veiled bribes designed to obtain precedence for the salesman's goods over those of his competitors which they might not gain on merit alone.

Most firms send gifts at Christmas time to their customers as an expression of gratitude for past favours, and to keep their names before their customers when future orders are being placed. But when such gifts take the form of poultry, cases of wine or spirits, and boxes of cigars sent to the private address of the firm's purchasing manager, he should be able to see that, unless he refuses them, it will be difficult for him to forget the taste of the port and the fragrance of the cigars when next he considers the firm's quotations. It must not be thought that all supplying firms use these methods to obtain business. A large number do not, but even so the salesmen sometimes try to ingratiate themselves with buyers at their own expense, because the expected order means commission to them or a higher place in their employer's sales quota competition.

### "TRICKS OF THE TRADE" THE BUYER SHOULD LEARN

THERE has for long existed an idea that certain men have a "flair" for buying which enables them to know instinctively when and where to buy. Analysis of this belief shows that such men depend on nothing more than lucky guessing, and the money involved in industrial purchases to-day is too great to be hazarded by either "luck" or "guessing." It is not denied that after years of buying in a certain market some men do develop a sort of intuition about the future price movements of the commodities in which they deal. But this only comes of long experience and of hard work, and is very different from what most people mean when they talk of a "flair" for buying.

To be a successful buyer a man must not only possess a high character: he must also learn the prime and subsidiary sources of supply of all the main materials he is going to purchase. He must know what is the special feature of each source of supply—for instance, that wool from some parts of the world is much dirtier than wool from other parts; that Belgian steel is cheaper than English, but for some purposes inferior; and so on. It is essential that he should be abreast of developments in each source of supply: which one is expanding and which diminishing, what substitutes are available, and what impurities are present in various grades. For example, in the manufacture of certain perfumes the essential oil must be free from all traces of chlorine. The buyer must appreciate the importance of this, and must make sure that the grade he is buying is marked with the letters which indicate that there is no chlorine present.

Not only must the industrial buyer know the sources and peculiarities of his materials, but he must know the organisation and customs of the market in which they are bought. He must know the average yearly consumption of the industry as a whole, and how far this is seasonal. He must be able to relate this to the present state of the industry in which he is interested. If he foresees an increase in trade, it may pay him to build up his stocks. At the same time, he must study the policy, present condition, and past history of his own firm. The buyer should know what his firm consumes in raw materials in a good year, in a normal, and in a bad year. But such knowledge is useless if he neglects to find out that it is proposed, for example, to discontinue a process. He may not get official notification of this change until it is too late for him to cancel contracts for supplies made in advance to obtain favourable terms. But if he keeps constantly in touch with the policy of the firm and learns all he can from the various departmental heads, then he will often be prepared for a change which will decrease or increase his firm's consumption of certain raw materials.

Finally, the buyer must know how the materials he buys are graded and tested. He may not be a skilled chemist or engineer, but he must know what simple tests are available to him when he is examining a batch of goods. He must also know the object and the normal results of the more complicated tests which can be applied to the materials he buys in his firm's laboratories. If he is buying lubricating oil, although he may never have tested for viscosity and flash-point himself, he should know how such tests are made and what results should be obtained. A supplier may take the buyer to his own test-room, and a knowledge of standard tests may save the buyer from making expensive mistakes.

### THE BUYER MUST KNOW HIS MAN

ALTHOUGH prices are cut very fine to-day in almost all markets, and the real "bargain" is seldom come by, there still remains a good deal of importance in good bargaining. This depends very largely on a knowledge of psychology. Every salesman shown into a buyer's office has two or more prices in his mind for almost all materials for which he may be asked to quote. The upper one he will mention first, and will get it if he can, if competition is not very keen. Some firms ask all salesmen visiting them to quote bed-rock prices, as they are not permitted to revise their quotations, but if the salesman thinks there is any chance of getting the order at once, he will get the highest price he can, which may not by any means be the lowest his firm would be prepared to accept. The buyer must be able to size up his man and differentiate between the percentage of "sales talk," which is part of every salesman's conversation, and the facts which are reliable and worth remembering.

Salesmen differ enormously in their methods of attack. There is the brisk, breezy, hail-fellow-well-met type who talks incessantly and half of whose conversation is extraneous to the matter in hand. There is the overbearing, domineering person who as likely as not walks straight into the office, disregarding "Private" notices, and attempts to bully the buyer by almost threatening him with the consequences of refusing the goods he offers. There is the suave type, scrupulously polite, who imparts inside information about his own business, his competitors, even the buyer's own firm, with a confidential air sometimes almost patronising. Lastly, there is the painstaking salesman who knows his product thoroughly, and who confines his attention while he is with the buyer to pointing out in what way his goods are suited to the buyer's purpose.

It may be thought that dealing with the last type of salesman exclusively would solve many of the buyer's problems, but it must be remembered that the other kinds of salesmen may serve excellent firms. They may have the power to make valuable concessions if handled well, and it is a most important part of a buyer's equipment that he should be able to sum up the particular salesman as a man and, if he thinks his goods are worth having, not let him go until he has obtained them at the best possible terms the salesman is authorised to offer.

## WHAT THE BUYER IS ASKED TO DO

A PURCHASING manager will normally be asked to buy four main classes of goods. First, raw materials, that is, those entering into manufacture either directly or indirectly. In a steel works the term would include both steel of various grades, and fuel, hardening compounds, etc. Secondly, there is plant and machinery, buildings, furniture, etc. These may be classed as capital expenditure, and the purchasing manager has a more restricted authority in this than in the preceding class of purchase. The board of management decides what capital expenditure shall be made; and although the purchasing office's statistical section and organisation for ordering and the purchasing manager's knowledge of markets will be of great value, the latter will find himself very dependent on the engineer and architect.

The third class consists of supplies for the office. These may run into considerable sums in a year, and should be given as careful attention as any other type of purchasing. Quite apart from the accounting department, the selling and distributive offices, and the secretarial section, there are offices, large or small, attached to every production unit in the factory, and unless all these are well equipped the efficiency of the factory is impaired. Finally, he will buy goods for resale. This mainly concerns the retail buyer, but it must be remembered that a number of manufacturing firms buy certain lines in which they do not specialise, so as to make their range complete. Another type of buyer deals in ready-made goods, usually branded lines selling at a fixed price to the wholesale trade, but his problems differ from those of an industrial purchasing manager, because he normally buys from a few selected firms only, very often foreign in origin.

### CAREFUL RECORDS MEAN QUICK DECISIONS

THE purchasing manager can only be of real service to the firm if he is given adequate staff and facilities, so that he can organise his own department with a view to efficient buying. Some buyers depend too much on their memory, or on scraps of notes, for vital information as to prices, grades, dates, terms, and so on. Even in the smallest purchasing office there should be provision for the recording of all quotations and tenders received, whether they were accepted or not. A salesman may offer a commodity which is not required at the moment, but it will often be found worth while to record his price, the terms and date of the offer, against possible future purchases. An index should be maintained showing who is the firm's regular supplier for each material required, with alternative suppliers, particularly if the latter could, in a case of emergency, make deliveries more speedily than the normal suppliers.

In addition, in all but the smallest offices, graphs should be made of the market prices of all the main materials bought, records should be kept of the factory consumption throughout the year, and files maintained of standard specifications and bench-test and inspection reports of all main materials. Any information obtained about customers' opinions of finished goods made from special purchases should be filed under the name of the material concerned.

Indexing is of the greatest importance in the maintenance of purchasing statistics, and time spent on cross-referencing, or on obtaining another copy of a document for filing under another section, is repaid by th greater ease with which the purchasing manager can be supplied with the information he wants. Decisions must be reached quickly in the purchasing office, and it is of great assistance to be able to lay hands on all the information needed at once.

The purchasing manager is responsible for the supplies and material used in his firm from the moment the requisition leaves the planning department, which decides how things shall be made, or the storekeeper, until the right materials are delivered to the stores. If there is a separate traffic department, then he is relieved of that part of his liability which exists while the goods are in transit. In a medium-sized firm he will have a clerk under his control who will deal with all traffic arrangements. In addition, there will be an assistant to examine and classify requisitions, to send out requests for prices where the requisitions are large enough, to check orders with requisitions, and advise the storekeeper, the accounting department, and the department requisitioning that the order has been placed. Deliveries must be obtained promptly, and suppliers must be reminded of their engagements. At the same time, the buyer's firm must not delay delivery by failing to send particulars of standard specifications, or to pay suppliers' accounts within the period recognised in the trade.

Even when delivery has been made, the purchasing office must see that the goods are checked on receipt with a copy of the order already sent to the storekeeper, and that they are correct and in good condition. Finally, the supplier's invoice must be checked promptly and sent to the accounting section. The purchasing manager must supervise this work, which, in a large firm, will, of course, be divided between a number of clerks. In addition, he must do the actual buying himself, which may involve attending a central market on certain days in the week, and he must interview all salesmen who can offer goods he might buy.

### BUYING THAT NEEDS A COOL HEAD: THE ORGANISED MARKET

CERTAIN commodities are dealt with in organised markets in some central place in a large city. London has its Baltic Exchange, where a variety of articles ranging from ships to old lead are bought and sold, its Mincing Lane for tea, and a number of other Exchanges for other commodities, while Liverpool has a very famous Cotton Exchange. It is chiefly in articles fairly easy to grade and sample that organised markets are found. To operate successfully on one of these markets requires a cool head, a good memory, and quickness of decision. On most of them will be found speculators, many of them performing a useful function in smoothing out the sudden fluctuations in prices which might otherwise occur, but some of them trying to "rig the market" by spreading rumours of failure in certain sources of supply. They have previously bought heavily, and hope to be able to sell at higher prices when the rumour of a coming shortage stimulates buying. At such times the atmosphere of a commodity exchange is electric, and a buyer may easily commit himself far more heavily than he would dream of doing if he had been sitting in his own office.

The "convention" or price ring has laid down prices for certain commodities below which its members, who are all the chief dealers in the commodities concerned, agree not to sell. This has deprived some of the commodity exchanges of a good deal of the volume of business formerly transacted, inasmuch as it is simpler to 'phone or write an order when bargaining as to price is not necessary. Buyers, nevertheless, do make an appearance at such markets, even if they do not expect to do business, for the market is an excellent clearing house for information, and contact between buyer and supplier can be made there more easily than elsewhere.

### HOW TO GET THE BEST TERMS

THE ultimate test of the worth of any buyer is whether or not he consistently gets the best terms for his firm. His success in this direction depends quite a lot on good organisation within his own department. In addition, he himself must have established the right relationship between other departments and his own. He can then depend on them to let him have only one requisition, where, without forethought, they might have had to send him two, and he knows that where possible they will wait for material so that he can combine several requisitions and obtain better terms for bulk deliveries.

The purchasing manager must know his market thoroughly and know exactly what he wants and how much to buy. If he knows this well in advance, he can choose the best times to lay in stocks. Coal is cheaper in the summer than it is in the winter, and even manufactured and semi-manufactured goods are sold in slack seasons at a price which is very advantageous to the buyer. The price is low because it is designed to cover only the cost of labour and materials and the whole, or even only a part, of the overhead expense the manufacturer is bound to incur, whether or not his factory is in production. The well-informed buyer can take advantage of these times.

When the importance of organisation and knowledge has been taken into account, however, there still remains something else necessary to explain the successful buyer's superiority over his less efficient colleague. His secret is good bargaining, and its principles are difficult to lay down. Something has already been said about the importance of being able to sum up the salesman and to winnow the wheat from the chaff of his presentation of his goods. But, first, the buyer can save himself a lot of time and energy, after he has had a little experience, by deciding whether to interview a salesman or to pass him over to an assistant. From some salesmen it is impossible to obtain any information of value other than the price of their goods, which could more easily be obtained straight from their firm.

### HANDLING THE SALESMAN AT THE INTERVIEW

WHEN the buyer has decided to see a salesman he should interview him, not in his own room, for there may be information lying about, or graphs on the wall, meant only for the buyer, but in a room set aside for the purpose. Such a room should be out of sight and earshot of any other salesmen who may be awaiting interview. It should be so fitted up with telephones, bells, etc., that the salesman need not be left alone during the interview while the buyer is called away, because, if he is given time to think over the bargaining that has taken place, he may determine to stand out for better terms.

The buyer should discourage talk on subjects other than business, but a garrulous salesman may be led to divulge useful information about his own or competitors' firms. Treatment suitable to one salesman will not extract the best from another. The buyer must try to find the weak spots, either in the salesman's goods, r in the salesman himself. If he suspects that the salesman does not know much about his product he should ask him a few searching questions. The answers may be glib, but if the salesman is conscious of the element of bluff in them, then he will be less inclined to stick to his highest price. If the buyer is convinced that the salesman can make a better price or give better delivery or payment terms, then he must not rest until he has got them.

He may stress the points at which the salesman's goods are unsuitable for the job in hand and compare them unfavourably with a competitor's goods. He may tell the salesman that his competitor's price is lower and his terms better, and although it is usually better not to reveal actual quotations, the favourable points of competitors' terms may be revealed. Finally, the buyer may try the effect of telling the salesman that he is wasting his time discussing the purchase on those terms and ushering him out, assuring him that no future business will be placed with him until his prices are revised. This often has the effect of producing the salesman's best offer, especially if the order is of a fair size, and is another argument for dealing with a few firms and giving them each reasonably good orders.

### THE RIVAL QUOTATION AS AN INSTRUMENT OF BARGAINING

ALTHOUGH opinions differ, it is thought, generally speaking, to be a mistake to divulge the actual amount of competitors' quotations to a salesman. First, it may be that his lowest price is considerably lower than the other quotation, in which case he can underquote and still not deal at his best terms. Secondly, there is a sound reason for the business custom of treating suppliers' quotations as confidential. It saves much time if suppliers can be persuaded to quote their lowest prices at once. But if they know that the buyer will use their price as a bargaining weapon against a competitor, and, when the competitor quotes a lower price, that they in turn will be asked to go still lower, then they will naturally leave a margin when fixing their first quotation.

There are, however, exceptions to every rule, and there may come times when a price is so completely at variance with other quotations that the buyer may tell the salesman what his competitor is quoting, in order to save time in bargaining. Normally, however, a buyer does best by giving a share of his business to each of a few firms, and treating them fairly. It must not be forgotten that, if a buyer is known to play one firm's quotation off against another in order to extract the last farthing, his firm is not likely to receive very favourable treatment when it is needing supplies urgently, or is short of cash and cannot settle promptly.

### A DAY IN A BUYER'S LIFE

THE buyer's job in a large firm is no sinecure. His mail is likely to be large and varied. Advertising matter will predominate and will probably contain some samples. Some purchasing managers read advertising matter, others throw it away unopened. While some is useless, a good deal is of real value and can be usefully filed for reference. There may be a contract to be read through, and, unless it is in standard form, passed to the firm's solicitors. Replies to correspondence needing the buyer's personal attention will be dictated, and his assistants instructed as to which requisitions received and classified the preceding afternoon are worth the trouble of special inquiries for prices.

The purchasing manager may then attend the periodic meeting between departmental managers, at which he will probably have to explain to an irate works manager that the delay in ordering the core-sand he had requisitioned was not intended as a personal affront, but was merely to obtain a better price. At the same time he will learn that one of his most trusted suppliers has been sending in unsatisfactory lathe-tool steel, and he will make a mental note to visit the shop where it is being processed in order to see if the steel or the methods used are at fault.

In the afternoon he will interview salesmen and read one or two trade publications, marking those articles and advertisements he wants his statistical section to file. He may pay a visit to a neighbouring supplier, personal contact with such firms being a great advantage to a buyer. Back at his own office he signs his letters and reminds his assistant to advise the traffic department of a big consignment of steel tubing which must be loaded up and dispatched for the North on the following day. So ends a day in the life of a man who is responsible for the expenditure of over a million pounds each year, and who could by neglect involve his firm in larger losses than any other man in the business.

## BUYING FOR THE BIG STORE

*by PAUL MAY, B.A.(Oxon)*

BUYERS of all kinds form links in the chain stretching from the raw material supplied by Nature to the finished product demanded by the public. Take, for example, a winter overcoat: to produce the wool the farmer must buy sheep to rear, food to feed them on, and labour to tend and shear them; the wool merchant must buy the shorn wool and transport it to the manufacturing centre; the cloth manufacturer must buy power, labour, and technical skill; the coat manufacturer must buy cloth, labour, houseroom, etc., and finally the retail buyer buys the finished coat and displays it in his shop to the general public.

The chain of buying naturally starts from the raw material and leads up to the retail store. As you advance along the chain, however, the bulk quantity of each item dealt in becomes smaller and the number of items increases. The farmer, for example, deals in raw wool only in bulk, the coat manufacturer deals in many different styles of coat, differently trimmed and made of different cloth, and the retail store deals in the produce of many different coat manufacturers.

While the principles of buying remain constant throughout, the work at the end of the chain is, at any rate apparently, more complex. The following section therefore gives a detailed account of the organisation and method of retail buying.

### SOME POINTS FOR THE RETAIL BUYER TO WATCH

THE buyer in a large retail shop has probably assisted the merchandise manager in preparing the estimates for the coming period, so that he knows at the start how much stock he needs to buy. When it comes to acting within the limits thus laid down, he must understand thoroughly the general policy of the shop and study this in relation to the particular goods which he is to buy. He must see clearly the type of customer for whom he is catering, and consequently the main price level of the goods which he must stock. There is a very definite distinction here between high, medium, and low-class trade. The shop which desires to trade in high-class millinery will place originality of style and fashion distinction above consideration of price, whereas popular-price stores aim chiefly, provided always they give good value, at achieving the right selling price. As the majority of shops cater for the various classes of customer to whom an extra shilling or two on the selling price is an important matter, we shall deal mainly with that side of buying.

Once the main selling price is decided, the subsidiary prices follow naturally, and the buyer must turn his attention to the problem of what he is to buy to sell at those prices. Unless the department is a very small one it will fall fairly naturally into certain divisions; for example, gloves may be leather, cotton, kid, etc. Within these subdivisions the buyer has to decide on the assortment of the goods, that is to say, how the various items that are going to compose the stock of the subdivision should be distributed over the different styles, colours, sizes, and so on. The tastes of the shopping public even within a fairly definite class are extremely varied, and the more fully a buyer can satisfy the multitudinous demands of his customers, the more fully they will have confidence in him and increase his turnover.

The buyer has to build up his assortment to some extent on the basis of past experience, and all figures which it is possible to obtain regarding the previous year's trading are valuable to him. Sometimes these figures do not amount to very much—for instance, only the weekly or monthly sales in sterling, the weekly or monthly stocks, the amount of money used in reducing goods, the average percentage difference between the cost prices and selling prices, the wastage figures and the resultant profit. Sometimes there is a lot more, such as item sales at various prices over a certain period, and item stocks at various prices at the end of certain periods, *e.g.*—the number of gloves sold at 6s. 11d., 8s. 11d., etc., during each month, and corresponding stock figures. Again the buyer may have information as to the item sales of the various sections, *e.g.*—deal tables and oak tables or of the various colours, such as red and green umbrellas.

All such information is extremely useful to the buyer in planning the buying for the coming season and in allocating the buying power which is at his disposal. He must also keep his attention on trade tendencies, fashion or otherwise, and read the past statistics in the light of these tendencies, rather than try to make future demand fit his statistics. He cannot rely solely on the past; to some extent he must predict future business.

### WHIMS OF FASHION THE BUYER MUST FORESEE

PREDICTIONS of the future course of trade vary in difficulty with the type of goods handled. If the goods are what are called "bread and butter" lines, the interest of the buyer will be concerned mainly with trying to foresee changes in the buying power of his particular type of customer. He must also consider probable fluctuations in the values of the raw materials and work, which together form the articles in which he deals. To do this he has to watch the raw material market, fluctuations in wages, and variations in the costs of transport, customs duty, etc., so that any large change is not a surprise. He must also, like the buyer of fashion articles, make certain that nothing new escapes his notice.

The buyer of goods which are affected in varying degrees by the changes of fashion has to watch prices and values in the same way, but he also has to go a great deal further; he must discern, if possible, in what direction fashion is likely to develop, or at least he must observe the actual development of fashion as soon as it first begins to appear. There are three main ways of doing this. The first is always to look at everything which a manufacturer has to offer, and to discuss with him probable trends and his reasons for sampling certain kinds of goods; the manufacturer has to be still further in advance of fashions than the retail buyer. Secondly, he should read any literature published regarding his particular goods, which has previously proved to be shrewd at discovering probable fashion developments; sometimes this can be supplemented by the advice of a representative at the fashion centre of the articles concerned. Finally, he must watch the trend of actual sales.

### DECIDING WHEN TO BUY

THE problem of when to buy is in theory simple; the answer is clearly "at such a time that the goods ordered will be delivered for display to the public when the public requires them, neither too early nor too late, and in such quantities as will meet the demand, so that good sales result and the stock turns over quickly." This should always be the buyer's basic object, but, besides the fact that the public does not buy by clockwork and is seriously affected by uncontrollable events such as the weather, there are nearly always complicating considerations to be taken into account. The following example will give some idea of them. A buyer who deals largely with a foreign country may feel certain that there is going to be a serious fluctuation in the monetary exchange, and this may lead him to buy before it is necessary, or to buy smaller quantities than he would otherwise have done. Similar factors might be an expected rise or fall in raw material, labour, or transport costs, anticipation of restrictive quotas or new duties, previous failure of manufacturers to keep to delivery promises, and so on. Again, a buyer may wish a certain line to be reserved to himself, and he may only be able to achieve this by buying early.

A buyer is, of course, influenced by the type of trade he is doing, and it may be more important to him to be able to show the latest novelty or fashion immediately it is produced than to start good sales of his new goods at once. Some goods are a safe buy, and so may be bought well in advance, and heavy contracts may be placed; other goods are dangerous, so that it is often better policy to risk losing a little of the early trade than to buy too soon. Every transaction really has its own special circumstances, each of which must be taken into account in deciding when to buy.

## THE BUYER PUTS HIS PLANS INTO ACTION

In doing his actual buying, the buyer must not only keep clearly in mind the details of all the planning and forecasting he has previously done, but he must always be prepared to readjust those plans and forecasts in the light of fresh developments that occur during the buying. In order to plan the actual course of his buying wisely, it is necessary for him to have a full knowledge of the markets available and the relative values of each market, and he must keep abreast of changes in these values. He may, therefore, have to visit each market at intervals and he must be sure to examine everything which that market has to offer.

To do his job properly, a buyer must understand the people with whom he is dealing. It is an accepted fact that to sell things effectively the seller must have a good understanding of what is in his customer's mind, what he wants, and why he wants it, and must look at his goods from the customer's point of view: in other words, he must understand the psychological attitude of the customer to this particular transaction, because his aim is to make some sort of profit out of the customer. Similarly the retail buyer must understand the point of view of his supplier, because he is always wanting to make some sort of profit out of him, whether it be a money or a service profit.

He must understand the individual with whom he is dealing, and he must appreciate what the supplier's main objects in each particular transaction are, and must be quick to perceive the right way in the circumstances of achieving what he himself wishes. He must understand the psychology of the situation and turn it to the best account he can. It is true of buying as of most things in life, that a more skilful handling of the same set of circumstances will produce a better result.

## COMBINING COURTESY AND FIRMNESS IN BUYING

It is a great mistake for a buyer to imagine that he is ever in a sufficiently strong position to deal unreasonably with his suppliers. He should always treat them with courtesy and keep on good terms with them; apart from everything else this will ensure him early information about tendencies of trade and good service. But this is not to say that he should not derive the most advantageous bargain possible

om his firm's point of view and keep his suppliers up to
ıe mark. What that mark is will depend on the nature of
ıe business. One type of buyer will be most concerned
ith style, effect, quality, or fashion significance, another
ith price, another with speed of delivery or general
rvice.

Whatever he wants, the buyer must firmly see that he
ts it to the extent to which he is entitled to it: this extent
epends in some degree on himself and his own personality,
ut in the main on his importance, not as a person but as
ıat particular buyer, in the eyes of the seller and the eager-
ess of the seller to do this particular transaction and to do
with the particular buyer. The buyer must be clever at
cognising the strength of the various factors in the situation,
ne of which will always be the terms on which similar goods
e offered by competitors and he must make his offer ac-
ordingly. A great deal depends on the trust and confidence
hich buyer and seller feel in each other, and the methods
y which the buyer seeks to achieve the terms required must
ary accordingly.

#### KEEPING THE SUPPLIER UP TO THE MARK

A BUYER must also, when he has bought, keep a keen watch
on the service given by suppliers and see that the standard
f quality and the punctuality of deliveries is good. He
ıust not risk his own trade by acquiescing in slackness in
ther direction. If goods are not up to standard, it means
ıat either the stock will be bad in quality or, if the goods are
turned to the supplier, in quantity, and lateness of delivery
ıay throw the stock out of proportion for a considerable
me. A buyer must also be very careful that he is getting
hat he wants, and must not get into the habit of taking
ıe first apparently suitable thing that is offered to him. He
ıust be full of energy and must see that he gets the best thing
ıat can be produced of the type he wants. It is very easy
lower the standard of his stock by lack of such energy or
throw it out of proportion by failing to realise exactly what
e is buying.

The technique of actual buying depends entirely on what
being bought. The buyer may place different emphasis
n the various qualities of the article concerned. For
ıstance, he may be interested in price almost exclusively
hen purchasing manufacturers' old stock or "job lots,"

and he may have almost no interest in price when purchasin
proprietary articles, that is, articles the retail selling price
which is fixed by the manufacturer. The fundament
point is for him to make up his mind exactly what it is
requires, whether this be some of the latest novelties in dre
materials or a pair of leather gloves to sell at 4s. 11d., and
make sure that he buys what is in his judgment the be
available thing of that kind.

### THE BUYER WATCHES THE RESULTS OF HIS PURCHASE

HAVING made his plans and forecasts and having put the
into effect in his buying, with any adjustments foun
necessary, the buyer must watch the result closely and ensu
that in his subsequent buying his plans are properly adjuste
to current events. Methods of doing this are very varie
in detail, but the main principles are much the same. Th
buyer must receive daily or at least weekly sales figure
The plan of his purchasing power already made has bee
based on the estimated sales, and if the actual figures a
differing from the estimate, the purchasing plan must natu
ally be amended. These sales figures give the buyer a gener
idea of how his buying is succeeding.

He must, however, endeavour to get much more detaile
information. He is concerned with discovering how far h
method of dividing his purchasing power over the differe
kinds of items that compose his stock is being successful.
some parts of his stock are selling at a very different spe
from others, it is obvious that some sort of proportion mu
be observed in the size of the stocks of those articles.
cannot be a strictly mathematical proportion in many case
but experience will teach a buyer what is the minimu
quantity of stock that will satisfy a demand which is sma
but worth catering for. If there is a heavy stock of son
particular article which is not at the moment selling we
unless his total stock is out of proportion to his sales, son
other part of his stock will be dangerously low in relati
either to the sales that he is actually doing or to the possib
sales.

There are three ways in which a buyer can watch how h
stock is comparing with his sales. First, it may be possib
for him to spend a part of his time in the department and s
either through selling himself or watching the staff sellin
get an idea of what the relation between the demands for t

various goods is. Then he can inspect the stock in the department, compare that with his impression of the proportion of the sales, and finally study the goods on order. Secondly, if he is able to spend only a small portion of his time in the department, he may go through the same process by questioning the members of the selling staff and the head of the department. Thirdly, if the nature of the goods stocked in the department lends itself to such a procedure, he may have fairly detailed lists of sales made out showing how the item sales of particular lines or particular prices are developing, and he may have a stock taken of the goods in the department under the same headings.

If he obtains figures in this way and compares them with what he has on order, making adjustments to meet changes in demand which he is led to anticipate, he will have a fairly clear picture of what is happening in the department. Besides these methods, it can be a great help to the buyer if each salesman, when he is asked for a certain thing by the customer and finds that he is unable to satisfy her demand, makes a written note of this and forwards it to the buyer. This method is most valuable sometimes for giving an indication of future large demand, but such records must be studied in relation to other sources of information.

Another point which the buyer must consider is the rate at which his whole stock is selling, that is to say, the proportion between his average stock and total sales over a given period. This is called the rate of stock turnover, and is considered more important in some shops than in others. If fairly complete estimates of stocks and sales have been made before the period starts, the buyer has merely to watch how his actual sales and actual stock compare with the estimate ; but in cases where the buyer has a free hand it is important for him to watch this relation between sales and stock.

### WHEN THE BARGAIN SALE BECOMES NECESSARY

THE question of making reductions in the selling prices of goods in order to effect a clearance is one in which the practice of shops is extremely varied, and the answer depends on the main trading policy of the shop, that is, the rates of profit, type of customer catered for, and so on. There are certain things, however, that it is important for all buyers to bear in mind. First, every buyer at times buys the wrong thing, that is, something which the public does not wish to buy, at any rate at the price at which it is offered for sale. The quicker the buyer recognises which items these are the better, whether he intends to make a reduction in the selling price at once or not: it helps him to keep the state of his stock clearly in mind. The selling staff can give him very good information on this point. Secondly, whatever the policy of the firm, there is a definite point at which the proportion of old stock (that is, stock which for one reason or another has not been sold within the period of time that seems reasonable) to new stock becomes dangerous, and a buyer must always be closely watching to see that this point is not reached.

On the other hand it sometimes appears waste of money to reduce the prices of goods which still have quite a good chance of selling at the existing price and are not dangerously affecting the total stock by the slowness of their movement. The best general rule, however, would seem to be that a reasonable reduction made early saves a larger reduction later. The average size of the reduction made depends chiefly on the policy of the shop, and on whether the total stock of the department has to fall sharply from its highest figure to a very low closing stock. But it remains true that the reduction made must as far as possible be neither so small as to be ineffective, nor so large as to result in an actual waste of the shop's profits.

The details of a buyer's practice in fixing prices depend on the shop's policy, and while some buyers might be very largely influenced in their buying by considerations of selling price, others might be very little concerned with this. The former will have a fairly close idea of the price at which they propose to sell the article, the latter will have a rough general idea. In both cases, however, the actual pricing must be finally determined by the quality of the goods when they are actually received, and the ultimate factors must be the amount which the particular public for whom the goods have been bought will pay for that particular type of thing, and the percentage profit which such a department ought in its particular circumstances to be able to make. In most shops the percentage added to the cost price will vary in the case of individual purchases, but in some shops an attempt is definitely made to keep the percentage in all cases practically the same. This latter practice, however, does not seem to make sufficient allowance for the human factor either in the buyer or in the manufacturing process or in the public.

### CHOOSING A PROFITABLE SYSTEM OF PAYMENT

In all kinds of buying and selling, making and receiving payment is a very important problem. A manufacturer has to pay for his raw materials, or at least pay out wages and other overhead expenses, while he is producing the goods ordered by the buyer and so it is important to him to receive payment for the goods as soon as he has delivered them. The buyer on the other hand does not generally sell all the goods at once ; he may have to hold some of them for a year or more, according to the nature of his business, and so it would suit him best to pay the manufacturer some time after delivery.

If, however, he delays payment, the manufacturer, in order to go on meeting his current expenses, has to borrow the money, either from an outside source, in which case he pays definite interest, or from himself, in the sense that he diverts to the use to which the money owed to him would have been put, other moneys which would otherwise have earned a profit in another use. Again, if the buyer pays at once, he may prevent himself from buying some other goods which he could sell quickly at a profit before making the payment in question.

The solution of these difficulties is that in calculating his cost price the manufacturer reckons that he will not be paid for a certain period, say, for example, three months, and includes the interest costs on his cost price. He then offers to buyers a small percentage rebate for early payment, the percentage varying with the amount of time that elapses between delivery of the goods and payment for them.

The buyer must see that he obtains as favourable terms as possible, but he must realise that if he requires too high a percentage he is probably, in effect, merely artificially raising the cost price from which the discount is deducted. Some manufacturers, on the other hand, quote their terms without promise of discount and charge interest if the amount is not paid within a certain time. The principle is the same. It is, therefore, open to the buyer to choose whether it will pay him best to use his money to get a discount on his purchase or to use it in some other way to get profit and sacrifice his discount.

## BUYING FOR A ONE-MAN SHOP

So far we have been dealing with retail buying from the point of view of the medium-sized store consisting of several different departments and big enough to carry a number of executive positions, rather than with the really big department store or the small shop. In both these cases the principles which have been outlined will mostly hold good with a process of multiplication in the former case and of simplification in the latter. There are, however, some problems peculiar to buying for a small shop which have to be considered.

The sales of a really small shop are not sufficient to support any non-productive executive posts, that is to say, any executives not engaged in either buying or selling. This means, in practice, that the proprietor or manager has to perform all the functions of management, merchandise management, staff control, and buying, which in a larger store are spread over a number of people. In other words he must be a jack of many trades and not a specialist, and in the modern world it is in many ways a great deal easier to be a specialist. It also means that he cannot be a buyer for two hours and then a manager for two hours more: he must be constantly interchanging his activities.

### THE PROBLEM OF GAUGING A SMALL SHOP'S REQUIREMENTS

The fact that the staff is small because expenses have to be low means that he cannot hope for statistics to help him in his buying other than bare particulars in money of his stock and sales; and even these may be single figures covering the whole shop. The result is that he has to plan his buying by looking at his fixtures and by his knowledge of what is selling. To balance this, however, his other activities mean that he must be in the shop a great deal and is thus able to see what is selling and to know roughly the amount of his sales.

Different considerations also arise with regard to stock. Let us suppose that in a certain big store doing a similar trade the sales are X on an average stock of Y and that the sales of the one-man shop are $\frac{X}{1000}$; yet it does not follow that the proper stock will be $\frac{Y}{1000}$; it is far more likely to be $\frac{Y}{800}$ or more, because in order to show the customers a reasonable assortment of goods, a fairly big stock must be carried, even if each line is represented by a minimum quantity. This means that the stock will not turn over so quickly, that is to say, that the yearly turnover divided by the average stock will give a smaller answer than in the case of the larger store, and therefore it will be more difficult to clear the old goods and keep the stock clean and fresh for the customers. In some small shops the clientèle is small and fixed and rapidly gets tired of seeing the same goods displayed.

As a result of carrying a small stock of each line, the small shop is made more dependent on the supplier than the large shop. It is essential that fresh supplies should be quickly available in many cases, and this precludes dealing direct with a manufacturer. Very often it becomes the best policy to deal in goods advertised by the manufacturer, which generally means selling them at a fixed price and so at a fixed profit.

The small buyer is more dependent on his suppliers than the buyer of a larger store in a further sense; he cannot afford to spend money on travelling expenses and so he cannot visit manufacturing or fashion centres. He is therefore compelled to form his opinion of future tendencies of trade from what his suppliers tell him and from any trade papers he may be able to obtain.

### SET-BACKS THAT PLAY HAVOC WITH CALCULATIONS

ESTIMATING is also more difficult for a one-man shop. A small disappointment in sales is a large percentage decrease and may quickly upset the balance of the stock. Such a trade is also probably more greatly affected by external circumstances, such as the weather, than that of larger shops. A year's bad sales made from a stock fairly large in proportion to the trade means a great handicap in the purchase of new goods for the next year.

Further, finance is a more difficult matter. A one-man shop must not be over-capitalised any more than a large store if it is to make an adequate return on the money, and a fairly large stock may make it difficult always to have an adequate supply of ready money. If this is so, the shop cannot take advantage of the discount terms offered by suppliers, which means that the goods in effect cost more than they would have done otherwise. Costs in general will also probably be higher, and so to make a proper profit with adequate allowance for clearing bad stock it may be necessary to charge higher prices to the public.

### THE SMALL BUYER AT A DISADVANTAGE

THE buyer of a one-man shop, on the other hand, has certain advantages through the unification of activities in himself. He can take quick decisions concerning all sides of the shop's activity and can co-ordinate more fully the various divisions into which the work of the shop falls. He supervises the selling as well as the buying, and therefore has first-hand knowledge of his customers as well as of their wants, for he has to exert himself to keep their goodwill and he is responsible for dealing with all complaints received. On balance, however, although the principles of buying we have discussed largely hold good for him too, he seems to be at certain disadvantages compared with the buyer of the large store.

## BOOKS THAT WILL HELP THE BUYER

THERE are comparatively few books dealing exclusively with industrial purchasing, although there are a number describing purchasing for individual trades. *Successful Buying*, by Eric N. Simons, published by Sir Isaac Pitman & Sons Ltd., is a good introductory book and gives examples of various records actually in use in purchasing offices. *Purchasing*, by H. B. Twyford, published by D. Van Nostrand & Co., New York, is an American counterpart of *Successful Buying* in scope and arrangement. It has, in addition, chapters on special types of purchasing, for example, " purchasing for a manufacturing and construction company " and " purchasing for construction work and operation of properties in widely separated localities."

Three American text-books designed for the serious student are *Scientific Purchasing*, by Edward T. Gushée and L. F. Boffey, published by McGraw-Hill; *Purchasing*, by W. N. Mitchell, published by Ronald Press, New York; and *Principles of Scientific Purchasing*, by Norman F. Harriman, published by McGraw-Hill. They are all hard reading, and it must be remembered that American commercial organisation is peculiar to that country. Many business men think that the attempt to reduce business factors to scientific formulæ, which is the American ideal, has gone too far. The last of these three books contains appendices on the organisation of the purchasing sections of various well-known American businesses, such as Western Electric Co. and New York Central Lines, as well as of the United States Navy.

An interesting collection of problems encountered in actual businesses in America is contained in *Problems of Industrial Purchasing*, by Howard T. Lewis, published by McGraw-Hill. The book is divided into sections, each devoted to bringing out some special factor in purchasing organisation. The editor is the Professor of Marketing at the Graduate School of Business Administration in Harvard University, and he was able to collect information about individual firms which it would be quite impossible to obtain in England.

# WHAT THE MIDDLEMAN DOES

*by R. L. de CHAZAL, B.A.(Cantab.)*

OPINIONS as to the relative merits of different branches of trade have varied from generation to generation. The canonist philosophers believed with the early fathers that all trade was sinful; though later, the pressure of economic developments tended to make them adopt a more realistic attitude and condemn certain undesirable features of trade rather than trade as such. Later still, in the seventeenth and eighteenth centuries, the physiocrats, who were the first to study Economics in a systematic manner, regarded agriculture alone as productive and considered those engaged in the crafts, in commerce and in the professions as the "sterile" class.

Adam Smith and the other founders of classical Economics were still engaged in long discussions as to what occupations were "productive"; and they found it difficult to include the services rendered, for example, by a jockey or by an opera singer among the "productive" occupations. A prejudice in favour of those who actually produced, that is, made, goods, as against those who merely dealt in them, thus lingered on. Such prejudices die hard, and even to-day there is a great deal of popular misconception on the question of the necessity, importance, and merit of those who trade in goods—a misconception which generally takes the form of various accusations against the "middleman."

## HOW THE MIDDLEMAN CAME INTO BEING

THE middleman is defined in the dictionary as "one who makes a profit on anything on its way from the producer to the consumer." This definition approximates to the meaning attached to the word in everyday language. But besides making profits, what does the middleman do? As a matter of historical fact, the development of the middleman is part only of the general growth of specialisation in economic life, made necessary by the growing and more diversified demands of larger populations and the increased productivity of modern industry. The earliest market can be conceived of as an impersonal middleman. The farmer and craftsman sold their goods direct to the consumer, but in the recognised meeting place of buyers and sellers. Out of this developed the general merchant, the pedlar, and hawker, and finally the shopkeeper. Others specialised in the mediation of foreign trade ; such were the Merchant Adventurers, the Merchant Companies, and the general exporting and importing houses which usually controlled their own fleet of ships. Others, again, specialised in warehousing, insurance, banking, and finance.

To-day the term middleman covers many types of individuals. We have merchants trading in the innumerable town and country markets as well as in the large and highly organised central markets such as Covent Garden, Billingsgate, and Smithfield. We have merchants, brokers, and various other kinds of agents operating on the specialised produce markets such as the " Baltic," the " Pacific," the Liverpool Corn and Cotton Markets, etc. We have the numberless merchants to be found throughout the country who are concerned with the direct importation and exportation of goods without acting through the intermediary of organised markets. We have jobbers, wholesalers, factors, and, finally, retailers, all of whom may be "free-lance" individuals working on their own account, or highly capitalised and elaborate joint stock companies.

### A WIDER DEFINITION OF THE MIDDLEMAN

As will be seen later, there are no clear-cut lines of demarcation between so great a diversity of "specialists." The commercial practices and regulations affecting such a variety of middlemen differ considerably, and cannot be treated here. The functions of the retailer and the produce broker, as well as certain aspects of marketing, are dealt with in other sections. In this one, therefore, we are concerned with the three principal remaining classes of middlemen—namely, importers, exporters, and wholesalers. We shall consider in broad outline what their occupations involve, and shall see to what extent post-War economic and political developments have affected the middleman's business. The submission will be that the middleman is much more than just " one who makes a profit on anything on its way from producer to consumer."

### IMPORT AND EXPORT: THE LIFE-BLOOD OF TRADE

In spite of modern complications and the use of money, trade is fundamentally still the barter of old. As the French say, *Plus ça change, plus ça reste la même chose.* Just as an individual offers a fair return for what he receives, so a nation cannot in the long-run import more than it exports. It is, however, not necessary for imports of goods to balance export of goods. Exports, for instance, may take the form of services such as those of shipping or insurance or accommodation of holiday visitors, but for the present purpose it is necessary only to consider transfers of tangible goods and not of services.

Until recent times, the importer was mainly a merchant who specialised in bringing into the country goods which he could sell at a profit. He usually had his own ships like those of Antonio in *The Merchant of Venice*: "Argosies with portly sail, like signiors and rich burgers on the flood, or, as it were, the pageants of the sea." Such were also most of the great merchants of London, Amsterdam, and the Hanseatic Ports, who went abroad themselves and bargained for foreign goods and sold those which they had taken with them from their home port. Such merchantmen had to go armed and be prepared to fight. Foreign customs and languages presented real difficulties, so that trading abroad was restricted to those who specialised in it.

Nowadays, however, commercial methods in different countries approximate more to each other. English is understood by most traders throughout the world; the standard of commercial honesty in observing contracts and in giving value for money has improved considerably during the last two centuries; information about goods available abroad is more easily obtainable through trade catalogues, general and trade papers, so that now even a private individual can make inquiries of the foreign manufacturer and ask for samples and estimates. Transport facilities have improved immeasurably. It has, therefore, become possible for almost anybody to place orders on the smallest or greatest scale, and importing is accordingly practised very widely. Nevertheless, the bulk of imports into Britain is still dealt with by specialists in this type of business.

### HOW IMPORT ORDERS ARE OBTAINED

THE earliest instances of importing occurred when merchants or their representatives went abroad and selected the goods. This method has been developed by importers having representatives or agents permanently residing abroad, who are continually on the look-out for goods which might be of interest to the importer. The more up-to-date method, however, is for producers and manufacturers to take the initial step themselves rather than wait till they are approached. This is done by advertising abroad; and the manufacturers send their representatives to canvass orders from importers in foreign countries, or employ agents to do this for them. Exhibitions and fairs have also played a considerable part in increasing imports into foreign countries, as when a number of British exporters organised a large exhibition of their goods in Buenos Aires.

A better method for many goods is for producers to have their own branches abroad, which keep in close touch with the demand of consumers and have travellers to canvass the trade; the goods are thus "marketed" and demand "created." This method of importing is most usual in the case of raw materials and foodstuffs in bulk, or specialities under trade marks, such as motor cars, tinned or packed foodstuffs, special machinery, etc. In such cases the importer does not buy the goods outright on "firm account" or "against orders," as it is termed, but receives them "on consignment": that is, they remain the property of the foreign producer until they are sold by the importer at a fixed price or at the best possible price. The proceeds of the sale are then remitted to the producer after deduction of expenses and commission.

Goods against orders form the minority of imports into Britain, whereas in the export trade they predominate. This is mainly due to the fact that three-quarters of British imports are composed of raw materials and foodstuffs in bulk, which are dealt with by the highly organised produce markets in this country, such as the Liverpool Cotton and Corn Exchanges; the "Baltic," Mincing Lane, the Metal Exchange, and Mark Lane in London; the "Pacific" in Hull, etc. These organisations enjoy such a fine reputation abroad that foreign exporters consider it safe and convenient to send goods on consignment to this country, although the goods are to a large extent exported again.

When goods are due to be sent to an importer in this way, the second stage comes when they are dispatched by the exporter (or *consignor*), who sends an advice to the importer that certain goods have been sent to him on a certain ship. If the importer (or *consignee*) is near the port where the goods will arrive, he will probably himself undertake the necessary formalities in connection with the removal of the goods from the ship, that is, the clearance of the goods. If his place of business is some distance away, he will probably prefer to have the clearance done for him by the shipping company or by shipping agents, as it is a matter which requires considerable personal attention.

The principal document is the bill of lading. This gives the consignee, or his agent, the right to claim the goods and is therefore the document of title, besides being an official receipt from the shipping company for the goods shipped, and a contract whereby the shipping company undertakes to carry the goods to the port of destination. The other necessary document is the invoice for the goods, giving the exact description, quantity, price, and total value of the goods sent, as well as the numbers and marks on the packages if the goods are not sent in bulk.

In addition, the importer may also require a Certificate of Origin to satisfy the Customs, who are responsible for seeing that tariff and quota regulations are complied with. Further, as it is usual to insure in the export and import trade goods in transit; the consignee will generally also receive an insurance policy, so that a claim can be made if the goods have been damaged or destroyed *en route*. The bill of lading, being a receipt as well as a document of title, must be endorsed, that is, signed by the consignee or by his agent. It is then lodged with the shipping company, who in exchange will issue a "Freight Release" or "Ship's Delivery Order" after all necessary shipping charges have been paid.

### GETTING THE GOODS THROUGH THE CUSTOMS

THE third stage in importing relates to Customs regulations, which are mainly concerned with the levying of Customs duties and the collection of detailed statistics as to description, volume, and value of all goods entering or leaving the country. For imports, the consignee must first prepare a "Customs Entry" form, giving, among other details, the name of the ship and her captain, a full description of the goods, and the place whence the goods were consigned. These details are checked by the Customs authorities, known as "the Customs" for short, with the details of the Ship's Report, which must be prepared by the Master of the ship, and which contains the description of the goods that are due for discharge. Only when the Customs are satisfied that all is in order, and that none of the goods are prohibited from entry (owing, for instance, to their being infected or being obscene publications, or lottery tickets), may the goods be landed from the ship.

Having arranged for the landing of the goods, the consignee must next prepare two, or sometimes three, copies of the " Free Entry " form for goods which are not liable to Customs duties, and, if the goods are required for immediate home consumption and are dutiable, of the " Entry for Home Use *ex* Ship." These forms are checked by the Customs: a Certificate of Origin may be required to be produced by the consignee, and the appropriate duties must be paid. When satisfied, the Customs initial one copy of the Entry form, which is presented by the consignee to the dock authorities. After the goods have again been checked by the Customs with this form, and after the Freight Release or Ship's Delivery Order has been presented to the dock authorities, together with any dock dues payable to them, the goods are finally available for the importers.

What happens to the goods once they are cleared will, of course, depend on the reason for which the goods were sent into the country. If the importer is a manufacturer, they will be transported by rail, barge, or lorry to the manufacturer's works. Goods on consignment may be warehoused at the port of entry or inland until they are sold, when they will be delivered to the buyers. Perishable goods, such as fruit, vegetables, and meat, will usually be sent immediately to some of the big markets in this country, such as Covent Garden and Smithfield, or sold by auction at the port of entry. Bulk commodities, such as tea, coffee, wheat, spices, rubber, and many other goods, will usually be warehoused by the docks companies on behalf of the importer until they are sold on the produce markets. Certain imports against orders may be sent direct to wholesalers and retailers for resale in shops to the public.

## HOW THE EXPORTER MAKES SURE OF PAYMENT

THE last and final stage of importing concerns the payment for the goods. When exporters in one country are quite satisfied as to the financial integrity and solvency of importers in other countries, they may be prepared to part with their goods and wait until the importers send them the necessary money in settlement. But it is obvious that there is always an element of risk in this procedure. Inquiries through information bureaux such as a Chamber of Commerce may show that the risk is small, but as trading houses are often working on extremely small margins of profit, a loss on one shipment may offset the profit made on a hundred shipments. In general, the risk cannot be run, so that safer methods are employed.

These are provided mainly by "documents on payment" bills of exchange (known as D/P bills) and by "documents on acceptance" bills (or D/A bills). Briefly, these methods ensure that the importer does not receive the shipping documents until he has either made a payment in respect of the goods, or has given a written promise to pay, in such a form that it can be legally transferred and "discounted." This is done through banks. Instead of the exporter sending the shipping documents direct to the consignee, he will send them to a bank in the importer's country, together with a bill of exchange drawn on the consignee.

The consignee must then "meet" the bill if it is a D/P bill, that is, make to the bank a payment equivalent to the face value of the bill. In the case of a D/A bill the consignee must "accept," that is, endorse, the bill, thereby promising to "meet" it. Not until he has done one or other of those things will the bank hand over the shipping documents to him. The bank, on request, will usually also "discount" the bill by making an immediate cash payment to the consignor. This payment will be less than the face value, so as to offset the risk which the bank runs of the bill not being met, and to offset the time which the bank will have to wait before being reimbursed by the consignee.

There is one important type of import trade which looms very large in British commerce, and that is the *entrepôt* trade. By *entrepôt* trade is meant the importation of foreign goods merely with a view to their re-exportation, as when in the tea trade the bulk of the world's crop is sent to London to be sold and subsequently largely exported again. This may appear an unnecessary complication, but there are many reasons why London is the largest *entrepôt* in the world, and of the great extent of British *entrepôt* trade generally.

Several producing countries have not a large enough trade with certain smaller countries to enable complete cargoes of their goods to be sent there; many producing countries do not export on a sufficiently large scale to set up selling organisations and markets of their own ; British ships, being the principal carriers of the world, naturally tend to converge on Britain in order to collect export cargoes of manufactured goods required by producing countries ; again, the organisation of British produce markets is so unique in its high standard that foreign producers find it safe and convenient to send their goods to Britain to be sold there at the best possible price.

### PLACING THE UNTAXED GOODS IN BOND

IT is only right that duties paid when goods are imported should be refunded when the goods are re-exported, but the amounts of duties paid may be very large, in which case the trader would have this money locked up unprofitably. To overcome this difficulty, "bonded warehouses" were authorised in 1802. By virtue of this provision, certain warehousemen may accept goods for storage before duty on them has been paid, but the warehousemen give a "bond" that they will not allow the goods to be removed without the Custom's consent.

When the importer proposes to place the goods he imports in bond, he must prepare an "Entry for Warehousing" instead of the "Entry for Home Use *ex* Ship." When he has arranged for their re-exportation, he must produce a warrant and a Shipping Bill, in which case the goods can be removed from the bonded warehouse.

The use of bonded warehouses is not restricted to the *entrepôt* trade alone, as by statute an importer may store dutiable goods in this manner, prior to their being released by the Customs for home consumption. Similarly, home manufacturers of goods which are subject to Excise Duties, that is, duties which are levied on certain goods produced at home, such as beer, packed tobacco, spirits, and patent medicines, may store their manufactures in bonded warehouses until they are required. In these cases, the payment of duties is merely deferred, as the warehouseman will not relinquish any goods until the Customs authorise him to do so, and until, of course, the warehousing charges have been met.

Such in outline are the main features and the procedure of importing goods into the country. It is a situation which is always changing in order to meet new demands and new conditions. The whole may be violently and unexpectedly distorted by international upheavals and internal political changes. The basic principles, however, remain fairly constant. There are many regulations, many complicated forms to fill up, but some may say, like Alice in Wonderland, "It is long but very, very beautiful."

### BRITAIN'S PLACE IN THE EXPORT TRADE

UNTIL the War, the United Kingdom was the greatest exporting country in the world, accounting for 14 per cent. of the combined exports of all nations. After the War the United States of America took first place, but even now British exports are approximately 11 per cent. of the world total. The importance of the trade to the country itself is illustrated when we remember that in 1924 from 23–24 per cent. of British production was exported: in 1930–31 exports had fallen to 16½–20 per cent. of the national production; in 1934 it was still lower. In other words, export cannot maintain the rate of improvement achieved in the home market. We export to-day, roughly, only one-sixth of our production.

Britain has, above all, been an exporter of manufactured goods, it being estimated that she supplies about one quarter of the world's total export of manufactured goods. These are composed principally of cotton, iron, and steel manufactures, woollen goods, machinery, and coal, which together constitute about half the total exports. The other half is comprised of an infinite variety—wearing apparel, chemicals, ships, pottery, electrical goods, leather goods, tobacco, spirits and cutlery, to mention but a few. These goods are carried to every corner of the earth, so that the scope for the British exporter is almost limitless; and almost limitless, too, must be his knowledge of oversea conditions, unless he specialises in certain goods or certain countries.

There are complications in the export trade which do not occur in importing. Tariff regulations of foreign countries are, in a large number of cases, more complicated than they are in Great Britain. Restrictions on exchange have not so far existed in Great Britain; traditions, prejudices, and habits of the home merchant are familiar to the importer, as are also the laws of the country, its methods of advertising, and its commercial conditions. These factors will vary in all oversea markets. The result is that exporting, to be success ful, is largely a specialist's job, whereas importing, as we have seen, can be undertaken by those who do not specialise in it. In the circumstances, it is not surprising that we find many types of exporters.

The oldest type of exporter is the merchant shipper who buys in the home market and ships abroad on his own account. This type is analogous to the general import merchant described in the preceding pages. Such exporters are, however, now less numerous than the export commission agent, who differs from the merchant shipper in that he buys only upon instructions received from importers abroad. The merchant shipper sells for the best price he can obtain, but the commission agent buys at an agreed rate of commission and has to inform the importer abroad at exactly what prices he bought. It is through the commission agent that most of the exporting of Britain passes nowadays.

Besides these two types of exporters there are others; the most important are manufacturers themselves who are in a sufficiently large way of business to set up a foreign marketing organisation, and to keep in touch with demand abroad through selling agents or through their own representatives or branch establishments. Other types are export associations of allied manufacturers, who combine for the purpose of securing export trade, and importers' buying offices, which represent several importers abroad, as, for instance, the buying offices of the great distributing firms of the U.S.A. which are to be found in London, Paris, and many other towns.

The procedure of obtaining orders is fundamentally the same as that already described for importing. Again, there are those who wait for the orders to be placed with them by visiting buyers from foreign firms, or in response to advertising through trade papers or through samples and leaflets sent to possible customers abroad. Alternatively, there is the more modern "go-getter" method of American repute. By this method the consumer and not the distributor is made the focal point. The up-to-date distributive system is a two-way channel which carries to the exporter (or for that matter, the importer and manufacturer in the home market) exact information about the wants of the consuming public, and carries back to the public the commodities which are wanted. Exporters thus create demand and do not depend on the importers' personal initiative.

### HOW PRICES FOR EXPORT GOODS ARE FIXED

ORDERS are delivered in various ways and prices vary accordingly. The most common method is c.i.f. (cost, insurance, freight), which means that for the quoted price the exporter agrees to ship the goods to a certain port overseas and also to take out an insurance against the risks of shipment. In such cases, the exporter must arrange for his goods to be carried to the port, and negotiate with a suitable shipping company for shipment of the goods. A variation of this method of quotation is when goods are sold " *ex* ship." In this case the exporter not only pays for the cost of insurance and transport to the port of consignment, but must also defray the cost of landing the goods from the ship on the other side.

Another common method of quotation is f.o.b. (free on board), which means that for the quoted price, the exporter agrees to load the goods on to the ship, thus leaving all subsequent charges to the importer overseas. In the circumstances, the exporter will not usually undertake to quote f.o.b. for shipment at any port, however distant from his warehouse or factory, but stipulates " f.o.b. London " or some other specific port. A variation of this quotation is f.a.s., that is, free alongside, but it must be remembered that any arrangement can be made, such as " delivered docks," or " duty paid," or " in bond," etc.

### WHAT IS MEANT BY AN "INDENT"

C.I.F. consignments are usually against " orders," but a large proportion of f.o.b. orders are against " indents." These, to all intents and purposes, are the same as orders, except that they are given by the importer abroad, not direct to the supplier of the goods, but to the importer's representative or agent. The term " indent " is an old one, arising from the custom for such orders to be made out in several copies and " indented " or torn irregularly at the edge, so as to prevent forgery or substitution. Nowadays, however, an " indent " is merely an indirect order which can be given by post-card, letter, or even verbally to the representative, that is, the " indenting house." Indents can be " open " so that it is left to the representative to select the particular brands or quality of goods, but, with the spread of advertising and the attempts of manufacturers to make their wares known abroad, indents are increasingly becoming "closed" or "specific," that is, the importer specifies exactly which goods he wants his representative to order.

When the orders have been received, they are first sorted, checked in detail, and the risk of executing them considered. In the case of direct orders, the necessary supplies of goods are selected from the exporter's own warehouses or bought from suppliers. They are then packed and marked in accordance with the importer's orders, and arrangements are made for their shipment. "Shipping Notes" are prepared for the shipping company, and forms are completed for the dock companies, or, alternatively, for the Chief Officer of the ship.

Next, the exporter must prepare his shipping documents. Besides the bill of lading and the insurance policy, he must prepare an invoice, which in most cases has to conform to intricate foreign regulations. Foreign countries have, almost universally, imposed import restrictions of varying severity. The two main kinds are import duties and quotas, for which purposes the Customs authorities in importing countries need accurate information in regard to the value or quantity of the goods. In the case of quotas or preferential tariffs, they must further have a declaration that the goods are wholly, or to a minimum of a certain percentage, produced within the country of origin.

Consequently certificates of value and of origin must be given by the exporter. These are sometimes printed on the back of the invoice, sometimes they are separate documents, but always they have to be certified as correct by a responsible person of the exporter's organisation. In many cases even this is not sufficient, it being necessary to obtain and pay for a further certification from the local Chamber of Commerce or from the local consul of the foreign importer's country. Invoicing, therefore, can be a troublesome matter, especially as varying regulations exist for different goods consigned to the same country.

Having prepared the shipping documents, the exporter will send them to the importer, or to a bank in the importer's country if the shipment is made "cash against documents." The significance of these points in the procedure of exporting is the same as in importing, especially as regards bills of lading and bills of exchange. In certain countries there are export duties and restrictions, or even prohibitions, on the export of certain goods, and in this case the Customs authorities are usually responsible for seeing that these regulations are carried out by exporters. In the United Kingdom no such regulations exist. The Customs do, however, collect statistical information about the description, quantity, and value of all goods exported, but these particulars, supplied on the "Customs Specification Form," are the shipper's responsibility and therefore do not concern the exporter.

### THE REPUTATION BUILT UP ON TRADE MARKS

THERE is a further matter with which importers and exporters are perhaps more likely to come into contact with than other traders, certainly in its international aspect, and that is Trade Marks. These affect trade of every character, and are becoming more and more important, not only to those who are anxious to avail themselves of the benefits conferred by them, but also to those who, maybe quite innocently and unwittingly, are in danger of infringing them. This is a convenient place to discuss them shortly.

From earliest times, producers have attempted to distinguish their goods from those of others by giving them a special name, or by placing a mark on them which could be readily recognised. In this way makes of goods, which had previously been found satisfactory, could be identified and bought again, with a reasonable assurance that they would conform to previous standards. Such names and marks were of obvious value to the producer, in that in time they acquired a reputation among members of the public and thus constituted an important part of the "goodwill" of the trader. Goodwill is, of course, primarily built up by the good name and connection of the business, but "trade marks" are an extremely valuable adjunct, especially in connection with manufactured goods.

Under English Common Law the exclusive right of a person to his trade marks has always been recognised, and when another person adopts or imitates any of these marks, that is to say, "passes off" goods as being those of the owner of the mark, the latter has a right of action against the infringer. But it is not always easy to establish "passing off"; moreover, it is often a costly business to obtain all the evidence necessary to satisfy the Courts. In order to help traders in this matter, the Trade Marks Registration Act was passed in 1875 as an introductory measure, and was subsequently supplemented by further Acts, especially that of 1905.

The purpose of Trade Mark legislation in Great Britain has been, on the one hand, to provide means whereby a knowledge of existing trade marks can be obtained, thereby preventing them from being unwittingly adopted by other traders, and, on the other hand, to enable an owner readily to establish his right to his mark without having to obtain the cumbersome evidence necessary for a "passing off" action. The first purpose was achieved by the institution of a Trade Mark Register, in which marks approved by the Trade Mark authorities are entered, and which is open to inspection by members of the public.

The second purpose was achieved by enabling a proprietor of a mark to institute legal proceedings for the infringement of his registered property. The importance of these provisions is that at present the owner of a mark need not produce evidence of "user," that is to say, evidence that the mark is actually in use, but need only show that the Trade Mark authorities have registered him as the rightful owner.

The choice of a mark is a very important matter. It should be striking, that is, have attention value; it must be suitable to the goods on which it is to be used; it must fit in with the language, customs, and ideas of the people who are to use it; it should indicate to the public that the goods emanate from a particular source, that is, be an indication of origin. Finally, the mark cannot be registered unless it is approved by the Registrar. In Great Britain a mark must fall within one of certain categories, if it is to be protected. It must either be an invented word, or a distinctive device, or a signature, or the name of a concern represented in a sufficiently peculiar manner to satisfy the Registrar, or an ordinary word. In the last case, the word must bear no direct relationship to the goods to which it is applied, and must not be a geographical name. Further, the mark will not, of course, be registered if it is likely to cause confusion with existing registered marks.

## HOW A MARK IS PUT ON THE REGISTER

THE Register is divided into fifty classes of goods, based on the classification of the Great London Exhibition of 1851, and application is made for registration in whatever class includes the goods on which the mark is to be used. Such an old basis of classification must necessarily have many practical drawbacks at present, as it may be desired to register one mark for a whole family of allied goods, which are often placed in several classes; in that case several applications must be made and fees paid in respect of each one.

The law and practice of Trade Marks is fairly simple as regards general lines, but it requires great experience and specialised skill to deal with the matter successfully, in view of the very large number of marks which have been registered, and which are mostly still protected, in Great Britain alone. The question becomes increasingly complicated in foreign trade, as nearly every country has a different code for trade mark protection. In the circumstances, specialist agents are usually employed, but no trader can safely neglect the subject, as it is so intimately concerned with the goodwill of his business.

In some countries marks are registered in favour of whoever is first in applying for registration, as in most South American countries. In others, such as the U.S.A., marks can only be registered if actually in use, whereas in Britain "marks proposed to be used" may be registered. In India and some other countries, there is as yet no Trade Mark law, but marks may be advertised in the press by the owner as being his property, and may be deposited with the Custom authorities, who will prevent the importation of any goods under a mark which is an infringement of the mark so registered. And so regulations vary. It is impossible to estimate what proportion of British foreign trade consists of "branded" goods, but it is both very substantial and increasing. In recent years even fruit, coal, and many bulk articles are sold under registered marks.

The function of the Customs in this matter is a valuable one. As we have already seen, they are not only concerned with the collection of duties and the compilation of statistics. They are also in the nature of Coastguards, watching that no goods enter the country that may be contrary to the public weal. Just as they may exclude dangerous and infected goods, so they prevent the importation of goods which might violate the established rights of traders in the country or be in unfair competition with native products.

There are at present tendencies at work towards the standardisation of Trade Mark law in the various countries

: the world. Some visualise a Utopia, when international rotection will be achieved without the necessity for obtaining ultifarious and expensive registration in each country, but ose days are still a very long way off.

## THE WHOLESALER: A LINK BETWEEN MERCHANT AND SHOP

WHOLESALERS differ from most export and import merchants, in that they buy in large quantities and sell in naller lots, whereas the middlemen we have dealt with so r, generally speaking, sell as well as buy in large quantities. is true, however, that wholesalers act purely as middlemen, rving as a link between the producers and import merchants 1 the one hand, and the retailers on the other. Their isiness is not merely that of buying from the one and selling the other; they also serve manufacturers and retailers in a iriety of ways. For example, they convey to the former formation about trends in the demand of the public, and to ie latter information about new lines of development on the irt of manufacturers.

They are, furthermore, important factors in stabilising rices, as they are large importers of goods, and therefore ust necessarily understand world markets and conditions order to buy at the best possible prices. Being specialists a restricted range of goods, and as there is strong competion among themselves, they are in a good position to safeguard oth the less specialised retailers and also the public at large ;ainst any price fluctuations which might result from faulty iying, or from a gross lack of anticipation in regard to :ely demand from consumers.

To be successful, a retailer must usually carry a great iriety of stock, but, owing to lack of capital and of space, : cannot possibly hold large quantities of every type of ticle which the public may require. Consequently he ders small quantities repeatedly, and he wants his orders ecuted rapidly in order to serve his customers well. In ie circumstances it is clearly extremely difficult for importers home producers to serve a retailer efficiently at a reasonile cost. The necessary link is found in the wholesaler, ho warehouses fairly large quantities of goods, which can : supplied to retailers in his district rapidly and in small iantities.

Wholesalers in their turn specialise in certain types c
goods, as even they cannot stock everything, so that a groce
may have a wide choice of home-produced foodstuffs fron
one wholesaler, of foreign foodstuffs from another, of beverage
from a third, of household goods from a fourth, and so on
Similarly, a retail drapery store may obtain small supplies c
clothing, hosiery, materials, shoes, etc., from wholesaler
who specialise in each of the articles concerned. The firs
part of the wholesaler's business is, therefore, that of ware
housing. The second part is to prepare the goods stored i
his warehouse for handling by the retailers. This can b
compared to the work of a transformer in the grid syster
for electricity : just as the enormous grid voltage has to b
reduced before it can be conveniently used, so goods in bul
are broken down into lesser units for distribution to th
public. Thus dried fruits are seeded, cleaned and packe
ready for sale by the retailers. Tea, coffee, and spices ar
blended to suit local conditions, and are packed in form
acceptable to the buying public.

Thirdly, the wholesaler is concerned with the payment fo
goods. The importance of this part of his business will b
realised when it is remembered that in Britain there ar
probably about 100,000 retailers in the grocery trade alone
If a manufacturer or an importer had to supply each one c
these retailers with some of his goods, he would have to se
up a very elaborate organisation to check their financi
standing. A wholesaler, however, is concerned with a muc
smaller number of retailers—usually only those in his distric
—so that he is in a much better position to decide whethe
he can execute their orders. It might be said that gooc
can be supplied only against cash payment, but moder
business conditions almost invariably demand some measur
of credit. Such is certainly the case amongst retail traders
who have little working capital and have usually to give cred
to their customers.

Actually retailers give less credit than do wholesaler
because credit must be based on confidence, and greate
confidence exists between wholesalers and retail customer
who buy regularly than between retailers and the member
of the public where buying is more spasmodic. This thir
activity of the wholesaler may, therefore, be subdivided into
first, his service to the large supplier in standing betwee
the latter and a horde of doubtful credits, and, secondly, h

service to the retailer in enabling him to carry on business with little working capital.

### WHERE THE SHOPKEEPER GETS HIS GOODS

FINALLY, we come to the wholesaler's fourth and last main activity, namely, that of selling to the retailer and buying the necessary goods from his suppliers. In practice, he has travellers who call on retailers, thereby assessing changes in public demand and influencing the retailers to order their supplies from him rather than from the other wholesalers in the same district. Whatever he can sell, or thinks he can sell, will be bought from suppliers, either by getting into touch with them and placing his orders, or, more usually, by placing orders with representatives of the suppliers who call on him. Here, again, there is the same tendency as applies in the case of importers and exporters. It is the seller who usually sets out to obtain orders from the buyer, and not the buyer who approaches the seller.

Import commission agents and representatives of foreign exporters are continually canvassing wholesalers with a view to orders being placed. When a wholesaler agrees to buy, the details of his order are usually sent abroad by the agent or the representative of the foreign exporter, and the exporter then consigns the goods direct to the wholesaler. The wholesaler is responsible for the landing and clearing of the goods. Thus in the motor trade, wholesalers, or factors as they are ordinarily called, usually have foreign motor cars and accessories consigned direct to them. Wholesalers in the grocery trade generally obtain supplies of certain foodstuffs direct from abroad. The warehousemen and wholesalers of the drapery trade often obtain direct supplies of foreign silks, gloves, etc. Foreign imported goods are, of course, to some extent supplied from stocks "on consignment" in the importing country, but this method is less prevalent than that of direct importation.

Wholesale selling is similar to the selling conducted by merchants who are concerned only with importing and not with buying of supplies from home producers. In both cases, books must be kept of the accounts of customers, whose financial standing must be carefully considered before orders are executed or canvassed. Invoices for goods supplied will be similarly prepared, and warehousing will again depend on the type of goods which the wholesaler or importer wishes to keep in stock. Wholesale ironmongers, for instance, under take to supply retailers with practically any article they ma require. Tools, cutlery, and similar smaller articles ar supplied direct from the wholesaler's warehouse, but th larger articles, such as gas stoves and mangles are usuall ordered by the wholesalers from the manufacturers who sen them direct to the retailer.

The majority of retailers deal largely with women, s that their premises must be compatible with feminine tastes but the wholesaler deals with commercial men. His premise are therefore not so important, provided they are reasonabl accessible to his customers and suitably placed for the deliver of orders. In practice they are usually located near eac other in the business centres of towns. In London, fo instance, we find the wholesalers in the grocery trade mainl concentrated round Eastcheap, whereas wholesale draper are in and around Wood Street.

### THE TENDENCY TO COMBINE WHOLESALING AND RETAILING

IN recent years there has been a marked tendency toward combination in the different stages of distribution. Th causes for this development (technically known as " integra tion ") are many. Retailers have found that with the im provement of transport, shoppers can be drawn from a muc larger area than was the case previously, and further, tha goods can be delivered more widely with the advent of moto vans than in the days of horse transport. The result has beer a large increase in the big stores of leading cities capable o carrying large stocks of many varieties, and a corresponding decrease of small shops for each small radius.

Retail organisations have also found it possible to run a chain of retail shops over an extensive area and buy their supplies centrally direct from manufacturers, etc., without relying on the wholesalers. A single retail organisation may thus have as many as 800 or 1000 retail shops in Britain alone. With this development, the business of the wholesaler has merely been assumed by the retailer himself, who may even have a separate department doing exclusively wholesale work. Conversely wholesalers themselves have opened up retail shops with a view to obtaining the considerable margin of profit which retailers must make on the goods they sell, if they are to keep well-stocked shops.

These causes for integration come from below, but there

are also causes from above, that is, from the supplier himself. Manufacturers have in the past often said that wholesalers do not "sell" goods to the retailers; that they are merely "order takers" without the drive to push the sale of goods. Consequently, many manufacturers and importers have set out to take over the activity of wholesaling as much as they could. This they have done by having their own salesmen calling on retailers, canvassing orders from them, and "advertising" the manufacturers' goods; and by reducing the minimum quantity which they are prepared to sell at a time, so that smaller buyers could buy direct. This development has been particularly pronounced in the sale of branded goods, as these are often extensively advertised and enjoy a steady demand from the public.

Conversely, wholesalers and even retailers themselves have undertaken packing, blending, or manufacturing, as is extensively the practice with tea, coffee, jams, and certain pharmaceutical goods. An important point to bear in mind when considering this development, is that with the increase in the circulation of newspapers, and in travel, films, etc., new fashions and tastes spread very much more rapidly, so that a strong case can be made out by those favouring integration, on the grounds that retailers and manufacturers must work together.

## SHOPS THAT STILL DEPEND ON THE WHOLESALER

In practice wholesalers are by no means dead. The large store has so far developed principally at the expense of the medium-sized store, such as the family grocer, but the importance of the small retail shop remains unaffected; for these small retailers at least, the existence of the wholesaler remains imperative. In the boot and pharmacy trades the wholesaler is being cut out to a great extent, but it is estimated that 90 per cent. of all groceries and 70 per cent. of all hardware and dry goods are still sold through the manufacturer-wholesaler-retailer channel.

An interesting sidelight on this question of integration was supplied from the U.S.A. in the years after the 1929 slump. Prior to 1929 there had been considerable criticism of the wholesaler, who was by some considered to suffer from blindness, lack of policy, and lack of a clear conception of his function. This resulted in manufacturers encouraging integration between wholesalers and retailers, and in manufacturers opening up their own retail shops. But once sales stopped increasing rapidly, they found that it was cheaper to employ the wholesaler again. Many of the manufacturers' retail shops were closed down and their creation was abusively referred to as "branchitis." In order to strengthen the wholesalers further, legislation has been introduced whereby advertising "allowances" and other methods, and "chiselling devices" for cutting prices to retailers, have been restricted, so that retailers and manufacturers are again finding it more profitable to employ the wholesale channel. (Yet sales of American chain stores rose rapidly so soon as conditions began to improve. Further, the previous trend towards integration showed signs of reasserting itself vigorously with the weakening of the codes' legal authority.)

A wholesaler's profits vary according to the lines he handles. On proprietary articles the average percentage is about 10 per cent.; on groceries 5 per cent.; on sundries, perhaps 12½ per cent., but on many foodstuffs, where there is keen competition, it is not usually higher than 2½ per cent. In certain cases wholesalers undoubtedly do make high profits on small sales, but these are to a great extent on farming and agricultural produce, where the risk of waste and decay is considerable. But as long as the field is open, and there is nothing to prevent the influx of new energies where profits are to be made with abnormal ease, wholesalers ought to continue to earn what is no more than a fair return for their work, their capital, and their risks.

### THE MANY SIDES OF A WHOLESALER'S BUSINESS

IN conclusion let us take a glimpse at the work of a wholesaler, choosing for this purpose a provision and drysalter wholesaler in the English provinces. He may have separate departments specialising in certain ranges of goods with an executive in charge who, on the one hand, will study his retail market and, on the other, will buy such goods as he considers can be sold at a profit. Taking the business as a whole, the wholesaler handles a wide range. Tea will usually be bought from a London merchant operating exclusively in Mincing Lane. Similarly, coffee is generally bought from some large London import merchant. The wholesaler buys his sugar from a refiner of cane sugar, or from one of the beet sugar producers, most sugar required for the home market being machined in Britain.

Home producers will also supply most drysalter's goods such as soap, soda, paint, etc., as also other manufactured goods such as patent medicines, flour, polishes, and many sundry articles. A large variety of foodstuffs, however, are imported direct on a c.i.f. basis from abroad through representatives or agents of the foreign exporter. Dried fruits come largely from Greece and Southern Europe. Canned fruit comes in the main from California, Australia, and the Malay States. Canned fish, such as salmon and crab, is imported extensively from Canada, Japan, and Siberia. Crayfish comes from South Africa, and sardines from France, Spain, etc. The United States supply the big majority of the lard required in Britain, and also export much tinned meat, many patent foods, and many varieties of prepared foodstuffs. And thus the list can be elaborated to a great length.

In recent years there has been a change in the activities of wholesalers when dealing with such goods. Previously, they had to undertake a great deal of grading, washing, packing, etc., before the goods they bought could be handled satisfactorily by retailers, but now much of this work is undertaken by the producers themselves. The tendency now is for such articles to be packed at the source into smaller and more attractive units, ready for sale to the consumer. This has resulted in prices increasing, as freightage and transport must be paid on containers as well as on the product itself, but, in foodstuffs at any rate, it is in the best interests of the community, on grounds of cleanliness, that packing should be undertaken as near the source as possible. In spite of this tendency, however, the wholesaler must still devote a considerable portion of his warehouse to "transformer" activities.

Thereafter the wholesaler becomes an ordinary selling machine. Travellers call regularly on retailers, in competition with those of other wholesalers. Orders are booked and executed in due course, invoices are made out, ledger accounts are entered, and money is received in settlement. Sometimes the matter of obtaining payment must be pursued in County Courts, but fortunately the big bulk of the wholesaler's business is of a more agreeable character. A retailer has more to lose than an ordinary member of the public by being involved in litigation and is therefore less likely to default.

The organisation of a wholesale house will in general follow this division of his activities. No hard-and-fast rules

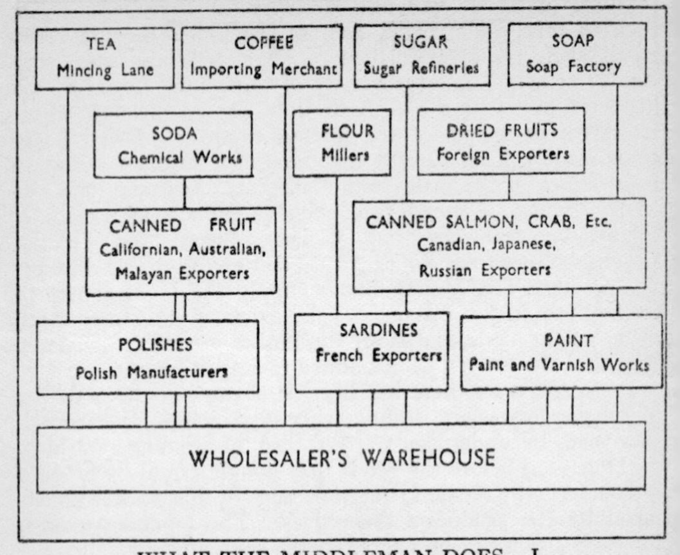


WHAT THE MIDDLEMAN DOES. I

*How provision and drysalter wholesalers collect their goods*

are in existence, but in practice there is usually a division into two main sections—administrative and executive—which are responsible to the directors or partners of the business. The administrative side may be subdivided into *the work done by the office Manager* who is responsible for the organisation and co-ordination of the various departments of the business; *the filing of records* and the collection of statistical information; *book-keeping*, including the personal accounts of the buyers and suppliers, and the cost accounts of the business; and *the cashier's department*, responsible for collecting and paying accounts, to the payment of wages and salaries and for keeping bank balances.

The executive side may be subdivided into: *selling*, comprising advertising and the management of the selling staff and market investigation; *buying*, covering the management of the buying staff, estimating and stock keeping; *the examination of orders*, consideration as to whether the orders shall be executed; and, finally, *forwarding*, comprising packing, the arranging for transport, and the supervision of

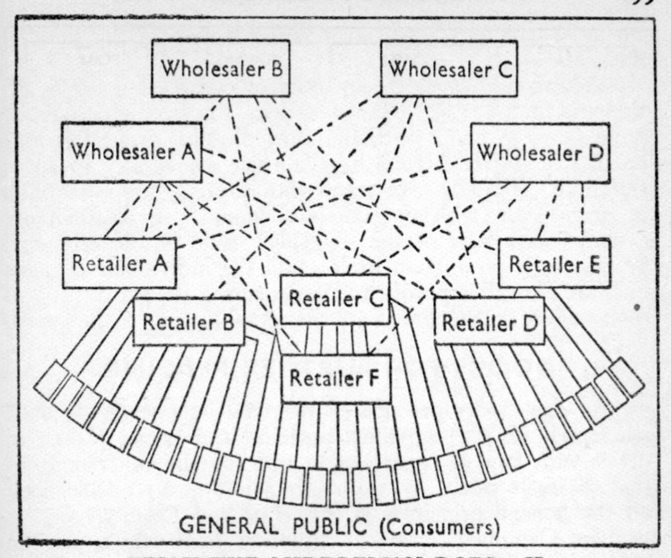


WHAT THE MIDDLEMAN DOES. II

*How the wholesalers redistribute their goods via the retailers*

warehouses. This organisation will differ in nearly every business, but such, substantially, will it be for every middleman whether in the export, import, or wholesale trade, provided he carries stocks of goods. Many, however, never carry stocks at all, being purely brokers, who operate mainly on the Produce Markets, just as brokers in stocks and shares, operating on Stock Exchanges, restrict themselves to buying and selling on behalf of clients. The organisation of such middlemen's businesses will clearly be different.

We have seen that middlemen are specialists; and from the point of view of the economist, specialisation is made necessary by the growth of the market, whilst at the same time, specialisation enables the market to grow still further. The complexity of the methods and organisation of modern production on the one hand, and the large and diversified nature of modern demand on the other hand, necessitate a market as wide and as perfect as possible. Yet the degree of perfection of the market depends on the ease with which supply and demand can meet. It is in this connection that we must look for the real economic function of the middleman.

Production changes the quantity of economic goods available and their physical characteristics. But from an economic point of view, goods with the same physical properties may be utterly different according to their availability in space and time. Trade is concerned with altering this availability in accordance with consumers' demand. It is therefore essential as a part of the "supply" side of the economic process as is production itself; and the individuals engaged in it are almost as productive in procuring the satisfaction of the wants of consumers as are the actual makers of the goods.

## BOOKS FOR FURTHER READING

THE day-to-day practice of the wholesale trade depends largely on the individual business, and books dealing in detail with any particular trade will contain an account of the wholesale side. An eminently sound and readable book on the general principles is *Wholesale and Retail Trade*, by William Campbell (Pitman). Another book which can be recommended as a lucid introduction to the subject is *Commerce, Its Theory and Practice*, by S. Evelyn Thomas (Gregg Publishing Co.). A more specialised discussion of import and export trade is contained in *Modern Business Routine, Vol. II. The Import and Export Trade*, by R. S. Osborne (Effingham Wilson), whilst a more specialised book is *The Importer's Guide to Customs Law and Practice*, by the Hon. H. Fletcher Moulton (Eyre & Spottiswoode). There is also a great deal of interesting and important matter contained in the admirable reports on industry and trade prepared from time to time between 1924 and 1928 by Sir Arthur Balfour's Committee, and published by H.M. Stationery Office. On Trade Marks a clear and practical guide is *Trade Mark Law and Practice*, by A. W. Griffiths (Pitman).

# HOW A SHOP IS RUN

*by PAUL MAY, B.A. (Oxon).*

THE shop exists to satisfy conveniently the needs of the public, and its function therefore is to bring together from different sources as wide a variety as possible of the goods it wishes to sell, so that the customer may obtain all the advantages of procuring goods from the different markets of the world without stepping outside his usual shopping area. In short, the dominant factor in retail trade is service.

In fulfilling this purpose the shop has three main activities : it has to buy from among the various goods offered to it by the manufacturing centres of the world those which it considers most attractive ; it has to sell what it has bought ; and it has to control and co-ordinate this buying and selling.

What a shop buys is determined by what it can sell—that is to say, by public demand, both as it is at the moment and as it is likely to be in the future. But public demand is so varied a thing that no shop can cater for more than a part of it. What this part is to be must be decided by the management, and we therefore see that the process is, first of all, determination of policy and realisation of what public demand such policy involves, and therefore what sorts of things the shop will be able to sell ; secondly, buying what the shop can sell ; and thirdly, selling what has been bought.

The detailed organisation of a shop, based on this threefold division into management, buying, and selling, is very varied. In many businesses there are only two main divisions—namely, the management, that is, either the owner of the business, the general manager, or a board of directors and managing directors, and secondly the heads of departments who are responsible to the management for selling arrangements in the departments under their control as well as for the buying. In other shops the organisation is much further subdivided, and there are a large number of executive positions on a level footing, each responsible directly to the management. In a general discussion, however, of the principles underlying the running of a shop, it is best to treat the organisation in its more usual threefold form. The diagram below gives a suggested organisation of a shop on this basis.

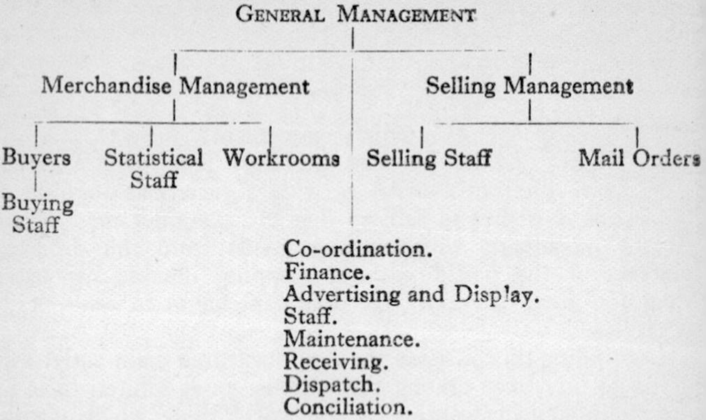


Co-ordination.
Finance.
Advertising and Display.
Staff.
Maintenance.
Receiving.
Dispatch.
Conciliation.

The activities of a shop being governed by public demand which is very varied, the first necessity is for the management to decide on the exact type of public for which the shop proposes to cater, and in exactly what way it proposes to serve that type. This aspect of management is often called Direction. The most important question is what the shop is to stock; its trade may be either general or specialised—that is to say, it may be content to stock a single commodity, for which there is already a demand that can be further stimulated, or it may decide that such a specialised trade is either too risky or too unlikely to find a satisfactory market in its particular case, and so make it its policy to trade in several of a large number of different lines. In some cases the fact that two or more types of goods are generally purchased together makes it economical to stock them all rather than a single line. It is necessary to decide, therefore, the main type of trade, and exactly how much of that type it is proposed to do.

### WHAT THE CUSTOMER WILL EXPECT

HAVING decided on the type or types of articles in which it is proposed to trade, it is then necessary to settle for what class of customer the shop is to cater. A decision on this point affects the whole scheme and running of the shop. The more wealthy type of customer will not only expect to find an attractive stock, but will also expect the building, decorations, service, staff, display, etc., to be in accordance with the type of stock. The less wealthy will probably be most concerned with questions of price and value, and, provided that these meet their wishes, they will not mind the shop being organised on a strictly utilitarian basis. Where a casual trade is expected, the shop will be differently run from one which depends largely on a credit trade. Similarly any other variations in the type of customer to be catered for will involve corresponding variations in the organisation of the shop. Naturally all decisions of this sort depend to a large extent on the amount of capital available, the type of address which this capital will justify, and the locality in which it is proposed to open the shop.

Decisions on the site and equipment of the shop follow the decision on the trading policy. The situation of the shop must obviously be convenient either in the sense that it is near the home of the customer, or in the sense that it is in a good position in a district where that type of customer habitually does the particular kind of shopping concerned. The floor space, window frontage, facilities for receiving and dispatching goods, and so on, must all fit in with the policy, and even questions such as the greater suitability of one side or one end of a street than the other must be very carefully considered, especially if the shop is to depend to any extent on chance trade.

The equipment and fittings of the shop when it is built will also depend on what the type of trade is to be. It is the customer who pays for this in the end, and the capacity of a particular type of customer to pay must be the deciding factor in determining the standard of comfort at which to aim and the proper organisation of the shop. An arrangement which would be economical in one type of shop might be completely unsuited to another; for instance, a shop which depended almost entirely on casual trade might find it good policy to double its window space by building arcades, with a consequent loss of selling floor space, whereas a shop whose policy it was to depend very largely on credit custom might find it more economical to keep the extra selling space and sacrifice display.

### WHERE FORESIGHT IS A VITAL QUALITY

THE policy on which the management decides must be a perfectly definite policy, but that does not mean that it must never come up for review. The management is concerned not only with what is actually happening in the shop, but also with what is going to happen in the future. It must, therefore, be constantly looking ahead and considering questions of commodity prices, market tendencies, standard of living, variations in fashion, developments in the ideas and ideals of various classes, the trends of international trade and the trade relationship between various countries, and many other such questions, and endeavouring to see how possible changes may react on the policy which it has laid down.

For instance, let us imagine a shop which trades in five different articles of ladies' wear ; owing to a change in fashion one of these articles becomes very little used. Unless the management becomes aware of this change of fashion early and fully considers the consequences, the shop will suffer—first, through having a heavy stock of this particular article which has to be cleared at a very low price, and, secondly, through the loss of a considerable part of its turnover. If the changing fashion is perceived in its early stages, the stock of the article concerned will be allowed to fall as the fashion disappears, and the loss will not be very great. Further, the management will consider whether the loss of turnover will be made up by increased sales in one of the other four articles, or whether it will be necessary, in order to maintain the turnover, to begin stocking another article. Similarly other changes, such as the change in the shopping district of a certain class of customer, a change in the standard of living, or a change in traffic routes, might necessitate a complete alteration of policy.

The management must plan ahead continuously in many other directions. For instance, it must estimate the probable future course of trade for a considerable period, and must compare the result with the facilities that exist in the shop for meeting with probable demands. In a business which is growing rapidly and is likely to go on growing, the management must compare the available selling space with probable future sales, and must estimate what sales are likely to prove the saturation point of the present building. If this stage is likely to be reached in the comparatively near future, plans must be made to have increased selling space available before it is reached, and the fact that growth in turnover affects the space required by every part of the organisation must also be taken into account. Again, the management must be constantly watching the markets for various goods, in order to see that the buyers have a proper knowledge of all fresh sources of supply and methods of production. It must watch for new inventions and discoveries which may help buyers in selecting their purchases. It must, in short, always be looking to see what is likely to go wrong and what could be done better in the future.

Besides looking to the future, the general management must also have an eye to the past. A business should learn from its past, but this can only be done adequately by organised research work. The investigation must be thorough if it is not to be misleading, and the results must be collected in a convenient form. There is a considerable amount of valuable research work that can be done, but this depends very largely on the size of the business. Research in a large business increases the overhead charges by only a very small percentage on turnover, but in a small business the cost may be prohibitive. The actual research done naturally depends on the circumstances of the business, but there are points of fairly general application.

The following are examples of topics lending themselves to such research:

> The rise and fall of the value of the average transaction, that is to say, of the average amount sold to an individual customer, and the relation of this to external circumstances.
>
> Advisable profit rates in different types of business for individual articles.
>
> Preferences and psychology of customers—the selling advantages of various parts of the shop, times of purchases; doors and lifts most used, etc.
>
> The relative values of various forms of advertising judged by their results.
>
> Trends of fashion.
>
> The methods used by competitors at home and abroad.
>
> Comparison of turnover and all percentage costs and results over a period of years.
>
> Comparison of methods of controlling stock.

## PUTTING THE POLICY INTO ACTION

Having decided what the policy is to be, it is necessary to see that it is fully understood by everybody and is translated into action by every department of the business. The management must manage in the literal sense of the word. This involves keeping a careful watch to see that the standard of the merchandise bought by the various buyers, the style of the shop and its internal arrangements, the type of the staff, etc., are all of the same character. It also involves seeing that the various other executives, such as the advertising manager, are working on the same basis and checking at once any new developments which overstep the limits set.

It is possible that such a new development would meet at first with apparent success. For instance, a buyer of one department might alter his bulk selling price to a lower level; this might result in an increase in turnover, but it is doubtful whether the extra sales would be made to the type of customer for whom it is the policy of the shop to cater. The result would probably be that within a few months the sales to customers of the required type had fallen off very considerably, and that a new type of customer was being attracted to the shop whom the other departments could not supply, while the old customers, whom this buyer could no longer suit, would make their purchases of other articles as well as the one concerned in a different shop. Thus, though the particular department would gain, its new customers would not bring fresh trade to other departments to replace that which had been lost through the departure of the old customers.

Besides seeing that all departments adhere to the main policy, the management must see that all departments work together in a co-operative spirit. It must set an example of open-mindedness and be always ready to listen to fresh suggestions regarding organisation. It is the duty of the management to adjust any differences which arise between the buying and the selling sides, to remove opportunities for friction, and to make sure that each executive has full opportunity to do his job as efficiently as possible. It is sometimes found that the best method of achieving this is to lay down clearly the exact duties and boundaries of each post in writing. This has been called a "job inventory."

## SHARING THE FLOOR SPACE BETWEEN THE GOODS

THE management is responsible for seeing that the business is run as economically as possible. For instance, it must plan the available floor space and distribute it among the various departments to the greatest advantage. In doing this it is a good plan to regard each department as renting so much space from the shop, and seeing that it is capable of meeting its liabilities fully. This means that the chief considerations in allocating floor space must be turnover, and the rate of gross profit which can be achieved on that turnover. The bulk of the stock held in a particular department must, of course, be taken into account, but it is clear that, if the value of a particular article is so low in comparison with its size that the sales resulting cannot pay the rent of the floor space used, such an article probably will not be worth stocking at all. The space on the ground floor will be more valuable in many cases than that on the first floor, and similarly ground-floor space near the front of the shop will be worth more than that at the back. Also in planning window display, settling the position and size of the various offices and service departments and similar problems of organisation, the same question of the return made to the business will have to be considered.

Other expenses of running the various departments must be watched in the same way. For instance, excess or lack of staff may seriously upset the results of a department, and it is clear that violent fluctuations in the trade of any department will make mistakes of this nature far more possible. The management has, therefore, not only to watch the sales to see whether they are justifying the money which they cost in staff, but it has also to endeavour to ensure that these sales are kept as level as possible throughout the year. Many frequent and spectacular bargain sales may produce an entirely contrary result and involves a good deal of fluctuation in staff.

There is also the question of wastage. In all retail businesses there must be a certain loss owing to the fact that many kinds of goods necessitate, or are open to, sampling by customers, and figures should as far as possible be kept, though the expense of keeping a full record of the cost of such loss would be far too high. Similarly the cost of pilfering cannot be ascertained. The management therefore has to be content to recognise such loss as wastage, but experience teaches what the reasonable limit of such wastage is, and the management must ensure that this limit is not exceeded. However, the limit must not be regarded as final, and the management must be constantly considering whether there are any methods by which the loss could be reduced without incurring extra expenditure.

The management must also watch the current results of the shop, not only the sales, stock, and profits, but all other figures produced, compare those with the estimates and take immediate action where the comparison calls for it. Speed in diagnosis and adjustment when anything is going wrong is of the first importance, and one of the chief qualities required for general management is the ability to appreciate a meaning in figures which is not apparent to the inexperienced eye. For instance, a change in the proportion of cash to credit customers might lead to the discovery that the general policy of the shop is being overstepped in some directions or requires alteration, or a small percentage disappointment in profits might lead to considerable revision of certain estimates.

## FINANCIAL PROBLEMS THAT MUST BE SOLVED BY THE MANAGEMENT

THE management must lay down its policy in general rules governing the financing of the business, and must see that they are carried out. It is for the management to prepare detailed estimates of what the expenditure is likely to be, and to control all expenditure on the basis of these estimates. It must deal with all questions relating to shares, capital, and dividends, and it must cover foreign exchange where necessary. It is also responsible for the proper keeping of all accounts, and for the preparation of all the necessary statistics based on these, and it must ensure that, in dealing with account customers, adequate provision is made for safeguarding the interests of the firm as well as the convenience of the customer.

In connection with finance, the management must determine the advertising policy and the financial allocation to be given to this purpose. Advertising policy varies enormously in different shops, and is closely bound up with the general policy of the business. Some shops depend almost entirely on the business which is brought to them through different forms of advertisement. Other shops advertise hardly at all but depend largely upon the goodwill which they secure hrough rendering some particular form of service to the public; for example, through selling goods at extremely cheap prices.

The central management is also responsible for maintaining he building and contents in proper condition. It must keep the structure of the building in sound repair, and for his purpose it is necessary to arrange for periodic inspections either by its own workmen or by an outside firm of every part of the shop. Repairs, repainting, and decorating must be arranged where necessary in order that the tone of the shop may not fall below the standard set by the policy, and must be carried out so as to interfere as little as possible with the sales and ordinary routine of the shop. They must also be within the estimates that have been made for the half-year's expenditure. Alterations have to be made to provide further selling space, if required for the further convenience of customers, and in each case the management must bear in mind the possibility of future growth.

Lighting and heating arrangements must also be considered. Some types of goods require fuller lighting for effective display; in other departments daylight lamps are necessary. Similarly it is necessary to adjust the heating arrangements to the conditions of each department. Again, it is essential that the fixtures and fittings are kept in a proper state of repair and efficiency. Old fixtures may accumulate dust and dirt more rapidly than new ones, with a consequent loss through damaged stock. They may also lower the whole tone of a department. Again, new types of fixtures must be examined and calculations made as to whether the cost of replacing old fixtures would be in proportion to the likely increase in sales.

## HOW THE GOODS ENTER AND LEAVE

THE central management must provide a suitable organisation for receiving deliveries from suppliers. In a shop of any size this is generally a separate department under its own management, and instructions are issued to all suppliers that goods are to be delivered to this department only. The manufacturer forwards with the goods what is called an invoice. An invoice is a statement showing details of the goods sent, the item value of the goods, the total value of the consignment, details of the discount allowed for quick payment, and, in the case of invoices from foreign suppliers, various

details required by the Customs ; the reference of the orde
given by the firm for the goods should also be quoted on th
invoice. It is the duty of the receiving department to chec
the goods received with the invoice and then to sign for thei
receipt. After checking with the invoice, the goods are sorte
out and placed in a position convenient for the buyer of th
department concerned, and the invoice passed to him to b
dealt with.

In cases where the shop deals with a number of foreig
suppliers and the goods are sent direct from the suppliers t
the shop, the receiving department may have to deal wit
queries raised by the Customs authorities regarding duty
and with expenses incurred in the carriage, handling, an
insurance of the goods. At the present time the increase i
duties and quotas may make this quite a large part of th
manager's job.

The department, however, receives not only goods whic
have been bought outright, but also goods which have bee
sent in by the supplier on approval for the buyer's inspection
The receiving department must keep a check on these an
ensure that, if they are to be returned, they are returne
within a certain period. The receiving department is re
sponsible for seeing that no goods which have not been bough
get into the shop.

## SENDING THE PURCHASES HOME

DISPATCHING goods is one of the ways in which most shop
give service to their customers. The general attitud
toward this depends in part on the policy of the shop, but i
is of the utmost importance that dispatch costs should b
kept as low as possible, and that no parcels should be sent i
the customer is ready to take them and there is no loss o
goodwill. The dispatch of the goods, like the receiving, i
generally in the charge of a separate department which ha
a fleet of delivery vans at its disposal. For our purposes th
department may be divided into two sections: the interna
and the external.

The internal dispatch department is responsible fo
collecting goods from the various selling departments, to
gether with instructions for delivery and payment, and checkin
the goods with the bill. It is extremely important that th
delivery instructions, which are generally attached to th
goods, should be written as clearly as possible, bad hand

vriting may cause either the goods to be sent to the wrong ddress, or a good deal of time to be wasted in deciphering he address. The delivery instructions should contain the ame and address of the person to whom the goods are to be ent; also information as to whether the goods are being harged to an account (in which case, sanction will have been btained from the accounts department), or have been paid or in cash, or are to be paid for on delivery.

Having collected the goods, the department next has to pack hem and label them, if this has not been done, with the name nd address of the consignee, and mark whether they are to be paid for on delivery or not. The parcel, if it is not to go by post or rail, is then listed according to the address and district on a sheet which will be given to the driver of the van, and is placed in a receptacle ready to be checked against the list and put into the van for the next delivery. In dealing with the parcels the utmost economy and efficiency in handling is necessary.

As in the receiving department, some goods received are not bought outright, so the dispatch department deals with some goods that have not been sold outright, but are sent out on approbation. These goods are dealt with in the same way as goods sold, except that a record must be kept of them and the goods called for after a certain interval, unless the department is notified that the goods have been bought and charged for. This point has to be carefully watched, as serious loss may result if goods which are sent out on approval are forgotten, and annoyance caused to the customer, if calls are made for goods which have been returned or purchased. The dispatch department must be responsible to the selling department concerned for returned goods.

The external dispatch department is responsible for maintaining the vans at its disposal in a proper state of repair and for seeing that they are as economical in running costs as possible. The manager of the department will probably find it wise to keep daily and weekly statistics, covering the cost of running each lorry, the number of parcels carried by each, the total cost of the fleet, the total number of parcels carried, the average cost of carrying the parcels in each van, and the average cost of carrying each parcel. From these figures he will be able to detect when the running of any particular lorry is becoming uneconomical; when the existing planning of delivery routes and allocations of vans to each district requires alteration; when it is necessary to increase or decrease the size of the fleet as the business of the shop fluctuates; when he is overstepping the limits of his estimated expenditure. The comparison of the total costs of delivery with the total sales is a matter for the central management, which must watch to see that the percentage relation does not become too high.

Besides maintaining the fleet, it is the duty of this department to ensure that the service runs punctually to a time-table. The van drivers must be given instructions as to the hours at which they are to collect goods from the internal department, and the districts which they are to serve. Each van driver receives with his load of parcels a copy of the sheet on which the parcels, with names and addresses, are entered, and this sheet must be checked with him. He then delivers his load, proceeding by the most economical route, and obtaining a signature for each parcel delivered and payment where necessary. If he fails to deliver any parcel, he must enter on the sheet the exact reasons for non-delivery, for the information of the internal department. If there are any goods to be called for, he receives written instructions in the same way.

### SERVICE THAT INVITES THE CUSTOMER'S CONFIDENCE

THE best asset of many businesses is their "goodwill," that is to say, the feeling of confidence in the minds of its customers that they will obtain what they want at the shop, whether this be quality of goods, a high degree of service, cheapness of prices, or large variety of stocks. If through inefficiency or accident a promise made to a customer is not kept, or the customer's expectations regarding what he will receive or has received are not fulfilled, confidence is shaken. It is for the central management—in some cases acting itself, in others acting through a separate executive—to see that in all cases the harm done is repaired to the greatest possible extent. Complaints received from customers, either at first or second hand, must be fully investigated and material restitution made in cases where this is possible, for example, by the replacement free of charge of a garment which has proved unsatisfactory.

This side of the management's work, however, should not be purely negative; it should also be positive in the sense that whoever is responsible should be continually investigating the methods used for inspiring confidence in customers and considering whether these can be improved and whether there are any further methods which might be employed for increasing goodwill.

## HOW THE STOCK IS BOUGHT

According to our original division of the shop into buying, selling, and co-ordination or management, the duties that will be ascribed to the merchandise manager belong to the general management, and in many shops they would form part of the general manager's work. For the sake of clearness, however, it is best to place merchandise management and buying in the same section, and to abandon to that extent the strict limits of the original division.

The merchandise manager must understand fully how the general policy of the shop affects each particular department. He must see that each buyer has a complete grasp of this, and he must co-ordinate the efforts of all the buyers on this basis. Thus a policy for each department will be evolved concerning all questions of stocks, profits, reductions, etc. This has to be discussed at intervals between the merchandise manager and the buyer, and comparisons drawn between the policy and what has actually been taking place.

It is of the first importance that reliable estimates of future profits should be prepared. If the management cannot rely on these estimates being as accurate as possible, it will be impossible for them to get the expenses of the business into the right proportion, and there will be a consequent disappointment in the profits, or else the service department will prove inadequate

The length of time for which estimates are prepared varies in different shops; we will assume here that the period is six months. The first point to decide is an estimate of probable sales. The simplest way of doing this is to make a comparison with the actual results of the previous year or previous years. The department, we will assume, has been showing a small but steady increase in the last few periods, and no reason is apparent for anticipating any change in the nature of the department's development. The merchandise management and the buyer consequently agree that a further small estimated increase on the previous period will not be far from the truth.

### HOW ESTIMATES ARE PREPARED

Having agreed on the estimated sales, it is then necessary to decide the estimated difference between the cost price of purchases during the next six months, and the selling prices at which they will be marked. This estimated difference is usually expressed as a percentage either of the cost price or the selling price; that is to say, if anything costs 5s. and is sold at 7s. 6d. this is either 50 per cent. on cost or 33⅓ per cent. of selling; the latter method is the more usual. This difference over the whole half-year is generally called the average mark-up, and it depends naturally on the general policy of the business and the nature of the goods themselves.

It is also necessary to estimate the amount of money which will have to be deducted from the selling price of various articles in order to clear them and for the purposes of sales, *i.e.* money for reductions during the half-year. This amount is also usually expressed as a percentage of the sales. Finally, an estimate must be made of the amount of loss which will be incurred in the goods in the department otherwise than through definite reductions, that is to say, through damage, breakage, pilfering, samples, etc. This, again, is generally expressed as a percentage of sales.

These figures, together with the sales figure, give the net amount of money which it is estimated the goods themselves will earn during the half year, and this is all that the merchandise manager is concerned with. The percentage costs of selling staff, buying staff, service departments, upkeep, advertising, etc., is a matter for the central management. In some shops the first step in preparing the estimates for a new half-year is for the central management to prepare all these figures on the basis of the estimated total sales for the whole house, and then to instruct the merchandise management that these estimated total sales will be required to produce such and such a total profit.

### HOW MUCH STOCK OUGHT THE SHOP TO KEEP?

HAVING decided the estimated sales, mark-up, reductions, and wastage for the department, the merchandise management has next to decide with the buyer what, in view of the particular policy of the department, is the right stock figure to aim at for the end of the period. This, too, is expressed as a percentage of sales or else as a definite fixed figure. The size of the stock varies enormously with the type of department and with the type of shop. A high fashion department in an exclusive shop will probably endeavour to clear practically the whole stock, and can generally afford to do so because of the high rate of profit which has been secured on the sales made in the earlier part of the half-year. In a department, on the other hand, which deals in non-fashion goods, which are not affected by a seasonal demand but sell at a comparatively level rate all the year, the closing stock will probably be relatively large, in order that no chance of making sales may be missed.

Besides fixing the closing stock, the buyer and the merchandise manager must agree as to what size of stock will be necessary adequately to meet the largest estimated sales, and to provide a margin of opportunity for exceeding these should a chance occur. On the basis of these two stock figures, the stock will rise and fall during the half-year in relation to the sales.

Estimates having been made in all these cases, it is clear how the buyer must arrange his buying, and in most shops the merchandise management proceeds to plan out how much money a buyer is justified in spending in any given period—a fortnight, a month, or three months—and to issue these figures to the buyer. Having made these estimates for each individual department, the merchandise manager can then produce a total estimate for the whole shop and can co-ordinate the total profit with that required by the central management.

The merchandise management is responsible also for providing statistics and supervising the control of his stock by a buyer. Details of the system used vary from shop to shop but the rough outline is the same. Having reached the estimated figures for the half-year, and issued to the buyer a plan of how purchases should be spread over the half-year, the merchandise manager must observe the results. He has to watch orders placed by the buyer and the total amount of money involved in his commitments in comparison with the suggested plan; to compare the actual sales and the actual stock with the estimate; to watch how far the buyer's pricing of his purchases agrees with the estimate; to see whether the reduction money available is being well used; and finally, to discuss these points at intervals with the buyer. Statistics giving information on all these points are prepared by the merchandise manager's staff and copies sent to the buyers.

## WHAT IS DONE AT A STOCKTAKING

WASTAGE, as we have seen, is a very important point, and by its nature a large proportion of it passes unobserved, or if observed, the calculation of its cost is so difficult as to be impossibly expensive. Certain elements of wastage such as breakage may be known and can be recorded, and all such must be reported to the merchandise statistical department as carefully as the moneys used in reducing goods. In order to keep a check on the wastage which is unknown it is necessary that stock should be taken periodically, in some cases monthly, in some cases half-yearly, as all stock figures obtained otherwise than from a physical stocktaking are merely estimates based on purchases, sales, and estimated losses. A physical stocktaking also helps the buyer to keep his eye on old and slow moving stock, and is useful for accounting purposes.

Methods adopted at a physical stocktaking differ. Each item in stock has two values, its cost price and its selling price, and consequently all figures relating to stock may be kept either at cost or selling price. Some firms have stocks taken at selling price and subsequently identify each article and ascertain its true cost, thus getting a total selling and cost value for the stock, from which figures of profit may be calculated very accurately. Other firms take stock at selling price and cost price, the cost price being written in code on the tickets on the goods as well as the selling price, while other firms take stock at selling price only and calculate the total cost value of the stock by deducting the average percentage mark-up. The stock is listed item by item, and the sheets are sent to the merchandise statistical department or counting-house. The resulting total stock figure, together with the stock figure at the end of the previous period, and purchases, sales, and reductions since, give the wastage figure.

It is essential that the utmost possible care should be taken to see that every single item in stock is listed, and listed at the price at which it is standing at the moment. Without the utmost care items easily get overlooked and a considerable percentage error may occur. If the wastage figures resulting from the stocktaking are in accordance with estimate or less, or even if a small surplus on the proper stock is shown, the stock figure may probably be accepted, unless there are any special circumstances that throw doubt upon it. If the wastage figure is much above estimate or a relatively large surplus is shown, the stock figure should be regarded with suspicion and the stock taken again and carefully checked.

### WHAT THE BUYER HAS TO DO

THE merchandise manager must be, to an extent varying with the powers given to him by the central management, responsible for the buying staff. In some cases he may be largely or partly responsible for dismissing and engaging buyers. In any case he must be constantly reviewing in his own mind the results obtained by each buyer, considering the suitability of each particular buyer for the post he occupies and his shortcomings, even perhaps discussing these with the buyer. He must also consider how external circumstances affect the work of each buyer. A substantial increase on sales, for instance, may be unsatisfactorily small in view of circumstances, while it may be a fine achievement in another case to have maintained sales at their previous level.

There are various items of routine which have to be handled by the buyer[1] or his staff. For example, immediately after a verbal order has been placed, a written confirmation must be made out to cover this in detail, and a corresponding specification of the order must be received from the supplier. Verbal agreements on such matters are dangerous to both sides.

When goods have been delivered and rough checked by the receiving department, the goods and invoice are handed over to the buying department. This department must then check the goods in detail with the invoice, examine them to see that they are up to the standard of the samples from which the purchases were made, check the cost prices, pass the invoice as correct to the counting-house for payment, mark the items with the selling price decided on, and any other particulars which it is the custom of the shop to put on the price tickets—such as codes indicating cost price, supplier, date of delivery, etc.

Besides selling to customers from the stock contained in the department, a shop also obtains goods specially to the customer's order. In some departments, such as men's tailoring, the trade is often almost entirely of this type. In this case, orders to suppliers are largely special orders, though often the " suppliers " are the shop's own factory. In other cases the special orders form only a relatively small percentage of the department's trade, and in these cases the buyer must make adequate arrangements to see that all such orders are dealt with promptly and their fulfilment to time carefully watched.

When the selling prices of goods are reduced or any sort of wastage occurs involving an ascertainable loss, for example, breakage of china, the buyer must make certain that a proper record of the loss is made. If this is not accurately done the stock figure of the department in the firm's books will not

[1] See " The Art of Good Buying " (p. 162).

present as true a picture of the actual state of affairs as it might and the unknown wastage figures at the end of the half-year will be large.

### STOCK-KEEPING THAT HELPS BOTH CUSTOMER AND STAFF

EFFICIENT stock-keeping is of very great importance in a shop. The stock must be arranged where it is easily available to the staff, so that they can quickly find the particular thing which they wish to show to a customer. Inefficient arrangement of stock leads to waste of time and loss of goodwill through keeping customers waiting. It is also desirable that so far as possible the stock should be arranged so as to make it easy to see how much of a particular item there is in the department. This can generally be managed without loss of efficiency from the selling point of view. Again, the stock should be arranged so as to present as pleasing an appearance as possible to customers. The more visible the various items are, the more easily and quickly can customers see exactly what they want, and they will appreciate this particularly if they have any difficulty in conveying their desire to the salesman.

It is generally necessary to make one particular person responsible for seeing that the arrangement of the stock fulfils these conditions, and he must also watch very carefully to see that the arrangement is not such as to lay the goods open to damage through bad storing, exposure to dust, heat, or anything else likely to harm the goods. The nature of this job makes the man who holds it likely to give valuable information to the buyer, and he is, therefore, often responsible for advising the buyer as to the state of the stock.

## HOW THE CUSTOMER IS SERVED

THE goods of a department can be displayed to the buying public in two ways, namely, in the windows and in the department. Part of the work of the management consists in seeing that the display facilities afforded by the window frontage are allocated to the various departments in proper proportion. The actual arrangement of the windows is dependent to a great extent on the firm's policy. In general, however, the head of the department, whether this be the buyer or someone else whose whole time is spent on managing sales, must pay particular attention to showing the right thing at the right moment. In part this will be arranged for the

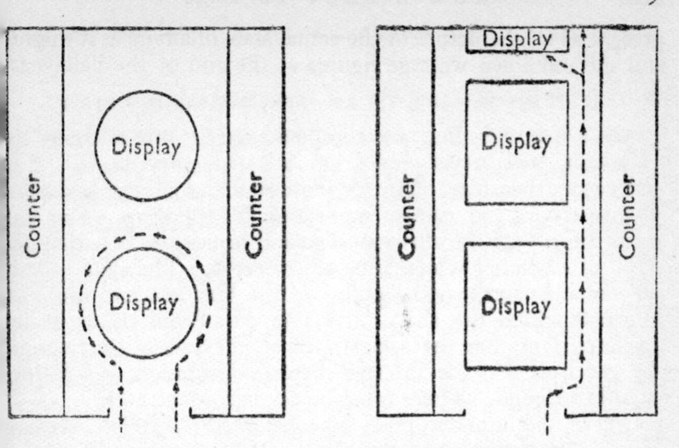


KEEPING THE CUSTOMER IN THE SHOP

Left: *People tend to walk round circular display stands; so that if these are placed near doors, they tend to lead the customer* out *of the shop.* Right: *The effect of long rectangular stands is to lead the customer further* into *the shop.*

departments by the management, who will vary the amount of window space allotted to each according to the time of year and the state of its trade and advertising considerations, but, outside these limits, the person responsible can influence the sales considerably by showing what is most likely to catch the public's fancy at the moment. In addition, window display is very useful for forcing sales, either of stock which is not moving as quickly as it should, or of stock which has had to be reduced. The same principles apply to displays in the departments. These do not draw the public into the shop, but they may attract the attention of customers passing through the department and must be arranged with that object in view.

It is very necessary for a shop that it should keep in close touch with customers' ideas, whether these relate to the changing trends of demand or to the satisfactoriness of the stock and service offered. It is a very important part of the duties of the head of the department to do this and to advise the buyers and the management of the conclusions he has reached as a result. In shops where the customers have, to any large extent, running accounts, this is even more important because the customers expect a certain amount of individual treatmen and recognition.

## THE IMPORTANCE OF AN EFFICIENT SELLING STAFF

BUYING and selling are complementary: one without the other will never build up a satisfactory trade. The provision, therefore, of an adequate staff and its proper contro is a matter of the utmost importance for the shop. The staf must fit in with the surroundings and be such as to satisfy the type of customer whom they are to serve. The type of staf depends, in fact, on the policy of the business and the class of trade which the shop intends to do. Similarly, it is just as important that the appearance of the selling staff should be good, as that the internal display, decoration, and fittings should be good. There must be no discordant note.

Again, the numbers must be considered carefully. We saw above that the costs of the selling staff are a very important factor in running a shop and must be kept in a constant relationship to turnover. It is the business of the selling management to forecast the needs of their departments for the near future, and to make sure that they are neither understaffed nor overstaffed.

The selling management must ensure a high degree of discipline. Unless the staff is accustomed to obey all instructions quickly and to subordinate themselves to the requirements of the department, it will not be possible either to get the ordinary departmental routine work done, or to achieve the requisite standard of courtesy and service. Slackness not only means losses due to waste of time and inefficiency, but also perhaps bad stock-keeping and consequent damage to stock.

## WHAT THE SALESMAN SHOULD LEARN ABOUT THE CUSTOMER

THE selling staff and their leaders are brought constantly into touch with the customers and enabled to see how the stock is selling and how far the customers are genuinely satisfied. They are in a position to give very valuable advice and help to the buyer and to the management. It is advisable for some system to be instituted whereby the heads of the departments can obtain from the selling staff detailed information of any cases in which they have failed to supply a customer. This can be done as we saw above by means of a daily written return from each assistant, the form of which will probably depend on the nature of the goods handled by the department. This return will enable the heads to supplement the ideas which they have formed during their visits to the departments under their charge and will enable them to make suggestions to the buyers. It will also help them to form an idea of the ability of each member of the staff to handle difficult situations, and of the initiative which each shows; in many cases where a bad salesman fails to satisfy a customer, a good salesman could do so from the same stock.

Similarly, the selling management should become familiar with the stocks in the departments under their charge, and should be able to form their own opinion as to what lines are selling slowly and in what directions the stock is heavy or light. They can thus give the buyer suggestions based on a different view-point from his; they can also determine more correctly what lines require special emphasis in display or in introduction by the selling staff, and what lines there are which should be given greater prominence at any particular time.

### CAUSES OF WASTE THAT CAN BE AVOIDED

JUST as the selling management have to keep a strict eye on the cost of the selling staff, so they have to watch very carefully for any source of wastage and to eliminate it, or, if this is impossible, to keep it down to a minimum. This is an extremely difficult business and provides an opening for every form of ingenuity. Ordinary matters of departmental routine appear on closer inspection to be really a form of wastage. For instance, the head of a department who encourages assistants to send goods out on approval, or merely agrees to their doing so, on a large scale is supporting a wasteful practice. In the first place, it encourages assistants to be slack; it is often the easiest way of dealing with a difficult customer to suggest sending the goods on approval, but it may mean that a probable sale becomes an improbable one. Secondly, if any large percentage of the stock is out on approval, it means that the assortment of the stock remaining in the department is not properly balanced, and a large amount of capital is being only partially employed over a period of days.

Wastage arises similarly from things such as pattern cutting and sampling, pilfering, breakage and damage, dirt and staining of stock and fading, unnecessary delivering of small parcels, wrong addressing of parcels, laziness of staff, under-charging. Many other individual points arise in each business. These must be controlled and remedies found to suit the individual requirements of the situation.

### CATERING FOR CUSTOMERS THROUGH THE POST

In a good many shops a varying percentage of the trade depends on what are called mail orders. Customers who either live at a distance from the shop, or who want to make preliminary inquiries before actually doing their shopping, write to the shop, often as a result of some form of advertisement, asking for details or samples of what they wish to buy, or ordering goods to be sent to them. In some businesses mail-order trade forms a very large percentage of the total turnover.

The selling management has to set up some form of organisation to deal with all letters received, and to obtain from the buyers or selling staff the goods or the information required in order to send an adequate answer. This side of the business has to be very efficiently run if it is to be successful, and, as customers often write at the same time to more than one shop, speed is a very important factor. Also, unless very well organised, such a department can be very expensive. The procedure adopted varies with the importance of the mail-order trade, but in many cases it is found that the most satisfactory method is for the mail-order department to act as a distributing centre and as censor to see that the letters are fully dealt with. The actual supplying of the goods and details should be done by the selling staff because of their more detailed knowledge of the stocks.

Car and motor-bus have brought the shop nearer to every type of customer in the past two decades ; yet the mail-order department still becomes increasingly important in every department store. Very large sales can be secured through newspaper advertising from those who are unable to come to the shop in person but can telephone or post their order. At the same time, further orders can be got through posting attractive catalogues and folders direct to customers or prospective customers with an order form enclosed. The method of using the newspaper is known as mail-order selling, that which uses the post only is known as direct postal selling. Both entail an elaborate and exacting technique of salesmanship by letter, of routine control, and of dispatch. Whether these systems are adopted depends naturally on the policy of the shop.

### HOW THE CUSTOMER PAYS HIS BILL

When the goods have been sold there remains the question of payment. A customer may wish the transaction to be settled in one of several ways. If there is immediate cash payment a bill must be made out, checked and countersigned by the head of the department or his deputy, and the cash received. If payment is by cheque a bill must again be made out, but sanction must be obtained from the proper authorities before the customer can be allowed to take the goods away, or before the goods can be sent out to the address given by the customer; in a good many cases the cheque has to be cleared before the goods can be sent to the customer. If an account is to be debited, the bill has in most cases to be signed by the customer and then sanction must be obtained before the goods are taken or sent.

Payment on delivery is applicable only in cases where the goods are to be sent and the assistant is responsible only for having the bill clearly marked to be paid on delivery. If goods are to be sent on approval sanction must be obtained in all cases. In the case of the goods being left until the cash is forwarded, the assistant must see that the goods are put on one side, that the correspondence department or other department responsible is advised to expect a remittance, and that the bill is receipted and the goods sent out immediately on receipt of the money. If hire purchase is resorted to, it is usual for the customer to sign an agreement with the firm containing the conditions of the transaction and rates of payment. The assistant is responsible for taking the customer to the department concerned.

A customer may bring or send to the firm an article belonging to himself which he requires to be altered or repaired —for example, a broken chair. The assistant must see that the order is carried out to time, and that in charging for the work done and returning the article to the customer it is made clear that the article is the customer's own property. If the article has to be called for in the first place by the firm, the assistant must be responsible for requesting the dispatch department to make the call. A customer may wish to have an estimate made out covering the cost of purchases he wishes to make or work he wants done. Arrangements must be made to have such estimates prepared quickly and accurately, and forwarded to the customer in writing.

### LITTLE WAYS OF EARNING THE CUSTOMER'S GOODWILL

THE customer may wish to purchase a number of articles in different parts of the shop and to collect these or to have them sent together and to pay for them together. Arrangements must be made to satisfy the demand either by permitting one assistant to serve the customer right through the shop, or, as in the case of the larger shops, by having a form on which the individual purchases are entered and arranging for all goods purchased to be labelled with an identification number and forwarded to a central clearing counter where a total payment can be made.

A customer who is having a purchase sent to his address may ask for a piece of his own property, a parcel, garment, etc., to be included in the package. In this case the assistant must make out a separate document to cover the customer's property and to show clearly that it is to leave the shop without charge; this document must be countersigned by the head of the department or otherwise sanctioned. Again, a customer may want to have an article delivered to him more quickly than is possible by means of the ordinary delivery service; and it may be good policy for the shop to accede to his request. A shop, therefore, must have some means of making such special quick deliveries, but, as this is a costly business, it must be done only under written authority countersigned by the head of the selling department.

The dispatch department must keep a check on goods kept on approval and returned from approval, but the selling management must also watch such transactions and ensure that charges are made where necessary, and that there is no risk of charging customers for goods which they have not retained. Similarly, in the case of goods returned for exchange, the selling management must deal with the customer and see that cash or account credit notes are made out when necessary. Goods returned with a complaint should be passed to the conciliation department.

In all the foregoing cases where a definite transaction occurs, either a bill or a credit note is made out, and it is from copies of these that the counting-house must derive their sales figures. It is, therefore, extremely important that no copies of bills should be lost, and that the contents of a bill should be easily readable. The selling management must pay strict attention to these points.

### WHAT MAKES THE DIFFERENCE BETWEEN FAILURE AND SUCCESS

To plan a policy for a shop and to draw a picture of its organisation is not a difficult thing to do. The difference between good management and bad does not lie in superiority or inferiority in this respect, but in ability or inability to make the plan work efficiently. It is true that a lot depends on the policy being drawn up to suit the shop and its position, or on the shop being built and fitted in accordance with the policy. It is also true that adequate capital is essential, otherwise the business will find itself unable to expand when opportunity arises and in difficulties about making fresh purchases at the right time, or it will be forced to borrow money at unsatisfactory rates. Nor must the capital be too large if the shop is to be able to pay satisfactory dividends. This merely means, however, that to have a true sense of proportion in planning and in action is as essential in running a shop as in any other business, but a sense of proportion alone will not make a shop run efficiently.

If a shop is to be successful, energy is also needed to keep its business steadily increasing. This energy, which finally determines the success or failure of the shop, ultimately derives from the leader of the shop and his immediate deputies. Without energy inefficiency soon arises, a feeling of contentment with things as they are and a disinclination to question the usual mode of procedure.

## HOW TO LEARN MORE ABOUT RUNNING A SHOP

THERE are a variety of good books for those who care to study the organisation and running of a shop in greater detail. *The Elements of Retailing*, by Ruth Leigh, contains an excellent treatment of the nature of a shop and the basic problems involved in running one. It gives special attention to questions likely to arise in the minds of beginners, and no previous experience is necessary in order to understand it. *Retail Management*, by Cunliffe Bolling, gives an instructive and detailed examination of the organisation and running of a shop which is applicable to the smaller as well as the larger stores. It is a very interesting book, both for those who hav had experience of executive positions in retailing and fo those who have not. *Department Store Organisation*, b Arthur Lazarus (Dry Goods Economist), is a more advance work in two volumes, the first dealing with general manage ment, buying, the direction of buying, and so on, and th second with accountancy, finance, and the control of expendi ture and stock. *The Model Stock Plan*, by Edward Filen (McGraw-Hill), deals in detail with the problem of keepin the right stock, which is the fundamental problem of runnin a shop, and sets out methods which have been found in prac tice to be the most successful by certain large stores in th United States.

*Chain Stores*, by Hayward and White (McGraw-Hill), give a very interesting survey of the principles of the Americar chain store and its special problems.

# HOW GOODS ARE SOLD

*y L. A. TERRY, B.Com.(Hons.), Cert. A.I.B., Principal of the Commercial Evening Institute, Hammersmith.*

THE development of mass production methods in anticipation of the possibility of selling the goods so produced has been characteristic of the last hundred years. Marketng—the actual sale of goods or their exchange against other goods—has, of course, existed since the time when specialisaion of labour was first practised, and man was no longer ble to satisfy all his own needs, but relied upon exchanging his surplus products with those of others.

Such a course led in the Middle Ages to specialisat on by craftsmen who made and sold goods for money. The essential differences between those times and modern times, however, are two: manufacture took place then very largely in response to definite orders, while to-day it is hoped that orders will be forthcoming after manufacture; and, secondly, the growth of competition between rival makers of the same article is, for a variety of reasons, keener to-day.

These changes in the selling process have been occasioned by the normal growth and development of the world. Trade, which was once confined largely to the village, has now developed so as to become world-wide. With the advance of education and culture, human needs have become greater and more insistent, while science has demonstrated cheaper and easier ways of manufacturing goods to satisfy these bigger demands. Cheapness in manufacture allows a larger variety of needs to be satisfied, since a given income can buy more. Humanity wants to satisfy as many needs as possible, and hence really insists on cheapness. But the manufacturer retorts that the cheapness indicated by science can be attained only by mass production of standardised goods.

Thus the world has to sacrifice some variety to gain the advantage of needs cheaply satisfied. Further, it has to agree to production taking place in anticipation of demand, for it would obviously be impossible for any manufacturer to wait before setting his machinery in motion until he had collected sufficient orders to give him the "straight run" required. Anticipation can never wholly coincide with facts, and there are thus possibilities of overproduction of goods for any one market at the price which the public is prepared to pay. Moreover, competition between different manufacturers will exist in the same market, which is limited in its buying power by the incomes of the consumers and the calls upon those incomes. Marketing in the modern sense thus becomes an attempt to promote a steady flow in the consumption of goods already produced, and to control production, both in regard to volume, quality, and style, in such a way that this steady flow is maintained as an outlet for the goods of the firm. Consequently, the marketing policy of any firm concentrates on the channels through which the flow is best directed and on gauging the extent and absorbing capacity of the market.

### WHAT A MARKET IS

TAKE the market first. The word has a variety of meanings covering entirely different aspects of the business of selling. In the sense of the economist it means that area in which the buyers and sellers are sufficiently in communication with one another for one price to exist, and one price only, for the same quality of an article. This, of course, sounds theoretical, but it is really closely allied to practice in the business world because the question of communication is important. The development of communications, both for the transport of goods and for the interchange of correspondence, has widened the market very largely indeed both for the sale of goods retail and wholesale. The wool sold in Britain in the Middle Ages was produced in this country and bought by people who lived here. The advent of cheap transport now brings wool from Australia, New Zealand, South Africa, and the Argentine (and even Iceland) to this country, while the buyers, who compete through agents acting under cable and telegraphic instructions, are domiciled in America and Germany as well as in England. The market has thus become world-wide, and producers of those commodities which now possess a world-wide market have to take into account the facts that competition is world-wide and that their buyers are also world-wide.

An example in retail trade is provided by the market-gardening industry. Before the advent of cheap transport fruit and vegetables had to be grown locally to meet home needs. This is no longer the case. Vegetables, in addition to being imported from France and Holland, are often grown in one part of England and sold in another, so that the tomatoes eaten in Manchester may well have come from the Hertfordshire glass houses.

The sphere in which competition may be met by the producer has thus widened. The essential factor in such widening of competition is cheap transport, and in a number of cases this transport is now easy to obtain. Thus even goods which have transport charges to bear may well make the task of the local manufacturer in marketing his goods even more severe. Against this he, of course, has the same advantage in a widened circle of potential buyers. A fair summing up of the position is that local advantages are no longer of such importance.

### WHAT THE BUSINESS MAN MEANS BY A MARKET

APART from the specialist meanings of the word, which will be examined presently, the business man in talking of his market means something more than the economist whose view has just been discussed. The market to the business man includes not merely the area over which he can sell his goods, but the spending power of the public in that area which can be used to buy his goods. Here, again, considerable difficulties are caused by the complexity of modern life. The purchasing power of an area may decline considerably if in its own productions it experiences a period of bad trade. Again, there is the question of how the surplus will be spent after necessities have been purchased. Luxury goods will all compete for the surplus, and the rival attractions of the home, the motor car, and entertainments are all there to persuade the consumer to use his surplus in different ways. Thus within any area, purchasing power, and the desire to use it in his favour, have to be estimated by the manufacturer in determining his marketing policy. This leads to some very interesting considerations to which reference will be made later.

The next meaning of the market is that of a special place where buyers and sellers meet together, and which is known as a regular meeting-place for the sale of certain types of goods. The familiar street markets, the markets held in the market places, and those held on market days in country towns are all examples of this kind. The Ministry of Agriculture has estimated that in this country there are well over 1300 of these markets. Marketing here is largely the problem of the dealer selling wares in competition with others, and reputation is therefore of more importance than advertisement. Enlargement of sales can come only at the expense of other sellers in the market, and not, as with a manufacturer, by an increase in the area over which he sells or by the introduction of a new product.

In the sense that there is a fixed place for the transaction of business the large wholesale markets are akin in character to these street markets. The main examples in England are the Cotton Exchanges of Liverpool and Manchester, the Wool Exchange, the Mincing Lane Markets, the Metal Exchange, and the Tooley Street Produce Exchange. These are what may be called primary markets in that the goods sold there are largely primary produce, and the buyers are manufacturers or wholesalers who propose to re-market the goods after manufacture or packing. They are the recognised raw material markets in which the producer sells his primary produce. Their working can best be understood by taking an actual example.

Wool is sold to manufacturers by auction at periodic sales. A good deal is thus sold in the producing country, but there is still a large amount sold by auction in this country. The wool is sent by the grower, or his bank which has advanced him money against it, to London, where it is put into the hands of a broker for sale. The broker is a member of the Wool Brokers' Association, who conduct the sales and have their own auction rooms for the purpose. There are six series of sales conducted by the Association during the year at advertised times.

The wool can be entered at any one of these sales by the broker, provided that it has been in London for a specified short period (usually eight days) before the sale starts. The option of entering the wool for the sale is left to the owner. He is guided by considerations of the price it is likely to fetch in the auction. This, of course, cannot be exactly foretold. An idea, however, is gained by the valuation which is sent by the wool-broker to the owner when the wool is put into the broker's hands for sale. This valuation is an estimate made by the broker of the price likely to be bid for the wool in the auction. It is based on an inspection of the sample of the wool which the broker has had drawn for him.

The wool itself is, of course, in warehouse, and the warehouse keeper takes from the bales, which in themselves are roughly cubes of four feet in side, a sample of the wool, which has to be representative of the whole bulk of it. The sample is usually about 1 lb. so that this is no easy matter. The broker judges from this sample according to the length or staple of the wool, its colour, the amount of dirt in it, and its resilience. A comparison of the wool with some recently sold, and his general knowledge of the conditions of supply and demand likely to exist at the next sale, then enable the broker to make his estimate. On the basis of this the owner decides either to offer the wool for sale, or to hold it in warehouse until a later sale if he considers a better price will then be obtained for it.

When it is offered, it is catalogued by the selling broker. Details are given of the quantity and the description of it, including distinguishing marks on the bales, its place of origin, and where it is at present warehoused. These catalogues are available for prospective buyers before the date fixed for the sale. Those who wish to bid for the wool then inspect it on the morning of the sale. In the warehouse the wool is arranged in the same lots as that in which it is catalogued. The bales are slit slightly to enable buyers to pull out the wool and examine it. This inspection goes on through the morning, and then in the afternoon the buyers bid for the wool at the auction sale in Coleman Street, London. The auctioneer is the broker to whom the wool has been entrusted for sale.

The buyers at such auctions come from our own manufacturing districts in Yorkshire, from America, and from the Continent. The sales are the recognised means of buying wool (except, curiously enough, English wool), and thus the producers are assured that all possible buyers are kept in touch with their offerings, and that through public auction the best price is realised. A further advantage, which will be apparent later, is that there is no risk of bad debts on such sales.

## HOW THE COTTON MARKET OPERATES

It is necessary in order to draw generalisations from this form of marketing to consider another case. The marketing of cotton is different from that of wool in that the sales are continuous and are not by auction. In the cotton exchange brokers conclude contracts for the sale of cotton with buyers all day long, and each contract is fixed at a price agreed between the buyer and the broker. The purchase is made on the basis of a definite "grade" of cotton and the actual cotton is not present at the time of the sale. This is an important difference from the case of wool. It is due to the fact that cotton as a raw material can be conveniently sorted into a number of qualities or grades, which are universally accepted when dealings in the material take place. These grades are so well known that it is not necessary to have the actual material present. Both buyer and seller know from the grade mentioned the quality of raw material which will be expected and delivered.

It is in connection with the " futures " market, however, that this grading system is important, for it enables the market to operate smoothly and to provide for manufacturers, and indeed for producers and merchants, a valuable device known as the " hedge." The " futures " market is so called because it comprises those dealings between buyers and sellers at which the price of the article is settled at the time of sale, but the actual delivery to the purchaser and payment by him is postponed until an agreed future date. Thus bales of cotton of a certain grade may be purchased at an agreed price for delivery in, say, three months' time. The purchase by grade enables this to be done. With wool it obviously could not be done except by storing the wool actually shown and purchased. With cotton no storage in this sense is necessary. In fact, the cotton to be delivered may not be in the possession of the seller at the time of the sale. He relies on getting it later, in time to fulfil his side of the contract.

### DEALING IN "FUTURES" HELPS BUSINESS TO RUN SMOOTHLY

THE results of this kind of dealing or its uses are at first a little difficult to see in their entirety. The system does more than assure to a spinner a definite price for the future purchases of yarn, although this in itself may be important if he is under contract for future deliveries of yarn at a specified price. The extra advantage which accrues is that the spinner is enabled to " hedge." If, for example, he is under contract to sell yarn in three months' time at a given price, there is an obvious chance that if he does not buy his raw cotton now its price may move in three months' time either against or for him, resulting in either loss or an unexpected gain on the contract. If at the present moment he buys for forward delivery at the same future date the amount of cotton he needs to fulfil his manufacturing contract at that future date, then these profits or losses are largely eliminated.

There is the further case where raw material is bought now and manufactured for future sale at the prices ruling later. In that case if prices of raw material fall later, so will that of

ıe manufactured article, and the manufacturer will be left
ithout profit on his sales of stock made from raw material
urchased earlier at a higher price. If, however, at the same
ıne that the purchase of raw material is made, a future sale
f raw material is contracted, then, when the time actually
omes and prices have fallen, the manufacturer can buy
otton for delivery against his sale at a lower price than he
ontracted to sell and so makes a profit. This profit compen-
ates for the loss or at least the lack of profit on his manufactured
tock, which he now has to sell on the basis of the lower
rices.

The planter in America or the dealer can take advantage of
his mechanism in a similar manner. The planter knows
hat his costs are and what profit he requires. If the price
efore his crop is ready would cover these costs and yield his
rofit, he can sell forward at that price about the amount
hich he considers his crop will yield. A fall in prices later
eed not then affect him.

The actual process is more complicated and not so ab-
olutely balanced in regard to profits and losses as this outline
uggests, but its purpose is always the same. It protects the
arious parties from the risk of large fluctuations in price, which
ould turn their ordinary operations into losses or unexpected
ains. In consequence this part of the marketing system has
he advantage of relieving manufacturers of risks outside
heir control, and they in turn do not have to cover such risks
y charging higher prices to the consumers.

Those who are willing to buy or sell such "futures" in dealing
ith manufacturers and merchants are known as professional
peculators. They take the risk of the losses, but actually the
sk to them is not so great as might be expected. In the first
lace they are willing to buy or sell only at their own price, and
his will be governed by an intelligent outlook on the future
rend of supply and demand, so far as existing information
ill furnish guidance as to that trend. In the second place,
hey are often asked to accept risks of an opposite nature
hich cancel one another out.

The essentials of this side of marketing are obviously the
rovision of "futures" facilities in these produce markets,
nd the extent to which grading of the product is possible.
rading and the future trade are largely interlocked. Without
ome grading system future trading becomes cumbersome and
omplicated, although not absolutely impossible. Unfortun-

ately all the commodities sold in these produce markets ar not capable of this grading. Wool is an example wher grading is out of the question. Tea sold in the Mincing Lan Exchange is another, as all sales have to take place again o the basis of sampling. Wheat is sold partly in one way an partly in the other. Ivory, again, is sold by auction.

### BENEFITS OFFERED BY THE PRODUCE MARKET

IN this form of marketing of primary produce, the produc markets are largely predominant. They have certain ver obvious advantages. As recognised centres all the chi buyers transact their business there; the prices realised ar those obtained by competition among buyers and sellers the prices are made public each day, so they serve as indicato to the producer. News of supply and demand, and any influ ences of these in the near future, is always given in thes markets, since the brokers make it their business to ascertai these matters. Finally, bad debts are obviated, since on a the exchanges there are strict rules as to payment for purchase on what is known as " prompt " day.

The rules of the exchanges for the conduct of business var both as regards membership of the exchange, settlement day methods of conducting business, etc., but in all cases gre care is taken to see that a high standard of professional condu among the members is maintained. The members are ofte made personally liable for the debts contracted when they a for principals. Machinery for arbitration in cases of disput is provided, and business on the whole goes through in thes exchanges very easily and without much documentation c litigation.

## THE CONSUMER IS THE FINAL MARKET

ALTHOUGH these markets are of importance for the specialised working, the main and the final market is, c course, the great consuming market of the general publi and it is on this that the manufacturer has to concentrate i competition with other manufacturers. This is, of course, market for finished or final goods, and its extent depends upo the national income or possible spending power of the publi

Actually to take the national income as indicative of th volume of the market is wrong, because this estimate neglec three points : first, that some market will probably be foun in the export trade; secondly, that the market is really a series of markets for different goods; and thirdly, that not all the national income is spent. English manufacturers in the past have specially concentrated on the export trade for a great portion of their market. The notices of commercial opportunities abroad in any issue of the *Board of Trade Journal*, even at times when restrictions on export trade are numerous, show that the importance of this market is still very great.

Each consumer splits up his income between a number of different uses. This means that only a part is available for the purchase of the goods of any manufacturer. In some cases the amount spent on particular articles is more or less fixed. The real necessities, such as bread, are illustrations of this. The food bill itself is usually a fairly fixed item in the spending budget. After this come the items of clothing and house room. The surplus left will then be divided between spending and saving. Most of the competition between manufacturers is to attract this spending surplus.

This does not mean, however, that there will not be competition to secure the money spent on different items in the food bill. The familiar "Eat more Fruit" and "Eat more Fish" campaigns are indications of this. Competition for a share of the market becomes even more narrow when different brands of the same article compete for places in the budget.

It is impossible to estimate the total retail trade of the country with any accuracy, and accordingly the monetary extent of the whole market is not certain. The manufacturer of an article is, therefore, confronted when it comes to marketing it, with the following questions. What volume of goods can I expect to sell? Where shall I sell these? To what type of the population? In what quantities? Through what channels? What competitors shall I have? What points in the public view are favourable in my product? How can I get these and the product better known? What services, if any, are needed by retailers or the public in connection with my goods?

### WHICH IS THE BEST WAY TO SELL?[1]

THE way in which marketing takes place in the face of all these problems is best seen by starting at the manufacturer's end. Assuming that he has decided what type and style of

[1] For further discussion, see "Sales Management" (p. 264).

article to make and in what size and at what price—all matters for further consideration later—how will he start immediately to market the goods? There are several channels of distribution through which he may elect to send his goods. He may decide to market them through wholesalers, who in turn sell to retailers, who in turn deal with the final purchase by the public. He may decide to cut out the wholesale trader and market directly to retailers. He may even go a stage further and decide to open his own retail shops. A stage further still leads him to sell straight to the public by what are known as direct mail-order selling methods, although this latter stage is not as a rule a development of selling through his own shops.

The main guiding reason that he will have in any of these courses of action is, of course, the biggest control obtainable over the ultimate sale of his goods. If he sells his goods to a wholesaler and leaves the wholesaler to find the final retail market, he has little control over the ultimate price at which his goods are sold, nor to whom they are sold, nor in what condition they finally reach the public. These are all matters of importance. What volume of demand the wholesaler finds in such circumstances will depend in part at least on what margin of profit he is making on the goods in comparison with other similar lines. Such a policy may result, too, in the wholesaler branding these goods with his own trade mark or brand. In such a case the manufacturer loses his freedom, because the popularity of such goods depends largely on the buying public recognising them by their brand. The manufacturer is then bound to continue his marketing of these goods through that wholesaler.

As a rule a manufacturer will not so tie himself down, but among the smaller manufacturers there may be some who are in part financed by the wholesaler and take their orders for manufacture direct from him. There is then little choice left to these manufacturers but to market through their source of finance. In such cases, too, the wholesaler is really entitled to the market and to any goodwill there may be, since it is his expenditure on advertising, etc., which has created and maintained the market. Such a policy as this in marketing is, however, probably best avoided by a manufacturer, since his own fortunes become too closely linked up with those of a wholesale house, and a change of direction in the wholesale house may bring about a number of other changes adverse to him.

The price consideration is also important, since in a number of articles the quantity sold depends upon the price charged. The principle of elasticity of demand assumes that reduction in price may lead to more or less proportionate increase in demand, according to whether the article is a luxury or a necessity. The obvious cases here are those of bread and motor cars. Changes in the prices of both have taken place. In bread very little increase in demand takes place through a lowering of price, since people want so much and no more of the article. The British motor-car industry, on the contrary, has benefited enormously in output through making continuous reductions in the price of the light car. This economic phenomenon applies to all articles to a greater or less degree. A manufacturer has thus a nice balance to strike between a small margin of profit on the sales of a large number of articles, and a large profit margin on a small set of sales.

The point can be illustrated by the following hypothetical example. The present sales of an article are 10,000 units a month. The cost of production on this small volume is 10d. per article. The gross profit per article is 6d. Will it pay to reduce the gross profit per article to 2d. on present cost if by so doing sales can be pushed to 25,000 a month, with a consequent reduction in production costs of 10 per cent. ? This becomes purely a matter of commercial arithmetic. In this case it would pay to alter the price. The difficulty is that in practice the directors cannot foretell exactly what sales will be under the new conditions. Much less is this possible if the selling is managed by wholesale distributors.

### THE PAY-WHILE-YOU-USE SYSTEM

COMPETITION for the limited spending power of the public has led to the development of another policy in marketing among manufacturers and dealers. This is the hire-purchase or instalment-trading plan, in which the consumer is persuaded to use a certain article which he could not always purchase outright, and pay for it by instalments while he is using it. While this trade grows, and more and more people are persuaded to adopt this method, there is, of course, an increase of sales ; but as soon as the trade has become stable it is doubtful whether any real increase in trade is obtained, except perhaps in the sense that the direction of purchasing power is altered, and people buy things which if they had been obliged to save the money first, they could never have afforded.

In practice the operation is always the same. The article is delivered on payment of an initial deposit and the balance is paid by instalments. In law, however, there is a difference, in that a hire-purchase agreement really leaves the user as the hirer and not the owner of the article until the agreed number of hiring payments have been made, while an instalment-purchase scheme makes the user the owner immediately, with the obligation to make a certain number of payments to complete the purchase.

The manufacturer adopting such a method of marketing must, of course, consider the question of finance. If the consumer does not pay immediately, the money must come from elsewhere. Is he prepared to advance the extra money himself or can he find some other business prepared to undertake the work? Who, too, will bear the risk of default in payments by the user?

To discuss these points thoroughly would be to embark on a detailed matter of law and commercial procedure. It is sufficient to say here that sometimes the manufacturer does provide the extra funds; sometimes he passes the matter over to a financial house to settle. If he deals with finance himself, it often results in his establishing a separate but subsidiary finance company to handle the work. This company will probably make dealers, who sell the articles to users on deferred terms, guarantee the final payment by their customers. The disadvantage of having the matter dealt with by a purely outside concern is that the connection between manufacturer and/or dealer and customer is broken, and the trade policy of the financial company, in so far as payment, etc., is concerned, may not be that of the manufacturer.

## THE IMPORTANCE OF GETTING FRESH GOODS TO THE PUBLIC

ANOTHER important point is that the goods should reach the public in a fresh condition. This is particularly true of the confectionery trades, and to practically the same extent of the food trades. If fresh goods are to be on the shelves of the retailer, then the manufacturer is really the best person to see that they are fresh, since the whole of repeat orders will be bound up in public preference for his goods. In such cases, again, the wholesaler has disadvantages as a channel of distribution, except that here the disadvantage is less real, since the wholesaler, too, has an interest in seeing that the goods reach the public in proper condition.

It is largely this question of freshness which is responsible, for example, for manufacturers of confectionery offering to replace any of their goods found to be in an unsatisfactory condition. All retailers who can possibly stock the goods in question must be induced to do so, in fact, if the trade is to be successfully carried out. In such goods the public insist on having near-at-hand supplies. For goods that are purchased less regularly it is possible to have fewer points of distribution, since in such cases the public are prepared to travel farther in order to buy the articles they require.

Elimination of the wholesaler as an unnecessary link in the chain of distribution has been talked of for a long time. Some of the reasons which make such elimination impossible have already been given. The wholesaler has behind him an army of retailers and in consequence a ready market. Often the cost of holding the stock of goods in the retail shops is largely borne by the wholesaler through the credit he grants. If the manufacturer seeks direct retail sales, is he prepared to replace these functions of the wholesaler? Is he prepared, moreover, to assume the risk of carrying a stock of goods which may prove more than the demand, or in the fashion trades, unfashionable? This risk-bearing aspect in the fashion trades is one of the chief reasons to-day for the persistence of the wholesale warehouses in this line of marketing.

Direct marketing to retailers in its turn brings its own problems. There is, of course, the quite difficult administrative problem of building up the necessary sales force to obtain distribution of the articles. This is essential, as any direct selling to retailers will undoubtedly bring in its train the antagonism of the wholesale trade, and the decision to market to retailers direct will in consequence probably entail an actual break with the wholesale trade.

Apart, however, from this, marketing through this channel brings other problems, such as the terms to be allowed to retailers by way of credit and discount, the number of stockists to be allowed in an area, the advertising to be done, the support to be given to retailers in their sales efforts, and the type of retailer through whom the consuming public is to be reached. If retailers are to sell the manufacturer's article, they will have to have their own sales efforts reinforced by efforts on the part of the manufacturer. This will lead the manufacturer as a rule to advertise his articles.

But advertising is not easily concentrated on his particular article, unless it has some distinguishing mark. Thus the practice of branding or using trade marks has been adopted. This enables the manufacturer's own particular product to be singled out and advertised with success. The branding is carried through all the advertising in national newspapers, on hoardings, etc., and is, of course, carried conspicuously on the article itself or on its packing. Such a policy of branding leads the public to expect a certain quality as standard. In the early days of the policy this standard quality was not always supplied, but in these days it is practically universal.[1]

### FIXING THE PRICE OF THE GOODS

A FURTHER advantage to the manufacturer who adopts this policy is that he is able to fix the price of his article for all retailers, since again it is usually carried conspicuously both in the advertising and on the article. This results in the profit margin of the retailer being limited, and in this connection the manufacturer has to consider what that margin of profit shall be. It must obviously be enough to make it worth the while of the retailer to push the goods. It must compare favourably, too, with the profit offered in similar goods by other manufacturers. On the other hand, the lower the price the more the public may buy. Ultimately the decision is probably made with an eye to the possible volume the retailer can be expected to sell, together with the absence or presence of competitive lines. Where the turnover is large, the margin is likely to be smaller than where the turnover is lower.

This consideration applies equally to the credit period to be allowed when the manufacturer sells direct to retailers. Formerly, it was said that manufacturers required immediate payment in order to finance purchases of further raw materials, etc., and to save the employment of additional capital out on credit. With the advent of the joint stock company as a form of manufacturing enterprise, the provision of extra capital for this purpose of financing has become of less importance, since it is more easily obtained.

Then comes the question as to how much extra publicity is required by the retailer to help him in selling the goods. Window display material and counter stands may be considered necessary, as well as the provision of either free samples or gift vouchers. This type of aid is usually more necessary in the initial selling stages of a campaign, than it is when the

[1] For further discussion, see " Sales Management " (p. 263).

product is firmly established, but even then it has to be kept well in mind and a certain volume of it provided. Advertisements, in which the name of the local dealer is included in addition to the main manufacturer's advertisement, have also to be considered.

The result is that while in this kind of marketing the manufacturer has obviously more control over the price of his goods and the volume of his sales, he has also to face more expense in doing the work.

The number of channels through which the manufacturer is going to distribute has still not been decided. The choice here lies between the ordinary private retail trader, the multiple shop concern, the department store, and the multi-department store. Choice must necessarily be made largely according to the type of article in question, and the place where the public will normally desire to buy it. The department store and the multi-department store are, of course, largely the centres of what may be called the shopping expedition trade. Thus for articles requiring a large distribution where purchases are frequent, they are not a suitable type of outlet, but they are good for the higher priced articles of less frequent demand. They are suited also to the fancy goods trade, where demand is largely inspired by the sight of the goods.

Where the department store and especially the multi-department store, in the suburbs and provinces is doing a less high class trade, these considerations lose some weight, but it nevertheless remains true that, as a whole, goods required frequently are better distributed through channels nearer the home of the consumer. The multiple shop is thus in a better position with regard to some goods. The difficulty then, however, is the general type of trade done by the multiple stores. Will the manufacturer find exactly his type of customer as a usual customer of the multiple store? Moreover, such companies may ask for special arrangements as to price, etc., as a condition of stocking such goods. In the one-price multiple stores, however, a large turnover may be found, since these shops are nearly always full of potential customers, and also because their policy is now to extend into the smaller towns. The danger here is, that if the manufacturer puts a special line into these stores, he may antagonise private retailers and damage the sales of his ordinary lines in their shops. Policy in marketing in this respect is thus sometimes difficult to determine.

Packing, transport, and delivery are other matters requirin attention in marketing direct to retailers. Packing must b of a kind to enable the dealer to make a good window c counter display, and yet be economical from the manufacturin point of view, and enable the goods to be closely packed fc transport.

Delivery must be so arranged that retailers are not bound t carry larger stocks than necessary. The tendency in reta trade to-day is more and more to practise hand-to-mout buying, and manufacturers have got to be prepared to provid retailers with frequent and small consignments of goods i they desire to keep their goodwill and obtain markets for thei products.

One of the best organised trades in this direction is probabl the London wholesale and manufacturing chemists' trade where any drug ordered in the morning by telephone is de livered the same day. A further endeavour to obtain mor efficient and cheaper marketing has been made recently by th railway companies and certain manufacturers in conjunction Bulk deliveries are taken by the railways to certain mai centres, where the railway companies have built warehouse which are let to the manufacturers. At these warehouses th manufacturers split the bulk consignments from the factory into individual orders for the district, and each order is ther taken from the warehouse and delivered by motor van. This has not only speeded up delivery of the goods but has resulted in saving of distributive costs.

## HOW THE PUBLIC'S NEEDS ARE INVESTIGATED

IN selecting retail outlets for his marketing the manufacturer is, however, handicapped to some extent by lack of knowledge of the type and volume of trade done by any particular re-tailer. In an experimental census conducted in 1926 in the U.S.A. (by the U.S. Bureau of the Census) some interesting facts emerged. One was that 37 per cent. of the independent stores examined accounted for 88 per cent. of the trade done by that type of store. Another showed the average *per capita* purchases. The inference is obvious to the manufacturer. Concentration of outlets should in some respects be kept in mind. We have, however, no census of trade done, apart from some Board of Trade figures, showing percentage changes in retail trade in different types of shops.

When a manufacturer has set in being machinery which

will fulfil all these necessary matters in marketing he has not, however, finished. For a time such machinery will ensure for him a share of the trade being done and a smooth flow of his goods to markets. But conditions are always changing, and the habits and tastes of the public are so flexible that continuous adjustments are necessary to meet new needs. Marketing is not complete when a certain number of retailers have been persuaded to stock goods. The final sale is to the public, and it is only if retailers find that they can sell goods that they will be prepared to place repeat orders. In other words, the manufacturer has to please the public, and it is necessary for him to be always in touch with public taste.

This is obviously a difficult matter, and it usually resolves itself into making periodic tests to determine public preferences and the reason for those preferences. The tests that are made are known as Market Research. A technique is gradually growing up in this branch of marketing which is replacing empirical by scientific methods. The type of information the manufacturer obviously requires to know, so as to maintain and extend the volume of his sales, is the trend of his competitor's sales, the areas in which his sales are strong and weak, the reason why preference is given to his brand of the article or to that of a competitor, the uses to which the public is putting his product, the price they usually want to pay for the article, their chief reason for its purchase, any complaints that there may be about its quality or uses that could be put right, any new uses for it which the public do not sufficiently realise, and the method by which the manufacturer can most economically convey all such information to his public.

Obviously it is impossible for a manufacturer to obtain all this information continuously from all sections of consumers. He must, therefore, make tests with certain sections of the population from time to time (often at the rate of once a year) to obtain the information.

In the main there may be three types of information desired. The manufacturer may desire to know his position in the market in relation to his competitors, and whether this is improving or deteriorating. Knowledge may be required in the second place as to why sales are stationary or declining, either in particular areas or over the country as a whole. Thirdly, the manufacturer may desire to know how to increase the sales of an existing product, or the best method of introducing a new one and its possible sales. An auxiliary use of such information is obviously to help the manufacturer in solving some of the marketing problems already discussed.

### THINGS THE MANUFACTURER WANTS TO KNOW

THE methods employed in obtaining information to answer these points consist of the isssue of questionnaires and the use of demonstrations. The questionnaire method is the one chiefly used but there are dangers in its application which require skill to avoid. Search should be made to see if the information required is published in any form. For example, if all that is required is to estimate the purchasing power of a particular new territory, it will not pay to spend perhaps £200 in conducting an investigation, when a sufficiently good pointer is available in the number of motor car licences issued, or in the rateable value of the district. Only if the problem relates to something concerning the manufacturer alone is it likely to be necessary to resort to the market research method.

If this is necessary, then the questions to be asked must be drawn up in such a form as to elicit easily and completely the information required. These questions will be put either personally or by post to a number of people who use or might use the article concerned, and also to a number of dealers in it. They must in consequence be easily understood and not ambiguous. Most of such questionnaires, too, should be short, as people will not be bothered to answer long strings of questions.

### WHAT SHOULD BE CONTAINED IN A QUESTIONNAIRE

THESE principles are best illustrated by taking a concrete case, for example, a manufacturer contemplating the introduction of a new domestic cleaner. The type of questionnaire would be as follows :

CLEANER INVESTIGATION

* District :
* Class : (A, B, or C)

1. Do you use a cleaner ?
2. What brand of cleaner ?
3. How often do you buy ?
4. What price do you usually pay ?
5. Why do you buy the particular brand ?
6. Where do you buy it ?

* To be filled in by investigator.

From this it can be seen that the questions are simple and limited, but each is directed to obtain specific information. From the answers knowledge is gained of the leading brands of household cleaners on the market in order of popularity and in magnitude of popularity, seeing that the number of users of each kind will then be known. In addition, the size of packet usually bought, the price paid and the main uses and reasons for use will be revealed.

### WHOM SHALL HE ASK ?

To whom are these questions sent? They cannot be sent to every household in the country for obvious reasons of cost. The object of the whole proceeding is to obtain as truthful a picture of the state of the market as possible. Thus, if every household cannot be approached, those that are asked must if possible be representative of the whole. The science of statistics shows that 5 per cent. of anything taken at random will give a view of that thing which is representative of the whole. Thus, 5 per cent. of households would give the answer. But if we assume a total in this country of eight million households, and an average over all cost per inquiry as low as 1s. 3d. we still should have to spend £500,000 to obtain the information. Such a course is then impossible. Random selection cannot be made. In consequence, a careful selection of a much smaller number has to be made so that the results from such inquiries may be representative of all.

To do this the classes of consumers are often split into A, B, and C groups. C represents those with under £250 per annum income—largely the weekly wage-earners in the manual and lower clerical grades; B, those with incomes between £250 and £500; and A, those with incomes above £500. If the article is used by all sections—as a cleaner would be—a number of inquiries proportionate to the numbers in each group will then be made in all three groups. If the article is used predominantly by one group—for example, foreign cruises in the A group—then practically all the inquiries will be concentrated into that group.

A further allocation is necessary geographically. The inquiries must be spread over the country as a whole, since in different parts of the country different habits and different preferences exist. Areas must be chosen to give results which bring out these preferences if they are important. For example, southern consumers prefer butter, as a rule, in packets and the

Empire or home produced variety. In the North-east, however, there is apparently a preference for butter from kegs and from Denmark. The areas chosen must, of course, be as representative of different occupations as possible. Actually this task is not so difficult as it sounds since most of the population of this country is concentrated in towns. Unless, therefore, the article is one predominantly used in the country (for example, an agricultural fertiliser) inquiries in a few well chosen towns will in most cases suffice.

From what has been said it can be seen that each inquiry must be considered by itself and a decision made as to the number, allocation, and areas of inquiries. Much research is successfully carried through by a really surprisingly small number of inquiries concentrated in about eight to twelve towns.

The inquiries may be made either in person or by letter asking for a return of the questionnaire duly completed. Personal inquiries by a special person known as an investigator are more expensive but produce better results, since the investigator, if he knows his work, is likely to obtain answers from at least 90 per cent. of the people on whom he calls. Postal requests unless sent to specially selected people rarely elicit a response of more than 15 per cent. even when stamped addressed replies are enclosed. In addition, the investigator often finds that in the course of his talk some new point of preference, some new use, or some unseen objection to the article comes to light.

### WHAT THE RETAILER THINKS ABOUT SALES

RESULTS from such inquiries are, of course, not mathematically correct, but they do give the manufacturer what he wants, that is the general trend of the market, and the relative position of his own product to that of competitors. In this country the procedure is comparatively recent and good results are obtained. In America the idea has been somewhat overdone, and the consumer is inclined to resent being asked and to refuse to answer.

Information obtained by this method is usually checked by a parallel investigation among dealers in the article. An investigator calls on them with a similar list of questions, and the manufacturer is thus enabled to get a view of the market from their angle, as well as to check to some extent the answers received from the consumers. Care has to be taken, however, to discount some of the answers. Thus, in answering a question as to why the public buys a certain brand of an article, the predominant answer from retailers will usually be because they push the sales of it. From the answers of the consumers, however, the reason for purchase that the dealer recommended the article will be much less frequently given. A dealer is naturally prone to attribute sales to his own efforts. An amusing instance in the opposite direction is given when the public are asked how often they buy such things as toothbrushes. A desire to impress the investigator with the cleanliness of their habits leads them to give an answer which shows a much greater frequency than the answer given by the dealer from his experience of public buying.

The tabulation of results and the combinations and permutations of the answers to questions is obviously a long work. The combinations of answers to questions can be illustrated by taking our supposed cleaner questionnaire and showing how some of the results from it may be obtained by arrangement and tabulation.

## TABULAR INFORMATION BY DISTRICTS

From Question 1.—Percentage of families using cleaners of all brands, together with investigator's remarks on class of family and the percentage in each class.

From Question 2.—Number using each brand in each class.

| Class. | A. | B. | C. |
|---|---|---|---|
| Brand A. . | | | |
| ,, B. . | | | |
| ,, C. . | | | |
| ,, D. . | | | |

Gives the class where sales are highest or indicates classes where more sales may be possible. May also show difference in class sales between different brands. If so, inquiry is started immediately as to what characteristic causes this.

FROM QUESTIONS 4 and 2.—Usual price paid for each brand.

| d. | Brand A. | B. | C. | D. |
|---|---|---|---|---|
| $2\frac{1}{2}$ | | | | |
| $5\frac{1}{2}$ | | | | |
| 6 | | | | |
| 10 | | | | |

FROM QUESTION 4.—Usual price paid by each class.

| d. | A. | B. | C. |
|---|---|---|---|
| $2\frac{1}{2}$ | | | |
| $5\frac{1}{2}$ | | | |
| 6 | | | |
| 10 | | | |

Gives generally the best-priced package, while price paid by each class will show (in conjunction with the first table) whether it is worth while concentrating on a particular price for one special class of consumer.

FROM QUESTIONS 3 and 4.—Amount spent per year (by calculation). Also whether there is a class of heavy and of light users or whether use is fairly regular.

| Times Bought. | $2\frac{1}{2}$d. | | | $5\frac{1}{2}$d. | | |
|---|---|---|---|---|---|---|
| | A. | B. | C. | A. | B. | C. |
| Weekly . | | | | | | |
| Fortnightly | | | | | | |
| Monthly . | | | | | | |

FROM QUESTION 6.—Distributive method by class.

| | A. | B. | C. |
|---|---|---|---|
| Grocer (private) . | | | |
| Oil shop . . | | | |
| Chain store . . | | | |

FROM QUESTIONS 4 and 6.—Distributive method by price.

| | 2½d. | 5½d. | 6d. | 10d. |
|---|---|---|---|---|
| Grocer (private) . | | | | |
| Oil shop . . | | | | |
| Chain store . . | | | | |

Gives information as to best distributive method, provided that that method has not got disadvantages from other points of view.

Such a tabulation is simple when compared with what is ·ften done. The point of any combination of answers to uestions is to give the manufacturer a specific piece of nformation which will be of use to him in directing his narketing policy. Often the combination of answers will e worked out by the use of key numbers to each question nd each possible answer, and then by the use of a sorting nd tabulating machine based on the Hollerith principle.

One obvious use of all such information is in the direction f advertising policy. The answers from each class of onsumer on why they use a particular brand can obviously orm the basis of the advertising appeal to that class of onsumer generally. This really leads to another use of the narket research idea, namely, finding out what papers are ead by the different classes of consumers and to what extent n each case in the way of circulation. Such information is ow available about some of the national and provincial laily and weekly papers as a result of questionnaire work and the use of business statistics of sales, etc. Advertise can also obtain such information from the Audit Bureau Circulations, which is an office set up for this purpose l the Incorporated Society of British Advertisers Ltd.

The work which this market research involves is real outside the normal scope of a manufacturer's activities. is usually, therefore, not undertaken by him directly, but performed for him by a firm of advertising agents who mal a speciality of collecting and having available all gener marketing data. They are, in addition, specialists in tl work of market research, and undertake it for manufacture as and when required for a given fee. A valuable adjunct such service is that they usually have an analysis of rece press advertising expenditure of each important manufactur of a proprietary line. Thus the manufacturer is made awa of the trend of the expenditure of his rivals.

## THE TEAM SPIRIT APPEARS IN TRADE

INTENSE competition between manufacturers of differe brands of the same article for the limited spending pow of the public has been a feature of this century. Whe one manufacturer has been strong enough, rivals have ofte been driven out of the market by "cut-throat" competitio and a virtual monopoly secured for the strongest man left.

In other cases, where strength has been more equall matched, competition has often been followed by agreemen Rivals have realised that further competition meant the rui of all, and have, in consequence, come to agreement among themselves as to the marketing policies to be pursued in th future. These agreements vary both as to their strictnes and as to their subject matter. Price-fixing, partition markets, selling organisations, output quotas, trust and cart formation, and organised marketing have all been brough into existence.

The stop to cut-price warfare is usually made when th competitors meet together and agree upon minimum price to be charged, or a division of markets in which each is to b left free from competition. The length of agreement depend often on the state of trade, and agreements which are nc strict at their inception are often broken as soon as trad opportunities increase; alternatively, when trade is ver depressed and the manufacturer feels that his output must b

›ld to cover part of his standing charges, he is tempted to
:ll below the minimum price either openly or by means of
:bates or discounts allowed.

### WHAT IS MEANT BY A CARTEL

A TIGHTER agreement then follows, and the cartel form of
organisation comes into being. This is usually an
rganisation which either shares out the orders received
nong the manufacturers in the agreement, or takes over their
utput and attends to the marketing of it. It may go further
nd control production by allocating to each manufacturer
the association a definite volume of output. This cartel
rganisation is governed, as a rule, by the manufacturers. It
ften forms a separate company.

In the cement industry in this country combination for
tionalisation of the industry took place as early as 1900
nong a group of companies. Another set of companies
as added to the agreement some years later, and the two
roups are known as the Associated Portland Cement Manu-
cturers Ltd. and the British Portland Cement Manufacturers
td. Together they have a selling organisation which is
ell known to the British public as the Cement Marketing
o. Ltd. The tobacco industry and the Light Castings
ssociation are other examples where agreements relating to
arketing exist.

A number of trades now have such agreements, and in
any cases they not only cover the home market, but deal
ith overseas markets and often with former rival manu-
cturers overseas as well. There are, of course, many
conomic arguments for and against any form of selling or
arketing agreements, but the fact remains that unregulated
mpetition leading to over-production, with its consequent
aste of effort, must definitely be bad and to the extent that
me form of agreement such as this does regulate the flow
f goods to market it must be considered good.

A somewhat different type of agreement on price-fixing
ists in certain retail trades where manufacturers and retailers
mbine to fix minimum prices at which all retailers must
:ll the articles concerned. Such agreements are prevalent
the grocery and drug trades particularly. The outline of
rocedure is that an association is formed of manufacturers
nd retailers who enter into an agreement, the manufacturers
supply only those retailers who agree to sell at a fixed

price, and the retailers not to sell below a certain price. An retailer who sells below the price, and is found doing s may have his supplies of that article completely stopped, c he may be fined by the association, or the more drasti penalty of complete cessation of supplies from all manu facturers may be imposed. The object of such an agreemen is to protect retailers from unfair competition and to enforc the price at which the manufacturer advertises the article.

A protection of a different form is given in the case c the newspaper distributing trade. Here, in order to ensur adequate trade to the retailers, their number in any particula area is limited.

## HOW ORDERLY MARKETING CAN HELP THE FARMER

ORDERLY marketing, as it has come to be called, has applie more recently in regard to the sale of raw materials an of agricultural produce. The primary producer has usuall suffered from the disadvantage that his crops come to marke at the same time of year as those of his competitors, and tha he is forced to sell them then in order to raise funds to con tinue the work ; he has to pay labour, buy seeds and fertilisers and often pay off bank loans. The result of this mass sellin at harvest-time by a vast number of producers is, of course to depress market prices against them. If it were possibl to hold some of the supplies off the market and sell them later, this depression of prices would not be so marked.

Private attempts to store harvest produce have been mad in various parts. In particular, schemes have been in exist ence and have worked well in Australia and Canada. Th main basis of such schemes is that a central organisatio (often on a co-operative basis) of the farmers themselves i able to raise funds against the security of the collective crop of the members. The members then deliver the crop to th organisation, which immediately advances against it a certai agreed percentage of its value. The crop is then stored b the association, and marketing takes place according to th demand and the prices ruling over the whole year. At th end of that time the balance-sheet is made up, and the balanc remaining over from sale is distributed among the member as the balance of payment for their deliveries of produce In this way a regular flow of produce to the market is assure and the schemes have often worked well.

One essential feature for success, however, is that th

whole of the crop shall be disposed of in the course of the crop year. Accumulations carried over, ruin the scheme, and not simply because they add to the supply of the next year. An accumulation of this nature means that the price has been maintained at an unduly high level by withholding part of the supply. The result of the high price obtained by the farmer is to cause him to think that such prices can continue, and, in consequence, he proceeds to produce more in the hope of getting the high price for the whole. Obviously the result of this is to overload the association with produce which it cannot sell at the level of prices required, and either prices have to be drastically reduced, or stocks accumulate, and the question arises as to whether some control over the acreage to be planted is necessary.

It is in connection with this organised and orderly marketing that Government interference has taken place. Apart from legislation with regard to shop hours and the quality of goods, the Government had not hitherto concerned themselves with marketing. Then, owing to the serious position in the coal industry caused by over-production, a change of policy occurred and the Coal Mines Act of 1930 was passed. This is a complicated measure dealing with a number of matters concerning the industry, but its interest from the point of view of marketing is that it establishes what is virtually a cartel form of organisation for the industry. A central organisation fixes the total production and allocates this to districts. In each district, a district organisation allocates the amounts to be produced by each pit. Any surplus production results in fines which go to compensate those who have not produced to the full. Minimum selling prices are also fixed, and are now co-ordinated by the Central Committee. Export and inland sales quotas are also fixed for each of the seventeen districts.

### THE "NATIONAL MARK" AIDS AGRICULTURE

WITH regard to agricultural produce the Government have taken steps to deal with both quality and marketing. The grading of produce has been brought up to a high degree of use and efficiency through the "National Mark," while marketing on an orderly basis is now being provided for a number of commodities under the Agricultural Marketing Acts of 1931 and 1933.

As far as Government policy is concerned, these Acts are

revolutionary. They provide for a form of joint marketing by all the producers through a form of marketing board, and, when this is in being, private marketing is disallowed; in some cases the proceeds of all sales are collected by the Marketing Board and distributed afterwards to the producers.

The system is that any body of producers of an agricultural article, who are the main producers of the article, may submit to the Minister of Agriculture a scheme for the marketing of their product through a marketing board. The Minister has to advertise the scheme and to hear objections to it according to the procedure set out. Modifications to the scheme may be made, and then the Minister, if he "is satisfied that the scheme will conduce to the more efficient production and marketing of the regulated product" (21–22 Geo. 5 Ch. 42 Sec. 1 (8)), puts it before Parliament for approval. After approval is gained, a board of the producers is set up with two co-opted official representatives. The duty of this board is to register all producers of the article who apply for registration, and to take a poll of all such registered producers to see whether the scheme shall be operated. If the voting on the poll shows two-thirds in number and two-thirds in quantity of registered producers in favour, then the scheme operates.

As soon as this is the case, a non-registered producer will be prohibited from selling the product. The Board which will now be responsible for the various parts of the marketing may, according to the width of the powers given to it in the scheme, buy the product, force registered producers to sell through the agency of the board, and fix prices, volume of sales, and grades.

A further provision is that Agricultural Marketing Reorganisation Commissions may be set up by the Minister charged with the duty of preparing schemes for the marketing of a particular product. Such schemes are then to be submitted by the Minister to the producers of the article for their consideration. Recent schemes so devised have been for live stock and poultry products.

The 1933 Act provides for the regulation through the Board of Trade of imports of agricultural products which are the subject, so far as home produce is concerned, of marketing schemes of the kind outlined above, or where such a scheme would be hampered if an import regulation order were not made. Under this Act, too, a Market Supply Committee has been set up to make recommendations to the Minister as to steps which should be taken for regulating the supply of agricultural products in the United Kingdom.

The 1931 Act has been implemented by the drawing up of schemes for the marketing of potatoes, hops, pigs, bacon, and, of course, milk. A feature of the milk scheme is the pooling of receipts so that milk producers in areas where much milk is sold for manufacturing are likely to obtain better prices for it than they would otherwise be able to do. The provisions of these schemes are complex, but the main purpose of all is to replace irregular individual marketing by a collective form. They have not yet gone far enough for it to be decided whether their working can be considered as satisfactory.

## BOOKS FOR THOSE INTERESTED IN MARKETING

ANY one who is interested in the details of these various Government schemes cannot do better than refer to the official publications issued by H.M. Stationery Office, namely, the Coal Mines Act, 1930, and the orders made under that Act, and the Agricultural Marketing Acts, 1931 and 1933, and the schemes formulated in accordance with those Acts. A good book on the produce market is *Organised Produce Markets*, by Prof. Smith, of Birmingham University (Longman). *Instalment Trading*, by C. Bolling (Pitman), is a useful book on that subject. *Market Research*, by Redmayne and Weeks (Butterworth), is a standard book in its field, and the books by R. Simmat on *Market Research* and *The Principles and Practice of Marketing* can also be well recommended. More general in scope is *Wholesale and Retail Trade*, by W. Campbell (Pitman).

# SALES MANAGEMENT BRINGS NEW STANDARDS INTO SELLING

*by CHRISTOPHER E. JACKSON, B.Sc.(Econ.), Lecturer on Marketing and Sales Management at the City of London College.*

SALES management, as a distinct branch of business administration, is a recent discovery. Not that selling is a new thing; but the emergence of selling as a vital business problem is new. For hundreds of years goods have been made, and made with the express object of being sold to others. The advent of machinery brought about an enormous increase in their number and variety. But for many years the selling of these products did not present any great problem to the producers. Sales did not need managing; they managed themselves. The manufacturer concentrated all his resources and his energy upon production—upon producing more goods, better goods, and cheaper goods. The best brains and the highest inventive genius were called in to his aid. Consequently, this branch of management reached a high state of perfection.

As the quantity and more especially the variety of goods increased, the more difficult became the task of getting rid of them. Consumers were finding themselves with a margin for expenditure over and above the bare necessities of life and with a multitude of new goods from which to choose. Demand for these newer types of goods fluctuated violently without apparent rhyme or reason. Unfortunately, industry, with its capital locked up in large factories and expensive machinery, had become much less able to adjust itself economically to changes in demand. This growing element of uncertainty in demand on the one side, and the increased rigidity of production on the other, made the problem of selling both more important and more complicated.

### SALES MANAGEMENT BECOMES A SCIENCE

THE manufacturer had perforce to turn his attention to this side of his business. Thus was born the sales manager. At first, the sole duty of this official was conceived to be the selling of whatever the factory chose to turn out. The degree of his success in achieving this end was the sole measure of his ability and of his value to his employers. How he was to do it was largely a matter for him to decide—presumably he was to rely upon a succession of bright ideas and schemes floating into his brain from the void.

Time and experience is helping the business world towards a clearer and saner conception of the functions of sales management. Production, sales, and finance are parts of a single unit—not separate and entirely unrelated activities. Sales management is no longer viewed as being a question of brain-waves, but as an activity of extreme complexity—a problem which demands the application of scientific principles—research, analysis, experimentation, and planning.

As yet, sales management has developed no accepted and well-defined technique. There is, indeed, no common agreement as to its scope. It is only within the last few decades that the subject has been studied with any semblance of a scientific approach. Certain American universities have done valuable work, but so far only the fringe has been touched. Its study bristles with innumerable difficulties, not the least of which is the extraordinary degree of reticence on the part of the business man, particularly in Great Britain. Nevertheless, whilst we have very much to learn—and unlearn—there are certain parts of sales management upon which light can be thrown and of which every student of business should have some knowledge.

### THE FUTILITY OF ENTRUSTING A BUSINESS TO FATE

It is the height of folly for any business man to rely on his luck in this respect and to allow the course of his business to be guided by the winds of chance. Success lies in the attainment of objectives. How, then, can a business succeed if it does not define its objectives and the general lines along which it intends to work ? The problem of selling its goods or services is common to all businesses. To some it presents a much less difficult proposition than to others ; but to all it is of paramount importance. It is not enough to say that the business is to sell cheese or motor cars or insurance—or even that it intends to make a profit by the sale of these.

The fundamental purpose of every business, manufacturing or distributive, is to render a service to the community. Profits are but the reward for doing so. That should be the foundation-stone upon which any sales policy is built. In order to carry out this object it is imperative to define clearly what precisely is this service, to what particular section of the community it is to be rendered, what the special needs of that section are, and, finally, how the task may most efficiently be tackled.

The policy may be written or merely understood. It may be brief or may be detailed. But it is clear that it should involve decisions upon such points as the nature of the goods or services to be sold; the type of consumer to be catered for; the channels through which the commodity is to be distributed; the general lines on which prices are to be determined; the general terms on which the commodity is to be sold. To give an example. "The firm will sell packeted breakfast foods to the lower middle and working classes in the United Kingdom through all retail grocers who order at least one case of six dozen at a time—otherwise through wholesalers. Sales will be made by personal visits of salesmen to the above, supported by advertising to both consumer and distributor. Retail prices are to be fixed and discounts for quantity allowed, providing a slight advantage to wholesalers for equal quantities. Net cash monthly account with 2½ per cent. discount for cash within seven days." This is merely a skeleton of a policy and could usefully be amplified.

It should be borne in mind that businesses are normally intended to have long lives. It is advisable, therefore, to lay down on broad lines a long-period policy to indicate the ultimate goal, as well as a short-period policy adapted to existing conditions. The latter should be so framed as eventually to lead up to the former. At cross-roads we must decide which of the several paths we are to follow: unless we know our ultimate destination and its general direction, we cannot choose aright. The line of least resistance is not always the one to take. It may, indeed, impede further progress.

## WHEN EXTRA SALES DIMINISH PROFITS

It might be thought that the aim of a business was to sell as much as possible. Beyond a certain point, however, extra sales may be secured only at a cost greater than the gross profit arising from them. It might with greater truth be said that the aim is to secure the maximum net profit. But methods calculated to produce the maximum net profit this year may easily reduce or even destroy our chances of profit in the future, so we must take a long view.

Continued progress is essential to the life of a business, and continued progress is dependent upon satisfied consumers and distributors. Proof that this fact is being increasingly realised is evident in the growth of the principle of service. The old idea that, once the goods have been handed over to the customer, whether he be consumer or distributor, and payment has been obtained, the sales department's job is finished, is fast going by the board. Selling organisations are following up their sales, educating the customer, and helping him by advice and practical assistance to get the best out of the product he has bought.

Whilst the sales department is a very important section of the business, it is not the whole of it. As in the healthy and rational human being, so in the sound business enterprise, every part must work in harmony with the rest. The co-ordination of the various sections of the business can only be secured where a definite policy exists.

For every factory there exists a certain rate of production at which it can work most efficiently and economically. Any variation of this, above or below, leads to a rise in unit costs. Hence, the factory looks to the sales department to maintain an even flow of orders at this level. But such an ideal is very rarely attainable. The demand for any given commodity fluctuates, often violently, not only from year to year but from season to season. It is obviously much easier and less costly for the sales department to secure business in conformity with this ebb and flow of demand.

Important questions of policy are involved in the task of reconciling these two opposing positions. Should the factory adjust itself to the normal inflow of orders, with all its fluctuations, or should selling effort be applied in such a way as to meet the full demands of production ? The former would involve a rise in the costs of production ; the latter in those of distribution. The decision will be influenced by the nature of the commodity and the market. The net profit for the business as a whole, due regard being paid to future progress, must be the criterion ; and this takes into consideration the costs both of production and of distribution.

With certain commodities the situation may most effectively be met by limiting sales or sales pressure during the very good periods, and increasing effort during bad ones ; or by adjusting prices or credit terms in order to attract orders when they are hardest to secure. With others, it may be possible and desirable to build up stocks during the off season, to be used up during the good season when sales are greater than current production. The balance may be achieved by finding new uses for the product during slack times or even by putting out new products with a reversed season, appealing to the same market and going through the same channels. It may be possible to discover a new market—perhaps a foreign one—where the season is different.

Therefore, whilst the best modern practice bases its production programme as well as its purchases of raw materials and other products required for the process of manufacture upon estimates of sales, a definite line of policy should be laid down and the estimates be drawn up in conformity with it.

### HOLDING THE BALANCE BETWEEN THE IDEAL AND THE PRACTICAL

A MULTIPLICATION of lines, varieties, sizes, and so on likewise leads to rising costs of production. So also do changes in old products and the introduction of new ones. But the salesman finds it easier to get orders if he can offer a wide range and satisfy individual requirements. This conflict between simplification and standardisation on the one hand, and multiplication and flexibility on the other, must be decided on broad lines by the general management and a true balance held between the desirable and the feasible. It should be remembered that the justification for production lies in the satisfaction of the wants of the consumer, and that those wants are ever changing. It is true that consumers do not always know specifically what they want. It is for the manufacturer, through his sales organisation and his research department, to foresee or discover those wants and to satisfy them.

The telephone met the unfelt want of being able to converse with people at a distance, the typewriter satisfied the need for more rapid and more legible writing, but it took many long years of education to make people realise the utility of these articles. But whilst new products are coming forward, old products are being modified to meet new situations. Furniture must be made to fit smaller rooms and to correspond with the style requirements of the present age the hurry and bustle of modern life demands meals which can be prepared quickly, and so on. For most commodities, too, there is room for great diversity of size, shape, colour, style and quality, and it is for each organisation to decide how wide the range of needs it proposes to serve should be.

We have so far dealt with the way in which the sales policy defines the relations between the sales and production departments. Let us now turn to advertising. This is normally used, not so much as a method of selling, but as an aid to it. To achieve any measure of success, it must be closely linked up with the activities of the salesmen. Both must direct their efforts upon the same market—the same type and class of consumer—and the features of the proposition put forward in advertisements must coincide with those stressed by the sales force. If the salesmen have been instructed always to emphasise quality, it would be bad policy as well as a waste of money to give prominence in advertisements to the low price of the article. Unless the objective is clearly defined beforehand, such a conflict between the selling and the advertising is possible, if not probable.

The organisation which is following a definite sales policy has cohesion and possesses a driving power which would otherwise be altogether lacking. Maximum results with a minimum of effort can only be achieved if every individual pulls his full weight—in the right direction and at the right time. The sales policy, together with the selling plan based upon it, tells him how and when his efforts are to be applied. An organisation without such a policy would be nothing but a disorganised collection of individuals; not, as it should be, a single unit, a team, working on set lines, with perfect understanding and complete co-operation, in order to reach a fixed goal. It might seek to sell to the wholesaler whilst undermining the latter's business by soliciting orders direct from his customers. It might be advertising to the wealthier classes when its goods are stocked only in shops rarely frequented by such people. It might be charging one customer a lower price and allowing him better terms than it allows his competitor across the street.

A policy firmly adhered to has an important psychological effect, not only upon the sales force itself, but also upon distributors and consumers. A firm which has no policy at all, or is continually changing the one it has, can hardly expect to enjoy the confidence of its customers. This does not mean that, once laid down, a policy must never be changed. A policy is a line of action designed to fit a certain set of conditions. Should those conditions change, the policy may need revision. On the other hand, whilst there is danger in holding to a policy too long, it should only be changed after very careful thought and after very cogent reasons for the change have been adduced.

### CHOOSING SOMETHING TO SELL

THE determination of a sales policy depends upon a close study of a number of factors. Some of these may determine quite clearly the lines of approach; others will afford a more or less limited choice. First of all comes the question, "What is the business to sell?" which seems on the face of it a very simple problem. In established businesses it is partly answered by what is already being sold. But only partly answered, for the demand for any commodity may weaken or cease entirely as a result of a change of fashion or purchasing power, of technical developments or new inventions. Again, whether it be a manufacturing or a distributive firm, the business must decide the grade or quality, the style, the degree of diversity of types, sizes, models, etc., as well as its attitude towards trade marks, guarantees and service.

If a business is large or is located in a district identified with cheaper quality goods, it will be unwise to attempt the sale of high quality goods which have a limited market. As we have already seen, in the manufacturing business great diversity of size, shape, colour, etc., is costly: it is equally costly in the distributive business, because it involves the holding of larger stocks for the same volume of business and a corresponding increase in interest on capital and in the expenses of warehousing and stock control. Diversity can be justified if those items with a smaller sale can be sold at prices high enough to cover all the extra costs incurred, or where the sale of those varieties with a large demand would be jeopardised by the failure to offer a full range. In the latter case, the offering of the unprofitable lines would be in the nature of an advertisement or special service. To come to a right decision on this point, it would clearly be necessary to understand the viewpoint of the purchaser—his buying habits and his possible reactions to any limitation of variety.

Sometimes it is desirable for a producer to identify himself with his product so that he is able, when he draws attention to it by advertising, to secure to himself the benefits accruing from any special merits his goods possess. Trade marks and brands have been developed with this object. It is clear that a business whose goods had nothing but low price to recommend them would be ill-advised to identify itself with them in this way. Some intermediaries are loath to sell goods bearing the mark of another firm. Should such intermediaries constitute the main channel of distribution, the manufacturer would have to decide whether to entrust his future to the caprices of these agencies or whether to take the slower and more difficult path—developing a market of his own under his own brand.

It may be that the product is destined to satisfy the personal wants of individuals; it may be for the use of industry, either as raw material or equipment; or it may be as supplies or equipment for institutions—schools, hospitals, banks, local authorities, and so on. This does not, however, carry us very far. Ideally, every sales manager would like to know the name and address of each prospective customer and a great deal more about him. In some cases one can be a little more definite owing to restrictions imposed upon the use of the product by law or by custom or by the nature of the article itself. Some of these restrictions are at once apparent; others can be ascertained only by a close investigation of the market. The likely users of perambulators, harvesting machines, miners' lamps, or plant for steel rolling mills are not hard to locate: it would be far more difficult to find out the users of hand-saws. The use of cigarettes, beer, and motor cars is restricted to those over a certain age.

But with these articles, as well as with most others, it becomes necessary to resort to a further definition. This results from special restrictions upon the use of the product such as may be imposed by lack of money, by the climate or the physical characteristics of particular regions, or by such psychological factors as the reasons which cause people to buy the particular product. It should be noted that a change of emphasis on such points as price, availability, service, style, economy, cleanliness, comfort, etc., will change the attitude of individuals towards any particular product, and hence alter the market as a whole.

### SELECTING A CHANNEL FROM FACTORY TO HOUSE

WHILST the majority of firms have not given much thought to the two questions already dealt with, all have been compelled to decide through whom the business is to sell. That is not to say that they have given full consideration to all the factors, or that they have chosen wisely. A study of the normal channels of distribution is the obvious first step, for it is through these that the product moves most smoothly. A decision to distribute through any but the orthodox channels will need strong reasons to justify it. Innumerable factors are involved, some pointing in one direction and some in another. The final decision will inevitably be a compromise dependent upon the relative importance of these different forces.

As regards goods bought by the general public for their own consumption or use, the usual method, other things being equal, is for certain types of goods to be sold to the retailer through the wholesaler. Such goods are staple products, especially those sold in bulk ; goods which are unstandardised and need much regrading ; goods in connection with which no special service or training is required ; goods which are not branded or advertised ; commodities which cover only a very small range of needs in their particular class ; products, the demand for which is temporary, uncertain, or merely occasional ; and those where the market is small and scattered, or where the risk of changes in style, fashion, or price is great.

A similar method would be used where production was on a small scale, unless it were for a very specialised market, or where the production was very irregular or uncertain. Such cases arise most commonly in agriculture. If the individual order of the retailer were so small as to militate against economical handling as well as raising the cost of obtaining orders, it would be found a better practice to sell through the wholesaler. But even then an antagonistic or even apathetic attitude on the part of the wholesaler, or a serious decline in his importance in the trade, might well justify different tactics.

It need hardly be said that just as these circumstances invite recourse to the wholesaler, so circumstances the reverse of these would, generally speaking, indicate the necessity for closer contact with the market. But even then, the problem would not be solved. Should the firm sell both to wholesalers and the larger retailers, or, if to retailers only, is it to be to every retailer who stocks that particular class of goods, or to a few selected ones, or to one only in every district? Or should it go further still and establish its own shops, or seek to sell direct to the consumer by house-to-house canvassing or through the post? It would take too long to discuss this complicated choice in detail. Suffice it to mention that, in addition to the points already indicated, the financial resources of the business and the normal buying habits of consumers would have to be considered. That is to say, answers should be found to the questions: "Where do the public buy it?" "How frequently do they buy it?" "With what other things do they buy it?" "What or who influences their choice?"

A single example will serve to illustrate the importance of these answers. Should a manufacturer of high class bedroom furniture open his own retail shops? High class bedroom furniture will be bought only in the largest towns. There will usually be one retailer who specialises in the high class furniture trade. The prospective purchaser does not, as a rule, know or want to know the names of manufacturers; even if he did, he would not be in a position to decide which was the best. He relies upon the merchandising skill of the retailer, knowing that the latter will have been in touch with all sources of supply and have chosen the goods most adapted to the requirements of his customers. The majority of these customers would much rather rely upon the specialist retailer than trust a manufacturer's advertisements or even their own judgment. What is more, it would be necessary to offer more than bedroom furniture, for people would not want to go to one shop to furnish a bedroom, another to furnish a dining-room, and yet another to furnish a lounge. These considerations do not, however, apply to medium or low-priced furniture or even to furniture of a very distinctive design or character.

### MEANS OF DISCOVERING HOW MUCH TO PRODUCE

A FURTHER point which has to be decided is the volume of business which is aimed at. Apart from the immediate productive capacity and the desire to maintain an even flow of orders which have already been mentioned, the degree of saturation of the market as a whole will indicate the advisability or otherwise of providing extra plant for the further growth of the business. Admittedly, the degree of saturation is not an easy thing to discover, but statistics of the output of the industry or the consumption of raw materials by the industry as a whole will serve as a guide. Should the demand for the product show signs of weakening, it would be unwise to incur further capital expenditure for the purpose of executing orders which might reasonably be secured in the forthcoming year. Even in a rapidly expanding market, too rapid an extension of business may lead to serious administrative difficulties and a disproportionate rise in costs. Some firms have indeed laid down for many years ahead a desired rate of growth for their business, and they do their best to keep to this, even if it means discouraging or actually refusing orders in times of excessive prosperity.

The problem of price is too complicated to deal with at length. An early decision should be made as to whether the firm intends to aim at large sales with a small profit per unit or small volume with a large profit per unit. The methods and scale of production as well as the size and elasticity (or responsiveness to price changes) of demand will be the main factors involved. It should already have been decided when examining the product and the market whether price was or was not to be the chief selling point. Also the conditions under which prices can be amended and the powers of salesmen in this connection should be clearly defined.[1]

A word may usefully be said here upon the question of discounts. Two methods of applying trade discounts may be distinguished—discounts which vary with quantity only, and discounts which, disregarding quantity, are based upon the position in the trade of the intermediary, so as to give wholesalers a larger discount than retailers. The quantity discount seems to be more logical in that large orders involve little more expense than small ones. Nowadays the large scale retailers are often in a position to place orders as large if not larger than those of the average wholesaler. The quantity discount, however, may induce many of the smaller retailers to order more at a time than their business justifies. Overstocking is one of the evils which a sales manager should seek to prevent, especially where the goods are likely to

[1] For a further discussion of these points, see " How Goods are Sold " (p. 240).

deteriorate in quality or to go out of fashion. Inferior, shop-soiled, or damaged goods will damage the reputation of the manufacturer in the eyes of the consumer, and a slow turn-over will tend to prejudice the retailer against his goods. Where the wholesaler is indispensable or renders a real service to the manufacturer or retailer, it is only just that he should receive payment for this extra service by being placed in a more advantageous position than the retailer. This may be effected by higher discounts for whole-salers, either alone or in conjunction with quantity discounts.

The conditions of payment decided upon by a business will depend mainly upon the custom of the trade and the possibility or desirability of extending the market by these means. Competition based on terms rather than on quality or service is, however, fraught with danger. But whatever the terms decided upon may be, they should be deviated from only in exceptional circumstances. As in other aspects of the sales policy, lack of firmness leads eventually to friction and loss of custom. And it is not always those who pay promptly who labour under a sense of injustice; it is often those to whom the firm has been most lenient.

### SHOULD A SALESMAN BE AN INVESTIGATOR?

ENOUGH has been said to show that a large amount of information is needed before a sound and comprehensive sales policy can be framed. From whence will this information be forthcoming? Much of it can be unearthed by expert analysis and interpretation from the records of the business itself, or from statistics issued by government departments and various trade organisations. But there remains a vast body of facts relating to distributors and consumers which can be collected only by direct contact.

Whether this work should be entrusted to the salesman is a debatable question. Although certain information can be gleaned from salesmen's reports and letters and they can be charged with the duty of making special investigations, the consensus of opinion is against it. For one thing, a salesman's job is to sell—and that is a full-time job. For another, the collection of information of such a delicate nature as the preferences and habits of individuals demands a special technique, an unbiased mind, and a certain amount of anonymity, if the results are to be of any value at all. This technique has developed rapidly within recent years under the name of Market Research.[1]

It is the duty of the Market Research department or agency to gather information about the market and its characteristics, and to analyse and to draw general conclusions from this information. This research should be a continuous, not a periodic process. Markets are in a continual state of flux, and it is for the intelligence department to keep the sales manager in touch with every important movement.

The basis of the activities of any business during a given year must be the sales which it is estimated can be made during that period. A forecast may be built up, roughly, from the individual estimates of salesmen or agents, or it may be arrived at by a careful analysis of the records of past sales, their general trend over a long period of years, their relationship to the alternating booms and slumps of general business, and their fluctuations from month to month throughout the year. Apart from any important changes in general policy or organisation, it is generally assumed that the long period movement and the seasonal fluctuations will continue as before. The most difficult task of all is to forecast the future movements of business in general, and to adjust the estimates in accordance with the relationship already disclosed. Various indices are used for this purpose, the most useful being unemployment figures, bank clearings, wholesale prices, wage rates, imports of raw materials, cost of living, credit rates, retail sales, and bank returns.

The forecast thus made should be expressed in terms of value for the benefit of the financial section of the business, and in terms of quantity for the production side. It should be split up as far as possible into the different lines or main groups of lines of goods dealt in, and, if sold to different markets, in accordance with these markets. The figures thus obtained must be adjusted so as to take into account, on lines laid down by the general policy, both the needs of production and the financial resources. It may, for example, be necessary to increase the general estimates in order to keep the factory running economically, or it may involve only increased estimates of certain lines in order to secure a more balanced production programme. To live up to the amended sales budget, together with the selling expenses budget, constitutes the main task of the sales department.

[1] See " How Goods are Sold " (p. 242).

### HOW A SALES CAMPAIGN IS LAUNCHED

BROADLY speaking, a selling plan or campaign means the definition of the minor objectives to be achieved within a short period, such as a year, and the precise methods by which they are to be attained. The objective may be a general one, such as a normal year's work, or it may be a special one, such as the introduction of a new product, the increase in sales of a single line, or the development of a new market.

If no particular market has been indicated, those markets which offer the greatest possibilities of expansion at the lowest relative cost must be determined. So must the degree of sales pressure required in the various sales territories or districts. It would be wasteful to concentrate selling effort, whether it be through personal selling or through advertising, upon districts where a full share of business has already been secured, or where there is special sales resistance, such as frequently occurs in the neighbourhood of a competitor's headquarters.

Decisions must also be reached as to the parts to be played by dealers, agents, salesmen, demonstrators, canvassers, samples, window displays, direct mail, press and other types of advertising, in building up the means to be employed. These different means should dovetail one into the other so that each receives added force. If new salesmen are required, when should they be engaged and trained? When should samples be ready, salesmen and dealers informed of the campaign, advertising copy be prepared, space booked, insertions made? When should orders be solicited, distribution be completed, dealer aids and window displays be ready? It is wasteful to advertise a product extensively before it is available for sale in the districts where it has been advertised and in quantities sufficient to satisfy the immediate demand anticipated.

When this plan of campaign has been worked out in detail and communicated to the sales organisation and the advertising department, operations can begin. Although advertising is dealt with in another section[1] and it is usually controlled by a separate individual, it nevertheless forms an integral part of the selling plan. That does not mean that the sales manager should dictate the copy or the media to be used, but it does mean that he should indicate the extent of the pressure he

[1] See "How to Advertise" (p. 342).

wishes exerted on specific markets, territories, or lines of goods, and when that pressure should be applied. He is the person ultimately responsible for sales, and he should, therefore, be in a position to control the general movements of all selling agencies.

The plan thus formulated and put into operation should be capable of adaptation to any special conditions which may arise. It is not possible, for example, to predict what one's competitors are going to do—their activities may necessitate greater pressure being brought to bear at a particular time or in a particular area. The general plan of campaign will remain substantially the same, but the element of flexibility is essential. Progress will need to be checked from day to day so that the necessity for any changes in tactics may be perceived at once. This aspect of sales management will be dealt with later in greater detail.

## BUILDING UP THE SALES MACHINE

An organisation has been defined as "a systematic union of individuals in a body, whose members work together for a common end." The common end is here embodied in the sales policy and the selling plan. The sales organisation is the machinery for carrying it out. Upon the efficiency and smooth working of that machinery depends the degree of success attained.

The work of a sales organisation may be divided roughly into its three main aspects—planning the work, carrying it out, and controlling the results. Each aspect comprises many tasks of great variety. Some of them, such as transport, dealing with complaints, and the keeping of accounts may be carried out by departments of the business not under the control of the sales manager. Others, like market research, may even be entrusted to agencies outside the business altogether. Nevertheless, whoever may be responsible for them, they still come within the broad classification of sales management.

As has been said before, there is no general agreement as to where the sales manager's duties begin and where they end. As in other kinds of work, modern practice is tending towards a greater degree of specialisation, thus limiting the activities and responsibilities of individuals.

Except in those businesses devoted to mail-order selling

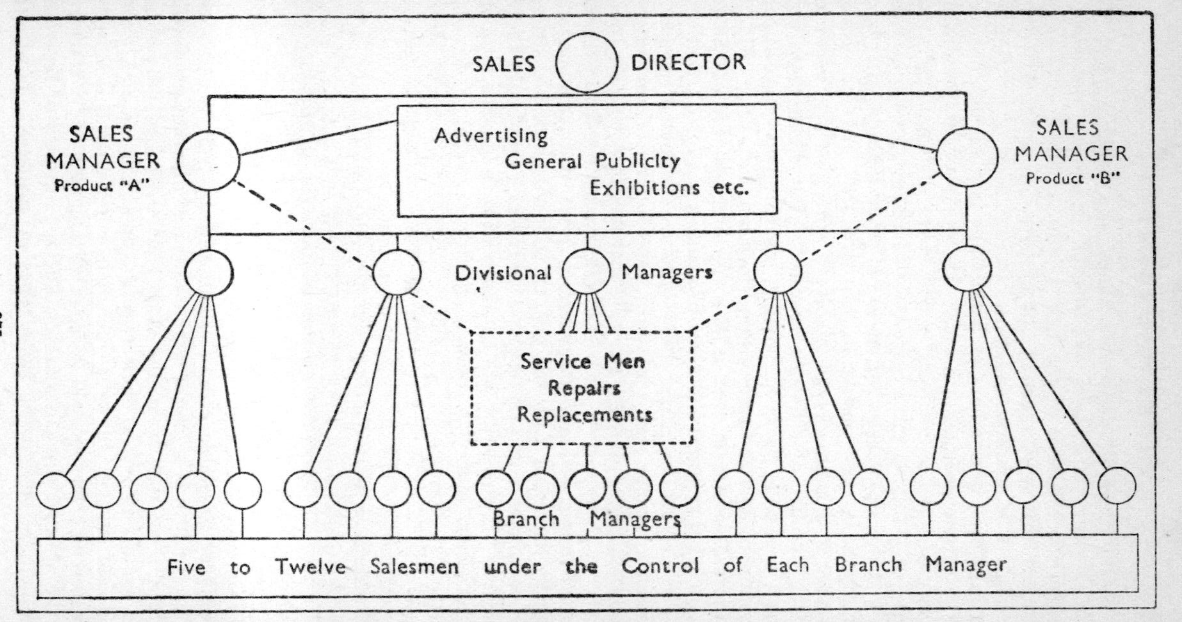


*Sales management plan of a large-scale selling organisation marketing two products, " A " and " B."*

or selling through their own shops, the usual method of contact with customers is through travelling salesmen. Unless the business of the firm is very small or extremely localised, this work must be shared by a number of different people. The simplest and most common basis of division is the territorial one, where each salesman is made responsible for a definite geographical area. He works under the direct supervision of headquarters, which, if the distance is not too great, or if buying takes place only at certain seasons, he will visit daily, or weekly, or at some other definite interval; otherwise he will reside in his territory. An increasing number of customers will involve a corresponding increase in the number of salesmen required. But when there are many salesmen, it is impossible to maintain that direct personal contact and supervision which is so desirable. Many authorities maintain that it is a full-time job for one man adequately to control and assist from seven to twelve salesmen.

The day-to-day supervision may be delegated to field officials known as senior salesmen, sales supervisors, or superintendents, thus allowing the sales manager to devote his time to the more important aspects of management and to general co-ordination. Should the necessity arise, district managers may be entrusted with the general supervision of a district, and divisional managers be given control of a number of these districts. A similarity will be observed between this type of organisation and that of an infantry regiment, with its battalions, companies, platoons, and sections. For this reason, it is often referred to as the "military" type of organisation. The line of responsibility is clear and well defined, each person being directly responsible to his immediate superior for the area entrusted to him.

Certain modifications of this simple type of organisation have been adopted to meet complexities of the selling problem. The first is the introduction of a further division of the work on the basis of different types of products. The object may simply be to enable greater attention to be paid to all lines when the firm is selling a large number of different products. Whilst these may be of the same general nature and sell to the same customers, their special characteristics and their uses will be very different. A single salesman will lack both the time and the special knowledge to bring each one effectively to the notice of his customers. The appointment of separate salesmen to sell to the same types of customers, however, may be for the purpose of introducing new lines which require special pushing, or it may be dictated by a fundamental difference in the selling problem. For example, the selling of an expensive duplicating machine is a very different proposition from the subsequent sale of supplies of stencils, paper, ink, etc., and calls for an entirely different type of salesmanship, different qualities, and perhaps a different method of remuneration.

The second modification is a division of the sales force according to the types of customers. Differences between types of customers may arise not merely in the size of the businesses or in the social and intellectual qualities of buyers, but in their buying motives and even in the uses to which the products are to be put. These differences may strike the sales manager as so important as to justify the employment of entirely different salesmen for certain of these markets. In other cases, the general management may deem it wise to go so far as to build entirely separate organisations—in some cases, even under a different name.

### PEOPLE THE "MISSIONARY" TRIES TO CONVERT

APART from the act of selling itself, other types of work must frequently be carried out in the field. Service, delivery, demonstrations, window-dressing, canvassing, and so-called missionary work all need to be organised. For these duties separate representatives are usually employed, sometimes working from headquarters and being moved from district to district as required; at others, definitely organised on a territorial basis. A word of explanation as to the meaning here of the word "missionary" may not be out of place. It is well known that certain products are purchased mainly upon the recommendation and advice of others. Baby foods, for example, may be bought on the recommendation of doctor, nurse, or hospital. The way to the purchaser's ear, therefore, is through these channels. It is the duty of the missionary salesman to secure the goodwill of those who influence the choice of the buyer.

The difficulties in the way of an ideal division of labour within the sales office are not so great as they are in the field. The three distinct types of work—planning, execution, and control—call for very different qualities of mind, and it is, therefore, desirable that they should be entrusted to different persons. Each of these main divisions consists of a variety of minor tasks. If any necessary division of work is made on the basis of the main divisions—that is to say, if each individual is allowed to concentrate on a small number of complete tasks—increased efficiency will result. Such an arrangement would not be possible in the field.

The nature of, and the lines of demarcation between, these separate tasks should be appreciated in the early stages of growth. Otherwise there is a grave risk that the organisation will grow up haphazard : important matters may be overlooked, because they are nobody's special responsibility ; conflicting decisions will be made and conflicting courses of action taken, because more than one person has had a finger in the pie. The result will be dissipation of effort, loss of efficiency, bad feeling between the staff, and, worst of all, dissatisfied customers. Every individual should know the limits of his authority and the extent of his responsibility. Responsibility for anything that goes wrong should be traceable to some one member of the staff.

Nothing helps more towards a clear understanding on this point than the setting down in writing—especially in the form of a chart—of the various tasks to be performed, the persons responsible, and their precise connections with each other. It enables a clear view to be taken of the whole field of operations ; it prevents needless overlapping ; it enables the individual to visualise his place in the organisation ; it facilitates the work of co-ordination ; and, finally, it forms the basis for further division of labour as the business expands.

Space does not permit an examination of all the various types of work carried out in the office—market and product research, planning, dealing with inquiries, orders, dispatch, correspondence, complaints, credit, collections, accounts, and so on—but reference may here be made to a person who is little known to the outside world, namely, the product manager. When a firm sells a large variety of products and it is impracticable or inadvisable to have separate salesmen, it has been found useful to appoint certain individuals at headquarters, called " product managers," to specialise in and be held responsible for the development of particular groups of related lines.

## INTERNAL FRICTION THAT REACHES THE CUSTOMER

ONE may be excused for repeating that the foundations of a smooth and harmonious working of the whole organisation rest on the existence of a sales policy and plan with clear-cut outlines and on an understanding of their implications by the entire personnel. Possibilities of conflict may be further reduced by the formulation of standard instructions. Certain situations and minor problems are continually arising. The lines on which these constantly recurring questions are to be dealt with should be set down in writing for the guidance of those concerned. This will ensure that decisions made and action taken on such matters are in accord with the general policy, and at the same time will avoid the waste of effort involved in thinking out the problem anew each time.

The chief defects of organisation exist in the relations between the sales department and other sections of the business, and in lack of co-ordination between the indoor and outdoor staffs. As regards the latter, it may reveal itself merely as a lack of sympathetic understanding or as a definite conflict of interests. It is contended—and with truth—that strict division of the different types of work, in spite of the most careful definition of policy, may lead to trouble. If different sections are allowed to give instructions to salesmen, what is the salesman to do if these instructions conflict ? Again, anything which causes friction between salesman and customer will make selling more difficult and naturally antagonise the salesman. For example, the collection department might write a sharp letter to a customer requesting immediate payment, although another section had received a complaint in respect of the goods supplied.

Some firms seek to obtain closer co-operation by bringing salesmen into the office for a time or, less frequently, sending members of the inside staff for a spell on the road. Several important firms in this country, however, have solved the problem by the introduction of sales clerks, whose duty it is to deal with all communications from salesmen and customers within certain geographical areas. In other words, the territorial organisation of the field has been reproduced on a smaller scale within the sales department. Every salesman and every customer can thus look to a single individual at headquarters for assistance and hold him responsible for mistakes.

Co-ordination between the sales department and other departments is provided for either by committees of the departmental heads or by a special official entrusted with this particular work. The committees suffer from many disadvantages, not the least of which is the lack of individual responsibility for decisions arrived at. Their greatest value would seem to be that they provide means for the discussion of new developments that may have arisen and of changes proposed in the sales policy or selling plan.

### SPREADING THE RADIUS OF SALES CONTROL

It has been seen that the supervision and control of salesmen is frequently decentralised where the sales force is large and unwieldy. But centralised control of a general character is still necessary to ensure an even development of the market and the efficient conduct of the business as a whole.

Within recent years there has been an increasing tendency towards the carrying out of other activities away from the head office. In its simplest form this decentralisation consists in the establishment of depots, warehouses, or showrooms, directly controlled from headquarters. In its most extreme form all dealings with customers and salesmen are carried out from a number of branch offices under the control of local managers, the work of the headquarters staff being confined to advice, general control of policy, and general administration. Between the two are many types of local offices with varying degrees of initiative.

Perhaps the most common activity thus decentralised is that of warehousing. The purpose of such local stocks may be to assist in effecting sales; that is to say, they would be used mainly for show or for demonstration. Many goods, however, are perishable, and stocks in the hands of dealers need to be kept fresh if they are to maintain the reputation of the manufacturer. In such cases, frequent orders rather than large ones should be the objective. But the cost of sending numerous small orders is high, and, more important still, goods must be available for delivery at short notice. These are part of the normal services of the wholesaler; but many firms have forsaken the wholesaler, and they must perforce render these services themselves.

The control of credit and collection of accounts are sometimes decentralised. It may be mentioned here that the practice of empowering salesmen to collect accounts is dying out. Where the number of accounts is very large and consists mainly of small businesses to whom the granting of credit is risky, closer contact than is possible from a single centre may be desirable. In such cases, not only the granting of credit and collection of accounts, but also, if local stocks are available, the invoicing and the sales ledger may be entrusted to the branch.

Service is usually decentralised. When it is a matter of maintenance or minor repairs and adjustments which are constantly being made, as in the case of typewriters, it is necessary to have a local service staff under the control of the local manager. Some commodities sold to industry, however, give rise to special difficulties, in that each industry has its own peculiar needs and problems. These may be so distinct one from the other that each major industrial area will require a technical expert on the spot to advise customers upon their problems and to investigate complaints. It is these conditions which most commonly give rise to the establishment in each major economic region of a branch possessing a wide measure of autonomy. The technical expert, however, whilst operating from this branch, would normally be under the general direction of the technical section at headquarters. In other words, it would be a projection of the technical element into the field.

The selection and training of salesmen, too, is sometimes left in the hands of local managers. This may be advisable in organisations whose personnel is constantly changing, or in those where the different customs, prejudices, and attitudes of mind which exist in different districts demand local knowledge for the satisfactory sale of the products.

## CHOOSING AND TRAINING THE MAN ON THE ROAD

THE selection, training, and maintenance of personnel is one of the most difficult, as it is one of the most important tasks which any section of a business has to deal with. In its general aspect it is discussed elsewhere in this book.[1] But it is necessary to deal here with some of the special difficulties which the sales manager of a large organisation has to face. Important as the inside staff is, salesmen are the real problem. The continual changes taking place in the sales forces of certain firms, especially those of a specialist character, are not only inimical to the efficient working of the

[1] See " The Art of Handling Men " (p. 87).

organisation and the development of an *esprit de corps*, but are also extremely costly. The cost should not be measured merely by the direct cost of securing, engaging, and training the men, but also in terms of the loss of immediate orders and permanent goodwill, due to interrupted representation as well as to bad or inexperienced salesmanship.

### LOGIC THAT HELPS IN SELECTING THE SALESMAN

THE method of trial and error is perhaps more harmful in selling than in any other job. Unfortunately, there is no way of telling whether an applicant will be suitable. His suitability rests not merely upon his ability to sell—and to sell that particular product to a particular type of customer and in a particular locality—but also upon whether he is able to adapt himself to the other members of the organisation, as well as with the policy and methods of the firm. Many sales managers still rely upon general impressions and intuition, but this is as likely to be wrong as right. A much greater degree of certainty can, however, be assured if the problem is approached in a logical way. The best available answers should be found to the following questions: What kind of a man is required? Where is he most likely to be found? What is the surest way of getting in touch with him? And, finally, how may he be recognised?

What characteristics, mental and physical, are conducive to success? Some of the larger businesses have sought answers to this question in a careful analysis of the records of past and present salesmen. Statistics relating to such things as age, height, education, intelligence, length of service, marital status and number of dependents, have been tabulated and compared with the degree of success or failure achieved. Some of the results have been helpful in indicating certain characteristics which seem to carry, whilst not a certainty, at least a greater possibility of success or of failure. For it is as important to be able to eliminate the unfit as to select the fit.

Some useful conclusions may likewise be drawn from an examination on similar lines of the sources from which salesmen have been drawn in the past. A distinction should here be drawn between experienced salesmen and novices. The former may have worked for competitors, or may have had experience in selling the same goods over the retail counter: they may have sold other types of goods to the same customers, or their experience may have been quite unrelated to that of the firm. The first of these is a much less popular source of recruitment than was formerly the case, and the second is not very common in this country. The third may be of value where the product is standardised and well advertised, and where a knowledge of customers is the most important requisite. The last, whilst not very common, has advantages where it is necessary to adapt the product to the requirements of different businesses.

As regards those without selling experience, the most useful source of recruits is the firm's own employees. This is especially the case when a full knowledge of the firm's organisation, policy, and methods or an intimate acquaintance with the product and its handling is essential. In the latter case, the factory or the warehouse will be tapped; in the former, the clerical staff. It is only natural that the sales department proper, especially branch offices, should be the most fruitful source, but occasionally other sections, such as the order department or the estimating department, provide recruits. Other possible sources are outside men with business experience other than selling, schools of salesmanship, and the universities and public schools. The first is unusual; the second is not very popular in this country; and as regards the third, experience has not so far been very fortunate, except for foreign markets.

### HOW TO FIND NEW SALESMEN

THE means adopted for getting in touch with potential salesmen will depend largely upon the source decided upon. In the case of non-employees, some of the larger firms find no difficulty in filling vacancies from those who have put in general applications. The majority, however, still have recourse to advertisements. Much has been written about the use of box numbers and other aspects of the advertisement, but it should certainly be so designed, both as regards where it is inserted and how it is worded, as to appeal to those sought and deter those who are not wanted. It is advisable to ask for information on some point which is considered to be a main factor in success or failure. This will facilitate the choice of those to be interviewed, if choice has to be made. Application forms are often used as a means of securing further vital information.

Innumerable different methods of carrying out the interview itself are in use. Sometimes it is left to the sales manager; sometimes his view is checked by a director; occasionally an applicant will be seen by three or four executives. Whatever method be employed, to secure all the best possible men for the work at the remuneration available depends on a combination of experience and intuition in those doing the work. Always the salesman interviewed should be given every opportunity to take hold of the conversation, in other words, to give a demonstration of his salesmanship in selling his own abilities. Further, a salesman should always be encouraged to talk, even if the result be that he talks himself out of the job. For only by allowing him to display his shortcomings as well as his capabilities can the most informed decision be made. Further, many capable salesmen are nervous about selling their own services, although they present fronts of brass in selling other people's goods or services. In this case, again, it is vital to place the applicant at his ease and to allow him to show the best and worst of himself as a salesman. Where possible, it is always worth while to interview a likely man twice before appointing him; this gives the manager an insight into the variations of health, temper and attack.

It is untrue to say that salesmen are born, not made. Not that there is no such thing as a born salesman. But they are rare, and it is better to deal with the rule rather than with the exception. The task of selling has become more complex and more exacting; more careful and more uniform methods are imperative. Training is often more or less casual; that is to say, the recruit is given the opportunity of picking up knowledge in the course either of tours of observation or of ordinary routine work in various departments. Less frequently, the training is organised on a definite plan, a certain time being allotted for the theoretical and practical study of specified subjects in a carefully chosen order. The training may last only two or three days, or it may extend over as many years.

The course may be designed according to the nature of the proposition, the character of the market, and the source from which the recruit has come: to provide knowledge of the policy and general methods of the firm; knowledge of the product—its production, its uses, and abuses; and, in particular, an understanding of the work of a salesman. The latter will include general work, such as analysing his territory, locating prospective customers, planning his route, credit, using advertising and sales promotion material, making out orders, reports, etc., and the principles of salesmanship as applied to the proposition in question.

This will to some extent involve the recruit spending a certain period in the offices. The aim is to give an outsider a general background and an appreciation of the needs and difficulties of sections with which he will have to co-operate directly or indirectly. Old employees are likewise given an opportunity of understanding the work of other departments than their own.

Only in technical products is anything beyond a general idea of the actual process of manufacture required. The salesman must look at the product from the view-point of his customers. The stress should, therefore, be placed upon its various uses and advantages, its correct handling, the diagnosis of the consumer's needs, and the way to deal with simple complaints. In certain trades, such as textiles, it is most important to know the range of products and prices, the methods of handling, and the feel of the goods. A fairly long experience in the warehouse is then essential.

### HOW THE SALESMAN LEARNS HIS JOB

As regards the actual work of the salesman in the field, experience in the offices, together with talks from important executives, serves to instruct new salesmen in the significance of carrying out the general preparatory and routine work, and in the best methods of doing so. The actual process of selling itself—salesmanship in the narrow sense—is dealt with elsewhere in this course.[1] Much can be learned from the experience of successful salesmen, and systematic training may be carried out at a central school or in the field. In the latter case, the recruit may be sent out on a special visit, and the details of this visit should be fully discussed on his return ; or he may be sent as an assistant to an experienced salesman ; or, again, he may be given a territory to work under the supervision of an instructor, who observes his methods, criticises each call after it is completed, suggests improvements, and demonstrates them in an actual interview.

Some firms have definite courses of training in the salesman's work, and arrange for old salesmen to go through a modified " refresher " course every few years with the object of tuning them up and of instructing them in improved

[1] See " Salesmanship " (p. 298).

methods. Opportunity is sometimes taken of salesmen's conferences to carry this out, or, at least, to deal with faults that have been found to be common to most of the sales force.

The sales manual is a booklet or handbook compiled for the personal use and guidance of the employees of the firm. It may consist merely of a few typewritten sheets, or it may be a thick, well-bound, and well-indexed book. Its use in this country is not as yet very extensive, and it has been designed almost exclusively for the use of salesmen. Sales managers might adapt it for the use of other members of their staff.

For salesmen, it serves as an epitome of their training. The more elaborate examples may contain a brief history of the firm and its main policies ; details of the product—its nature, uses, and special advantages ; types of customers and their characteristics ; general instructions and rules for the salesman regarding the methods of carrying out their work, and, perhaps, in the case of specialities, a model sales presentation.

Contracts with salesmen should be set out in clear and concise terms. In order to avoid any possibility of dispute, the contract should contain the conditions under which the salesman is engaged, and the notice to be given by either party, together with a full statement of the work the salesman is expected to do, including the extent of his authority and his responsibilities. Provisions should also be made for safeguarding the interests of the firm in the event of the salesman leaving it. This usually provides that he shall not call upon the firm's customers in his old territory with competitive goods before the expiration of a defined and reasonable period. It is also necessary to specify the territory allocated to him, and to provide for revision of this agreement.

The remuneration he is to receive must be stated, and how it is to be arrived at, and when it is payable. If it includes payment on a commission basis, the orders on which it is payable should be made plain. They may be all orders from his territory, whether through him or not, or only orders sent by him personally, or, again, all orders introduced, whether delivered to his territory or to some other. A statement of the powers of the firm to accept or refuse orders is usually inserted. The responsibility for expenses is also important, as it involves such questions as: What expenses and how ıuch will be paid by the firm? If a motor car is used, who ; to provide it, and who is to pay the expenses of running nd repairs? Finally, mention must be made of the deposit r security required, if any, and provisions for its return or ›rfeiture.

### THE PROBLEM OF HOW TO FIX REWARDS

THE remuneration of salesmen is a question of great complexity and one where there has been much experiment. No one method seems to fit every situation. The objects of ny system should be first of all to attract and keep the right ype of man; secondly, to reward him according to the value f his services; and finally, to be reasonably easy to understand and administer.

The problem bristles with difficulties. Even within the ame business, some things are easier to sell than others, and ome yield a bigger gross profit than others. It is easier to sell luring a boom than in a slump, in season than out of season. Some territories are much easier and cheaper to work than ›thers. Again, how is one to measure and reward that work vhich is intended to build up future sales rather than to bring mmediate results?

Payment of a fixed salary is simple, but it fails to provide ın incentive to hard work. Nevertheless, it is the only suitable nethod where a large amount of development work must be carried out, where orders vary considerably in size, or where hey are infrequent.

Payment by results is commonly interpreted as a percentage commission on sales. But, whilst this will prove an incentive o obtain more and larger orders, it may do this only to the letriment of future business. A salesman paid on this basis ılone will be in a position to earn only when he is in front of a ›rospective customer. He will be loath to undertake other vork, unless he happens to be unusually far-sighted and is, noreover, sure of retaining the territory for a considerable ime. "A bird in the hand is worth two in the bush" will be ıis maxim. He will resist reductions of his territory or transerence to undeveloped areas, however desirable they may be n the interests of the firm. He will be tempted to ignore the langers of over-selling, to which reference has already been nade. Payment by commission alone is, therefore, justifiable ›nly where a strong incentive is needed, where the risk of ›ver-selling is slight, and where other kinds of work—for example, specialities of a non-repeat kind—are entrusted to different set of individuals.

In the great majority of cases, firms have tried to combine the advantages of these two methods by giving a fixed salary and a commission. Where the salary is very small, the objections to commission only are not met except in so far as the salesman is relieved from immediate financial worry. But however small a part commission plays, it is inequitable as between territories of differing degrees of development or productivity.

To meet this objection, recourse is frequently had to sales quotas. Each salesman is allotted a certain volume of sales, depending upon the relative prosperity of his territory, the degree of development, and the difficulty of coverage. It is obvious that great care must be exercised in fixing these quotas. Some firms give commission on all orders, with a higher rate when more than a certain percentage of the quota is achieved others give commission only upon orders over a certain percentage (say 80 per cent.) of quota.

The realisation that a salesman's work comprises many tasks has led some firms to attempt an estimation of the relative value of these duties to the firm. Marks or points are allotted to such factors as value of orders, number of orders, number of calls made, new accounts secured, and demonstrations booked. The number of bad debts incurred and complaints received may be given negative marks. The salesman's activities are valued in accordance with this schedule, and payment is made on the basis of the total points scored. It is obvious that this system may be very complicated and difficult to administer.

Attempts have been made to get at the roots of things by making the profits contributed by each salesman the basis of payment. Some firms have taken gross profit, whilst others have taken into account all expenses over which the salesman has any control. Profit-sharing of this nature is especially difficult to administer. It presupposes a willingness on the part of the management to reveal their profits ; otherwise it is purely arbitrary as far as the salesman is concerned. It makes no allowance for differences in productivity or development And what is to happen if there is a loss—a loss probably not attributable to the salesman at all ? Quite apart from this very few firms indeed have succeeded in working out the profit derived from each territory.

## THE VEXED QUESTION OF EXPENSES

If a salesman is expected to pay his own expenses, he will naturally be less amenable to control of his movements. He will avoid any activity which involves expense without an immediate compensating addition to his remuneration. Such a procedure amounts, indeed, to an attempt on the part of the management to shift on to the shoulders of the salesman a responsibility which should be its own. It may be justifiable, however, in connection with the sale of goods of a non-repeat character, where the profit must of necessity cover the immediate cost of securing the order. It may be excusable where the territory is small and concentrated, and expenses are therefore negligible, and where the actual movements of salesmen are not controlled.

On the other hand, where the firm pays all expenses, only the closest check upon the various items of expense can detect extravagance or the over-statement of expenditure. To obviate the necessity for this, the payment of a fixed allowance is frequently resorted to. In such a case, the allowance should be fixed only after a very careful study of the nature of the territory of each salesman. But here there is a risk that some salesmen will seek to make a little extra by economies of various kinds, which might easily damage the prestige of their employers. Certain organisations encourage the cutting down of expenses by giving a bonus for such savings. But these may be bought at too high a cost. It is part of the sales manager's job to know where expenses may safely be cut, and to place the onus upon the salesman is an admission of his own incompetence.

The necessity for the use of motor cars will arise from physical considerations, such as the carrying of large quantities of samples or small stocks for immediate delivery; from motives of prestige; or from the desire for economy. Economy does not mean simply cheapness in comparison with other means of transport. It is equally effected when an extra outlay brings in a more than proportionate increase in results. Orders secured bear a direct relation to the number of calls made. If the extra number of calls made possible by the use of a motor car will produce business showing a gross profit greater than the cost of depreciation and maintenance of the car, it becomes an economical proposition. In congested areas this is not likely to be the case.

If the question has been studied aright from this point of view, the sales manager should have a good idea as to the cost for each territory, and there should be no difficulty in the company providing the car and paying all expenses. The original estimates, duly adjusted from time to time, would constitute an adequate check. Some firms expect salesmen to provide the car; sometimes a fixed allowance is made for running expenses; sometimes salesmen have to pay all expenses.

### WHY THE IDEAL TERRITORY IS SO HARD TO KEEP

In few businesses is a free hand left to salesmen or agents as to the area of their activities. Planned distribution is impossible unless some individual is made responsible for every single part of the country to be covered. The territory allocated to a salesman should be large enough to keep him fully employed, yet small enough to allow him to work it with the desired intensity and efficiency. The balance between these two ideals is difficult to secure. Conditions are never stationary for long: customers may increase or decrease; competitors come and go; the value of the region as a market may grow and justify more intensive cultivation, or it may decline to such an extent as to become no longer profitable to work; or the policy of the firm may change the immediate market. The position of equilibrium is, therefore, always in a state of flux. While frequent changes of territory involve serious administrative difficulties and should be avoided, it is clear that territories should not be considered as fixed once and for all.

The allocation of territories is complicated by many factors, all of which must be carefully considered if the basis is to be a sound one. It takes much longer to secure orders from new customers than from old; for many lines than for few; for a vacuum cleaner, duplicating machine, or some technical product than for Bovril, Cadbury's chocolate, or Dunlop tyres. A larger area can be covered if goods are sold to a few large wholesalers than if they are sold to numerous retailers; if customers are scattered than if they are close together; if the article is of a non-repeat character than if calls have to be made every two or three weeks; if little beyond actual selling is required than if investigations, servicing, window-dressing, and other work has to be carried out as well.

Much will depend, too, upon the general development olicy of the firm. A small firm may secure a given volume ither by concentrating on a small area and working it in- nsively, or by covering a wide area superficially, limiting self to the most important outlets. Growth in the first case ould involve simply the addition of new areas ; in the second, would mean a continual process of division and subdivision f the whole field. Another factor which is often overlooked the rate of expected growth within the territory. Salesmen ust be allowed time to devote to this aspect of their work. onvenience—involving a consideration of the transport cilities available, and the ease with which certain points can e reached from different centres—may, however, indicate he advisability of a division not entirely compatible with ome of the above factors. The importance of securing some niformity within the territory may demand some other form f division.

Some businesses selling consumer goods of a general haracter direct to retailers base their territory roughly on opulation. Should the commodity appeal only to certain ections, a rough estimate of the numerical importance of hese sections will form the main basis of division. These stimates are made in a similar manner to those designed to ndicate the size of the market.

It has been seen that salesmen paid wholly or mainly on a ommission basis are likely to resent a readjustment of their erritory, which takes away some of their best customers. ven those paid on salary are not likely to view with complac- ncy the loss of old and tried customers and the task of having o seek out new ones.

Before any readjustments are made, it is essential to secure he salesman's goodwill. They should be shown why it is ecessary, where and how extra business may be secured, nd how they may benefit by the change. It is unjust to xpect the salesman to bear any immediate financial loss that nay result from such an adjustment.

If he is paid on a quota basis, the new quota should fully neet the case. If not, he might be guaranteed his last ew years' average income for a period long enough to nable him to build up his business to its former size. The same result might also be achieved by a bonus liminishing each year according to the estimated rate of rowth.

## HOW THE OFFICE FOLLOWS THE SALESMAN'S PROGRESS

THE essential elements of any proper system of control an direction, whether it be of an airplane or an organisation are, first, a precise knowledge of its objective and the best wa of attaining it; secondly, the devising of adequate means c checking progress and detecting faults whether of speec direction, or general running; thirdly, the ability to interpre the meaning of any signs of error, locate the cause, and appl the appropriate remedy. Although the two must inevitabl overlap, for the sake of convenience it may be advisable t consider the control of selling from two aspects—the contro of selling operations in general and then the management c the sales force.

Is progress being maintained at the desired rate and o sound lines? The most obvious indicator will be the volum of sales and their distribution over the various lines an markets, as well as over the different months of the year, compared with the sales budget. But future progress depen upon the present satisfaction of customers. An unduly hig ratio of returns and allowances to total sales will serve as warning. The fault may lie in the goods, in the price polic or in poor salesmanship. An analysis of the alleged caus of such returns and of complaints regarding the goods ma afford a valuable insight into the causes of the trouble. Quali may be poor, the goods may be unsuited to the particul purpose, customers may lack the necessary knowledge facilities for their correct use or treatment, service may l inadequate, or the goods may have been in stock too lon Flaws in the method of delivery are one of the most prevale causes for dissatisfaction. It behoves the management n only to provide for its control in building the organisation, b to keep a check on it through a record of orders on hand.

Effort is perhaps being applied to the right markets, but a the most productive sections of these being attacked? A f in the average value of orders, whilst not conclusive evidenc may suggest that they are not. What is the smallest ord that pays? If expenses are estimated at £10,000 f 20 000 orders, their average cost will be 10s. eac With an average gross profit of 25 per cent. on selli price, a minimum order of £2 is needed to avoid los

Again, it is useless selling to customers who do not pay. The ratio of bad debts to sales will indicate whether salesmen or the credit department are taking unnecessary risks. A disproportionate rise in the number and value of overdue accounts would indicate the necessity for tightening up the collection of accounts. For the longer accounts are left, the greater becomes the risk of bad debts.

An unsatisfactory general position would naturally demand closer investigation. But even though the position may appear satisfactory, it should be borne in mind that it may not be so throughout the organisation. Defects in some parts may be masked by exceptionally good results in others. Comparisons between actual results and quotas will quickly reveal the territories where effort is not being properly applied, or where development is taking place on wrong lines. Having located the faults, the cause or causes must be found. Before putting the blame upon the salesman, it should be ascertained whether local conditions—a depression in the main industry, local strikes, and so forth—have diminished sales possibilities. If advertising is an essential part of the campaign, has the district been adequately covered? Should sales be through retailers, what percentage distribution has been achieved, and is it in the right type of shop?

### THE STORY THAT THE FIGURES UNFOLD

PROFIT, though not the sole criterion of efficiency, must be the measuring-rod of success in the long-run. A firm would not normally continue selling in territories which resulted, and were likely to continue to result, in a loss: at least, it would seek to adjust its methods so as to turn the loss into a profit. Although the indicators already mentioned throw some light on the problem, accurate knowledge on this point is obtainable only from profit and loss statements for each territory. This is the province of accountancy.

Within the factory, cost accounting has reached a high standard of efficiency. It is possible, without much difficulty, to discover the cost of producing a given article, or of carrying out a single contract or process, and the profit arising from it. It is only within the last few years, however, that any serious attempt has been made to do the same thing for distribution. No technique has yet been evolved, but a number of firms are experimenting with solutions of the problem.

The essentials are an estimate of the gross profit arising

from the sales in each territory and a careful allocation of expenses to each salesman or district. If different products are sold or different prices charged, sales will have to be analysed in accordance with the gross profits earned. Expenses may be divided broadly into the cost of the selling process itself, of carrying local stocks (if any), of delivery, of advertising and sales promotion, of service and overheads. In each category certain expenses, such as travelling expenses, salesmen's salaries, and commission, present no difficulty; others like carriage, cost of packing, etc., may be allocated without much trouble; but the rest, including sales office expenses, market research, and so on, which apply to the market as a whole, must be allocated on the most logical bases possible.

The profit or loss thus calculated, before including the last item of general expenses, will show by how much the company is better or worse off for the business secured in each territory. General expenses would still go on if the firm ceased to work this territory. The fact should not be overlooked that a territory showing no profit or even a small loss may still be profitable to work if the extra sales thus secured enable the goods to be produced at a lower unit cost. A similar approach might be made to products in order to discover which were profitable to sell and which were not—subject to the same proviso.

### VALUABLE CLUES TO REASONS FOR FAILURE

VALUABLE clues as to causes of loss or abnormally low profits may be secured by expense ratios, which express the various types of expenditure as a percentage of sales, and comparing these with some standard, such as results from previous years or from other territories. A very high ratio for delivery, for example, would suggest certain possible remedies dependent upon the market and the commodity—use of the wholesaler, selected or exclusive agencies, partial or complete substitution of personal visits by the post, the opening of a local depot or its closing down, the fixing of prices *ex* works, the fixing of a minimum order, and so on.

In those firms which have not as yet evolved any system of sales cost accounting, certain rough indicators are still open to the management. In respect of those expenses which can be allocated to the several territories at sight, average ratios for the whole firm can be calculated to indicate the selling cost per call, per order, or per £1 sale. Comparisons between these ratios and those for each territory may afford valuable information.

In the absence of sales and production budgets for different lines, the rate of turnover is a valuable gauge of efficiency. The rate of turnover may be estimated by dividing the actual sales for a year (or for any less period calculated on an annual basis) by the average stock held throughout the year. A fall in the rate of turnover, if the total sales themselves are satisfactory, would suggest that too much stock is being carried, or that goods with a high margin of profit are being neglected for those with a low margin, or that the purchasing department is at fault.

Salesmen carry out their work far removed from the vigilant eye of the management. The selling process is affected by numerous and ever-varying factors. Not the least important of these is the human factor represented by the customer and the salesman himself. The peculiar nature of his work, as well as his distinctive temperament, makes the problem of management especially difficult.

The scientific management of the sales force involves certain steps—the planning of work, the devising of standards of performance, the keeping of records and measurement of performance, the discovery and correction of errors, and the improvement and stimulation of performance. The link between the sales manager and the salesman is most commonly the postman. In larger firms it is true that senior salesmen, supervisors, branch and district managers are entrusted with the immediate supervision of salesmen, but they cannot be with every salesman all the time. Moreover, they themselves must be controlled. Management from a distance is therefore unavoidable.

The sales manager can judge only by results. Unfortunately for too many, the word " results " is synonymous with sales. But what matters is not merely how much has been sold, but also what particular items, to whom, in what manner, at what cost, and, often, what other things have been done besides selling. Sales, however, are obviously of primary interest and must claim first attention.

### THE QUOTA: A MEASURING ROD OF EFFICIENCY

SALES quotas have already been mentioned as a device for providing an equitable basis for remuneration. They serve a more important purpose by defining the share which each part of the country is expected to contribute towards the total volume of sales. Assuming that this allocation has been made, as it should have been, with due regard to all relevant factors, it will inevitably constitute a measuring-rod of efficiency.

The potential consumption of each area will form the main basis of division. The figures thus obtained require adjustment according to special local conditions and characteristics, such as the predominance of large or small customers, the local prosperity as revealed in unemployment statistics, etc., and account must be taken of the differing degrees of competition met with, the degree of development as revealed in past sales, the extent of coverage, the degree of saturation and projected local sales campaigns, and, finally, the character of the individual salesmen. The annual quotas thus arrived at should be split up into monthly, or even shorter period, quotas in order to provide for the normal seasonal fluctuations of sales, or the flow which has been decided to be most desirable.

It should be mentioned that many firms employ simpler but less accurate methods of arriving at quotas. In some cases a purely arbitrary addition of, say, 10 per cent. is made to the previous year's sales. In others, salesmen or agents are asked to state what they anticipate selling during the following year, and these estimates are altered up or down according to whether the sales manager considers the salesman to be unduly pessimistic or optimistic. The opinion is sometimes held that it is advisable to indicate to the salesmen a higher figure than is really expected, with the object of making the salesmen work harder, but such a policy usually fails in its purpose. It should be realised that continued failure to reach the quota not only leads to discouragement of the salesmen; it also tends to rob the quota of any significance whatsoever.

A difference of opinion exists as to the advisability of broadcasting the achievements of individuals in relation to quota. It is contended on the one hand that the competitive spirit—the desire to be first in the field—is stimulated by letting every salesman see how his own results compare with those of others. On the other hand, it is maintained that those whose results are poor but not the worst are more likely to console themselves by saying, "at any rate, I have not done as badly as Smith, Jones, and Robinson."

### INVESTIGATING A DROP IN SALES

AN appreciable falling off from quota in any territory calls for immediate investigation. Before attaching blame to the salesman, other possible causes should be looked for. If nothing can be found, the salesman's activities must be examined. It is little use hauling the salesman over the coals unless one has a fairly clear idea of the nature of his delinquency.

An examination of the quotas for different lines and markets, and of his percentage of old and new accounts, should indicate whether he is carrying out the general policy of the company or not. Is he making the best use of his time ? In this connection, the result of an investigation carried out by a well-known American firm is of special interest. This investigation revealed that on the average 40 per cent. of a salesman's time was taken up in travelling, 25 per cent. in clerical and miscellaneous duties, 20 per cent. in waiting for interviews, and only 15 per cent. in actual selling. Closely related to this question of the use of his time is that of whether he is doing a full-time job or is taking unofficial holidays. The answer to both of these should be found in the number of calls he has made. But it is not unknown for salesmen to report calls that were never made. How is the sales manager to detect this without making inquiries from customers or checking it on the spot ? He might find a clue in the average number of calls per sale. But a rise in this figure may be due to other causes.

As regards the salesman's methods, whilst it is not possible to form any definite conclusions without an investigation on the spot, such points as the number of calls per sale, the average sale, the average sale per call, the number of old accounts lost, returns and allowances, complaints, bad debts, and overdue accounts, as well as an analysis of the reasons the salesman gives for not making a sale, may suggest definite faults or weaknesses.

### KEEPING A CHECK ON THE SALESMAN'S ACTIVITIES

THE management needs to know where the salesman is, what he is doing, and how he is doing it. Some of this information is obtainable from the ordinary records of the business ; the rest must be secured from the salesman himself. Ordinary letters are admirable for reports of local conditions or for dealing in detail with specific matters. They are not usually suited, however, to the reporting of the normal activities of a salesman. Details of importance to the management may either be overlooked or be considered of no account. On the other hand, a lot of time may be wasted in needless repetition, or in the giving of information which is readily obtainable from other sources.

The sales manager should do all in his power to increase the time his salesmen can devote to customers. With this object, printed forms are often supplied to salesmen. These forms usually involve little writing but elicit information needed to help in the formulation of future action, to control the activities of the salesman, and to increase his efficiency. The information called for will naturally vary with the type of business, but it should be limited to the absolutely essential—names and addresses of people called on, the result of the call, reasons if no sale has been made, advertising material or help required from headquarters. In the case of a new customer, other information may be required, such as the nature of his business, estimates of his credit standing and his purchasing capacity, competitive goods in stock or in use, and the name of the person to be interviewed.

These reports are sent in daily or weekly to headquarters, where they are scrutinised, and action taken where necessary. The information is entered on customer record cards, and a general summary of the salesman's work noted on a card bearing the salesman's name. These cards are filed for ready reference and kept up to date. Where salesmen decide their own route and the visits they make, it is necessary for them to keep a record of each customer (preferably in loose-leaf form) and the dealings the firm has had with him. Since communications may have been received from or sent to the customer by the head office, it is essential for the salesman to be kept informed, usually by the sending of copies.

A great deal of time can be saved and unpleasantness avoided if the salesman is in possession of the complete history of his firm's dealings with any customer to date before he calls on him. This may be ensured, and the salesman's time saved, by issuing a type of report form which can be used over and over again. For example, the towns to be visited during the next week being known, the reports relating to all customers and prospective customers in these towns are brought up to date, any points of special importance noted on a separate instruction sheet, and the whole dispatched to the salesman, preferably in a loose-leaf binder. At the end of the week the salesman returns the reports; they are examined in the sales office and any special matters dealt with, the customers cards are brought up to date, and the reports are then filed away again.

### HOW THE SELLING STAFF CAN BE STIMULATED

CERTAIN firms, especially those dealing in specialities, make extensive use of sales contests for the purpose of stimulating salesmen to greater efforts. It is a practice which does not appeal to all types of salesmen, and it should be adopted only after very careful consideration of its repercussions on the sales policy. Space does not permit an examination of the *pros* and *cons* of the matter. It should be pointed out, however, that volume of sales is not necessarily the objective (although it usually is), nor need prizes be restricted to one or two individuals. The basis may be a certain percentage increase in sales, either in general or of a particular line, or a certain number of new customers, or a certain percentage of cash orders, and so on, and a prize or bonus may be given to all salesmen attaining a certain minimum.

Cyclostyled or printed publications are freely used to maintain contact with salesmen or distributors and build up an *esprit de corps*. Some of these maintain a very high standard both as regards general make-up and literary style. Their contents are designed to impart general information regarding the policy, organisation and personnel, progress that is being made, the activities of competitors, general business conditions and details of selling schemes, contests, and so on. They may also give general instructions on points, where statistics have revealed a general failing, or provide more detailed information about certain aspects of the salesman's or distributor's work. They assist by indicating new uses or outlets, describing new methods, or dealing with difficulties of common occurrence. Occasionally, editorials of a purely stimulative character are inserted. House organs circulating amongst distributors are of a more formal character, and discuss problems of special interest to dealers such as stock control, accounts, buying, etc.

Sales conferences and conventions are sometimes organised, ranging from daily, weekly, or monthly meetings of a mainly local character, to annual conferences for all salesmen in the country. Opinion is divided upon their value. The latter are without doubt costly, and they should not be held unless they serve a very useful purpose, a purpose, moreover, which is clearly envisaged by the sales manager. They should be carefully planned so that no time is lost and the full benefits may be derived from them. The sales manager has here an excellent opportunity to review the past year's progress and outline his plans for the period ahead. He can develop the theme with a greater wealth of detail and in a more convincing manner than would be possible in a sales bulletin or a letter. He is able to explain and remove misgivings or even hostility regarding changes in policy, methods of remuneration, and methods of arriving at quotas. He is in a position to deal fully and forcibly with any general faults either in attitude of mind or in method. New lines can be explained and demonstrated. And finally, the whole organisation may be inspired by a greater sense of responsibility, a new spirit of co-operation, and a renewed confidence in the firm, its products, and themselves.

## WHERE TO READ MORE ABOUT SALES MANAGEMENT

Some readers may feel inclined to make a closer study of sales management and would welcome a little guidance on further reading. Unfortunately there are few good books on the subject, and most of these are American and obviously apply specially to American conditions. C. L. Bolling's *Sales Management* (Pitman) gives a good general outline of the many aspects of sales management, whether sales are made through agents, travelling salesmen, retail shops, or by mail order. It covers a wide field, and has the added merit of dealing exclusively with British conditions and methods. *Intensive Sales Management*, by J. C. Ashley (Dartnell), deals in a practical manner with all the aspects of sales management.

The marketing section of the *Handbook of Business Administration*, published by McGraw Hill for the American Management Association, contains a series of useful contributions by leading American experts on such subjects as market research, price policy, sales quotas, selection, training, and control of salesmen, marketing costs, etc. A new American publication, the Dartnell *Sales Managers' Handbook*, although containing much information which is of no value outside the United States of America, nevertheless deals fairly fully with many aspects of the sales management problem.

Sales forecasting is still in its infancy, but a number of books have been written dealing with the methods of procedure and the various factors which influence the trend of trade. Wm. Wallace, a director of Messrs. Rowntree, has written an instructive book, *Business Forecasting* (Pitman), which gives a general survey of the principles of forecasting as applied by the most progressive firms in this country. *The Selection and Training of Salesmen*, by Kenaghy & Yoakum, deals very fully with the various methods adopted in America for discovering and developing good salesmen. The results of experiments are given, and many types of forms and tests are reproduced. The book deals less fully with certain other problems involved in the management of a sales force. *The Control of Distribution Costs and Sales*, by W. B. Castenholz, is one of the only two books which deal in anything like a satisfactory manner with this difficult question of control. Although American, the general principles of the work apply alike to all countries, and it may very usefully be studied by an English reader.

# SALESMANSHIP

*by BERNARD M. CONYBEARE, F.R.Econ.S.*

THERE is no position more essential to the well-being of the community than that of salesman, and no work which, if both honestly and vigorously done, is more satisfactory to the doer. The salesman should take no small view of the important nature of his duties, for it is essential to the health of the business world that they should be conscientiously carried out. There have never been so many goods and services offered to the public as there are now, with the purpose not only of satisfying the bare needs of existence, but of saving time or money and of helping people to make a fuller use of leisure. It is the business of the salesman to make all these goods and services, drawn from all parts of the world, readily available for the public.

His functions are manifold. He acts as the medium through which ideas can be exchanged between the customer and the supplier, in order that any goods for which there is a public need may be provided by the manufacturer. It is his business also to present to the public any new goods and services for which there have been little or no demand, but for which a satisfactory demand can, in the opinion of the supplier, be created.

The salesman should look upon himself not wholly as the servant of his employers, but also as the servant of the public —who are his ultimate employers—and he must do his best to see that the scales are always evenly balanced between his employers and the customer. It is his duty to see that the customer is not supplied with a product which is unsuitable for the purpose for which it is required, or is over-supplied with a suitable product. In fact, he has to be ready to act as guide and counsellor to the customer whenever the situation calls for one.

It is of great importance that every effort should be used to accelerate the speed with which products are turned over, in order that overhead expenses—the proportion that standing charges bear to the total trading profit, or to the total turnover in cash—may be kept down, and that the trading profit may be increased. When goods are kept turning over quickly nd selling costs are kept low, every section of the community enefits. No matter from where the investor, pensioner, vage-earner, or salaried worker draws his income, whether rom industrial, government, or municipal sources, he will eel the benefit, if not in increased income, at any rate in ncreased security. The machinery of business is fully ccupied, there is less unemployment and distress, and enefits are felt all round. The credit for this, when it is chieved, belongs in large measure to the salesman.

### A WRONG IDEA OF SALESMANSHIP

SOME salesmen actually feel an inward dislike for their job, because they say that they are "not actually producing nything." This idea, which springs from a completely nsound conception of the marketing of goods, has no justiication in fact, and is absolutely fatal to really successful elling. The producing and selling of goods are complemenary to and bound up in each other, even though an artificial listinction may sometimes be made between them in the ame firm, for the purpose of business convenience or bookeeping. An extreme case is that of a well-known firm in which the production department sells the goods to the ales department, even though both concerns have the same lirectors and the same capital.

The printer of a ten-shilling note has not "produced" ten hillings by printing the note: it remains only a cheap bit of aper with a design on it, unless it is known that it can be put nto circulation at any moment and that it can always be xchanged for goods or services. The case of goods and ervices is somewhat similar. Goods may be very nice to ook at, or services may be very convenient, but they have no commercial and social value or significance unless and until hey can be sold for a commercial return. If they cannot be, hen they must cease to be produced or offered. An article nay be produced by a factory either as a result of the work of ts own design department or as the result of information supplied by its own or some other selling staff, but whether it continues to be produced depends on the salesman who sells the article to its ultimate consumer or user.

Further, the principal cost of an article by the time that it s actually sold to the public is often not the cost of actual proluction; sometimes by far the greater part of the selling price s due to the actual cost of selling, whether this consists of factory charges or whether it is in respect of a shop. This applies particularly to specialities, and the more difficult the speciality is to sell, the higher the proportion of selling cost is likely to be. Typewriters, for instance, of which the actual factory cost of production in the United States of America was some thirty-five shillings, have been sold in this country for twenty-five pounds. The actual net profit may, even then, have been less than in the case of many articles more easily sold. If, therefore, there is an efficient sales staff which can very materially reduce the selling cost of an article, its activities are of immense benefit to the public.

The salesman can also help to create demand by faithfully recording and sorting the various demands of individual customers which together go to form public demand. He can often save his employer's money, which is itself a negative form of production, by seeing that the customer does not obtain some unfair advantage. He can put forward his employer's view with dignity and present the firm in the best light, and there is no business in which he cannot fill an intensely useful and worthy part.

### THE INEFFICACY OF THE "SHOP FRONT" MIND

THE salesman should try to avoid developing a "shop front" mind which has all the apparently attractive qualities on display, and nothing in reserve for the rush periods, when there is a run on his mind. Deep reserves are required, reserves which will keep him cheerful and courteous at all times and under the most trying circumstances. All customers like to see a cheerful salesman, and one often hears them remark that they look forward to seeing some particular salesman who has a reputation for cheerfulness. The salesman should be careful how he deals with the customer who is always full of woe; by quiet cheerfulness he can very often get him to change his opinion.

Courtesy requires habitual exercise: it is useless for a salesman to expect that he can pick and choose, and that he need not always show courtesy towards his colleagues and subordinates, while always being able to show it to his customers. If he has not habitually practised showing it to all, the time will come when the varnish will crack and he will find that he is not able to show it to some particularly trying customer and there will be trouble. Courtesy, like charity, should begin at home, in the firm itself and between its members.

Self-control, it goes without saying, is most important, but it is doubtful whether it can be described as a quality. The salesman should realise that the term "self-control" rather implies that, before the control has become fully operative, there has been some degree of conflict, even though it may happily have been of short duration. A mind in which such an internal conflict is taking place is hardly likely to be in its best form for concentration and good salesmanship. He should aim not so much at establishing self-control for the ordinary things of life as at cultivating an even-tempered mind, which will call for the exercise of self-control only in the most exceptional circumstances.

One sometimes hears a salesman say that such and such a thing or person gets "on his nerves." This is very often because he is thinking all the time that the situation or person is annoying, and that he must exercise self-control in order not to show his annoyance. The more he tries to exercise self-control, the greater he assumes the annoyance to be, and so the vicious circle goes on. Sometimes all irritation goes at once if the salesman simply says to himself that it is all in the day's work, that it is entirely normal, and that he is bound from the nature of his work to take the rough—sometimes the very rough—with the same good temper as he takes the smooth. An even-tempered mind does not mean a lazy mind. Some people who are mentally lazy prefer not to think about anything worrying or sad, or which involves any responsibility which may shake them out of their self-centred ways or penetrate their insulation from the shocks of everyday life. But an equable mind should feel deeply and yet not lose a sense of proportion or place feeling above what is fair to firm, colleagues, and self.

### EXAGGERATION: THE SURE SIGN THAT SOMETHING IS WRONG

THE salesman should be truthful, even though the immediate result of this may seem, at times, disappointing to him. It is gravely doubtful whether the use of exaggeration is advisable at any time. Without entering into a discussion on the ethics of the question, it may be said that exaggeration is harmful to the character since its user may lose his sense of proportion and become unfitted for any higher sales position, where a sales campaign may have to be planned in a strictly accurate and truthful manner. Indeed, those who use exaggeration frequently end by being dishonest with themselves, and develop what is more or less a "split" personality—they enter into a competition with themselves, and each time they tell a story they add something to increase its interest.

The sole result of exaggeration is a negative one—its use is always an indication that there is something wrong which should be put right. The salesman may think that the product which he is selling is inferior and that it requires over-praising in order to sell it, or he may be conscious of inferiority in himself or his employers and may think that he or they require something stronger than the truth to make them appear in a good light. Exaggeration may be regarded as a desperate attempt of the mind to disguise some trouble which should be removed. The salesman should also be a good mixer and at his ease with all sorts and conditions of customers—otherwise they will not be at their ease with him and will probably want to get rid of him as quickly as possible, with the result that he may lose a sale which he might otherwise have got.

Punctuality is most important, and the salesman should show at least the same degree of care about arriving at work as he does about leaving. Very often there is an unofficial period of grace, perhaps of five minutes or perhaps more, allowed to the salesman on arriving in the morning. It does not look well if the salesman invariably takes advantage of this, but leaves with extreme punctuality in the evening. Every salesman knows of such cases, and also knows that salesmen have been sent for by the Managing Director, who has said, "I observe, Mr. ——, that you are not as punctilious about the time at which you arrive as you are about the time at which you leave." Unpunctuality is one of the worst trainings that a salesman can possibly give himself and is one of the deadly sins, showing, if others are inconvenienced as well, the most complete lack of consideration. The salesman should always remember that even if his own time is valueless—supposing that he takes this low view of it—the time of others may be of considerable value.

Perseverance is one of the first essentials, especially in the case of an outside salesman. The writer knew of one case where a travelling salesman had called on the same firm for twenty years without getting an order. In the twentieth year, the son of the principal of this firm asked his father to give this man an order, saying that he thought that he deserved it. The salesman got the order.

## PATIENCE AND METHOD GO HAND IN HAND

TACT is likewise essential, and is really a combination of various qualities, good judgment, consideration, imagination, and patience, all of which are necessary. All these are active qualities, even patience. Some people have the idea that patience consists in waiting for something to happen and smiling bravely if it doesn't; but this is entirely wrong. Patience consists largely in holding one's hand so as to act more effectively when the right moment arrives. There is no better training for the character, if the object for which the salesman waits is a good one. The salesman of understanding mind is always patient and ready to see the other person's point of view and to help lame dogs over stiles—or even to help trying customers to select their goods. He will also forbear to press the customer more than is wise when trying to effect a sale.

Honesty of purpose is really covered by saying that the salesman should be truthful. He cannot talk convincingly unless he has high selling ideals and faith in the goods which he sells, and unless he honestly believes in the importance and value of his work. He cannot hold the attention of his customer when he is talking as if he doesn't quite understand, or believe in, what he is saying. Method and routine are essential. It is sometimes the fashion to decry both of them, but this is only because their use has not been understood and has been abused. They are not intended to do away with the necessity for thought, but, on the contrary, to free the mind from worrying about things which should be done as a matter of course, so that it may be better able to observe any new facts and to make deductions from them and to do really creative work. The use of method and routine removes a good deal of mental strain since it becomes easier for the mind habitually to take definite action at the time when it is called for, rather than to leave this to the whim of the moment or the chance promptings, perhaps, of an overloaded memory. But method and routine should be the eager servants of the salesman, not his harsh taskmasters.

Another thing to learn is the importance of the correct balance of detail. There are some salesmen who have intelligence to which they undoubtedly join application—yet they do not meet with any great measure of success, certainly not a success which is equal to their abilities. They do give great attention to detail, but do not consider the job as a whole and allow themselves to become side-tracked, discussing some relatively unimportant point at the same length as some far more important point. An artist, in filling in the background of a picture, would not paint it in such detail as the foreground; yet there are salesmen who miss the broad sweep of the brush in trying to paint in every part of their job in equal detail, so that their work instead of being all one piece is a series of isolated events, even though they may be doing the same piece of work the whole time. In writing letters they will give more attention to the exact wording of the letter than to the effect which the letter is intended to produce.

The salesman may have every good quality, but he will not go far unless he also has the power of continuous application, that is to say, perseverance plus judgment. Many of the outstanding figures of the business world are not what is generally known as "brilliant"; but they have worked and observed and their success may well be attained by others.

## THE MAN BEHIND THE COUNTER

BEFORE discussing in detail selling in a retail shop, or indoor selling as it is called, and selling on behalf of a producer or wholesaler, or outdoor selling, it may be useful to mention some of the main differences between the two. The problems which the salesman has to face in each case are not by any means the same, and in some ways the work of the indoor salesman is the easier, while in others the advantage is definitely on the side of the outdoor salesman. The balance of advantage is hard to strike.

The main difference lies in the approach, which may be divided into two parts—the physical and the mental. The potential customers of the indoor salesman do actually appear before him, whereas the potential customer of the outdoor salesman may never appear before him—he may only hear the vain repetitions of voices over the internal telephone or from inner offices, announcing what he has come about, and considerable ingenuity may have to be exercised by the outside salesman in securing even a glimpse of, let alone an interview with, his potential customer.

As regards the second, or mental, part of the approach, when the salesman has actually met his potential customer the important difference is that the majority of those who enter a shop have in their minds the general idea of buying, and of buying some particular class of product or service. Many enter the shop or department prepared to ask for some particular article manufactured by one particular maker or company. In this case the indoor salesman will encounter practically no sales resistance on any of these points. The outdoor salesman, on the other hand, may have to enter a shop, the proprietor of which may have decided not to buy anything at all at the time of the salesman's visit. This resistance he will first have to overcome. Again, the buyer whom he is seeing, though decided that he is going to buy some particular class of product, may have decided that he does not want the special product which the salesman happens to be offering, if he is confined to one particular line, or make, of articles. This resistance, too, the salesman will have to overcome.

### SALES RESISTANCE HAS MANY FORMS

THE salesman of the wholesale merchant or factor may not have to deal with resistance on this score, as he will be able to offer the products of a number of makers. But he may have to encounter an additional sales resistance, peculiar to his business, which arises from the buyer saying that it will pay him better to go direct to the manufacturer, who may also be offering "sale or return" stock.

The salesman may be offering an established product of a type for which there is a steady demand, and he will then have no resistance to meet as regards selling that type. One sometimes hears something like the following: "Smith a salesman? Why, he never had to sell a thing in his life," meaning that the demand was already created before he came on the scene and that his selling is of a mechanical nature. This is one of those sayings which sound acute, but which are sometimes very far from the truth. Considerably more sales resistance may have to be overcome in the case of an article which has to be sold against fierce competition, however well established that type of article may be.

The inside salesman is, again, in a considerably stronger position than the outdoor salesman as regards the display of stock, and will often be in a position to show any number of complete and full size articles, rather than samples which are incomplete or are not full size, or which can be reinforced only by photographs or by a catalogue.

The balance of advantage up to this point has been with the indoor salesman, but from now on the balance is probably to the advantage of the outside salesman. He is in a much better position in most cases to obtain repeat orders, since usually he will not be selling to the ultimate consumer. The outside salesman is, again, usually in a position to do a much larger turnover and, if his area is large, has a better chance of keeping a steady yearly average of sales than has the inside salesman, who may be in a shop or department which serves a fairly small area.

The outside salesman, also, generally develops rather closer personal relations with his contacts than does the inside salesman. Thus, in following up inquiries, or in following up work which has not resulted in a sale at the time, the outside salesman, again, has an advantage over the inside salesman, in that his contacts do not move about and are usually more easily got hold of than those of the inside salesman, who may have to deal with a rather nebulous inquirer.

### THE SHOPMAN EXTENDS HIS RANGE OF PERSUASION

SINCE retail selling over the counter employs far more salesmen than are employed in selling retail outside, or in wholesale selling, this branch of salesmanship calls for consideration first. The trend of modern retail salesmanship is much more dynamic than it used to be. The customer is, in the first place, put to much less trouble than formerly in choosing goods and services, being told of these very often by post, personal call, or telephone. Furthermore, after a sale has been effected, there is more free service offered than formerly. The result is that the day when retail selling consisted chiefly in standing behind the counter and waiting for the customer to come into the shop has gone. The retail motor trade, in particular, used to wait in their showrooms for the buyer to come in and inquire about a car until the drive of competition made them go out to see their prospective purchasers.

Departmental representatives can make outside calls in person, as well as by telephone. It is easy to get a personal hearing by telephone, but it is also easy to have the conversation terminated without having done anything, and this method should be used in very strict moderation. The salesman may be only one of many, and the prospective customer may display considerable irritation if this method is abused.

The caller should say who he is, mention the article concerned, and explain why he has rung up; there may have been a sudden run on the stock of some particular article, deliveries may be slowing up, and he has reason to believe that the potential or actual customer is interested.

Events which necessitate a more or less considerable expenditure on goods and services are engagements, marriages, births, and the building of or moving into new houses and flats. Early information of building projects can usually be got from the building trade papers, which can be consulted at any public library, and very often the name and address of the actual owner of the new building is given, or can be obtained from the architect's office if asked for tactfully. Where contact can be established there is the opportunity for effecting a much larger turnover than is usually possible, especially in the case of new hotels and similar large buildings.

It is assumed that window-dressing has been properly attended to by experts, and that the customer has actually entered the shop. The next point that has to be considered by the salesmen of a department collectively is the question of "tracking," *i.e.* the route which the customer takes, to their department, from the various entrances. The salesman should make a point of asking for permission to inspect this tracking sometimes, and of going from the department to every entrance of the shop; if he always uses the staff entrance, he may never see that some direction sign is badly posted, and this is too often considered nobody's business. Attention to the posting and legibility of signs should be given in order to make certain that a customer will have no difficulty in finding the way to the department required. Sign posting should be co-ordinated by some central authority in order that competition between the various departments may be controlled.

An attractive display of stock should be arranged near the entrances to the department, which may invite customers passing to other departments to look in. Similarly, attention should be paid to the display in the department, so that customers who have come in may be tempted to linger. A buyer who has come for one thing can in this way be reminded of other things he wants, or even lured into getting something it had never previously entered his head to buy.

## HOW TO RECEIVE A CUSTOMER

A CUSTOMER'S reception should not be in any way effusive—effusiveness puts many customers off, when they are of a reserved type, no matter whether they are nervous or quite at ease—but at the same time the reception should be cordial. A slight bow from the supervisor or any senior salesman, who happens to be near the entrance when the customer comes into the department, pleases many customers who do like to feel that their entrance has not passed entirely unnoticed. Even those who had intended walking straight through the department may sometimes stop to ask a question which may even lead to a sale.

Salesmen who may be having any private conversation, no matter what it is about, should break it off immediately if there is a potential customer anywhere near them. A diffident customer may be tempted to linger, to choose, and to buy, if he or she sees that the sales staff are alert, but may be put off by the casual attitudes of the sales staff.

The salesman should endeavour roughly to classify what may be the interests of his customer, bearing in mind age, appearance of bodily activity, style of clothing, and so on. It is true that this is a little difficult in an age when grandfathers and grandmothers take to dancing with vigour, or to going on cruises. But the salesman may find that if he exercises his powers of observation, his time in making suggestions is sometimes saved and he may secure a sale which would otherwise be missed.

He should know the position of all the stock in the department so that he can find it easily and quickly, without fumbling, and without having to keep on turning over piles of articles. He should make as little noise as possible in moving the stock about, and should aim not only at the appearance, but at the actuality of quiet efficiency. He should remember that the customer receives his impressions by means of sight and hearing—and to a very much less degree, touch—and that the customer very often does not use both at the same time. He should be careful not to distract the customer's attention too much by talking when the stock is being examined, or by moving the stock under examination when the customer is talking to him.

He should be in a position to advise his customer as to the suitability of the product, its practicability—that is, whether it does what it is supposed to do, or what the customer would like it to do, and in the case of some products, how it does it. He must also be able to advise on the behaviour of the product in use and, what is often an important consideration, its appearance in what are to be its normal surroundings.

### THE CONVERSATION THAT HELPS A SALE

HE should always make a positive suggestion, and should not say " May I show you " . . . to the customer unless he is certain that the answer will be " Yes." This question implies a certain amount of doubt in the salesman's mind and, if he is only drawing a bow at a venture, he may miss a chance by giving the customer an easy opportunity to say no. He should say " I should like to show you," and the customer will usually consent to be shown.

The salesman should take care not to be too technical as the customer may get bored and thus refuse to buy. This is not to say that the salesman should not be able to discuss technical matters in an interesting way with those who want to know about them ; sometimes he may have a customer who is of an inquiring and scientific mind, and who is interested in hearing about the origin of the raw material, the various qualities of raw material, how they are made into the finished product, and so on. But it must be remembered that there can be no discussion longer or more endless than a scientific one, and the salesman should not allow an undue amount of time to be spent in this way.

He should not overtalk to the customer. The ideal sale is one in which the salesman does not have to talk to the customer at all, and the nearer the salesman can get to this ideal the better. He will then be able to deal with a greater number of customers, and the bigger will be his turnover in consequence. After a salesman has settled down in a department the proportion of sales that he makes to the number of customers or inquirers dealt with, will remain at a fairly steady average. If he wants to increase his turnover, then, he will have to increase the number of demonstrations of articles which he gives.

Sometimes, when showing an article, it is a good plan for him to stop talking for a moment or two so that he can see how things are going. He may have a customer who is not saying much and he may not be sure what impression the article he is showing has made. The customer will, very often, make some illuminating remark and the salesman can then go on again, if he finds that the customer is not yet ready for a sale. On the other hand, it may pay, with the good-humoured or sporting type of customer, to try to get a definite decision by asking what quantity the customer may be put down for, or, rather, suggesting some quantity to put him or her down for. Once the salesman has decided that the article is, in fact, suitable for the customer, he should not allow the least doubt to appear that he is taking a sale other than for granted.

### KEEPING AN EYE ON THE SALE OF THE FUTURE

If a sale does not result, the salesman should enter the reason given in his book, and, if it appears that a sale may subsequently be effected, should try to get the inquirer's name and address for placing on the Departmental Mailing list. Even in the case of a small cash sale when the goods are taken away, the customer's name and address should be obtained, if possible, so that it can be added to this list. The list can then be brought up to date each month by adding new names at the end in alphabetical order. Twice a year, or at any time thought suitable, an up-to-date mailing list is compiled, which includes all such additions to the list. With this list will be filed any notes made by the salesman in cases where he did not effect a sale at the time, with the date on which the customer may be written to. After the matter has been brought forward twice without result, it may usually be regarded as dead, though this will vary according to the type of article.

The suggestion book kept by the salesman should contain suggestions from customers as to size, shape, appearance, and quality. At regular intervals the supervisor should make a note of any suggestion which appears to have merit, or any suggestion which, while not appearing to be very good, is brought forward by a number of customers, and send the note to the Sales Manager.

Every effort should be made by the salesman not merely to open new accounts, but also to see that existing ones are fully worked. The word " account " is used here to denote any customer who buys in the department, whether it is a cash sale or a credit account. There is no doubt that, in very many shops, the existing turnover could be largely increased by giving closer attention to the working of old accounts.

## MAPPING A ROUTE THROUGH THE SHOP FOR CUSTOMERS

FAR more attention might be given to team work between the various departments, and salesmen should remember that, although they may have finished serving the customer in their own department, other departments may not have done so. The salesman should keep himself informed as to the " lay-out " of the other departments and their position in order that he may be able to direct customers by the shortest way. Any changes made in the position of departments should at once be marked on a plan, which can then be posted in every department.

The salesman should know the period of maximum seasonal appeal of all the other departments—or as many of them as he can—so that he can work in co-operation with them. It may be the dull period in his department, but the " season " may be in full swing in the department next door, and the salesman may be able to do them a good turn which they will repay later.

The salesman cannot work effectively with other departments if he only knows one or two departments, and the business of his firm will undoubtedly not reach its highest possible turnover if there are many in the same position as he is. A salesman, unless he is in a key position, should try not to spend too long in one department, provided that he can be moved in a series of gradual stages from his own department to one that is closely allied to it and so on ; he will then quickly pick up the selling points of his new stock and there will be no loss in selling efficiency. The salesman who is not able to pick up new details quickly, however, must not expect to be moved by his employers, as there is then likely to be considerable inefficiency in his new department. It is essential, then, that the salesman should learn all that he possibly can about the work of all allied departments. Some firms give evening talks, which are open to all salesmen, about the technical points and work of the different departments, and the salesman who wishes to get on will be well advised to attend these. It is desirable that the work of all departments be covered during the year. Sometimes it is possible to arrange for a supervisor from some other department to attend one morning a week, before the customers arrive, in order to give a short talk on the work of his own department, and indicate to the salesmen of the department which he is addressing how they can help his department.

When the salesman has finished with the customer in his department, he should ask if the customer will visit another department, mentioning one which sells a similar product, or —working either backwards or forwards—one which sells a product which normally follows or precedes that sold in his own department. The main idea is to keep a close connection between the product suggested and the particular product which the customer has just bought, so that the mind of the customer is attuned to a similar sale and the next salesman on the job will not have to meet too much sales resistance. Salesmen who know each other can often arrange to interchange customers, and they then keep a note of their joint turnover. Where a customer is attracted by the idea of visiting another department to see a particular product, the salesman should make sure that he actually does arrive in that department.

Personal recommendation is most important as a means of increasing turnover, and an opportunity will often occur for the salesman to ask the customer to bring some friend to visit the department in order to see some particular article in which the customer's friend might be interested. Sometimes a customer will recommend that a friend be written to about some special line of goods.

### HINTS TO BE FOUND IN COMPETITORS' METHODS

THE salesman should try in every way to increase his store of general information. He should make a point of looking at the windows of similar shops which serve a similar public, and should make a note of any articles which, while of quality equal to that of some article in his own department, are being sold at either a higher or at a lower price ; any information worthy of record which he gets in this way, the supervisor can pass on to the Sales Manager.

The salesman should aim at being able instinctively to estimate the current appeal of the goods which he sells— —an appeal which is a combination of seasonal influence and of any current fashion or thought—so that he may know to what portions of his stock to give prominence. He should try to look at the newspaper thoroughly each day, as valuable information can be gained in this way, not only as to what the public are buying, but also as to what they might be induced to buy, when it has been brought to their notice.

The bargain sales, especially, are regarded by the daily papers as having a definite news value.

### MAKING SURE THAT THE CUSTOMER IS RIGHT

THE salesman should remember that the thoughts and actions of his customers are governed by instincts, and that they might deny this—even with some show of indignation, in case these instincts might be considered petty or discreditable—if it was suggested to them. Nevertheless, allowance often has to be made for such instincts. According to the saying, the customer is always right: the highest form of salesmanship is for the salesman to make sure that the customer really *is* right. If the salesman thinks that the customer is about to make what will be, in the circumstances, an entirely wrong choice or is choosing a lower priced article when able to pay for a higher priced and more durable article (which would be more satisfactory in the long run), he should try to lead the customer away from this choice.

In doing so, he should avoid the least appearance of "pushing," and, in giving the true reasons for the customer making another choice, it is as well, with the obstinate type of customer—who disagrees with any definite suggestions put forward—to put these reasons actually in the form of questions. The customer may then think that he or she alone has made the choice, and unconsciously co-operates instead of disagreeing the whole time. If the salesman ever has flatly to disagree with a customer—which is usually bad business—it will very likely mean that he has made no serious effort to secure this co-operation on the part of the customer.

Another type of customer who isn't really right, but whom the salesman should endeavour to make so, is the pessimistic type. This type is more often met with by the travelling salesman, since people who are in a pessimistic mood do not enter shops, to any large extent, to buy. The salesman should never agree with such a customer directly, but should try to persuade him or her that there is such value for money ready for inspection that pessimism cannot exist beside it. The salesman who agrees with a pessimistic customer is hardly likely to get an order.

It is advisable to show a higher priced product before a lower-priced one, at any rate where the customer has given no very clear indication of a price range. No ordinary customer will be annoyed at being shown an article at a higher price than that which he or she is prepared to give and will often, on the contrary, be inwardly gratified. On the other hand, there are many customers who feel slightly hurt if the salesman shows them an article at a lower price that that which they are prepared to give, and who think that the salesman has formed a view of their position other than that to which they think they are entitled. Furthermore, it is perfectly easy to come down in price, but always much more difficult to go up and to show a rising price range. Considerable sales resistance may be encountered and a higher-value sale may be missed. Even where the customer has given a clear indication of price range, there is no harm in putting a higher-priced article forward with the others and saying nothing about it; the customer may ask about it and the salesman may book an order for the higher priced product.

### LULLING THE DOUBTS OF THE SUSPICIOUS CUSTOMER

THE type of customer who looks suspiciously at everything and everybody, including the salesman, requires handling with great care, and if the salesman thinks that some line which he has on view will not be suitable for the customer, he will be well advised to keep it in the background. Whereas the ordinary customer, if told that some particular line is not suitable for the purpose for which he requires it, is usually grateful, the suspicious type is apt to assume that there is something wrong about the whole of the stock, and has been heard to remark afterwards, "That salesman is a funny man, he tells one not to buy things!"

When the decisive and abrupt type of customer—usually a man—is met with and the salesman has just given a reason (which has been accepted) why the customer should choose a particular article, let him beware against giving additional reasons, though they may all be equally good. Some people, especially these who pride themselves on making up their minds very quickly, get very irritated if they are given additional reasons, as they regard this partly as a waste of their time and also, perhaps, as an indirect reflection on the rapidity of their decision. This type usually moves, talks, and behaves abruptly.

It is always worth while taking that extra bit of care with the troublesome or over-critical customer, who inspects stock at great length and seems rather annoyed about it. This type s often just as ready to sing praises as curses and, if pleased, o tell all her (or his) friends about it.

### FAILURES THAT IRRITATE THE CUSTOMER

ONE of the chief causes of friction between salesman and customer is the giving of delivery dates which are not cept. If there is any doubt at all on the part of the salesnan as to the delivery date which he wishes to quote being in accurate one, he should obtain confirmation from some-body who knows. If his supervisor does not know, then he can use the internal telephone. If the salesman has quoted a irm delivery date, and it is subsequently found that owing, perhaps, to unforeseen circumstances the promised delivery date cannot be kept, then the customer should receive a letter of apology at once. The goods may have been ordered for some special function or event, and the non-fulfilment of a lelivery date should always be looked on as an event of serious mportance, and every possible effort should be made to ninimise any inconvenience caused. The supervising salesnan should enter the reason given for non-delivery in his book.

Customers may sometimes become very irritated—especially the self-important type, or the type which is always ooking out for slights, real or imaginary, at the incorrect spelling of names or addresses, or the transposing of initials. A customer will sometimes go to the trouble of returning a form or invoice, and pointing out that two initials have been transposed, but that he or she does not mind, etc. It is always safest to assume that the customer *does* mind, and to get him or her to confirm the name and address after it has been written down by the salesman.

If the customer is of the chatty type and, owing to some unavoidable reason, has to wait after the order has been dealt with, with the result that a conversation on general topics is started, certain subjects should be avoided or discussed in an entirely non-committal manner. Religion and politics are both subjects which may stir up considerable feeling, and salesmen have given great offence to customers on occasion by thoughtless remarks.

### THE DISPLAYED ARTICLE THAT IS "SOLD OUT"

IF there is a display in a window or show-case away from the department, the salesman should know exactly what is being displayed there, and typewritten lists should be available in his department detailing the products shown. If any of them are sold out, the salesman should inform the super- visor, who will then take steps to have the article removed from display if this seems desirable. It is as well to do this in the case of articles on which there is a considerable run friction is likely to be caused if a customer has had to make a tedious journey to a department, only to find that the article desired has been sold out. In the case of less sought-after articles, there may not be the same urgency about removing them, and the view may be held by the supervisor that it is something to get the customer into the department or shop where he or she may be smoothed down if disappointed and shown something else. In the case of a shop where the customer has to walk a short way from window to counter getting the customer in may be the first consideration, and friction as the result of a short walk should hardly be a serious problem.

There should be a note in each department stating where deliveries are made by van in the various areas, together with a note showing the latest time that the Dispatch Department can receive goods from the various selling departments. Friction is sometimes caused when a salesman promises to send articles which a customer could easily carry, and just misses the last delivery of the day in that area.

The salesman should be very careful, when selling any goods which carry a maker's guarantee of replacement in certain circumstances, to see that he does not promise replace- ment in any other than these particular circumstances. If he does, and the makers of the goods refuse replacement then the salesman's firm will be bound to replace if they wish to avoid unpleasantness with their customer ; but the unpleasantness will still be there as far as the salesman is concerned.

Care must be taken in matching colours and in showing colours by artificial light, as mistakes may be made over this ; and even though the customer may have been just as mistaken, he or she may feel a sense of grievance against the salesman. Most counters, where coloured articles are shown and where accuracy in colour choosing or matching is desir- able, have " daylight " lamps, that is, lamps in which the ordinary gas-filled metal filament bulb has a piece of blue glass in front of it. This glass absorbs the excess of red rays which are present in the electric light to a greater extent than in daylight. These lamps do not really produce more than an approximation to daylight, but are much better than the uncorrected electric light; daylight bulbs can also be obtained, in which the glass of the bulb itself is blue; these bulbs are, of course, much cheaper than a complete lamp, but are not quite so well corrected, because the glass of the bulb is very thin.

### SHOWING MATERIALS IN THEIR TRUE COLOURS

THE principles of reflection and absorption of colours should be understood by the salesman of materials. A white material reflects all the colours of the spectrum, and a black material absorbs them. A red material reflects red rays and absorbs the others, a blue material reflects blue rays and absorbs the others, a purple material reflects both red and blue rays, and so on. If they are to appear, then, in their true colours, the light which they receive must be similar to daylight, or otherwise the balance will be upset. If a yellow material is shown in the light of a sodium flame, for example, which gives off only yellow rays, it will appear in its true colour, since it is getting the particular coloured ray which it is capable of reflecting. But if a material of colour other than yellow is shown in the light of this flame it will appear black, since it is absorbing the yellow rays and has no supply of just those colours which it is able to reflect.

The matching of colours has been dealt with at some length, since ignorance of its principles has at times led to considerable friction. "Rush" colour-printing jobs, for instance, have before now had to be thrown away when morning came, simply because the printer has chosen his colours under uncorrected artificial light, worked on the job all night, and only found out his mistake in the morning.

It may not always be necessary to display a colour by natural or artificial daylight; it may be some material which is required for display, when sold, almost entirely under artificial light, in which case it is far better to show it under the conditions which it will have to meet.

Another cause of possible friction is fading, and, though the onus will usually be put on to the manufacturer, a certain amount may rest on the supplying shop, and it is desirable that the salesman should have some knowledge of the conditions which, other things being equal, make for fading. The important factor in fading is moisture. A material which is placed in bright sunshine in the Egyptian desert for three months may show very much less fading than a similar piece of material which has been for only three days in a room in which there is a certain amount of steam, as in steam pressing. Even if it is on the shady side of a street in England, behind thick plate glass it may still fade very much more than in full sunlight in Egypt, owing to the fact that the air here contains very much more moisture.

This problem should not concern the salesman as much now as formerly, as so much more is now known about dyes, but he should satisfy himself that a dyed material which he is selling for a cruise will be satisfactory under the conditions in which it will be worn. The sun's energy is very high round about the green region of the spectrum, and some dyes which absorb rays in this region may be liable to change in the presence of moisture.

## THE MAN ON THE ROAD

WHOLESALE selling may be either on behalf of the manufacturer to the factor or retailer—sometimes both—or on behalf of the factor or wholesale merchant to the retailer. The travelling salesman may be confined to quite a small area where his calls are highly concentrated and there is no distance to travel between them, or he may have a very large area involving considerable expenses on account of travel and hotel bills. It is essential that the salesman should receive all travelling expenses and all reasonable hotel expenses, travelling expenses being paid to and from his recognised headquarters wherever they may be—his home or some depot or office—on his way to and from the particular area that he is working. The salesman may be asked to take over an area where there is an existing connection and which has been worked for some time, or he may have to develop a territory which has been quite unworked as far as his product is concerned. In the latter case, the average cost of travelling (salary, expenses, and commission) of the firm's travelling staff may be allowed to be considerably exceeded for some time. The employer may often find it necessary to subsidise in such a manner the salesman who is working new ground, and the salesman will find it necessary to accept such a subsidy for a time ; but it is not desirable for either side to continue such an arrangement for too long, as it is apt to spoil the salesman's sense of practical values.

If the salesman is working entirely new ground for himself ut not for his firm—who already have an existing connection here—his position is much easier than if he is called upon to vork new ground for a new product. In the latter case, he will ave to do what he can to create demand, which itself comes rom the user or ultimate consumer of the product. It is a low process for the salesman to create demand, and this is robably done most quickly with the majority of products by isplay and newspaper advertising. The salesman can in-luence demand to some slight extent by seeing that the retailer ives his goods display and that he exhibits show-cards, vindow-strips, etc.

The retailer himself will not do much more to influence ublic demand, even if he is very well disposed towards the alesman and his firm, unless he receives a higher rate of profit, ince his selling costs are likely to be raised by stocking an rticle which requires more selling. A small firm which makes n article for which there is little demand may be able to offer slightly higher rate of profit to the retailer without sacrificing uality, because they often do very little advertising, and have atisfied themselves that it is not from this cause that their sales ave remained small. But the retailer, with the best will in the vorld, is powerless beyond a certain point. Some few years go the writer was in the shop of a cycle agent, watching with nterest his efforts to sell a small boy one of the lesser known rands of cycle tyre. The small boy finally assented, and the ycle agent winked at the writer, over the boy's shoulder, when he boy suddenly said : " Oh no, I forgot, mother says I must ave a . . .," mentioning a well-known brand of cycle tyre.

## THE FIRST STAGE IN THE ATTACK

IF the salesman is trying to open a new account and is writing for an appointment, it will often pay him to write that he will e coming to the prospect's town on such and such a day or days, nd that he would appreciate an appointment, even if he has no ntention of going to that particular town except to see the erson to whom he has written. He will often be rewarded by letter saying that, while it is not worth a special journey, the vriter will give him an interview if he is coming that way. Some rincipals and buyers, partly out of consideration for the sales-nan, sometimes refuse an appointment which they would therwise give if they think that it will mean a special journey n the part of the salesman, who may then miss the chance

of " getting in " and coming into personal contact with th
firm.

In writing for an appointment, the salesman should read th
letter through—assuming that the prospect of whom the inter
view is asked is not familar with the salesman's product o
products—and ask himself whether the information given i
the letter is sufficient for the reader to come to a decision t
grant an interview. This may sound very elementary, but it i
a fact that otherwise experienced salesmen will sometime
write a letter asking for an interview, and, quite forgetting tha
they themselves know all about the product or products bu
that the prospect does not, will not provide any of the essenti
details on which a decision can be formed.

The prospect will want to know what the product is, what
does, and—sometimes—how it does it, in as brief a letter a
possible. It is true that " snap " interviews may sometimes b
obtained by a salesman who has given only the vaguest in
formation of what he has come about and who has used som
concealed method of approach, but this method is hardly likel
to be successful with a letter. The reader may not have an
time to spare during the day for the gratification of mer
curiosity, or if he does allot a few minutes each day for th
purpose—on the principle that he may otherwise miss some
thing which will be of assistance to his business—such dail
time may already be fully booked up.

If the salesman has occasion to write to a customer with whom
he has been in business contact for some time and who know
all about his product, asking the customer to do something o
suggesting a certain line of action, he should still read his lett
through critically, although from a different angle, and shoul
make sure that he has given a clear summary of what he think
might be done. It is disconcerting to a salesman to arrive at
call, after he has written to a customer at some length, only t
be greeted with the question, " Well, Mr. . . ., just what is
you want us to do ? "

Postcards are sometimes sent, in the case of a salesman wh
is on a fairly regular journey, informing customers of a
impending visit ; these postcards have sometimes even ha
a photograph of the salesman put on them !

In some firms, where the working principal or buyer
accessible, the salesman can often get an interview withou
previous notice and may not have to wait long. With othe
it is possible by telephoning to arrange a definite intervie

the same day. Others, again, will not make an appointment other than through the post. In every case where an interview is refused, the salesman should make a note in his book of who has refused it, and why it has been refused, the particular method that has been used in requesting it, and whether every method of approach has been used.

### WHEN IS THE BEST TIME TO CALL?

SALESMEN who are calling on large business houses sometimes say: " Oh, it's no use calling on large firms much before eleven a.m., they don't want to see you." The wish is often father to the thought, and some salesmen like a cup of coffee before they settle down to the serious business of the day. Again, one sometimes hears it said that it is no use calling on a large firm after five p.m., because they do not want to see the salesman after that time. This may be because there is another English institution which may be connected in the salesman's mind with five p.m.—tea. The salesman will certainly lose business if he accepts this generalisation. It is obviously impossible to lay down any hard-and-fast rule as to the time for first and last calls, since this often depends on the nature of the business and whether it is done in works or offices; before 9.30, when the post has not been sorted, is sometimes a very good time for catching a principal, and works directors may often be caught much earlier than this.

On arriving at his call—if it is a first call—the salesman should make a note, which he can transfer to his book afterwards, of the situation, class of business done, and any other points of importance; he will also note, both in the case of first and subsequent calls, whether there is a display of his firm's products, and if prominence is given to window-cards, strips, or metal signs—where these are used by his particular class of business—which advertise his firm's products. Also, if any boxed goods of his firm are displayed, he will note whether the appearance of the boxes is attractive. Many firms pack their products in drab boxes, when colours would cost very little more and would be well worth the extra outlay. Similarly, if he is working in conjunction with a lorry or van which is actually distributing goods, he should see that some use is made of the vehicle for the display of advertisements. A van or lorry is a most valuable travelling hoarding on which it costs nothing to display an advertisement, and it is most surprising how little use some firms make of their vehicles.

If a salesman is already being interviewed in the shop or department, in a public position, it is customary, and indeed good manners, for other salesmen either to wait out of hearing distance, or—if the shop or department is a small one—to wait outside.

### OLD CUSTOMERS WHO MUST NOT BE NEGLECTED FOR NEW

THE opening of new accounts is very valuable, but the salesman must make sure that all his existing accounts are being fully worked. He must obtain the confidence of his customer before he can work an account to its fullest extent. Smaller firms can sometimes be " pushed " by the salesman into giving a larger order than they had originally intended or wished to give, and one sometimes hears them complain to other salesmen that Mr. —— is a " pusher." But the salesman should not take this too seriously or think that he will shortly be getting the orders which formerly went to Mr.——. A " pushing " salesman would soon be sent about his business if it was found that his goods did not sell well and that a large supply of them was still on the shelf on the occasion of his next call.

In the case of new accounts, references are usually asked for, but, in any event, the salesman's firm will get a report from some trade protection society. This report makes general remarks as to the status of the customer, probable or actual rental, and whether there has been any slowness of payment on his part such as to require any means of collection other than that provided by the suppliers of the goods themselves. Too much attention should not be paid to isolated cases of slowness, as sometimes a customer who has a sense of grievance against a supplier may be deliberately slow in settling the account over which the trouble has arisen. But any County Court judgments against the customer, all of which are recorded on the report, are indications for the exercise of extreme caution on the part of the salesman in attempting any extension of the account. Though the ultimate responsibility for accepting any order belongs to the employer, the salesman is morally bound to take as much care with his employers' money as he would with his own. In any case, bad debts cannot be included in his turnover or rank for commission, so that they represent a loss for him, even though it may not be quite so direct a loss as it is for the employer.

The salesman may find that there are some areas or towns

in which he does not seem able to do much, and he should be careful not to spend too much time there " pegging away " to the detriment of other areas and of the extension of existing accounts. Such areas or towns may be influenced by filtration of customers into the district from areas where his product is already well established, and in this case the salesman should give special attention to these backward areas during the time of year when they receive the greatest number of visitors.

Care should be taken, when a range of samples is carried, to see that these are up to date, that they are varied slightly, and are not always shown in the same way. Samples are very useful sometimes, in acting as a concrete reminder to a customer who may know the salesman's whole range of goods, but who may not be able to recall each single item to mind. The sight of samples stimulates the mind of the buyer, even if it is only an attractive box with the article which it is made to contain shown on the outside. If, however, the buyer sees the same samples time after time, he is apt to remark, " Oh yes, the same old samples," and they lose the suggestive force that they should have.

## WHY THE SALESMAN SHOULD KEEP A REGULAR TIME-TABLE

REGULARITY in making calls is important, and the salesman should work as far as possible to a time-table so that his customers know that they can rely on seeing him at regular intervals. Customers will often save up orders for a salesman whom they may not have seen for some months, but who they know will be round at the usual time, and with whom they are friendly. At the same time a certain margin must be allowed each day for development work and contingencies, so that the whole schedule is not thrown out if the salesman has to wait an unusually long time at a call, or if he has to spend some time in opening new accounts. Method and routine are excellent things, but must be governed by intelligence ; if the salesman's time-table is so rigid that his supervisor knows exactly where he is to be found at any hour of the day, then his work is hardly likely to be of a high order.

Regularity in making calls is especially important in the case of salesmen who also act as collectors of money, but the turning of a salesman into a collector is much to be deprecated from the point of view of efficiency. Lower-salaried employees at the customer's, whose time is of considerably less value than the salesman's, could in nine cases out of ten send on the money to the salesman's firm for the customer.

Alternative journeys should be mapped out, and the most economical, both in time and money—which are usually the same thing—should be chosen. The traveller should resist the temptation to go on to the next town during business hours when he has not finished working the town that he is in, and may not be able to make any calls by the time when he does arrive in the next town. If he is travelling with some product the retailers of which close at normal hours, he can get on to the next place after they have closed. On the other hand, if he finishes up early in a town, or finds that he is going to do so, he should try to get ahead of his schedule, and should ring up his calls to see if they can arrange to see him earlier.

It is usual for salesmen who are travelling the whole week to arrange their journeys so that they are as near as possible to their base at the end of the week and do not have to spend the whole of the last day in getting back, so wasting valuable calling time. This applies equally to the first day. Salesmen may sometimes have to do a good deal of late report writing, but on the whole the average salesman does not make enough use of late trains or car drives.

He should complete on the same day as they arise all the jobs which can be definitely finished and got rid of, and in this connection should not hesitate to make free use of the telephone for trunk calls; this may sound expensive, but it is very often the cheapest policy. He should never let the sun go down on jobs which could have been finished the same day, but which have been left with "tags" sticking out all over the place. There is a time to "sleep on it," but the salesman must be careful not to make undue use of this. However, if he gets towards the end of the day a troublesome letter or paper to deal with, or if some trouble arises which can be deferred until the morning for a decision, it is often best to leave it until then and to put it out of his mind for the time being. Matters which appear very serious or difficult at the end of the day, when the salesman is tired, may take on quite a different aspect in the morning.

### "JOY-RIDES" THAT HINDER THE BUSINESS OF SALES

THE salesman should discipline himself at least as much when he is out on journey as he would be disciplined if he was working inside; indeed, the successful salesman usually observes a far higher discipline. The practice sometimes adopted of taking round relatives when travelling by car is much to be deprecated unless the work is being done purely on a commission basis. Employees in an office or works are not allowed to have their friends and relatives about on the premises the whole day, and, however much the salesman may try to delude himself, friends and relatives when taken on journey—unless treated with an utter lack of consideration—do slow up the salesman appreciably and sometimes make the difference between a salesman finding a call in or not, or arriving in a town before early closing.

The same applies to any work outside his business which the salesman may do after his normal business hours, in the way of writing for profit or anything similar. He is bound, if he is receiving a salary, not to push any such work beyond the point which, when passed, leaves him too tired to attend to his work properly the next day. Such work, in moderation—like any other change of work—may sometimes be recreative, but this is a matter for the salesman's knowledge and conscience.

## KEEPING ON GOOD TERMS WITH THE WHOLESALER

SOMETIMES a salesman may be calling on a wholesale customer, and, at the same time, may be calling on a retail customer, who also goes to the wholesaler; he may even be offering to the retailer such terms as will pay him to cut out his wholesaler, if he can place a large enough order. This, rather naturally, sometimes leads to friction between the salesman, or his employers, and the wholesaler. The wholesaler has the remedy, such as it is, of withholding his orders, but to do so will often inevitably lower his own turnover since this dual method of working is chiefly resorted to by large and powerful manufacturers for whose goods there is a regular demand, so that the wholesaler must stock them. In areas where the wholesalers are large and cover the ground well, the manufacturer may decide to leave all but the largest retailers to them, but in other areas and with many products the salesman calls on the wholesaler's customers wherever he thinks fit. The salesman is in a difficult position, and the wholesaler is likely to listen unsympathetically to any explanations from him. It is up to the employers of the salesman, if they think that the wholesaler is acting fairly by them, to act fairly by him and not to lower his turnover by calling indiscriminately upon his customers. The salesman will bear in mind that the wholesaler is in some ways saving the manufacturer money, by supplying his product to smaller buyers, the filling of whose orders by the manufacturer might be more trouble than they were worth. The wholesaler, also, is in such cases taking what risk there may be of any bad debts.

Where the salesman is selling what may be regarded as a non-perishable commodity, he may be asked to supply goods on sale or return. This method was much in use at one time in the motor tyre trade and is used by various trades. It is often attractive to the retailer who is not actually invoiced for the goods until he has sold them, and who is thereby enabled to carry a larger stock at the expense of the manufacturer. The responsibility of the salesman, however, is increased by this method. Sale or return stock must be turned over faster than an equivalent amount of ordinary stock to obtain the same amount of profit since the manufacturer's costs have been raised ; he has had to put more money into his business to produce much more manufactured stock than he would normally require, and this will have raised his overhead or fixed charges. It is the salesman's responsibility to see that the retailer also plays his part, and that he keeps this stock turning over at a faster rate.

The prices of many commodities are strictly laid down, and the salesman is not allowed to give any discounts other than those laid down as standard by his employer for particular classes of buyer and for certain quantities.

## CHECKING RESULTS

ONCE a year the salesman should receive a list from his firm, in duplicate, of all accounts on his ground, showing the total turnover as compared with that of the previous year ; he can then return the copy to his firm, together with any comments in the case of customers whose turnover has shown a decline as compared with the previous year. Many firms also hold a sales conference once a year at which all their managers and often the entire staff of travelling salesmen are present. The sales policy for the coming year is then discussed, together with any observations from the sales staff as to requests from the public, products to be supplied, the activities of competitors, and so on. These conferences are often very valuable, but sometimes demand a compromise between what the salesmen ask for and what it is possible to give them.

### METHODS WITH ARTICLES THAT ARE DIFFICULT TO SELL

THE method adopted by the manufacturers of most difficult specialities—such as automatic machines, weighers, slicers, duplicators, typewriters, and similar articles—is for the salesman to make a " cold canvass," *i.e.* a call without any definite inquiry having been made as to the probability of getting an order, from door to door of an office building, or street of shops, calling on every potential user of their product, or on the ultimate user of the product, wherever he may be. The tendency, in other words, is for the makers of such articles to go direct to the ultimate consumer—irrespective of whether or no their products can be obtained from a middleman—since they often take the view that their business is so difficult, that, if it were entrusted chiefly to the retailer, sales would not be sought after with sufficient energy.

It is customary for specialty salesmen to use the " concealed " method of approach, that is to endeavour to get their product—if it is sufficiently portable—in front of the prospect before he knows what he is to see or even just what the salesman has come about. Where it is difficult to get a demonstration, this method is undoubtedly successful, in the hands of salesmen who know how to use it, in the case of smaller firms and private or professional men, but it is hardly likely to succeed in the case of larger firms. The number of demonstrations given bears a fixed relationship to the number of sales, and this relationship remains fairly steady for any given area ; the greater the number of demonstrations, the greater the number of sales.

In some of the large towns, and especially in the central postal district of London, it is difficult to obtain permission to make demonstrations owing to the very intensive working which has been done, and to the material being highly concentrated ; hence the resort to the concealed method of approach for obtaining demonstrations. Such a method is not congenial to every salesman, and when it does not appeal to him it is best left alone. In country areas or towns with a fairly low density of population per square mile it is usually much easier to get demonstrations, but, on the other hand, the proportion of sales to demonstrations is usually higher, so that the number of sales may still remain the same. When the salesman has given a demonstration of his product, he fills in a card, and if a sale has not been effected at the time, his supervisor may subsequently take any cards and call on any of the prospects which look hopeful; any prospects which then appear dead are scratched off the monthly prospect list.

The sale of difficult specialities demands an entirely different treatment from the sale of commodities and is more of a "snap" nature, the work which leads to a decision often being done in the first minute or so. Moreover, the speciality salesman, when he has once sold his product, may not see his customer again, unless and until he comes back to try for a "Trade out" (see below), since the business of supplies and the servicing of machines, apparatus, etc., is usually taken over by another department. The salesman of scientific specialities is in a different case and it is not necessary to resort to any concealed methods of approach, as his prospective customers are usually of an inquiring type of mind and are always ready to see anything that he may have to show.

## PUTTING THE FINISHING TOUCH TO A SALE

In closing a sale much the same method is employed as in retail selling, but is applied more intensively. If the prospect is hesitating it may pay the salesman to show that he at least feels no doubt as to whether there is going to be a sale; he can then take some accessory which goes with his product and ask how much he may put the prospect down for. The prospect often assents, or says "not so fast," when the salesman knows that things are, at least, still in train. Quite long silences may sometimes occur between the salesman and the prospect, and it often pays to let the prospect break silence first.

In the case of a "Trade out," where some new product is sold to the owner of a previous model, which is then taken away and an allowance made for it, the method of working is fairly simple. Any out-of-date features of the old product are pointed out in turn by the salesman—usually the user of the old product, who may be standing by, will back him up heartily—and, after a brief recapitulation of them all, the new product is shown and it is pointed out that in this the old undesirable features are lacking. After that, any entirely new features can be shown.

### THE MAN WHO PREPARES THE WAY FOR THE SALESMAN

SOME firms employ both propagandists and travelling salesmen and it is advisable, in any discussion on salesmanship, to include some notes on propaganda work. The propagandist often carries matters right up to the point where it only remains to take an order, calling sometimes on the supplier—whether wholesaler or retailer—and sometimes direct on the ultimate consumer, who may be one of the general, as opposed to the professional, public. The propagandist is usually employed for some product of a technical or scientific nature which the ordinary salesmen of the firm are not capable of explaining adequately, or where it is thought that the taking of orders might interfere with the correct carrying out of propaganda.

Propaganda and the taking of orders demand the exercise of slightly different qualities or, rather, an alteration in the normal balance of sales qualities. The propagandist cannot pretend to be entirely detached, as he works in close co-operation with the sales staff and takes a keen interest in what has happened as a result of his work, yet his mind should not be as concentrated on present sales as must be the mind of the salesman. A propagandist who is moved back to the sales side must usually increase his *tempo* and *vice versa.*

When public speaking is done, the best months for meetings are from October to the end of April. After April it becomes increasingly difficult to get good attendances for evening meetings, especially on fine evenings. Where the product which is being brought to the attention of the consumer is of public interest and admits of treatment in general terms, the representative can usually arrange to give talks to public and professional bodies and to Rotary Clubs. These last meet once a week for a luncheon, which is followed by a talk of about twenty minutes' duration and some ten minutes for the asking and answering of questions.

There are also numerous business associations, such as hotel associations, which are powerful in some areas. Many of them are willing to give a short time for a talk at one of their meetings, if the subject matter can be presented in a manner interesting to their members. The propagandist should not allow himself to be affected by any person who shows mock horror at a talk which has as its basis some particular business product. Most associations are vitally interested in business and the wheels must be kept moving.

Where public meetings are to take place twice in the day, an afternoon meeting about 3 p.m., followed by an evening one at about 8 p.m., are probably the best choice and secure the the biggest possible attendances. A canvass before such meetings must usually be somewhat discounted, as the number of promises of attendance which the givers are not able to keep is sometimes high. Printed cards, with a tear-off portion to be returned through the post, can be handed to those attending the meeting; the names and addresses of those interested can also be taken.

Newspapers will seldom insert free advance notices of public meetings even in the case of matters of public interest. But they will usually report a meeting when they are sent a notice of it. Press publicity agents can sometimes get a good many paragraphs into the paper about an article which is of public interest, but directly the product becomes commercialised to any extent—this may not mean that anyone has made any money out of it—the papers stop giving free publicity in order not to spoil their market for advertising. A notable exception to this is the case of bargain sales, which the papers always regards as news. Only the simpler forms of publicity will, however, concern the travelling propagandist.

The propagandist usually makes out his reports to his employer in triplicate, one copy being sent to headquarters, one kept for reference, and one being sent for the information of the salesman who works the place which is reported on. The propagandist reports regularly and fully. He will also frequently be required to attend exhibitions at which some firms have displays, not for the purpose of taking orders direct from the public, but of handing them on to the trade suppliers. Exhibitions should be chosen with care, and the cost of a stand at some of them, together with the cost of attendance, can be rather disproportionate to the financial results obtained. In cases of the addition of new goods and services, or extensions of old goods and services, some exhibitions are a very useful means of showing new articles or uses to the public. The "Health Market" is one that has been extended in recent years and the public is constantly being educated to demand a wider range of beverages, health foods, tonics, etc. These lend themselves to effective introduction at exhibitions for the general public as well as at trade exhibitions.

## THE SCIENCE OF SELLING INVISIBLE GOODS

THE selling of services is a vast field, and comprises the selling of anything other than concrete goods. Generally speaking, everyone who is in receipt of an income sells something or other; even the individual who is in receipt of an income from investments provides, in effect, a service for which he is paid by the recipients of the invested money. Here, however, the selling of services is regarded in a rather narrower sense, and some of the more intangible services need not be considered, since they do not provide a large outlet for the practising salesman. The hotel industry, for instance, provides a service which is of great national importance and does an invisible export trade—which is of great value to the business world—when it caters for foreign visitors to this country. The various invisible exports are extremely valuable to the national well-being and go far towards correcting the adverse balance of the trade of this country.

Such a service as that provided by the hotel industry calls for just as much care and skill as must be shown by any salesman who actually hands goods over a counter or who takes orders for them; and there are many other industries which in fact demand the exercise of the same balance of qualities as those used by the salesmen, but which never advertise for salesmen or propagandists and need not therefore be considered further here.

The railways and the road transport companies of the country provide essential services, and show an example of the old and the new both engaged in providing the same services. They both have many inquiry depots throughout the country, and the railway companies have made great advances in the direction of better advertising of their services and closer co-operation with the public; these inquiry depots tend to become more and more "shops" where services are sold. The railway companies do, in effect, employ outside salesmen, and thus the last stronghold of business conservatism may be said to have fallen.

## THE MARKET WITH A LIFE-LONG APPEAL

MANY towns, more especially the spas and coastal health resorts, have inquiry bureaux, which are, in one or two cases, situated some distance away from the resorts themselves. These deal with a very important service, that connected with the appeal to health. This appeal is one of the strongest appeals of all, ranking probably in importance with that of food and housing. It is desirable that the salesman who is dealing with this appeal should know something about physiology and hygiene. This market is limited only by the total number of the population, since the appeal concerns every member of a family, while other appeals are limited to those who are actually able to use the product concerned. The health appeal is concerned with goods, the necessity for which starts at birth and continues throughout life.

Recreational services absorb many salesmen and are often organised on an extremely business-like basis. A tea garden and amusement park near one of the large centres of this country employs a whole-time representative at a considerable salary and commission to go round interviewing Sunday schools, associations, and similar organisations, with a view to inducing them to go to the tea gardens for their annual outings. The various large health resorts have not yet started sending round travelling salesmen—the funds which they could employ for such a purpose are limited by Act of Parliament—but this would seem to be a logical development of their activities, which are connected with recreation as well as health.

Again, there are the various services such as insurance, which deal mainly with provision for the future, or with the living of a fuller life beyond the needs of mere existence. Their development is bound to employ more and more salesmen—for this is what they are, whether they work in inquiry bureaux or elsewhere—and to require a high degree of salesmanship.

The salesman of services is selling, not a concrete object, but an idea; nevertheless he is faced with much the same sort of problems as the salesman of concrete objects, with this difference, that the counter where he shows what he has to sell is the other person's mind. The salesman must make the service that he is selling take form and shape there, so as to become something vivid to his listener; he must appeal to the mind of his prospect, by means of the sense both of sight and of hearing. He may start by trying to sweep the counter more or less clear, so to speak, by presenting a contrasting idea. The seller of insurance, for instance, speaks about the evils of non-insurance and lack of providence for oneself and for one's relatives. The seller of recreational facilities may instance the evils of non-relaxation for oneself and for one's family. In the former case, tables may assist the salesman to build up his idea ; in the latter, photographs. He must proceed just as logically and progressively as does the seller of concrete goods.

## BOOKS FOR THE STUDENT OF SALESMANSHIP

For those who wish to pursue this subject further there is a large number of books from which to choose. Among the smaller ones *Efficient Salesmanship*, by Frank W. Shrubsall, and *Salesmanship*, by W. A. Corbion and G. E. Grimsdale, provide useful epitomes. The principles are admirably discussed in *Personal Salesmanship*, by R. Simmat, a book which is warmly recommended, and there is much interesting matter in William Maxwell's book on the subject, as well as in the books of Charles C. Knights, *The Technique of Salesmanship* and *Training for More Sales*. Outdoor work is dealt with in *Commercial Travelling*, by Albert E. Bull, in *The Outdoor Sales Force*, by P. E. Wilson, and in *Practical Commercial Travelling*, by Ronald T. Lewis. *Retail Salesmanship*, by Cunliffe L. Bolling, gives a comprehensive and readable account of that part of the subject in all its aspects.

# CAPTURING THE ATTENTION OF THE PUBLIC

## The Psychology of Advertising

*by R. SIMMAT, M.A., of the National Institute of Industrial Psychology. Author of " Personal Salesmanship," " Market Research," " The Principles and Practice of Marketing," etc.*

WHEN the engineer constructs a machine he can foretell with some degree of accuracy what it will do under certain conditions and circumstances. More recent advances in psychology have enabled scientists to predict how living organisms will react to the combination of stimuli making up their environment. Studies in comparative psychology have given us a knowledge of the factors affecting animal behaviour and this has helped us to understand human behaviour to some extent. However, human behaviour is rendered more complex by reason of the fact that while man has as the fundamental basis of his behaviour all the impulses and tendencies to reaction that other living beings have, yet at the same time his primitive tendencies to reaction are more easily modifiable by his experiences, and they are also controlled by that exclusive characteristic of man—" volition " or " will."

William McDougall has explained the development of " volition " probably more clearly than any one else. He regards man as being a mass of impulses to reaction : reflexes such as the involuntary withdrawal from pain, instinctive acts such as are aimed to preserve either the individual or his species—for example, the instinct of pugnacity—and finally, a composite of individual tendencies or dispositions to reaction that are clustered about what he terms the " self-regarding " sentiment and which constitute volitional behaviour.

Briefly, his theory is that in man primitive tendencies to reaction are modified in accordance with his idea of what he " ought " to do, but it is these primitive impulses which provide the motive power or energy for reaction to any given set of circumstances. It is this complication that has made it difficult to predict the behaviour of any one human individual. Probably if we knew the whole background of his experiences, his behaviour could be predicted with a reasonable degree of certainty. But in any case the backgrounds of each individual in a community differ, and thus a very difficult task would confront any one attempting to predict human behaviour by this means.

### USING THE GENTLE ART OF PERSUASION

ADVERTISING is a means of influencing the behaviour of groups of individuals so that they buy certain types or brands of merchandise—that is to say, to behave in a certain way. A knowledge of psychological principles is of great assistance to the business man in ensuring that he employs the most effective ways of persuading people to use his particular goods.

The first factors that must be taken into account are sociological as well as psychological. For example, the mental attitude of people in various areas differs. Thc psychology of the Scot is different from that of the man in Wales, the Yorkshire man is different from the Londoner. Each type must be persuaded to do a certain thing in a special way. Their habits, their modes of living, their outlook upon life are all different. The business man who makes a study of their psychology and applies it to his advertising is going to be more successful than the one who does not.

Many advertising men, as the result of their experiences, have developed an intuitive sense of what are the most effective ways of influencing different types of individual. Until a few years ago they relied solely on this intuition. Recently more scientific studies have been made of the habits of the persons to whom advertisements are designed to appeal. These studies have become known as market researches, and represent statistical compilations of sociological, economic, and psychological facts in relation to groups of people. They afford a scientific basis for predicting the reactions of these groups to certain types of advertising. However, knowledge of the many factors involved—especially the psychological ones—has not yet advanced to the stage where such predictions are infallible. But market researches of this kind do represent an effort to put advertising and selling on a more scientific basis than was the case some years ago.

In addition to the socio-psychological factors important in considering the groups of people whom it is desired to influence by advertising, there are other purely psychological factors in human behaviour which have been studied in experimental laboratories for many years. Traditional psychology has been conducting researches into the phenomena of attention, memory, and the association of ideas for many years. The laws which have been formulated are of great significance in advertising—indeed it was in their practical application to his problems that the advertising man first realised how much assistance psychology could be to him.

An analysis of the process of persuasion as the result of an advertisement shows that there are three clearly defined stages:

1. Attracting the Attention.
2. Driving the Message Home.
3. Encouraging the Decision to Act.

In connection with the first of these stages, psychologists have outlined certain laws as determining whether any phenomenon will attract the attention or not. They have formulated certain other laws with regard to how and why things are remembered or forgotten. The third stage is a more complicated one, but laboratory studies have been made of the mental processes involved in, first, making a decision, and secondly, in acting on the decision.

### HOW THE MIND SELECTS THINGS OF INTEREST

It is not difficult to understand the general meaning of the term "attention." Technically it may be defined as a mental process as the result of which the mind perceives one or more items out of several simultaneous impressions. The first factor of importance to be noted, then, is that attention is selective, the second factor that it is limited. The number of things to which we can attend at any one moment is limited, and the mind makes a selection in accordance with certain laws from the many presented to it. The advertising man's concern is that his particular message shall be the one that will be selected as the object of attention. The attention oscillates or changes rapidly from one item of experience to another. He is thus concerned that the attention, in addition to being attracted by his advertisement, will also be concentrated on it and held by it.

Primarily attention is of two types—involuntary and voluntary. It is the phenomenon of involuntary attention that is of most importance in advertising—that is, the controlling of the individual's attention without his being immediately aware that he is attending. Subsequently the interest of the advertisement must be so great that the interest is held by it to the exclusion of other items. Involuntary attention is secured by a variety of devices—large lettering, brilliant colours, striking illustrations, and so on. Attention is then held by exciting the curiosity of the individual or else embodying in the advertising matter some meaning that is of particular relevance to his needs.

There are four factors governing attention, which may be stated as the laws of:

INTENSITY.
CONTRAST.
INTEREST.
NOVELTY.

In accordance with the law of intensity, the greater the intensity of the stimulus the greater the degree of attention excited. Thus a loud noise will attract the attention more readily than a whisper, a large advertisement more readily than a small one, big heavy black letters more readily than small lightly printed ones, and so on.

The law of contrast lays down that items in great contrast with their surroundings will attract the attention more readily than those in harmony with their surroundings. The coloured advertisement surrounded by a mass of advertisements in black and white will attract more attention than if it were surrounded by a mass of other coloured advertisements, and so on.

In accordance with the law of interest, individuals will attend to items of importance which relate to their immediate interests and needs rather than to those that do not. If the individual is interested in cricket, an advertisement relating to cricket will attract his attention rather than one relating to golf. If he has influenza, he will not attend to advertisements describing cures for lumbago. If wheat prices are of importance to him, he may not attend to news about the discovery of a new species of coral in the Pacific Ocean, and so on. Lastly, it is easier to attend to something that is new or something that is continually changing than to something that is always the same—in advertising the attention can always be attracted by novelty or change. This is why new posters and all kinds of new devices are constantly employed in advertising.

### INTEREST: THE FIRST STEP TOWARDS REMEMBERING

When the attention has been attracted by an advertisement, the next step is to ensure that it should be remembered. As the amount to which we can attend at any one moment is limited, so the amount which we can remember is also limited. The more an object of experience has attracted our attention and the longer our attention has been held, the greater the period of time will be for which we can remember it. But unless other factors operate we shall, after a time, always tend to forget the item to which we have attended. There are thus two important steps in the memory process: retention of the item attended to, and recall of the item originally retained. A good or a bad memory is to some extent a matter of the native ability of the individual, but so far as the retention and recall of advertisements is concerned, they can be controlled by making use, first, of repetition—repeating the advertisements at intervals to ensure they will not be forgotten—and, secondly, by making use of the mental process known to psychologists as the association of ideas. By the association of ideas is meant the recalling of one item of experience by reason of its association in our mind with some other item. For example, the word "pills" might recall in our mind the name Beecham, or the word "cigarette" might recall the Imperial Tobacco Company. One of the objects of advertisers is to create these associations between a type of product and their own particular name.

There are three ways of developing an association of ideas between two items of experience, by contiguity, by similarity, and by contrast. The association can be strengthened by repetition of the items associated in these ways. According to the principle of contiguity, items of experience may be associated in this way either in time or in space. If we see the words Players and Cigarettes associated in an advertisement for a sufficient number of times, either word will tend to recall the other. Similarly, if we hear the words Boots and Chemists at the same time sufficiently often, either one of these words will also tend to recall the other.

Likewise, if two items of experience are similar, one may tend to recall the other, though probably not to the extent of items associated by reason of their contiguity in time or space. For example, if we have experienced an enjoyable meal at a particular restaurant in one town, the sight of a similar restaurant at a later date in another town may recall the original experience.

Lastly, if two items of experience are in contrast to each other, one may tend to recall the other, though probably to a lesser degree than in the case of association either by contiguity or by similarity. For example, if one year we spent an enjoyable holiday at one seaside resort, then a depressing holiday at another resort may recall the former experience.

### MAKING THE PURCHASE OF GOODS A HABIT

An advertisement may attract attention, its details may be easily remembered, but from a practical point of view it is of no value unless it causes people to come to a decision to buy the goods advertised. When a decision to act has been made several times, it tends to develop into a habit, and the mental process becomes mechanised. It is the object of all advertisers to transform a voluntary decision into the mechanised habit of purchasing their particular goods.

Psychologists have classified voluntary decisions into five types: the reasonable type; decisions influenced by external stimuli; decisions influenced by spontaneous emotions; impulsive decisions; and the logical reasoned decision. Of these five types some are of little importance to the advertising man. The fifth type particularly is of small significance to him, since one of his objectives is to try to influence the consumer so that he will not consider the claims of competing articles.

The first method of decision is the most important, especially in relation to the more expensive and less frequently purchased types of product such as motor cars, houses, etc. The process involved in this "reasonable" type of decision is that the reasons for purchasing a certain product seem gradually and almost insensibly to settle themselves in the mind, and, finally, as a result a clear-cut decision to act becomes formulated, without consciousness of any great mental effort being involved in the process. The importance to the advertising man of leading up to this type of decision is that the majority of people make most of their decisions in this way.

The second process of decision is related to the reasonable type, but approaches to the type of action resulting from what is known as "suggestion." To stimulate this process the advertisement must suggest action, and by so doing simplify for the potential purchaser the process of making a decision. Many people will not search newspaper files to read advertisements describing all the brands of the product they wish to buy. They are too mentally lazy. They will purchase the one presented to them at the moment. Thus it is probably in some degree true that any kind of advertising will succeed if it appears often enough and large enough. But advertising depending on size and frequency alone is extremely wasteful.

The third type of decision is essentially dependent on suggestion and the process of coming to a decision relies upon a sudden emotional impulse. Women decide more in this way than men do. The advertising man can do little. It is almost wholly a chance decision, whimsical and uncertain. He can do most by endeavouring to stimulate emotional spontaneity by creating an artistic or sentimental background.

In making a decision of the fourth type the individual passes from one mood to another often diametrically opposed to the initial state. The practical application of this can be seen when a person reads certain advertisements for years and may never be stimulated to action. Suddenly the advertisement material coincides with his mood and needs and creates an all-powerful impulse to purchase.

The importance of the analysis that has just been made is very great. The enormous differences in the mental structures of individuals and the complicated mass of motives combining to influence every single person would make it appear a difficult task to influence communities by any mechanised mass appeal such as advertising. Yet our analysis has shown that human action is governed by certain laws. We do not yet know all about these laws, but from what psychologists have already discovered we can to a certain extent study the nature of social groups and plan a course of action that will have results which we can to a degree foretell.

## SOME BOOKS ON BUSINESS PSYCHOLOGY

A GREAT deal of literature exists on the psychology of advertising and selling. Much of it rapidly becomes out of date. Among the older writers Scott and Poffenberger are the best, and their books recommended are *The Psychology of Advertising*, by W. D. Scott, published by Pitman, and *Psychology in Advertising*, by A. T. Poffenberger, published by A. W. Shaw. Other useful books directly describing the relation of psychology to advertising and selling are *Psychology in Personal Selling*, by A. J. Snow (Shaw Publishing Co.), and *Psychology as a Sales Factor*, by A. J. Greenly, published by Pitman. Some more recent books showing the application of modern psychological technique are *The New Psychology of Advertising and Selling*, by H. Link (Macmillan); *The Principles and Practice of Marketing*, by R. Simmat (Pitman); *The Applied Psychology of Advertising*, by A. P. Braddock (Butterworth); and *The Principles and Practice of Advertising*, by R. Simmat (Pitman).

# HOW TO ADVERTISE

*by F. McDONALD, Member of the Incorporated Society of Advertisement Consultants, and Lecturer on Advertising at the City of London College.*

It is a far cry from the big-drum-beating methods of the "bad old days" to the studied and carefully planned and executed methods of advertising to-day. The idea that the loudest proclamation, whether by word of mouth or by the printed word, made the biggest impression upon the public mind and pocket has been replaced by more subtle and reasoned methods, and advertisers to-day are supported by an army of experts trained in all the various phases of advertising operations.

Advertising in the early days was defined as "Printed Salesmanship." To-day that definition is inadequate; the art of advertising is practised in many ways other than by print—for example, illuminated signs, still and moving; cinematograph films, skywriting, radio, and countless other innovations.

Just how far the alliance of advertising with the sales department, and indeed with other departments, of a business should be religiously maintained will be outlined later on. For the moment it is necessary to deal shortly with advertising as related to business in general. There are many who say that advertising is an evil. That may or may not be so. In any case, it is a necessary evil. That it is economically justified is proved by the growth of such firms as Oxo, Rowntrees, Kodak, Angus Watson (Skippers), and countless others whose names are household words. That they continue, and indeed increase, their advertising every year is convincing proof that these firms at any rate have unfailing faith in its efficacy.

### THE PART THAT ETHICS PLAY IN ADVERTISING

Advertising can also be vindicated on ethical grounds. In ordinary life, ethical conduct is the carrying-out of principles of human morality and duty, based on a study of our fellows and sympathy for their feelings. It is much the same in advertising. Having something to sell is all right, but it must give continued satisfaction to the consumer if sales are to be repeated. A man might be fooled once, even twice, but not all the time. In business a dubious article might be sold once, even twice, but not all the time, and all the advertising in the world will not achieve such an impossibility, however doggedly it is attempted.

In brief, advertising must be allied to goods ethically right, and the tone and character of the advertising must be equally right in order to ensure success. The vulgar tone, the "cheap and nasty" type of advertising, does not attract in the favourable sense of the term, and it does not sell goods more than once, or twice at the outside, even if the goods themselves are above reproach. The character of the advertising must reflect the character of the house which is marketing the goods.

The old code of business conduct, *caveat emptor*, which being translated means "let the purchaser beware," or, in other words, "the purchaser buys at his own risk," does not govern advertising to-day. It is the seller who must beware of making promises in his advertising which he cannot fulfil. The law is jealous for the public, and the reckless advertiser can easily fall into legal traps which will probably cause him immediate financial loss, and will very likely do irreparable damage to his business generally.

Advertising aims at fulfilling a variety of different purposes which can be classified conveniently as primary and secondary. Among the primary purposes, the first is to secure wider distribution of goods. More dealers can be persuaded to stock the goods by advertisements in the trade press, and a wider public can be reached by means of media such as window display at the dealer's shop, or through the press, or by posters, etc.

Secondly, advertising aims at increasing consumption by attracting new buyers from among the public, or by introducing new uses for a commodity. The public can be taught new ways to use soap, or new methods of cooking foods so as to make a breakfast article suitable for lunch as well. Advertisers are always on the look out for new ideas, and prize offers and competitions and schemes are constantly being organised to discover new uses for a product.

Thirdly, goodwill can be established and a form of trade insurance effected. A brand name or trade mark serves to identify the goods with the producer, and accordingly goodwill is created by advertising the name or trade mark. Similarly with patented articles; after a period of time the patent may expire, and competition may become more intense. Advertising can replace the protection which the Patent Office no longer affords by the faith which has been instilled in the mind of the public.

Fourthly, dealers can be materially assisted. Advertising not only enables the manufacturer to sell to the retailer. If it does that for any length of time, it means that the retail dealer is finding it possible to pass the goods on to the public. In other words, the very advertising which is designed to assist the manufacturer also serves to assist the retailer by clearing his shelves and increasing his turnover.

### ADVERTISING THAT BENEFITS THE PUBLIC

FINALLY, advertising can be of real benefit to the consumer himself. Goods and services which were at one time luxuries have become by wider use almost necessities. This has been made possible only by the wider distribution and consumption which advertising has fostered. Wider distribution means increased production, and increased production should mean production at lower costs. As a result, increased benefits accrue to the advertiser, and these are passed on to the consumer by the wise advertiser, either by a reduction in the purchase price or by an increase in the quantity, and possibly also in the quality, supplied at the original price.

Among the secondary purposes of advertising is the moral support it lends to the salesman, "the man on the road." The salesman, despite all that may be said to the contrary, is a temperamental creature both by nature and training, and is subject to the vagaries of the weather, the people he meets, the surroundings in which he has to work, and so on. Thus, although he has the prestige of the goods, and of his firm, behind him, he feels at times the need of a greater confidence in himself and his sales message and his goods. This is particularly so when he finds himself in front of the buyer, and advertising can then supply the necessary urge.

Moreover, benefit is also conferred on the executive and on the staff of the business. Goodwill gained by advertising is a present asset and a form of insurance for the future. A successfully advertised business provides substantial and increasing financial rewards for the executive ; to the worker, whether in the factory, the store, or the office, continued distribution through advertising means steady work and consequent prosperity.

Simple as all this may sound, it must not be supposed that all that is necessary is to have the goods and a little money to spend on advertising, to put out some advertisements, and then to sit back and watch the sales grow. All advertising effort does not succeed, nor does all the advertising of successful firms hit the mark every time. There are certain causes of waste, and care should be taken to eliminate them. The major cause of waste is undoubtedly failure to predetermine the objects which your advertising is to perform. Similarly, the failure to make an extensive preliminary survey of the market, of competitive lines, and of possible new channels of trade can, and often does, result is advertising waste. These investigations must naturally determine the sales-advertising policy of the business, and, by eliminating the guesswork, are of great assistance in framing the first essential in advertising, namely, the aim.

Again, lack of consistency in policy will cause waste. The chosen plan must be given a real chance to work ; it should not be altered unnecessarily while in the course of its run. Having determined the policy carefully at the outset, have faith in it, and let it run the course. Other causes of waste in advertising are poor presentation of the advertisements themselves, such as buying " ready-made " instead of " made-to-measure " plans ; trying to cover too much territory without an accompanying distribution of the goods adequate to meet the demand ; extravagant and exaggerated (though not necessarily untruthful) claims for the goods.

### FOLLOWING UP ADVERTISEMENTS WITH ADEQUATE SUPPLIES

An important part is played by the extent of distribution. Should distribution be inadequate, and advertising be commenced inviting the public to obtain supplies " from your dealer " in a district where few, if any, dealers are stockists, the results are bound to be damaging to the campaign. People acting upon the invitation of the advertisements are naturally going to be disappointed when they are unable to obtain what they want, and few will go to the trouble of trying other dealers in the district until they are successful. Many will even voice their disappointment to others. Thus the sale of the goods when they do become available in the district, perhaps long after your advertising has appeared, will be seriously prejudiced, and considerable waste will have occurred.

These are some of the chief causes of waste in advertising. It will be seen that to a considerable extent they can be prevented by a careful preliminary survey of the ground which is to be covered. Such a survey, primarily designed to safeguard the plan from any possibility of waste, is also of great assistance in choosing the proper medium, and is thus the fundamental cause of ultimate advertising success.

## WHO'S WHO IN THE ADVERTISING WORLD

IN military parlance a campaign is a connected series of operations forming the whole or part of a war ; an organised effort or struggle. Similarly an advertising campaign is a connected series of plans and an organised attack upon a discriminating public by way of advertisements, designed for the accomplishment of a definite business purpose, namely, to sell a commodity or service.

Three important considerations have to be faced when planning any advertising campaign. First of all, there is the aim, or what it is expected to achieve. This must control the organisation and administration of the advertising. Secondly, the best way of achieving this aim must be decided. This raises the question of the various advertising media available and their relative values. Thirdly, there is the question of costs, and the means by which the money essential for advertising is earned and spent.

That there is a definite need for careful organisation and administration of advertising has now been clearly shown. In order to understand " how the wheels go round," it is necessary to become acquainted at once with the personnel involved, the departments concerned, their scope and the connection between them. This will give the reader a glimpse of the wide ramifications of advertising as a business.

### THE ADVERTISING MANAGER'S JOB

FIRST of all there is the Advertising Manager. He may be the owner of the business or he may be an employee. Among other things this executive is the liaison officer between the advertiser and the advertising agent handling the campaigns.

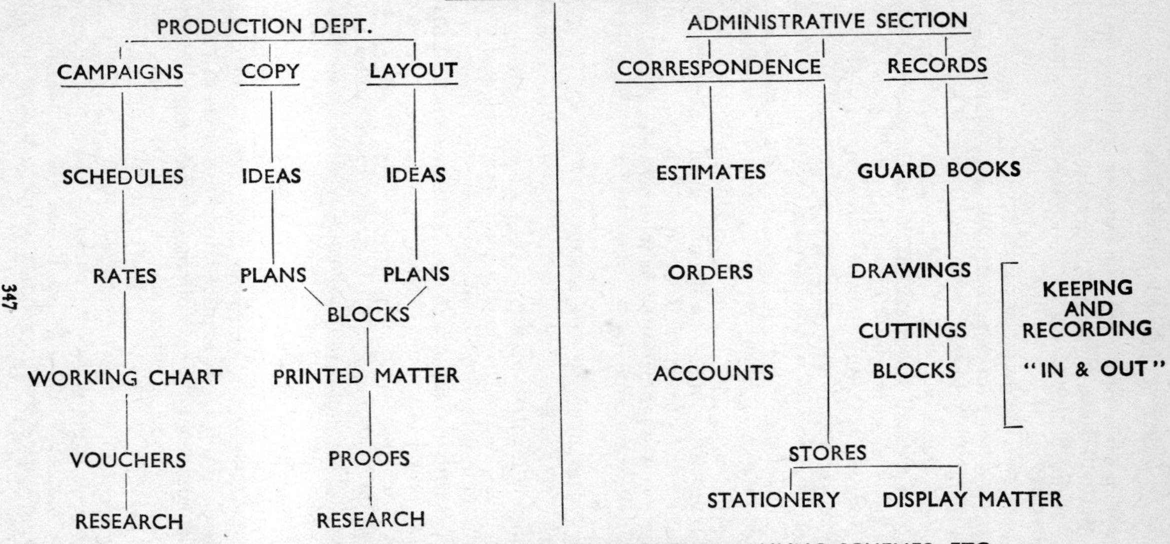


1. THE ORGANISATION OF AN ADVERTISING DEPARTMENT

He is usually a man of wide all-round advertising experience, technically qualified, and able to check up the agent's activities by way of media, production, and campaign schedules as to time and cost. It is his business to see that the agency does its job to the requirements of the advertiser. It is essential, therefore, for him to work in close co-operation with the agent at all times.

Sometimes the Advertising Department is a one-man affair, especially in a small business, but in the larger concerns it may include assistants in different sections of advertising work—copy, lay-out, campaigns, records, routine work of a clerical nature, and so on. Fig. 1 is a specimen of departmental organisation for a large manufacturer.

From this chart it will be seen that the department is controlled by a manager or responsible director, and the work is divided into sections. The main division of the department is into two groups: Production, involving the employment of one or more artists, copywriters, and other technical assistants; and administration, employing clerical and other routine staff for correspondence, filing, orders, records, etc.

### THE WORK OF THE ADVERTISING AGENT

SECONDLY, there is the Advertising Agent, who is directly responsible for the "placing" of the advertiser's campaigns whether press, outdoor, vehicular, or in any other form. He is usually equipped with an organisation efficient in service, and staffed with assistants who are each expert in a particular phase of present-day advertising production. He is in constant touch with the advertising manager on matters, of campaign planning, production, and presentation, and must keep plans and announcements on time according to determined schedules.

His remuneration comes in the first place from commission, which he receives from newspapers and from other publications and activities for which he is a "recognised" agent, on all bookings for space placed by him on behalf of his client, the advertiser. This commission may vary from 10 to 15 per cent. Some agents work on what is called a "split commission" basis, meaning that half of the commission received is credited to the advertiser. Whether this is a desirable proceeding is rather a controversial subject between "straight commission" and "split commission" agents.

A second source of remuneration is that derived from what

MANAGEMENT

BOARD OF WORKING DIRECTORS

| ACCOUNTS DEPT. | RATES DEPT. | PRODUCTION DEPT. | | SALES DEPARTMENT. | |
|---|---|---|---|---|---|
| | | STUDIOS. | COPY. | | |
| Checking and Invoicing A/cs for Advertising Blocks and Printing. | Rates, Schedules, Records of Costs per reply, etc. — Checking dispatch of Copy and Blocks, Collection of Proofs, Vouchers; Checking and Forwarding. | Original Layouts; Rough Sketches, Finished Drawings; Lettering for Press, Posters, Showcards, Folders, Booklets. | Copy for Press Advertisements, Booklets, Folders, Letters, Editorials. | Market Investigation. Collection of Market Facts from Trade (Retail & Wholesale) Sources, and from General Public. By Questionnaire and in person. | Sales Organisation. — Sales Policy and Planning Sales Records and Systems. — Engaging and Training of Travellers. — Sales Conferences, Bulletins and Portfolios. |
| | | LAYOUT. | PRINTING. | | |
| | | Printed Layouts; Proof Reading and Correction; Ordering Blocks, Matrices, Stereos. | Estimates for Booklets; Folders; Showcards; Posters; Form Letters. | | |

2. THE ORGANISATION OF AN ADVERTISING AGENCY

is termed a "service fee." Here, again, the fee varies, and may be anything from 2½ per cent. to 5 per cent. on all gross business handled by the agent for the client. By this means the agent obtains payment for his services in the preparation of ideas, copy, lay-out, campaigns, in the production of blocks and art work, in the placing of printing blocks with newspapers and periodicals for publication, and in performing all the incidental work entailed in the smooth running of a campaign. It should be noted, however, that the fee does not include the cost of blocks, type settings, art work and the like, which form charges additional to the "service fee."

The formation of an agency may vary in detail, but generally speaking it is on the basis shown in Fig. 2. Here the management is in the hands of a Chairman and working Board of Directors controlling a series of sub-departments, *i.e.* Accounts, Rates, Production, and Sales. These in turn are usually under the immediate charge of departmental managers, who handle work relative to art, copy, printing, etc., in the production department, campaigns in the rates department, and sales or accounts in their respective sections.

### THE ADVERTISEMENT MANAGER'S JOB

THE Advertisement Manager, the third figure in the advertising world for us to consider, is engaged by the publisher of a newspaper or periodical to let and control the quantity and quality of space allotted to advertisement. He has to sell this available space to the advertiser, and is assisted by a selling staff. Most of the space he lets is booked through the agent and not by the advertiser direct. "Promotion matter," as it is termed, is sent out to the advertiser in order to give him information as to the quantity, quality, and area of circulation of the journal, and to announce special features of the paper likely to be of interest to him.

All publishers of journals have space to sell and circulations to maintain, and the advertisement manager, therefore, has to meet fierce competition. When the space is let and the time comes for it to carry the advertisement, he is responsible to the owners to see that no questionable advertisements appear, such as those making extravagant claims which stand little chance of being fulfilled, dubious financial offers, immoral or "daring" announcements, and so on. These are likely to impair the prestige of the paper or abuse the confidence of its readers. Some proprietors of newspapers and journals even go so far as to guarantee the refund of purchase money to readers who suffer disappointment as a result of acting upon advertisements which have appeared in their publications.

It is a part of the advertisement manager's job to see that as far as possible the advertisers' announcements are inserted in the paper so as to give them the most effective display, and, while it is impossible to please every one, it must be said that advertisers usually have little to complain of in this respect.

### THE EXPERT WHO ADVISES THE ADVERTISER

THERE remains the Advertisement Consultant. He may have an agency organisation, through which he can buy and fill space and run an advertising campaign himself, but usually he does not do this work, merely acting, as the name implies, as a consultant. He is generally a man widely experienced in all forms of advertising practice and sales problems, and with a sound knowledge of production and of the cost and technique involved in any plans he may submit to clients, he can and does save prospective, and even old-time, advertisers a great deal of money by means of his researches and recommendations.

He is remunerated by fixed fees ; for an initial consultation a nominal fee is charged, and then, if instructed to produce plans for the "cure," he is awarded a fee in accordance with arrangements made at the first deliberations. His plans may include suggested campaigns, copy and art ideas, marketing plans, sales policies, and the like, and he can produce recommendations which it would cost his client much time, worry, and money to discover by other means.

## LAUNCHING AN ADVERTISING CAMPAIGN

THE advertising manager, then, the advertising agent, the advertisement manager, and probably the advertisement consultant, are the persons who have to collaborate in the creation of an advertising campaign. At the outset it is most essential that a general outline of the position should be given by the manufacturer to any outside agency he calls in to help him with his advertising. Usually, a preliminary meeting is held between the manufacturer and his responsible executive—that is, the advertising manager, and the advertising agent or his director.

At this meeting the state of distribution attained by the manufacturer will be discussed ; his existing policies with regard to sales and advertising will be looked over for possible errors of commission or omission ; his production facilities will be examined to see how far they are suited to meet the increased demands the advertising is expected to create ; and finally it will be determined, as far as possible, what object his advertising is intended to achieve. Without some basis of understanding on these lines it would be unreasonable to expect an agency to submit any effective campaign to meet the manufacturer's requirements. It would, in fact, be almost impossible for the agency to do so.

Armed with this preliminary and essential information, the agency director holds a conference, which is attended by the head of the agency, the director who has interviewed the client (termed the Accounts' Director), and the sales' director. All are made acquainted with the available information as to the client's position, and they proceed to discuss the situation, and form preliminary plans for the agency's different departments to work upon.

The departments concerned are the Market Investigation department, the Production department, and the Sales department. These departments may be given different titles in varying agencies, yet in operation they are fundamentally the same in all.

## GATHERING INFORMATION ON WHICH TO BASE ADVERTISING

THE work of the Marketing department is to proceed with investigations amongst the wholesale and retail trades and the buying public, in order to acquire facts and data which will influence the plans for advertising and selling the product. The information thus acquired is placed before the production department, which proceeds to outline the advertising policy, and before the sales department in order that the sales policy may be suitably framed.

All these preliminaries take time, but when, in the opinion of the agency, the plans are in reasonable shape, the first general conference is held. This conference will be attended by the manufacturer and his advertising and sales managers, the head of the agency, together with his accounts' director, and his sales and production managers. The preliminary findings of the agency are submitted to the manufacturer, and a full discussion takes place as to the lines to be followed in the preparation of complete advertising and selling campaigns. When the decisions have been arrived at, and the conference is over, the real work of preparing the campaign begins.

The work of the market investigation department is ended for the present, and the work now devolves upon the production and sales departments, with the addition of another department, the rates department, or, as it is called by some agencies, the campaigns department. The production department proceeds at once with the preparation of lay-outs, that is, advertisement designs, whether they be " copy " or a written story, for press advertisements, posters, show matter (showcards, bills, etc.), literature, and plans for window displays ; demonstrations and exhibitions ; or other determined forms of advertising media.

Meanwhile the sales department prepares a detailed sales plan. This involves the mapping of territories, or " routeing " as it is sometimes termed, and the production of sales letters, record forms, portfolios and bulletins, that is to say, Sales Talks, for the salesmen. The rates or campaigns department is responsible for the selection of the actual media to be used, and prepares estimates and schedules showing the papers suggested, the size and number of the insertions, the proposed dates of appearance, and the total cost of the scheme, including all technical charges.

It is in the matter of rates that the advertisement manager is most in evidence, for among many other things he sees to it that advertisers and agents are kept constantly up to date concerning the prices of the different sizes of space which he has to offer in his paper. This information is contained on a Rate Card, which gives not only prices, but other relevant information concerning technical requirements, circulations, frequency of issue, special features, page sizes, and column width and depth. All this information is useful in the choice of media, as it shows the limitations or possibilities of the journal for the advertiser's product, the comparative cost per thousand of circulation, the area coverage, and the class of public appealed to.

When the plans prepared by these three departments are ready, a second conference between the advertiser and the agency may be necessary ; at any rate the plans will be submitted to the advertiser for final consideration. This produces discussion, and probably amendments ; ultimately, however, the advertiser decides that the agent is to go ahead.

### OBSERVING THE EFFECT OF THE CAMPAIGN

THE production department of the agency is thereupon set to work making finished drawings for the advertisement designs, ordering blocks for the drawings, and preparing lay-outs for the printer. Booklets, folders, showcards, posters, etc., are put in hand, proofs checked and instructions for printing issued. All this work necessitates highly skilled assistants in order to obviate printing errors, keep costs down to a minimum, and obtain the best results.

The sales department co-operates with the advertiser's own sales department in the engaging and training of travellers and in the inauguration of systems to record territorial sales and travellers' reports on work done, " prospects," and competitive activities. The advertising portfolio which has been prepared by the production department, and any letters and bulletins it has been decided to use, have to be issued and explained to the travellers.

In the meantime the rates department has been actively booking the necessary space in the various newspapers and periodicals selected for the campaign, issuing copy and blocks to these journals, and finally checking the insertions according to the time schedule agreed upon. When the insertions appear, the various publications send what are termed voucher copies of the paper to the agent. These vouchers are the issues containing the advertiser's announcement, and are usually submitted in duplicate, one being retained by the agent as a voucher to support the publisher's account when it is received, while the other copy is sent to the manufacturer as a guaranteee that the advertisement has appeared according to plan.

When the campaign has been launched, it does not follow that the work of the agent and of the advertising manager is ended ; that they can then just sit back and watch the sales mount up. There is still the work of watching the effect of the advertising, checking the pulling power of the different media in use, noting the effect of one style of " copy " as against another in the various areas covered by the campaign, and finally computing the costs of the advertising as against resulting sales during and after the campaign.

A useful chart for the use both of the agent and of the

| PAPER. | No. of Inserts | WEEK END. FEB. | | | WEEK END. MAR. | | | | W/E APL. | | | TOTAL COST FOR SPACE | | |
|---|---|---|---|---|---|---|---|---|---|---|---|---|---|---|
| | | 12 | 19 | 26 | 2 | 9 | 16 | 23 | 1 | SPACE | COST PER SPACE | | | |
| DAILY X . | 8 | M.* 1† | M. 7 | M. 2 | M. 8 | M. 3 | M. 9 | M. 4 | M. 7 | 10″ d.c. | £120 | £960 | 0 | 0 |
| DAILY Y . | 8 | W. 2 | W. 8 | W. 3 | W. 9 | W. 4 | W. 7 | W. 5 | W. 2 | 10″ d.c. | £110 | | | |
| DAILY Z . | 8 | Tu. 5 | Tu. 8 | Tu. 6 | Tu. 9 | Tu. 7 | Tu. 10 | Tu. | | | | | | |
| EVENING X | 8 | Th. 6 | Th. 4 | Th. | Th | | | | | | | | | |
| WEEKLY Y | | | | | | | | | | | | | | |
| | | | | | | | T | OTAL | COST | OF SP | ACE | 4,000 | 0 | 0 |
| | | | | | | | | | 5% S | ERVICE | FEE | 200 | 0 | 0 |
| | | | | | | ART, | TYPES | ETTIN | G, BL | OCKS, | Etc. | 326 | 0 | 0 |
| | | | | | | | | | GRAN | D TOT | AL £ | 4,526 | 0 | 0 |

3. PRESS ADVERTISING RECORD.

* *Indicates day of week on which advertisement appears.* † *Indicates the number of "copy" used.*

advertising manager is what is termed a working chart, an example of which is given in Fig. 3. This chart gives at a glance all the vital information the manager requires regarding his campaign, such as the papers used in the campaign ; the number and sizes of the advertisements used in each paper ; the dates and days of the week on which they appear ; the " copy " used ; and the individual, as well as the total, costs of the insertions, together with all technical charges. This ready grouping of facts saves endless delving into files, estimates, correspondence, and the like.

It is also of considerable assistance in keeping on date with insertions due, copy to be used, and so on. This chart, minus the costs, forms the frontispiece of the Advertising Portfolio issued to the travellers, and in addition the portfolio has reproductions of the various advertisements which are being used in the campaign. In this way one of the important co-operative links between the advertising and sales departments is supplied.

## HOW THE DEPARTMENTS SHOULD CO-OPERATE

IT is one of the first essentials that the advertising department should co-operate not only with the sales, but also with the production, or actual manufacturing, department. Friendly rivalry between heads of departments is right up to a point, but when it threatens to interfere with the smooth running of the individual departments, there is great danger of the best-laid schemes going awry. Unfortunately it is not an unusual thing to find acrimony where harmony should prevail. One of the first things, therefore, which an advertising manager should do upon taking up his job is to get into touch with the heads of other departments in order to establish friendly co-operation.

Perhaps the most important relationship in his first days should be with the production or manufacturing department. No salesman, however anxious to start selling, would dream of going out to his prospective customers until he had learned as much as possible about his goods, the policy behind the firm, and the service available. Similarly, whilst technically expert as an advertising man, no advertising manager can hope to sell to his public without a thorough preliminary analysis of the production side of the business.

He should learn all about the product, the raw materials from which it is manufactured, and the method of production which is used. He cannot see his " prospects," but they can see him and judge him by the messages he puts into his advertising.

There are many ways in which co-operation with the production department can help the Advertising. One, for example, is with regard to a Brand Name or Trade Mark. Very possibly the lines to be advertised are new to the market, and have no name or mark designed to identify them from other competitive lines already well established on the market. One of the first things, therefore, to be done is to provide the goods with a suitable name or mark which is capable of registration, so that it cannot be copied or imitated by competitors without infringement.

This is extremely important, for the goodwill of a Trade Mark is one of the most valuable forms of property ; it is in effect the foundation of the business with which it is associated. Instances such as Kodak, Hovis, Glaxo, Sunlight, Cerebos, Quaker immediately leap to mind. All expenditure on advertising, with a view to the development of the mark in connection with the goods on which it is used, is an investment in the value of the mark.

### SELECTING AN ATTRACTIVE PACKING

ANOTHER means of identification is the style of packing, and this involves considerable care, thought, and research. Here again wise co-operation between advertising and production can lead to a successful solution of this by no means easy problem. Research should be made, for instance, into the size and style of the package which is to hold the product, so as to decide the shape or form to be adopted ; the material of which it is to be made, whether glass, cardboard, wood, bakelite, or other substance ; and whether it should be large or small, or of varying sizes.

There are many points to be considered by the advertising department in this connection, such as the shape, size, colour, lettering, illustration, the use of the trade mark, harmony with the product and, where desirable, novelty. These may be called the designing factors.

It is also necessary to bear in mind the " tie-up " with other products already in use by the firm ; the value as advertising display in dealers' windows or on counters and shelves ; ease of handling, both by the consumer and by the dealer. Originality should also be aimed at so as to produce a striking difference in design as compared with packings used by competitors.

Another factor which has to be considered in packing is the outer container holding a number of the individual packages. This " outer " has to be designed so as to meet the various requirements of transport and storage. Ease of handling, elimination as far as possible of pilferage, ease of storing in dealers' shops, suitability of shape so that only the minimum of storage room shall be required are all matters to be taken into account. These outers also afford an outlet for advertising ; bold printing of the name or mark or a brief slogan can be put on them, so that they act as silent salesmen in the course of transportation.

### HOW TO KEEP THE PRODUCT UP TO DATE

PERHAPS one of the most important forms of co-operation between these two departments lies in perfecting, improving, and even changing the product, in order to keep abreast of the needs of the consumer. The necessity for anticipating the needs of the public is shown by the constant changes of size, utility and form of radio, gramophone, and motor products. No one man has the monopoly of ideas, and two heads in this instance are definitely better than one.

This inter-departmental co-operation can also prove extremely valuable in the persistent search for new uses for a commodity. It has been said that sales are limited—not by the few uses to which a product can be put, but by the few uses the manufacturer has discovered for them. New ways of preparing foodstuffs ; divers uses for soap and soap powders ; olive oil used as a lubricant and polish ; reptile skins for making shoes, coats, and hats ; steel, not only for cutlery and industrial purposes, but for home and office furniture ; oranges, not only for refreshment, but for medicinal purposes, such as gargling, etc., are just a few of the new uses which, once investigation brought them to light, have been exploited by advertising with resulting increased sales.

Just how the advertising and sales departments can co-operate in actual practice may be seen in a variety of details. For example, the advertising department lends its aid in the careful preparation of Press Advertising portfolios for issue to the travellers, to aid them in discussing the product with the buyer. Similarly as regards show matter ; as new pieces of display material come to hand from the printers, the advertising department arranges for specimens to go to the travellers. Each traveller examines them and makes his comments, which are sometimes very helpful, and supplies of the display matter, calculated to cover his likely requirements, are then allotted to him.

Window displays are possibly put into the shops of selected dealers by the advertising department on the recommendation of the sales department. Often, where displays are not actually put in, suggestions are given to the traveller for the dealers' benefit. Other assistance is afforded to the sales department by advertising in handbooks or price-lists to be sent out by dealers, or by lending printing blocks for this purpose and for the dealers' own advertising in the local press.

On the other hand, the sales department co-operates in return by supplying the advertising department with statistics showing the strength or weakness of the selling in different areas. Such statistics may have a decided influence on advertising projects. Also, through district managers, agents, or travellers, the sales department passes on useful information about market conditions throughout the territories they cover, and reports upon the selling and advertising activities of competitors there. The sales department can also supply reports on dealers' opinions of the advertising, the effect of the media chosen, the reception of display material, and comments by the public on the advertising, which the agent may overhear or have passed on to him from other sources. All these provide extremely useful information for the advertising manager.

## THE MEDIUM AND HOW TO CHOOSE IT

MEDIA is one of the most important studies of the Advertising man. They are, in fact, the means by which the pre-determined aim has to be achieved, and the right choice of media is, therefore, vital to the success of a selected campaign. Sound appeal presented through the right medium constitutes, of course, the ideal advertisement. If the medium is unsuited to the aim and commodity, the appeal, however sound, runs a grave risk of missing the mark. Even appeals which are not altogether good can, in the right medium, get results, though perhaps not up to a hundred per cent.

A medium, as defined in advertising, denotes any publication, poster, sign, or any other of the multitudinous forms of advertising service designed to convey the message which the advertiser expects to reach his buying public, with the ultimate aim of inducing them to purchase his goods or service. It is, in fact, an intermediary between producer and consumer.

Every business has its own peculiar problems, ills, and needs, and a medium might suit one business but be altogether unsuited to another. The fundamental problem, is, therefore, how the advertisements may best be brought to the public notice, in order to receive the maximum of favourable attention and stimulate the maximum of action among the largest number of prospective buyers ; in other words, what is the best medium to use for the particular business in question ? After all, the real test of successful advertising is not the skill shown in presenting the advertisement in the design, for example, but the influence it has on sales once it is published.

There are a great many kinds and classes of media in general use in present-day advertising. All have their own particular values and uses, and it is the business of every advertising man to choose the medium or media best suited to his particular business needs. The media in current use to-day may be classified under the following heads—which are not, of course, intended to be in order of merit. Press ; Direct Advertising ; Outdoor Publicity ; Dealer Helps and " Other " Advertising, such as Films, Radio, Novelties, Handbooks, and Directories.

While there is little doubt that at the present time the Press is the most potent force in advertising, yet it is impossible to lay down a hard-and-fast rule to suit every business in the use of any medium. It is possible, however, to give principles underlying wise choice. It will, perhaps, be useful to give one or two examples of representative trades showing how the media have been selected in each instance. It must be remembered that these, while actual instances are not to be taken as definitely applicable in all cases, individual circumstances may make a great difference. The details set out below show the percentage allocations to the various groups of media :

TRAVEL.

| | Per cent. |
|---|---|
| National Dailies | 12·5 |
| Sunday Newspapers | 5 |
| Provincial Mornings | 12·5 |
| Provincial Weeklies | 5 |
| Magazines | 12·5 |
| Trade and Technical | 5 |
| Posters | 5 |
| Signs | 5 |
| Films and Slides | 5 |
| Dealer Aids | 10 |
| Miscellaneous | 12·5 |
| Advertising in European Markets | 10 |

PERFUMERY.

| | Per cent. |
|---|---|
| National Dailies | 11·5 |
| Provincial Mornings | 2 |
| National Weeklies | 8 |
| Magazines | 8·5 |
| Trade Journals | 0·5 |
| Posters | 20 |
| Signs | 4 |
| Dealer Aids | 21 |
| Advertising Overseas— | |
| Press | 16 |
| Outdoor | 8·5 |

DOMESTIC ELECTRICAL APPARATUS.

| | Per cent. |
|---|---|
| National Dailies | 50 |
| Provincial Dailies | 10 |
| Trade and Technical | 5 |
| Electric Signs | 5 |
| Dealer Aids | 30 |

PAINTS.

| | Per cent. |
|---|---|
| National Dailies | 43 |
| Provincial Dailies | 17·5 |
| National Weeklies | 8·6 |
| Trade Journals | 2·5 |
| Other Publications | 0·7 |
| Direct Mail | 0·7 |
| Dealer Aids | 27 |

COCOA AND CHOCOLATE.

| | Per cent. |
|---|---|
| National Dailies | 21 |
| Sunday Newspapers | 2·5 |
| Provincial Mornings | 1 |
| Provincial Evenings | 4 |
| National Weekly and Monthly Magazines | 8 |
| Posters | 3·5 |
| Coupon Gift Schemes | 23 |
| Films and Slides | 4·5 |
| Samples | 2 |
| Dealer Aids | 11·5 |
| Miscellaneous | 19 |

## QUALITY A FACTOR IN CIRCULATION

IN this connection it is necessary to consider a question upon which the value of a medium largely depends. That is, circulation. Generally speaking, circulation is accepted in terms of figures. This is right up to a point, but, while circulation may and does include the number of people reached by the medium, there are several other allied factors which have also to be considered. Circulation, to be brief, comprises the quantity and quality of the medium, the area of distribution, the quality of advertising carried by the medium, the periodicity of issue, and flexibility.

No doubt the value of a medium depends largely upon the quantity of circulation—upon the number of people who see it, or hear it, or hear of it. Until recent years, statements of the circulation of printed media were utterly unreliable. Nowadays, however, publishers of most reputable journals issue what is called a " net sales certificate," that is, an authentic statement over a period of three, six, or twelve months, showing the actual number of copies sold, less free copies, returns, sporting, and other special editions. At the least, journals now give some fairly reliable statement on the same lines, instead of the ambiguous : " Largest Sale in the West, East . . ." or wherever it may be circulated.

The A.B.C., or the Audit Bureau of Circulations, has done, and is still doing good work in this connection, and although by no means as effective an organisation in this country as is its contemporary, the A.B.C. of the United States of America, it is hopeful of a still more useful future. Briefly, the object of the A.B.C. is to have among its membership all publications willing to give certified statements of their circulations in respect of quantity, quality, and coverage, and any other relevant details useful to the advertiser. It is, after all, the latter who pays the piper, and he should have a little say in calling the tune to his, as well as to the publisher's, satisfaction.

Secondly, the value of a medium depends upon the quality of its circulation; in other words, upon the class of people it reaches. For example, *Punch*, *Tit-Bits*, and *Peg's Paper* go to very different classes of the buying public. It is necessay, therefore, to glean all the information possible concerning the financial, social, professional, and educational standard of the readers of the particular media proposed for your campaign. This information is given by quite a number of publishers themselves, but this is not yet general practice, and a great deal has to be collected by the advertiser. He has to rely on his experience of keying advertisements (so that each reply tells him which advertisement has produced it), on correspondence, questionnaire, and other similar means. Doubtless when the A.B.C. is stronger this information will be more readily obtainable.

Common sense must enter a great deal into this diagnosis of distribution of publications, for some media yield better results owing to the quality of their readers than do others possessing probably a larger circulation. It is obvious that it is a mistake to attempt to advertise beer in *The Methodist Recorder* or sausages in *The Vegetarian News*. Equally silly choices have been made and can still be made by the unthinking.

## CHOOSING A CIRCULATION TO MEET YOUR NEEDS

THE next important point in circulation to consider is that of area coverage, that is, the districts in which a particular medium is distributed, and the extent to which it penetrates into the homes of the public. For instance, *The Yorkshire Evening Post* is published in Leeds, but it circulates not only in and around Leeds, but all over Yorkshire and parts of Lincolnshire, Lancashire, and Durham; *The Daily Herald, The News Chronicle, The Daily Mail, the Daily Express*, and other national newspapers, published in London, are not sold there alone but throughout the length and breadth of the country, and in Wales, Scotland, and Northern Ireland. Therefore, if it is necessary to cover only a section of the country with advertising, a local medium is chosen, and not the large national dailies which cover the whole of the land, and carry an area coverage in excess of requirements. This would be merely so much waste circulation.

A further factor in circulation is the quality of the advertising carried by the medium. This weighs greatly in determining the utility value of a medium. Reputable advertising issued by regular advertisers consistently in certain publications cannot but influence other people in the selection of media, particularly when considered in conjunction with the volume of advertising regularly carried by these papers.

The value of a medium depends also upon the periodicity or frequency of issue. In the case of a newspaper it may be a morning or evening publication; in the case of periodicals and magazines, they may be weekly, fortnightly, or monthly. Thus it is possible to gauge the medium which will be best suited for the particular time or season at which an announcement should appear. If, for instance, it is desired to intimate to the public an immediate change of price, it is no use contemplating a monthly publication which would be issued too late for the purpose; a daily paper would be the proper medium to choose.

## THE POWER OF THE PRESS ADVERTISEMENT

THE Press, by which is meant all publications, daily, weekly, etc., and the Daily Press in particular, is one of the most potent forces of international life to-day. It can mould public character and sway public opinion; controlled in the direction of good, it can work wonders, for example, in improving living conditions and relieving distress, but in the hands of the unscrupulous it can work incalculable harm. In advertising, the proof of its potency lies in the fact that it is the most effective means of reaching the largest possible number of people in the shortest possible space of time and, comparatively, for the least expenditure of money.

Through one of the leading national dailies alone, such as *The Daily Herald*, *The Daily Mail*, or *The Daily Express*, it is possible to reach in a day approximately two million potential buyers of your product; while *The People* and *The News of the World*, issued on a Sunday, claim a circulation of over three million, the reputed largest circulation of any newspapers in the world. It can safely be reckoned that by the judicious choice and use of the large London dailies (nationals), the Sunday Press, and a selection of the leading provincial dailies, it is possible to introduce a message in the speediest and cheapest way to the entire population of Great Britain and Northern Ireland, approximately 44,000,000 people, excluding, perhaps, the few inhabitants of the remoter villages and hamlets.

### THE TYPES OF TRADERS WHO ADVERTISE MOST

It is interesting to note what kind of advertisers use the newspapers. First of all there are manufacturers of articles sold through retailers to families. These are big users of newspaper advertising space. The tie-up is often included in the copy by inserting lists of local dealers, or, perhaps, the announcement itself makes it quite clear, as it should do, of course, what classes of dealers handle the product.

Secondly, advertisers and distributors of motors, pianos, and similar products, sold to a smaller proportion of the population, are great newspaper advertisers, despite the fact that there must be a certain amount of waste circulation, as not all classes of the community use these products. This waste is counteracted if the advertising stimulates the probable buyer, the " when I can afford it prospect," to desire to buy later on. Furthermore, it is argued quite reasonably that local distributors are encouraged and assisted by the appearance of manufacturers' announcements in the local press.

Thirdly, makers of office and labour-saving devices are realising more and more the value of the big nationals and transferring their allegiance from the specialised press.

Operatives, that is, the ordinary rank and file of businesses, are nowadays interested as actual users in the devices, and in the advertisements issued, and so comprise a definite factor in the ultimate purchase. Advertising of these devices shows that the copy appeals are directed mainly to the users who, while not actual buyers, are yet the consumers.

Fourthly, the Mail Order Houses agree that the Press is invaluable, particularly when they are breaking new ground; in other words, when the "prospects" are as yet unknown. Where they are known, Direct Mail is the most effective mode of attack, though even to the known customers Press advertising acts as a stimulant, reminding them of bargains secured at a previous date.

Fifth come the Mail Order "smalls." Most people are acquainted with these advertisements, "Bargains by Post," as they are often headed, appearing usually on Saturdays. Special offers of lino, gardening utensils, and so on are some of the regular displays, and, judging by the frequency of use, no doubt the advertisers find these spaces profitable. Bundled all together, as they are, in one apparently conglomerate mass, they continue, nevertheless, to make favourable appeal each week-end.

Finally, a big source of advertising revenue is afforded by Store Press advertising. Departmental Stores desire great assistance from Press advertising, which must not be confused with Mail Order advertising pure and simple. By advertising in the national dailies the large West End London stores move considerable stocks of bargain items, and, in addition, draw attention to personal shopping facilities for those living in the London area and for visitors from the provinces who are in town on holiday.

## THE DIFFERENT APPEALS THAT JOURNALS POSSESS

IN classifying the Press the popular daily newspapers must be put first. Such papers as *The Daily Herald*, *The Daily Mail*, *The Daily Express*, and *The News Chronicle* all have a regular following of their own particular partisans attracted by the varied political appeals and other topical features. Also in the National class on popular picture dailies like *The Daily Mirror* and *The Daily Sketch*; they dominate in picture news and have a distinct appeal to women. These may be termed the National daily newspapers as they circulate all over the country.

In the next category is what may be termed the semi-National Press. This includes *The Times*, *The Daily Telegraph*, and *The Morning Post*, and also the well-known Provincial paper, *The Manchester Guardian*. These papers, while of National importance, do not enjoy the extensive countrywide circulation and penetration of the National dailies, but represent the quality rather than the quantity circulation of the newspaper world. They comprise the " class " as opposed to the " mass " publications.

Another important group of newspapers still in the National class is the Sunday Press. Of those published in London and owning large circulations are *The People*, *The News of the World*, *The Sunday Express*, *The Sunday Dispatch*, etc. ; these are the large-paged type of newspaper. In the illustrated class are found *The Sunday Referee*, *The Sunday Graphic*, and *The Sunday Pictorial*. In the " class " type, with readers who are fewer in number but are buyers of the more expensive types of goods, are *The Sunday Times* and *The Observer*. The Provinces also have widely circulated Sunday weeklies, notably *The Empire News* in Manchester ; and *The Sunday Sun* in Newcastle-on-Tyne. In Scotland there is *The Sunday Mail*.

Issued on the day when 99 per cent. of people are enjoying their longest leisure period in the week, the Sunday Press reaches almost every part of the kingdom, and is almost certain to enjoy the attention of every member of each home it enters at some time during the day.

Of the Provincial newspapers it is only fair to say that in the main the morning papers are not, as far as circulation is concerned, in as healthy a state as their evening contemporaries. This is greatly due to the increase in the strength of the National dailies, with their improved facilities for rapid distribution all over the country, and their " up to the minute " news service and feature writers. Nevertheless the Provincial morning paper has its use, especially when intensive localised campaigns are contemplated. It would be impossible here to list all these publications, but it is sufficient to say that Leeds, Manchester, Glasgow, and most other leading provincial towns, have their own morning newspapers with widely varying circulations and importance. The Provincial evening papers are in a much more prosperous state, and again almost every large city and town has its paper, in some cases more than one.

Full consideration must be given to this section of the Press, whether for inclusion in a National campaign, when they serve as a strong link-up, or more especially in the case of intensive local or zonal advertising, where the wide circulations of the National dailies would be superfluous to requirements.

The London Evening papers are also important media, their penetration not being confined to London, but radiating beyond Greater London to the South and South-East Coast towns.

### HOW THE ADVERTISER USES THE WEEKLY PAPER

THE last group of newspapers to consider is the weekly Press, including London and Suburban papers as well as a large number issued in the provinces. The weekly newspaper is frequently issued in connection with the " local " daily, but more often than not it is published in districts where no daily appears. Specialising in local topics, district news and personalities, it is essentially a family paper, and affords a good opportunity for the large advertiser to link up with the local retailer and consumer at a low cost. The advertisement columns are largely filled by the local retailer's own advertising, and they are indeed the retailer's best medium both from a cost and circulation point of view. London may be taken as an example, comprised as it is of a group of small townships rivalling in population in many cases some of the large provincial towns ; Wandsworth, East and West Ham, Croydon, Hampstead, and others, each have their own weekly Press. In the Provinces there are also hundreds of similar publications, with equal advertising advantages at low costs.

The weeklies may be divided into classes, first of which is that of the Illustrated Weekly, such as *The Illustrated London News*, *The Tatler*, and *The Bystander*, appealing to the more leisured and moneyed classes. Luxury, or better-class articles are well advertised in their pages. These journals have the advantage that goods can be advertised in more than one colour. Publications in the Illustrated group, appealing exclusively to the wealthier women, are *The Lady*, *The Queen*, and *Vogue*, the latter a fortnightly paper, where colour as well as black and white can be used in advertising. Among those appealing to the " mass " feminine public are papers like *Woman's Weekly*, *Home Chat*,

*Home Notes*, etc., and advertising of more popular-priced articles in this medium finds a ready and profitable response.

Popular weeklies of the *John Bull* and *Passing Show* order, humorous publications like *The Humorist*, with *Punch* as the premier in this class, and other specialised weeklies which deal with such subjects as Education and Child Welfare ; Medical and Nursing work ; Outdoor and Indoor Sports, Games, and Hobbies ; Temperance ; Horticulture and Agriculture, etc., all go to make up this vital section of the Press.

The monthly magazine is almost as ubiquitous as the library book. It is read during leisured and happy hours, and caters for almost all classes of advertisements in monotone or colour. In the general interest class are found *The Strand*, *Nash's*, *Pearson's*, and *The Royal* magazines ; fiction predominates in *The Novel*, *The Grand*, and *The Argosy* magazines ; humour finds outlet in *The Happy Magazine* and *London Opinion*, while domestic interests are well covered by *Ideal Home*, *Good Housekeeping*, and *Homes and Gardens*.

## THE TECHNICAL AND TRADE PRESS

THE technical press is that which appeals to the production side of trade, while the trade press satisfies the distributive side. In one sense the Technical Press may be called Trade Press, but not generally so, for, while in one respect it appeals directly to the Trade, in a broader sense the bulk of the appeal is to the production man, the expert, the technician—it is in effect, as far as advertising is concerned, a medium of direction, advice, and suggestion to the professional man, and as such must be treated with especial care. The appeal in the technical press will be to men like mining, civil, and consulting engineers, to architects, chemists, and other executives who, while they may not do the actual ordering of the goods, yet are employed by their firms in a consultative capacity, and what they think about goods and services will weigh considerably when orders are placed. Journals such as *Engineering*, *The Electrical Review*, *Chemistry and Industry*, *The Shipbuilding and Shipping Record*, *The Mining Journal*, *Gas World*, and many more, are naturally small in circulation, but every reader has a particular, exclusive, and specialised interest not only in the editorial but also in the advertising pages from start to finish, and anxious to miss nothing affecting his professional status.

The Trade Press is designed for the shopkeeper and his assistants, who form the distributive side of trade, the actual link between the manufacturer and the buying, consuming public. Almost every trade has its particular paper, and its circulation is limited only by the number engaged in the trade it represents. In the editorials as well as in their advertisements, these papers keep the reader *au fait* with the latest developments in their trade, and strive not only to advise him what and how to buy, but also, as the late Thomas Russell once said, to teach " the grocer how to groce." There are an enormous number of them covering, for example, bakery and confectionery, chemistry, grocery, hardware, the motor and cycle trade, the ice-cream industry, meat and fish trades, and many others besides.

### THE MESSAGE FOR THE PASSER-BY

AN advertising medium, almost equal in importance to that of the press, is what we may term outdoor publicity—that is, the poster, hoarding, electric sign, etc. While advertisements in the press give a fairly detailed story of the goods—why to buy them, how to use them, their values, etc.—outdoor publicity and other activities dissociated from the press are designed as auxiliaries to keep in mind the messages that the press has put forth from time to time.

Perhaps one of the most useful forms of outdoor publicity is poster advertising or billposting, as it is commonly termed. The advertiser's message can be spread throughout the length and breadth of Great Britain and Ireland by means of posters, in sizes varying from double crown (or one-sheet bills) up to forty-eight sheet posters. The unit of all posters on the hoardings is what is termed double crown, a sheet measuring twenty inches in width by thirty inches deep (the width is usually given first), so that a sixteen-sheet poster is made up of sixteen double crown sheets. The diagram in Fig. 4 shows the relative sizes of poster units. The only deviations from the accepted double crown unit for poster sizes are in the case of auctioneers and estate agents, who generally use the double demy, *i.e.* 22½ inches by 35 inches, and in the case of railway and shipping advertising when double royal, *i.e.* 25 inches by 40 inches, is often used.

The rent for poster sites is per double crown sheet, which varies from a farthing to twopence a week or more in the Provinces and from twopence up to fourpence a week in

London, excepting, of course, for the mammoth sites seen in the West End of London or for special positions in leading provincial towns. In the latter case they may vary from £5 to £50 or more a week for a single mammoth poster.

One of the arguments in favour of the poster is its size, aggressiveness, colour, and simplicity of design, so that "he who runs may read." Moreover, the poster cannot be overlooked or consigned to the waste-paper basket as can newspapers, mailing shots, etc. People not only see but involuntarily read posters.

A good poster should be designed to attract the favourable attention of the person who sees it, to interest him, and to remind him of the goods it advertises. Whether in one or more colours, it should be simple and legible, and should show the name of the product, picture the product itself or at least its use, and bear a terse and concise message (of about three words, and certainly not more than five), commonly termed a "slogan." Well-known examples of effective slogans are: "Prevents that sinking feeling"; "Keep that schoolgirl complexion"; and "Players please."

The long days of summer with its usually fair weather are of greater value for poster advertising than are the short, wet, winter days, for two reasons. First, because there is better and longer visibility in the summer months, although many of the more modern poster sites are floodlit during the winter, or situated in well-lighted streets. Secondly, in the summer the weather is more favourable to the life of a poster. On the average, the life of a single poster is about five to six weeks, so that when ordering posters from the printer it is not sufficient to order the exact quantity required to fill the number of sites taken. Few campaigns are of less duration than thirteen weeks: in fact, except in special circumstances, results cannot reasonably be expected under this period of time.

Generally speaking, poster contracting in this country is in the hands of a number of contractors owning their own hoardings. They are in competition one with the other, and as their organisations often overlap, this makes competition all the keener, to the benefit of the poster advertiser, who gets better sites and increased facilities.

### THE COST OF A POSTER CAMPAIGN

LET us suppose that we wish to occupy 2000 sixteen-sheet poster sites for a period of thirteen weeks; we must

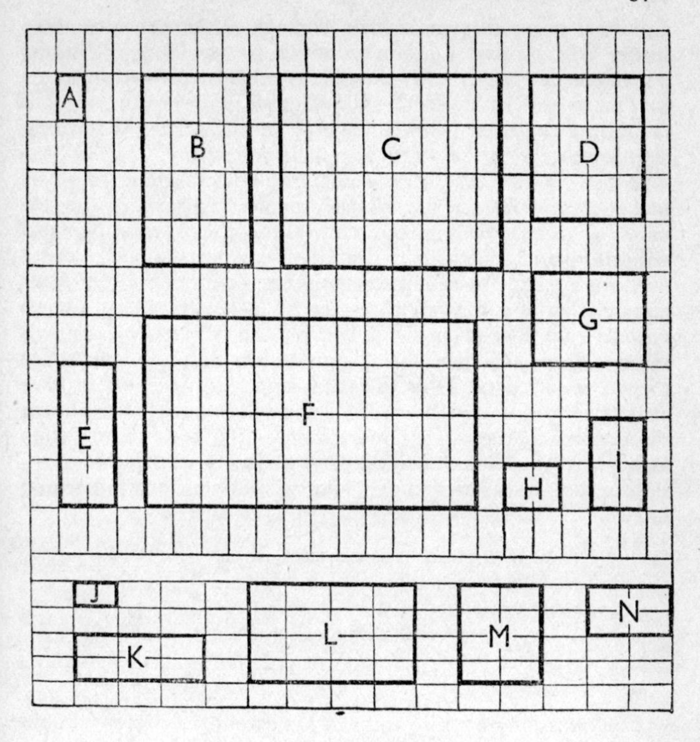


4. POSTER SIZES

A *Double crown :* 20″ × 30″ (*see also* J).
B 16 *sheet upright :* 6′ 8″ × 10′.
C 32 *sheet :* 13′ 4″ × 10′.
D 12 *sheet :* 6′ 8″ × 7′ 6″.
E 6 *sheet :* 3′ 4″ × 7′ 6″.
F 48 *sheet :* 20′ × 10′.
G 8 *sheet broadside :* 6′ 8″ × 5′.
H 2 *sheet :* 3′ 4″ × 2′ 6″.
I 4 *sheet upright :* 3′ 4″ × 5′.
J *Double crown broadside :* 30″ × 20″.
K 6 *sheet broadside :* 7′ 6″ × 3′ 4″.
L 16 *sheet broadside :* 10′ × 6′ 8″.
M 8 *sheet upright :* 5′ × 6′ 8″.
N 4 *sheet broadside :* 5′ × 3′ 4″.

reckon the cost in some such way as this: One sixteen-sheet poster site at, say, $1\frac{1}{2}$d. per double crown sheet per week, equals 2s. per poster site per week. It is reasonable to assume that for this number of sites, allowing for renewals, the number of posters required would be 4500, and 2s. each for printing the posters would be a fair average for this quantity.

Added to the cost of the posters and site rents must be reckoned the service fee, that is the fee charged by the advertising agent placing and controlling the billposting with the billposting contractor. Rarely, if ever, does the advertiser on a large scale deal direct with the contractor: he deals through his agent, who, for a fee (usually about 5 per cent. on the total cost of sites booked for the advertiser) arranges for the distribution of the posters to the various contractors in the areas covered by the campaign, arranges for reports on the condition and position of the posters erected, submits his reports to the client, and instructs the contractors when and where to change positions and make renewals.

The cost of our campaign, then, would work out something like this:

| | |
|---|---|
| 2000 sixteen-sheet poster sites at 2s. per site per week for thirteen weeks . | £2600 |
| 4500 sixteen-sheet posters at 2s. each . | 450 |
| Plus, say, 5 per cent. Service Fee . | 130 |
| TOTAL for Scheme . | £3180 |

The question of where and to what extent the posters should be distributed depends—first, upon how much money there is available; secondly, whether the campaign is to be national or local only; and, finally, upon the length of time they are to be posted, whether for three, six, or twelve months.

While most of the poster sites available at the present time are of reasonably good appearance and in suitable places, all outdoor sites—and this applies equally to painted, electric, and other outdoor signs—are subject to legislation. The Advertisements Regulation Act, 1925, and the Town and Country Planning Act, 1932, enable Local Authorities to regulate and restrict advertisements so as to prevent disfigurement.

A form of advertising medium rather allied to the Poster is the Poster Stamp or "Sticker," as it is sometimes called. It is really a miniature poster, often a replica of a firm's successful large poster, and measures, roughly, $1\frac{1}{2}$ inch wide × $2\frac{1}{4}$ inches deep. It can be used in many ways, for example, as a sticker on invoices, correspondence, existing literature, or in connection with exhibitions, conventions, or similar activities. The trade and public are thus consistently reminded of the advertiser's goods. By virtue of their diminutiveness, designs for poster stamps must be extremely broad in treatment to allow for the considerable reduction in size when they are reproduced.

### THE PAINTED SIGN STILL A FAVOURITE

PAINTED signs constitute an outdoor medium that is still largely used both in London and the Provinces, despite the odium they arouse. They are chiefly to be found on buildings or boards facing traffic routes and busy public thoroughfares. In some cases the advertisement is painted direct on to the wall of the actual building; in other cases it is painted on canvas mounted on wooden boards and surrounded by a frame and then affixed to the building. The treatment may be varied by using a cut-out painted sign. Some of these are composed entirely of lettering, while others include the use of human figures as well as lettering.

As most of these cut-out signs are erected on the roofs of buildings and project above the actual height of the building, they constitute what is called a "Sky Sign" (which is not to be confused with sky-writing). Consequently, permission has to be obtained from the local authorities before one of them is erected. A nominal fee is payable annually in respect of such signs, and permission for renewal must be sought each year.

The use of the painted sign is not necessarily confined to building spaces specially set aside for this purpose. Advertisements are also painted on the walls of dealers' stores, inside railway stations, on football and other sports grounds, and on tobacco, newspaper, and sweets kiosks. They can also be put up in fields, along roads, and beside railway lines. In that case they are called Field Signs. Notable examples are Hall's Distemper, Beecham's Pills, and the displays of several other large advertisers. The essential thing with regard to the painted sign, as in all advertising media, is to see that the visibility, legibility, and attraction are as good as possible.

Enamelled iron plates are frequently seen in railway stations, along railway routes, on the embankment walls leading to and from stations, on large gable ends of buildings, and, on a smaller scale, on the fronts of shops, where the articles in question are sold. Iron plates are strongly made and should last three or more years; they are washable, and since they can withstand the weather, are used principally out of doors. The cost of these plates varies according to their size, and the number of colours they carry. In pre-War days the cost was 7d. or 1s. per square foot; nowadays they may cost 2s. 6d. per square foot or even more. The rent for the exhibition of these plates is between 1s. 6d. to 2s. per square foot, and, particularly with the railways, contracts are not available for less than three years' showing of the plates.

A cheaper plate for under-cover use is the tin plate, which is less durable than the iron variety. It has, however, cheapness in its favour and the capacity to take more colours in the design. Both these plates serve purely as reminder advertisements. In order to be effective they must be kept clean; if they become rusty or otherwise damaged, they should be replaced at once.

### ELECTRICITY AS AN AID TO ADVERTISING

ELECTRIC signs are of two kinds—still and moving. The first has the attractions of light and colour, while the second has also the attribute of movement. Some electric signs once lighted are used merely for illuminating the advertisement, particularly in the case of box and screen signs outside dealers' doors, and are lighted by means of lamps only, in one or more colours. The next improvement is an adjustment to the sign which causes the lighting to be flashed on and off according to the time adjustment on the flasher, which is worked by a small motor. Finally there is the continuously moving electric sign, either fitted with coloured bulbs, or with discharge tubes containing neon. Neon lighting is the most recent sign-lighting improvement, the glass tubing being filled with neon or another gas at a low pressure and made to glow by passing through an electric discharge. The tubing is shaped to the design of the advertisement, and can be obtained in various colours.

Of course signs vary in size according to position. There

are box and screen signs for shopkeepers; others, both still and moving, are erected along the fronts of shops, or over the windows, and are either exposed or encased; they can be supplied with reflectors or backgrounds or any intriguing devices of the sign-maker's craft. In particular, mention must be made of the mammoth signs displayed on the buildings of places like Piccadilly Circus and Leicester Square in London, and on the buildings of important thoroughfares in the larger towns in the Provinces. In these positions both lamp and Neon signs are used, but are, probably without exception, of the moving variety.

Advertisement through this medium is again mainly intended to serve as a reminder to the public. It is, however, questionable whether it is more profitable to be part of the scintillating, conglomerate mass of signs in places like Piccadilly or to be solus in some less important thoroughfare.

### THE COST OF ADVERTISING BY ELECTRIC SIGNS

THE cost is a big factor in advertising by signs. In the case of box or screen signs over dealers' doors, a few pounds will cover the cost of the sign, the lighting must be paid for, and probably, though not always, a small rent of a pound or two will have to be paid to the dealer for the use of the site. The larger signs across the fronts of shops cost more to make and erect, probably £40 or more, according to size and to whether they are bulb or Neon; lighting must be paid for, and again a rental of £25 or more per annum has to be paid to the shop-owner.

The mammoth signs are far more expensive, and the advertiser will have to consider seriously whether the cost is proportionate to the advertising value likely to be obtained. The cost of the erection of the sign, the sign itself, and the wiring, etc., may be £100 or even £300—£400, according to size, and the running expenses will be appreciably higher if Neon is used. There is also the rent of the site, varying according to whether it is in London or in the Provinces. The rent for a site somewhere around Piccadilly will be £100 or more a week; for a good site in a large provincial town, it will probably be a good deal less. On contractors' sites the rent usually includes rates and taxes, but where the site is on dealers' premises or on privately owned property, these items are additional to the rent, and the advertiser has to pay for them.

Finally, no sign of these proportions and composition can be put up and left to its own devices, for it usually happens that now and then, for technical and other reasons, they refuse to work. Therefore, in the case of these larger signs, it is essential to have a maintenance contract either with the sign-maker or with a signs maintenance firm, and this may cost £50 or £100 a year more. This maintenance is essential to keep the sign always in good working order; the electrical installations must be regularly inspected, repaired or adjusted; the bulbs or tubing need to be kept clean; the paint-work has to be washed or repainted when necessary; the time switches require regular attention; and a thousand and one other worries which signs advertising brings in its train have to be dealt with as they arise.

### ADVERTISEMENTS TO CATCH THE TRAVELLER'S EYE

ALL the big provincial towns as well as London have large public transport services, including trams, buses, railways, coaches, and carrier vans, both motor and horse drawn. In the London district alone, under the London Transport merger of 1933, London Transport covers some 2,000 square miles, extending well into the Home Counties. It owns some 3 000 railway cars, 2,660 tram and trolley cars, and 5,300 motor buses. This gives advertisers an immense circulation and the cost is fractional.

Positions for advertising on the trams and buses are available on both the outside and the inside of the vehicles. On the outside of the trams the space on the sides is usually occupied by enamelled iron plates in painted or printed strips; the platform and staircase fronts are covered with small enamelled iron plates or tin plates, as also are the seat backs and doorway finger plates, the latter being of the match-striker type of advertisement. The rear and front ends of the platform cabs carry bill-board positions, double crown size, which are usually filled with posters of the newspaper contents bill type, such as "Lyons' Cooling News," etc. The windows bear on the inside transparencies, window bills, glass plates, and sometimes window cards of very light board. Space for roof cards is also available on the insides of some of the vehicles. The positions afforded by buses are much the same, except that the sites cost a little more.

For Railway advertising there are, first, the Main Line and Suburban steam trains; and, secondly, the Underground and other electrified trains in and round London. The facilities afforded by the former are by no means comparable with those of the latter: in fact, the only positions available inside the coaches are on the right and left of the centre mirror, photograph, ventilator-handle, or whatever else it may be that adorns the centre of the coach's seat-back, according to the antiquity or otherwise of the coach. Of course, there are various facilities offered in the stations themselves: platform, booking-hall, waiting-room, kiosk, and refreshment-room positions are available.

On the other hand, advertising on the electrified railways, particularly in London, has been brought to a fine art. Inside the carriages the spaces available are the seat backs, roof spaces, side panels, carriage door panels, and ventilator positions. On the stations, the platform walls, the subways leading to the lifts, the lifts, booking-halls, and escalators, all provide splendid positions for the advertiser's display.

Last, but by no means the least of vehicular advertising comes Van advertising. Divided into two classes, Horse-drawn and Motor-driven, they may be regrouped once more into Carrier Vans, like Pickfords, Carter Paterson, etc., Railway delivery vans, and the advertiser's own commercial vehicles. The van posters or bills, which form the medium used on van sides, are much larger than any which can be displayed upon trams or buses. The chief dimensions of bills that are acceptable are 120 in. by 80 in. broadside; 63 in. by 25 in.; 60 in. by 40 in, 30 in. by 20 in., and 30 in. by 40 inches.

The cost depends upon the size of the bills, the length of contract, and the class of vehicle, but one can reasonably reckon that the price for 100 sides on vans for one month would work out at about 15s. per side per poster per month. One thing greatly in favour of van-side advertising is that short contracts are possible, a three month's "try-out" is often given on the basis that if satisfied the short term becomes chargeable on the long term rate which may ensue.

### THE MESSAGE TOLD BY SCREEN AND SKY

An advertising medium which has now come into its own and which grows in power almost daily is constituted by the film. To-day, many large advertisers, who used to look askance at the screen as a vehicle for their publicity, are now making film advertising a definite part of their programme. This is no doubt due to the enormous improvement in the production and distribution of the publicity film. As the ordinary " box-office " film has improved through the agency of new methods, healthy competition, and a greater degree of technical skill, so has the advertising film improved also.

There are approximately 4,500 cinemas in the United Kingdom, of which 1,000 are considered useless for film advertising. The remainder are graded as " A," that is first rate cinemas with an average seating capacity of 1,250 ; " B," that is second and third rate cinemas of the suburbs and small towns, with an average seating capacity of 1,000 ; and " C," the smaller third-rate cinemas with a seating capacity of say 500 to 600. Taken together, these cater for 20,000,000 people weekly.

The average figures of a six-day screen rental are : for a Grade " A " theatre, £6, 10s. ; for Grade " B," £4, 5s. ; and for Grade " C," £2, 10s. To these must be added the cost of the original film—and this may be between £200 and £2,000, but on the general average should be about £550—and the cost of copies at about 1d. per foot for silent films, and between 1¼d. and 1½d. for sound films ; thus, the cost of a copy of a 500-feet sound film at 1½d. per foot is £3, 2s. 6d.

A fairly normal rate of exhibition is that of eighty cinemas per month for a period of six months, making a total of roughly 500 exhibitions. For this, 25 copies would be needed, allowing for two or three spare copies, and the cost would be £78, 2s. 6d. For incidental distribution costs, such as carriage, a sum of 2s. 6d. per exhibition should be allowed. A service fee of 10 per cent. on the whole cost must also be included.

There remains Sky advertising to be considered. By means of the latest development in sky-writing the aeroplanes used in this form of advertising are enabled to produce much clearer images by writing at 20,000 feet instead of 10,000 feet. The higher altitude tells very much in favour of the sign, because the range of visibility increases by the square of the height. The message is written across the sky by means of a smoke trail, so that it is only successful as a day medium. The sky banner, flown between two planes, is the latest development here.

## GIFT SCHEMES THAT MAKE THE SALES FIGURES SOAR

ONE of the most rapidly effective and most difficult of sales methods to control is the gift scheme. The gift scheme is normally designed to increase the sales of a commodity already on the market. Gifts may be either supplied free on purchase of a given quantity of a commodity; or gifts may be supplied in exchange for a given number of coupons, checks, certificates, labels, box tops, etc., enclosed with or forming part of the container holding the goods. Further gifts may be awarded in exchange for part coupons and part cash.

The premium system of selling is not new, but it comes in cycles. It enjoys its greatest vogue at the depth of a depression. In other words, it is normally a fairly expensive method of selling, which has the advantage that it will secure sales where most other methods have failed. It is not uncommon to find that the sales of a well-known line which always fail to go beyond a certain figure can be increased by from 20 to 50 per cent. through a gift scheme. There have been cases where even new products have been marketed almost overnight and brought to high sales purely by the result of gift advertising. The sales of one cigarette were raised from 500,000 to a total of 300,000,000 after a period of three years' gift-scheme advertising. The possibilities of the gift scheme were very fully illustrated in the case of the cigarette trade during the slump of 1931–3. During that period by the use of gifts a number of independent tobacco concerns built up enormous sales in the teeth of competition from the Imperial Tobacco Company which did not offer gifts. Eventually, however, an agreement was come to between the independents and the Imperial Tobacco Company to stop gift schemes entirely.

These schemes, however, are particularly useful in the sale of newspapers, periodicals, soaps, foods and household equipment. Further, they appeal to men as well as to women. The desire to get something for nothing is alive in all classes, from dustman to duke. It is no uncommon thing to find applications for gifts coming from members of the peerage. But such schemes require very careful consideration by the sales department before they are launched. For, if gifts can be obtained by purchasing certain goods, the danger is that a competitor may give an even better gift or that the sale of the goods without gifts becomes almost impossible. In other words, gift schemes are high-pressure sales methods, and they must be used with great care in handling both new and established products, if they are not to damage the normal sales organisation and to increase costs dangerously.

### METHOD AND PROMPTITUDE MEAN SUCCESS

SCHEMES launched by inexperienced people soon become prey to the many problems evidenced in all gift-scheme advertising. It should be borne in mind that in schemes of this nature you have to cater for almost every class of the general public, which is discerning, critical, and ever-suspicious, from the labourer to the peer : even the latter has the human desire to get " something for nothing."

Briefly summarised, the system for dealing with a gift scheme must comprise the reception and recording of applications and checking of coupons ; the preparation and dispatch of gifts ; correspondence, filing, " mailing " lists, and " follow-up " ; complaints ; and records showing numbers and nature of gifts required, area popularity, etc. The scheme department should be divided at once into two sections, receiving and dispatch, and under no circumstances should the two be permitted to merge for obvious reasons. There will also be a buying section, but as buying generally has been dealt with elsewhere, that section need not be considered here.

One clerk, at the start, will be sufficient to receive applications. These must be dealt with the same day as received, for delay means ultimate confusion and dissatisfied applicants. The letters are opened, and the contents carefully examined, the letter is then marked to show at a glance the number of coupons received and the nature of the gift or gifts required. This can be clearly done by ringing round the essential points with coloured pencil. Discrepancies should be placed with " complaints " for immediate attention. As the scheme grows, this work of checking entails more staff, and, in order to track " error " to its source at a later date, each clerk should have a differently coloured pencil for the work, or else a code-number or initial. This helps in the early settlement of possible queries.

When the letters have been checked, they are passed to the typist for labels to be addressed. A plain label, excepting for the firm's address and the legend, " if undelivered, please return to . . .," should be used. This will minimise risk of pilferage, as otherwise the name emblazoned on a label may lead the curious to investigate. Another method of typing labels found useful by one large firm both to the packer, and also as a check in case of future query, was to use a code along the foot of the label thus: 28 : 3 : H : U, meaning label typed the 28th March, by Harris (typist), and covering gift "U" (umbrella, perhaps). All labels should be addressed in triplicate so as to provide one for the gift parcel, one for the dispatch file, and one for the mailing cabinet.

## LAYING THE FOUNDATION OF FUTURE SALES

THE addressed labels, accompanied by a summary of the day's gift requirements should be sent to the dispatch department for attention. Again promptitude of attention is necessary to ensure success. No label should be held over to the following day, excepting where gifts are out of stock, in which case the receipts department should be advised and the applicant written to without delay. The nature of packing materials, storage, etc., are things with which an experienced store manager can help, as they need careful organisation.

Correspondence, filing, registration of records, complaints, etc., must be carefully supervised. The third copy of the label should be filed for mailing "shots" and other "follow-up." It may be placed in expanding cabinets either alphabetically or geographically, according to business requirements. This cabinet of names and addresses can be invaluable, one firm having built up by this means a reliable mailing list of nearly half a million people, representing already interested prospects for the future.

## THE PRIZE SCHEME AS A SALES BUILDER

COMPETITIONS may be either tests of skill, like painting, designing posters, and "slogan" building, or genuine puzzles, free from chance. All these are useful promoters of sales and therefore come within the ambit of advertising. The same care in organisation should be taken, although, of course, the question of dispatch of prizes does not necessitate the same amount of work as in coupon schemes. It is important, however, that awards should be scrupulously fair and in accordance with the terms outlined in the press or other announcements. Prizes, whether in money or kind, should be dispatched at once, and due prominence be given in suitable media to the results.

This type of advertising is always open to suspicions in the public mind, and the object of the manufacturer should be to allay this by rigid adherence to terms, and close attention to organisation and appreciation of the public requirements.

### DISPLAY ADVERTISING THAT HELPS THE DEALER

So far we have dealt only with the media which reach and teach the vast consuming public, and not—with the exception of the Trade Press—with those which affect the dealer, calling for his aid and support, and lending him aid and support in return. It might well be asked why it is necessary to help the dealer at all. Surely, if he receives sound goods, that should be sufficient. On the other hand, the dealer is the point of contact between the advertiser and the consuming public, and many advertisers have been unsuccessful simply because they have failed to realise the importance of dealer influence in respect to their goods.

Display advertising helps the dealer to move the goods, which the advertising and selling has placed on his shelves, into the consumer's hands—their rightful place. It includes such things as mechanical and electrical window devices, models, package displays, cartons, dummies, sets, etc., and also showcards, cut-outs, window bills, price tickets, and counter cards.

Showcards vary considerably in form, shape, style, design, size, and nature. They can be flat—that is, they can consist of oblong or square-shaped cards, fitted at the back with struts and hangers, or they can be cut flush, which means that the edge of the printed card is cut through or guillotined; or they can be made so that the printed edge of the paper is turned over to the back of the card and strengthens it. Again, a card may be cut out—shaped so as to form a figure or anything else that is desired. Cut-outs, however, cost a little more than flats because of the extra cost for the special cutting of the edges.

Window bills and price cards may be flat or cut out, and both cards and bills may be preserved by varnishing the printed surface, or, in the case of cards, by covering them with gelatine. The extra cost per piece is small and is especially worth while in the case of material going overseas to tropical climates.

No matter what display material is used, it must be attractive and adaptable. Above all, when ordering the material, it is important to have in mind the classes of shops the display will be used in, and the amount of space it will, in the main, be accorded. It may be that a minimum height is a factor to be considered, or that width has to be limited, or that both height and width are restricted in the class of trade in question. Large, unwieldly pieces may either be too big for the dealer to use, or out of all proportion to his display space, and it is necessary to consider the dealer in these matters if he is to give satisfaction by good sales.

### THE APPEAL THAT GOES STRAIGHT HOME

We now come to the last important advertising medium, that afforded by Direct Mail. A plan has to be worked out which will provide an indication not only of the amount of money required, but of the manner in which it should be spent. Given an acquaintance with the proposition and the advertiser's general objectives, it is necessary to consider the territory to be covered ; the classifications of customers or "prospects" ; the numbers in each class to be approached ; the correct sequence and series of mailings ; the literature and materials to be employed. It must be decided whether sales letters, booklets, cards, folders, broadsides, novelties, or leaflets are to be used ; whether to have a sequence of any one kind of approach or an alternation of different kinds ; what kind of envelope, reply card, order forms or inquiry forms to use. Nor must the method of printing and the postal rate be neglected.

### HOW TO PREPARE A MAILING LIST

In settling the mailing list, it is necessary to find out whether there are distinct classes of individuals who should own the product ; whether their names and addresses are available and authentic ; whether they have got the money to buy with. Their geographical position must be favourable, and it must be known how many of them can be supplied. If there is more than one distinct class to be reached it may be that different handling will be necessary for each, or that what suits the one class will not answer for the other. Inasmuch as the mailing list represents the prospective market, these points should be the first and foremost consideration.

The main object of Direct Mail is not only to sell by Mail, but to break down sales resistance ; it acts as an advance guard for the salesmen, and a follow-up to their visits, and will often tell a story when and where a salesman cannot. Direct Mail reaches only the persons whom it is desired to reach. It is an economical medium, dignified, flexible, and selective.

The following is a sketch of a specimen campaign, with its estimated costs. It is a proposed insurance mailing shot to 75,000 professional men, and comprises a personalised form letter and a small booklet, enclosed in good quality wallet envelopes, bearing halfpenny stamps :—

| Item | £ | s. | d. |
|---|---|---|---|
| Art Work, Copy, and Plan of Scheme . | £100 | 0 | 0 |
| Printing Blocks . . . . | 50 | 0 | 0 |
| Printing a series of 6 booklets (75,000) . | 900 | 0 | 0 |
| ,, ,, 6 letter headings (75,000) . . | 337 | 10 | 0 |
| Envelopes, 450,000 . . . | 348 | 15 | 0 |
| Facsimile Work. A series of six quarto letters reproduced by facsimile typewriting process . . | 675 | 0 | 0 |
| Indexing. Creating a grouped card index of 75,000 names and addresses, including cost of cards, 5″×3″, feint ruled . . . | 75 | 0 | 0 |
| Addressing, by typewriter, 450,000 envelopes . . . . | 393 | 15 | 0 |
| Dispatching. Folding and enclosing 450,000 letters and booklets in envelopes, tucking-in flaps, affixing stamps, checking, bundling, and mailing . . . | 174 | 7 | 6 |
| Postage at a halfpenny for 450,000 . | 937 | 10 | 0 |
| Grand Total of . | £3991 | 17 | 6 |

## WHAT TO SPEND ON ADVERTISING

THE classic advertising cost is that which averages 3 to 3½ per cent. of the actual retail price. A few advertising percentage costs of representative trades are as follows :

|  |  |  |  |
|---|---|---|---|
| Collars . | 3.5 per cent. | Dentifrice . | 2 per cent. |
| Cameras . | 3 ,, | Motor cars | 1.1 to 2.6 ,, |
| Soft Drinks . | 10 ,, | Rail Travel . | 2.5 ,, |
| Suits . | 2 ,, | Cigarettes . | 5 ,, |

There are several ways in which the money can be allocated to advertising, but not one of them can be accepted as definitely suited to any one product. Here again the product and the sales policy must be taken into account. One method is by taking a percentage of Sales. In this case, sometimes the figures for the past sales year or half-year are used, sometimes the anticipated sales for the oncoming year or half-year form the basis of the computation. This is the method most commonly used, perhaps on account of its mathematical simplicity. It should not be overlooked, however, that the percentage of sales used by one trade is not necessarily applicable to another.

Another way is to make an assessment on a certain unit of the product. Here again the number of units taken into account is that founded on the sales of the period corresponding to the one under review. Thus, many advertisers find it more convenient to take a case or packet of their product as the basic unit for measuring their advertising appropriation, and they budget everything on this basis. Salesmen, for instance, are allowed so much per case for salary, so much for expenses, etc. The reason this method is used by some people is because the money value of the product fluctuates widely, or the money value is not known until the returns are received from the Trade. This form of allocation is more common in co-operative advertising than in individual campaigns.

Some firms put all the money that can possibly be obtained into advertising as an investment in future sales. This is merely a demonstration of pure faith in the product, and is hazardous, to say the least of it. The amount of money spent may be out of all proportion to the immediate sales, and the method is therefore not to be recommended.

The Budgetary system is not too common in this country as yet, but it is gradually becoming more so. It is a simple method which needs no explanation, as it is merely an amplification of the ordinary housekeeping budgeting, according to the apparent money available.

Again, a certain percentage of the previous year's profit can be appropriated to advertising. Many firms are in favour of putting a good proportion of the profits back into the business through advertising. The profits of a company may be budgeted and turned over to the various departments of the business, a certain amount to sales promotion, a certain amount for addition to plant, and so on, and some to advertising. This plan has much to recommend it.

## WHERE TO READ MORE ABOUT ADVERTISING

QUITE a large number of books are available for the further study of Advertising, some going into details of the many different aspects of the science, and others dealing more widely with the subject as a whole. A reliable and exhaustive American survey of the whole matter is Starch's *Advertising Principles*, and an efficient English treatment is given in Thomas Russell's *Commercial Advertising*. The place of research in modern business is readily recognised, and is of great importance in advertising. White's *Advertising Research* contains a fund of useful information on this side of the subject. A full treatment of Media is to be found in Eley's *Advertising Media*; while other specific phases of the Advertising Art are obtained in *Effective Postal Publicity*, by Max Rittenberg; *Advertising Lay-out and Copywriting*, by Watkins; and *Advertising and the Law*, by Bishop. These are all recommended to the reader as practical handbooks on their respective subjects.

# HOW GOODS ARE CARRIED

*by ROGER CHAPMAN, M.A.(Cantab.), Fellow of the Institute of Chartered Shipbrokers*

THE economic and business development of the present-day world dates from the discovery of cheap and expeditious methods of transporting passengers, goods, and messages. Without the ability to do this the mass production made possible by machinery in almost every line of industry and trade would be useless, since the reason for the success of mass production is not so much the making of enormous quantities of goods at a very low price, as the ability to deliver these quantities to customers all over the world, cheaply and expeditiously. It is therefore apparent that a very important part in present-day business activities is played by transport over land and sea and by the business firms of all kinds who facilitate the transport of passengers and goods in various ways.

The immense volume of raw material and finished articles which are exchanged at the present time between countries in different parts of the world, and the cheapness of transport by water as compared with transport over land, make it proper that sea transport should be dealt with first. The main difference between sea transport and land transport is the great diversity of the former and the comparative sameness of the latter. This diversity in the business of shipping is caused by the different classes of goods to be carried, the greatly varying distances over which they have to be carried, and the different docks, ports, harbours, and rivers in which they have to be loaded or discharged. For this reason shipping has to be dealt with more fully than inland transport.

### TYPES OF VESSELS THAT ARE USED: LINER OR TRAMP?

IN dealing with shipping it is first of all necessary to get some idea of the various types of ships that are available for the carrying of cargo. It is also necesssary to remember that since the advent of the motor vessel it is no longer possible to class all vessels indiscriminately as steamers. But all these varying types of ships, while very numerous, can be divided for general purposes into the following main groups : passenger liners ; cargo liners ; cargo tramps ; oil tankers ; small and coastal cargo and passenger vessels.

All types and classes of vessels can be fitted into one or other of these main groups, although there will naturally be considerable over-lapping between one group and another. For instance, large passenger liners all take cargo to a greater or less extent, usually valuable goods which can pay a high rate of freight for the extra speed or safety of shipment by these special services. The quantity of cargo they take depends on the relative values of the cargo and passenger traffic offering between the ports or countries to which they trade.

On the North Atlantic, where there is the largest and most remunerative passenger traffic of any trade, passengers are catered for almost exclusively by these large liners, and only high-paying and quick-handling cargo is considered. Speed in dealing with the vessel at each port of call, in order to maintain perfect regularity of service, is more essential than securing large quantities of cargo. On other routes, for example, from the United Kingdom to the East Coast of Africa, the passenger traffic of itself is not enough to keep the regular liners going, and cargo traffic becomes of increasing importance.

Just as passenger liners take a cargo to a greater or less extent, so the cargo liners which are trading regularly between different countries or ports will nearly always take a few passengers, to whom cheapness or the health value of a longer voyage is of more importance than speed, or in cases where the passenger traffic is not large enough to warrant there being regular passenger liners on the route.

These liners, whether passenger or cargo, give regular sailings on definite dates in all directions all over the world wherever the traffic is sufficient to warrant them, and maintain their services whether traffic offers or not, in exactly the same way as a railway company. Naturally the cost of transport by liners is higher than that by tramp services, as the steam-ship company takes the risk of having to sail the vessel nearly empty, while an absolutely full ship is a comparative rarity. The services are, however, of such advantage to passengers and shippers of goods, who are able to decide on the vessel that will suit them weeks or months ahead, that liner services are always tending to increase as compared with ordinary tramp services ; and wherever a steady flow of passengers or goods becomes apparent on any particular route, a liner service will gradually come into being, and the tramp will gradually retire.

## CARGO TRAMPS: THE VAGRANTS OF THE SEA

THE cargo tramps fall into an entirely different group, being, as their name implies, the vagrants of the seas, and going from one end of the world to another, wherever the most remunerative cargo offers. In all ports and harbours of the world the tramp is to be seen, from ten thousand tons of cargo down to no more than a hundred tons. Whereas the liners are becoming little more than large floating trains, the tramp has a romance all her own. She has no regular course or time-table ; she may be away from home for three months or three years ; she will sail anywhere with anything.

Some tramps are built specially for bulk cargoes, such as coal, grain, or timber, while others are built more particularly for general cargo of one sort or another. Those built for bulk cargo have open holds and large hatches to facilitate rapid loading and discharge, whereas those built for general cargo have smaller hatches and two or three decks on which cargo can be stowed in such a way that the vessel can load for several ports of discharge, and can carry damageable goods in safety.

There are, in addition, cargo tramps built essentially for particular kinds of cargo, as, for instance, a fleet owned in Norway specially designed for carrying railway material, such as engines, tenders, coaches, rails, and sleepers ; each ship has derricks or cranes fitted on board, capable of lifting up to 100 or 150 tons, for loading and discharging these particular goods at ports which have no facilities for lifting such heavy loads. In this class of specialist cargo ships are oil tankers, which, as their name implies, are used for the carriage of oil in bulk, and, owing to their special construction, are suitable only for this cargo, and do not enter other markets to any extent. As a result, they are of interest only to ports and firms dealing with oil, and seldom appear in ordinary shipping business.

The last main class of tramps—the coastal vessels—is small in actual quantity of tonnage, but, owing to the short distances usually covered and the large number of cargoes lifted each year, its importance is greater than might appear. Coastal vessels can be subdivided into liners and tramps ; but as from the point of view of transport they really are more competitive with rail and road than with overseas carrying, they are classed together under the one heading. They usually cater for passengers who wish to travel across stretches of water, such as the Bristol Channel, which cannot economically be crossed by bridges or ferries, or for pleasure cruises, and for goods in cases where cheapness is comparatively of greater importance than speed. Even round the coasts of Great Britain, where the rail and road distances are small, the quantity of goods carried by coastal services is much greater than is generally realised.

The average speed of the cargo tramp is about ten knots, a knot being one sea mile per hour, and a sea mile being slightly greater than a land mile, that is, ·151 more than a land mile. Cargo and passenger liners are much more speedy, ranging, as a rule, from fifteen to thirty knots.

### THE FOUR TONNAGES USED TO DESCRIBE A SHIP

IN ordinary shipping use there are four tonnages to be considered, and when the size of a vessel is given it is necessary to state which tonnage is being referred to. First, there is *displacement tonnage*. It is well known that a floating object displaces its own weight of water; and as salt water weighs one ton per thirty-five cubic feet, the number of cubic feet displaced by the vessel divided by thirty-five gives the displacement tonnage, or weight, of the vessel and her cargo. The builders usually give a displacement scale when they build a vessel, showing her unloaded displacement, her displacement when fully loaded, and the number of tons of weight per every inch of immersion.

*Deadweight tonnage* is the tonnage of cargo, stores, and bunkers that the vessel can take to load her down to her Plimsoll marks. It is the difference between the unloaded displacement and the loaded displacement, and is of great importance to a shipowner, as it represents the amount of cargo he can carry and on which he gets paid freight in the case of deadweight cargoes. *Gross tonnage* is the total underdeck space of the vessel, including in some cases certain enclosed spaces above deck, including all holds, engine-room and bunker space, divided by a hundred cubic feet to the ton.

Finally, the *net tonnage* is the gross tonnage less all spaces not used for carrying cargo, such as engine-room and bunker spaces, also divided by a hundred cubic feet to the ton, and is frequently the tonnage on which dock dues, tonnage dues, towage, and pilotage charges have to be paid. It is, therefore, to the shipowner's interest to build vessels with the largest possible deadweight tonnage and the smallest possible net tonnage when the ship is intended for carrying deadweight cargoes.

In the case of non-deadweight cargoes, where the holds are full without the vessel being loaded down to her marks, it is important to have the holds of as large a cubic capacity as possible so that a good quantity of such cargo can be carried. Thus vessels for this type of cargo are built with extra width or beam and full lines, and, therefore, with a larger net and gross tonnage compared with the deadweight tonnage, the bulk of cargo carried being of more importance than the weight. As a rough approximation, net tonnage is about 60 per cent. of gross tonnage, and deadweight tonnage about 150 per cent. of the gross.

Reference has just been made to the ship's "marks." These are the Plimsoll marks on the side of the vessel below which she may not be loaded. There are actually five marks: Freshwater (when the vessel may be loaded deepest), Indian Summer, Summer, Winter, and Winter North Atlantic, for each of which the ship must have increasing free-board. Free-board is the distance from the water-line to the main deck of the vessel, and is the margin of safety reckoned to be necessary according to the structure of the vessel and the time of year. Thus in the winter, when the weather is rougher, she must have more free-board, or a greater distance from the main-deck to the water-line, than during the summer.

## HOW A SHIP IS PROPELLED

THE particular trade of the vessel largely determines the form of propulsion to be used, as well as the type of construction. There are two main forms of propulsion—steam and motor—the steam being raised in some cases by coal fires and in some cases by oil fires, and the motor engines, as a rule, being run on crude oil. The advantages of oil-burning steamships and motor-ships are cleanliness and saving in crew and space; no firemen are required, less space is occupied by fuel, which can be carried in the vessel's double bottom, and, in the case of motor ships, less space and less weight are taken up with the engines. The advantages of coal-fired steamers are that coal is in most parts of the world considerably cheaper than oil, and that the Scotch boiler, which is generally used, is amazingly reliable in service, and is being tended to-day by the third generation of engineers. The steamer is safer and more reliable year in and year out; it does not need constant or expensive attention, and sea-going repairs, if necessary, can be more easily effected by the vessel's engineers than is the case with the motor engine.

As a rule, the liners are users of oil and the tramps are users of coal, speed and cleanliness being necessary for the liners, and cheapness and reliability being the chief requisites of the tramps. As the liners are on the average much faster than the tramps, and as the increased power required for increased speed varies as the cube of the extra speed required, great importance attaches to the extra weight of the engines required for increased speed and the quantity and weight of the fuel to be carried.

There are other methods of propulsion in use, such as Diesel-electric, and, of course, the almost out-of-date sail, but none of these are to-day of much competitive importance. The shipowner weighs up the pros and cons of these methods when ordering a new ship, and decides on whichever he thinks is best suited to his particular trade.

### CARGOES ARE OF INFINITE VARIETY

THE cargoes to be carried are of paramount interest to shipowners, and vary to an almost infinite extent. They can, however, be roughly grouped in three categories. First, there is *general cargo in small parcels*, consisting of small lots of case goods, bale goods, hardware, iron and steel finished products, etc. Part or whole cargoes are made up of lots of all sorts and sizes, coming from many individual manufacturers to many individual customers. A manufacturer wishing to send ten or twenty tons of finished goods, for instance, to America, books space at a scheduled rate of freight with a passenger or cargo liner company for a sailing on a specified date. These goods have to be shipped in this way as the individual manufacturer has not sufficient quantity for shipment at the one time to be able to charter a vessel on his own. The liner company books as many of these lots as possible, and the vessel then sails with as much or as little as is supplied.

Naturally such a method costs more in proportion than chartering a special vessel, as the shipping company has to take the risk of the quantity of cargo offering for each sailing being very small, and the vessel duly sails whether she has ten tons or a thousand tons. By far the greater quantity of manufactured and finished articles are shipped in this way; the manufacturer has the advantage of knowing exactly what rate of freight he will have to pay, and the dates of the vessel's sailing and of her arrival at the discharging port. In this way the service offered by these regular general cargo liners approximates very closely to the service given by a railway company.

The second category is *general cargo in large quantities*. Where a person has a quantity of goods to be carried at one time sufficient to fill a ship, it is cheaper, as a rule, for him to charter a special vessel for the purpose. An exporter of large quantities of finished iron and steel goods, for instance, may have three thousand tons to ship at one time from the United Kingdom to Italy or Spain. He, therefore, gets a shipbroker or cargo agent to put the cargo on the market and find a vessel of suitable size and position to take it at the lowest possible rate of freight. The vessel is then chartered for a date which is mutually agreed between the merchant and the shipowner, and takes the cargo to its destination.

The liner companies, if they have a suitable sailing for the required destination, may make a special bid for the traffic, in view of the substantial quantity; and as the liners are, as a rule, more suitably built for carrying such general cargo, shipments of this nature frequently go by general cargo liners, unless they are from or to a port at which the liners do not make a regular call, or are not prepared to make a special call, in which case the tramp service is the only alternative.

## BULK CARGOES: THE BASIS OF SHIPPING PROSPERITY

THE third category, *bulk cargoes*, forms by far the largest tonnage of cargo carried by sea, and consists, as a rule, of raw materials of one sort or another. It is on the quantity of these bulk cargoes that the prosperity or otherwise of shipping as a whole largely depends. As an example, if there happens to be an almost world-wide drought, which will have the result of seriously lessening the grain harvests, particularly in European countries, it will be reasonable to expect that there will shortly be large movements of grain from such countries as Argentina, Canada, and Australia to Europe; this will cause a strong demand for suitable tonnage for this purpose, and the effect of this will be seen in increasing freights in almost all directions. Bulk cargoes can be divided into several classes, each class forming a market between shippers and shipowners. Tramp vessels are chartered for the various cargoes offering all over the world, usually on a standard form of charter agreed between the Chamber of Shipping of the United Kingdom and the shippers in each particular trade.

To tramp shipping coal is the most important cargo, by reason of the enormous tonnage carried each year and the diversity of destinations and sizes of vessels required, ranging from a hundred tons for coastal or near ports to ten thousand tons for countries six thousand or ten thousand miles away. Coal is approximately a deadweight cargo, and suitably built colliers will, as a rule, carry their full tonnage. A great quantity of shipping is specially constructed for carrying coal and other deadweight cargoes, with large open holds, big self-trimming hatches, and moderately fine lines. Such vessels can be loaded and discharged very rapidly and easily, with the minimum of handling of the cargo, and the comparatively fine lines have the effects of saving in engine power and fuel consumption.

Grain is almost as important to shipping as coal, and a large number of ships, varying in size from five thousand to ten thousand tons deadweight, are built specially for the trade. The diversity in size of tonnage required is not so great as is the case with coal, but the distances to be covered are on the average greater. Grain carriers are built on much the same lines as colliers, as grain is also approximately a deadweight cargo. The holds may not be quite so open, since grain in bulk shifts very easily, and shifting boards have to be fitted to prevent this. Frequently cargoes consist partly or wholly of bagged grain, and vessels with two or more decks are suitable for this and are often engaged in the trade.

The chief shipping trade of the world is perhaps that between the River Plate and Europe—out to the Plate with coal and home with grain—and the quantities of grain to be shipped have a vital effect on all other markets. If the quantities are large, tonnage has to be attracted from other trades by higher rates, and the influence is eventually felt even among small five-hundred tonners, which have less competition from the larger vessels on the margin between two trades, and so are able to get better rates. Similarly, a poor demand for grain tonnage usually means lower rates in other markets sooner or later. Other deadweight cargoes, consisting chiefly of iron and other ores, phosphate, sugar, rice, salt, pitch, etc., are carried with similar tonnage and in approximately the same way as coal and grain.

## TIMBER CALLS FOR SPECIALLY DESIGNED VESSELS

A FOURTH large and important group is *timber*, and a large proportion of vessels is built particularly for this trade, which requires special design of ship. In the first place, timber is not a deadweight cargo, and a vessel cannot carry anywhere near her full cargo of timber in her holds. As a result, part of the cargo is shipped on deck, in some cases as much as three-fifths, and vessels are built on fuller lines and with greater width or " beam " than for coal or other deadweight cargoes. This enables them to carry a large cubic quantity in their holds, and also gives them increased stability, which is vitally necessary in view of the cargo piled above the main deck to a height of twelve or fifteen feet. The hatches are usually smaller, which gives added strength to the whole structure, and the decks are made as clear and open as possible. The bulwarks are higher, to give strong side-support to the deck cargo, and there is what is known as a " well-deck " forward, and possibly also aft, so that the cargo can be stowed on deck much more safely than would be the case with an ordinary collier.

The main deck of the vessel can be imagined as a flat surface, with the forecastle, the bridge space amidships, and the poop (aft) raised well above the main deck level, to give what is known as a three-island type of vessel; the deck cargo then fills in the spaces or " wells " between the " islands." The vessels range from a thousand to five thousand tons deadweight, and freight is usually paid per standard of 165 cubic feet. As a deadweight ton occupies approximately 45 to 50 cubic feet, it will be seen that a vessel will carry in standards of timber somewhat less than one-third of her deadweight capacity. The question whether she is a good timber carrier or not largely depends, therefore, on the quantity she will carry on deck, while maintaining a safe margin of stability.

Timber vessels usually carry coal in the direction of the timber loading port, but are not so suitable for coal cargoes as regular colliers, owing to their smaller hatches. Similarly, colliers carry large quantities of timber homewards, but a timber vessel will carry anything from fifty to a hundred standards more than a collier of the same deadweight capacity, owing to her special construction, and so can make a profit out of a timber cargo where the average collier could not do so.

## CARGOES THAT REQUIRE SPECIAL SHIPS

FINALLY, there are general bulk cargoes of all sorts—cotton, beans, fruit, esparto grass, flax, generals from India, etc.—which are regularly carried by tramp vessels. What is known as the Mediterranean trade largely consists of such cargoes, and requires vessels of from three thousand to six thousand tons deadweight. Cargoes of light goods and case or bale goods, such as cotton, fruit, and generals, are not really suitable for open hold vessels, and some owners specialise in tramp vessels for these particular cargoes, with smaller holds and hatches and full lines to give the best possible cubic space and usually two or more decks for stowing special lots, and thus preventing the full weight of the cargo from resting on that stowed at the bottom of the ship.

There are innumerable other kinds of cargo to be carried, but not in sufficient quantity to form separate markets of their own, and tonnage for these is usually chartered in London, or on the spot, as and when the occasion arises.

## HOW CARGOES ARE ARRANGED AND CARRIED BY LINERS

IN all cases of carriage of goods by sea there is a contract arranged between the shipper and the shipowner, and certain terms are in everyday use by these parties. The arrangement of cargoes can be separated into two sections—general cargo carried by liner services and bulk cargo carried by tramp steamers. The contract of carriage in the first case is arranged on a bill of lading only, as the shipper is not chartering the whole of the vessel, but is only booking the necessary space for the parcel he has for shipment. The merchant with cargo for shipment to an overseas destination, to which there are regular sailings, makes inquiries from the shipping company, either direct or through an agent, for a rate for the particular material, which is usually quoted from f.o.b., the loading port, to c.i.f., the discharging port.

*F.o.b.* means " free on board," and the merchant or his agent places the cargo free on board the vessel, paying all costs to that point, such as railway rate, wharfage or quay dues on the cargo, and loading from truck or quay into the vessel. The shipping company receives the material on board, and pays the stowing charges as part of the quoted rate of freight, the line of demarcation between shipper and shipping company being considered to be the side of the vessel, so that when the cargo passes over the side, or, as is frequently stated, "over ship's rail," it passes from the hands of the one party into the hands of the other. The actual division of the total loading and stowing charges between the shipper and the vessel is determined by the custom of the port of loading, and, although there are variations at different ports, this division is usually made as stated above.

*C.i.f.* stands for "Cost, Insurance, Freight," and is not strictly a shipping term, being a term in general use between seller and buyer, the price paid by the buyer on a c.i.f. sale covering the cost of the goods, together with the insurance and freight to the point when the shipping company delivers the goods at the discharging port. C.i.f. has, therefore, been adopted as a shipping term to refer to the point at which the vessel delivers, which is usually over the vessel's side or rail, all discharging costs being paid by the vessel and included in the freightage quoted. All subsequent costs, such as receiving, landing, and wharfage or quay dues, are paid by the receivers of the goods.

The liner company books as much as possible of various sized lots of general cargo for each date of sailing at the scheduled rates, sometimes making a special cut in the rate for large quantities. If required, goods can be booked for transport on a through bill of lading, which means that the shipping company arranges to collect or deliver from or to an inland destination, and also undertakes the work of passing the goods through the Customs and forwarding by rail or other inland transport. It is a general rule that, though the rate quoted covers the costs from or to the inland point, the responsibility of the shipping company in such cases begins and ceases at the "ship's rail" point of loading or discharge, and all inland forwarding is done on the conditions of the inland transport company.

The regular liner companies have their agents in all large business centres to book traffic for their services, and are usually able to rely on getting steady quantities of merchandise of all sorts. Rates are governed in most cases by liner conferences, in which competing liner companies of all nationalities, serving the same routes, agree to schedule rates of freight and conditions. There are frequently non-conference lines running, and giving lower rates, but the conferences have been found to be of real advantage to shippers, even if it sometimes means a higher rate of freight, because they ensure absolutely regular services, and prevent the constant fluctuation of rates, which usually result from unfettered competition. Nothing kills business so surely as uncertainty, and merchants quoting a c.i.f. price for goods to be supplied some time ahead need to have some guarantee that the rates on which they base their quotation will not be suddenly altered, and that the services on which they rely will be maintained.

### THE TRAMP STEAMER'S CARGO

A MERCHANT having a quantity of cargo to ship, sufficient to enable him to charter a vessel for his cargo only, will quote his order on the appropriate market, either direct or through an agent. Shipowners with a suitable vessel, or their agents, then approach the shipper and make him an offer of the vessel, or else ask him to give them an offer at a definite rate of freightage for the ship, if he finds that she is suitable for his purpose.

In this case the contract of carriage is by charter party, and the goods are shipped on a bill of lading which incorporates the terms and conditions of the charter party. The charter is signed by both parties, usually on a standard form, and insertions to suit the particular cargo and vessel are made in spaces that are left blank for the purpose. A date is named on which the vessel and cargo must be ready, and a later date, known as the cancelling date, is also given, so that if the vessel is delayed and is not ready to ship the cargo by the cancelling date, the charterer has the option of cancelling the charter if he wishes to do so. When the cargo has been shipped the bill of lading is drawn up and signed, and the vessel then proceeds to the discharging port, and delivers the cargo there to the holder of the bill of lading, which has been forwarded by the shipper.

### HOW A QUOTATION IS MADE

A SPECIMEN quotation on the market of a coal cargo, taken from the South Wales coal market, is :

2500 *Cardiff/Newport Rouen, May* 15*th*, 84 *hours*, 500, 1 *franc*, 3/6.

This means that the shipper is requiring a vessel to carry 2,500 tons of coal from either Cardiff or Newport, at his option, to Rouen, about May 15th. Eighty-four consecutive hours are to be allowed the shipper for loading the cargo, and it is to be discharged at the rate of 500 tons per day, the vessel paying 1 franc per ton as her share of the cost of discharge. For a suitable vessel for this cargo the shipper is prepared to pay 3s. 6d. per ton, and it is understood that the vessel also has to pay the cost of trimming at the port of loading in accordance with the schedule trimming rates. A vessel may offer at 4s., and the cargo be finally arranged at 3s. 9d. The charter is then drawn up with May 15th as the date of loading and, say, May 22nd as the cancelling date. Provision is made for the charterer to pay the shipowner what is called demurrage, that is, a certain sum per day if the time allowed in the charter for loading or discharging is exceeded. Similarly, it is provided that the shipowner is to pay the charterer dispatch, as it is called, at half the demurrage rate, for any time saved on the time allowed in the charter. In the case of the cargo quoted above, it is a rule of the trade that dispatch is paid on discharging time only, although frequently it is paid on loading time as well, particularly with cargoes other than coal. Sometimes there is no dispatch clause in the charter at all. On a cargo of the size mentioned, the demurrage rate would be about 16s. 8d. per hour, and the dispatch rate about 8s. 4d.

Tramp cargoes of all sorts and sizes are arranged every day in the same way in the different markets of the world. Here is another typical example, this time for a timber cargo :

750 *max.* 15*th Oct.* *One Bay Chaleur W.B.E.I.* *All Spruce try about* 50/–, $1.75 *stevedoring.*

This means that the shippers have a cargo of spruce timber, maximum 750 standards, requiring about a 2,400 to 2,500 ton deadweight vessel, for loading about October 15th. from one port in the Bay of Chaleur, on the Canadian Coast, say Campbellton or Carleton, to one port in the West Britain and East Ireland range, including Glasgow, Liverpool, Manchester, Preston, Garston, Dublin, Belfast, and Bristol Channel ports, for which they are prepared to pay 50s. per standard, this rate to include one dollar seventy-five cents loading charges for account of the vessel.

Loading is usually arranged at about a hundred standards per day, and discharging at the rate customary at the port of discharge, also, as a rule, about a hundred standards per day. The vessel with such timber cargoes always pays part of the cost of loading, varying from $1.50 to $3.25 according to the port of loading, and also pays the usual share of the cost of discharge, in accordance with the custom at the port of discharge, which varies to a considerable extent. The shipowner, therefore, needs to consider very carefully the ports at which he will be required to load and discharge, as otherwise he may find that he has to pay more for these services than he estimated when the freight was arranged.

Although it is usual with bulk cargoes for the vessel to pay something for both loading and discharging, in some cases cargoes are arranged on an f.i.o. basis, which means "free in and out," the cargo being loaded and discharged without any cost to the shipowner for these services. This is a method which commends itself to shipowners who are not familiar with a particular trade.

Each trade has its own conditions regulating the loading and discharging of cargo and the cost to the vessel of these operations. These conditions are known to shipowners, or to the agents they employ to watch their interests, if the trade is one of which they have not had previous experience. For this reason it is found that, as a rule, most shipowners stick to their own particular trades with which they are fully conversant, as it is impossible for any one shipowner to have adequate knowledge of all trades and forms of Charter Party. Some shippers have their own particular form of Charter, and, as a rule, these are found to be quite fair to shipowners; if they were not, it would soon be known, and it would be difficult for those shippers to get offers of tonnage.

### THE CHARTER PARTY: A CONTRACT FOR HIRING A WHOLE SHIP

NATURALLY with all shipments, whether by liners or by tramps, there is a contract of carriage, usually drawn up by representatives of shipowners and shippers in each particular trade. The first of these to be dealt with is the charter party, which is the contract form when a vessel is chartered to take a cargo for shippers who require the use of the whole vessel.

Charter parties are usually printed, in accordance with the agreed standard form, with spaces left for filling in the details of each individual contract. They require a sixpenny stamp, which is usually cancelled by the last party to sign them. The form is filled in with the details of the names of the shipowners and of the charterers, the name of the vessel and her size and position, and other chief points such as the quantity of cargo, the rate of freight to be paid, the time allowed for loading and discharging, the ports where loading and discharging will take place, agency at these ports, and commissions and brokerages payable to charterers and agents for arranging the cargo.

The ordinary charter is for a single voyage only, but charters for several voyages, or time-charters for a stated period, are also regularly used, and the principles are the same in all these cases, the aim being to provide a fair contract for the use of the vessel for the stated purpose or period.

### THE PURPOSES SERVED BY A BILL OF LADING

IN addition to the charter party there is also a bill of lading for each shipment of goods, and a bill of lading is used also to form the contract of carriage where there is no charter party, as in the case of a small parcel of goods being shipped by a liner service. The bill of lading is the most important shipping document, and great care is required in making it out and in using it. When the goods have been shipped the bill of lading is drawn up and signed by the captain or his agents, giving the quantity and description of the goods that have been received on board the vessel. In the case where there are several bills of lading, particularly with liner services, the ship's officer who receives the cargo on board gives what is known as the mate's receipt, and the bill of lading is subsequently made out from the mate's receipt by the shipowners or their agents, or in some cases by the shippers themselves.

The bill of lading, when finally made out, is the receipt of the vessel for the goods on board, whether these are a full cargo of coal or a case of manufactured articles, and the vessel is required to deliver at destination in accordance with the bill of lading. Any loss or damage noted during discharge becomes the vessel's responsibility, with various exceptions for heavy weather, fire at sea, etc., which are covered by a marine policy of insurance on the goods, taken out by the owners of the goods. It is, therefore, very important that all goods received on board the vessel should be carefully checked so that the possibility of the vessel being called upon to deliver against bill of lading, goods which were never actually received on board, is avoided.

Secondly, the bill of lading is a document of title to the goods, and the vessel is only called upon to deliver the goods at destination against the bill of lading, and must on no account deliver them to someone who cannot produce the bill of lading or give satisfactory proof that he is, in fact, the holder of it. It has not infrequently happened that the vessel has delivered the goods without production of the bill of lading and that someone else has come along afterwards with this document to demand the goods. In such a case a claim would be made against the ship for the value of the goods.

As a document of title to the goods the bill of lading also becomes a negotiable instrument when it has been duly endorsed by the party named upon it as the shipper. Frequently it is sent by the shipper of the goods to the buyer or receiver through a bank, and the buyer can take up the bill of lading only by payment for the goods to the bank. In this way the transfer or sale of the bill of lading, once it has been endorsed, is equivalent to the transfer or sale of the goods on the vessel, which is probably at the time on the high seas. An endorsed bill of lading for a full cargo of eight thousand tons of wheat, for example, is equivalent to an open cheque for the value of the cargo, and so is an exceedingly valuable document.

When the vessel arrives at her port of discharge, the receiver of the goods presents the endorsed bill of lading to the shipping company or their agents, and in return the cargo is delivered to him, and the bill of lading is cancelled by the shipping company. In the case of freight not being paid on arrival of the vessel at the discharging port the shipping company is entitled to hold the goods, which is called exercising a lien on the goods, until the freight has been paid. In this way the owners are able to protect themselves against non-payment of freight by selling sufficient of the cargo carried to make good the deficiency. In the case of a bulk cargo, freight usually has to be paid concurrent with the discharge, so that there will always be sufficient cargo left in the ship for the owner to be able to exercise a lien for the freight outstanding.

### HOW CARGOES ARE LOADED AND DISCHARGED

As there are innumerable ports of different kinds throughout the world, including harbours, wharves, docks, and rivers, so there are many different ways of loading and discharging cargo. The first method, and that most in use at up-to-date ports, is for the cargo to be loaded or discharged by shore cranes fitted with appliances suited to different kinds of cargo. Modern cranes have an arm, or jib, that can be raised and

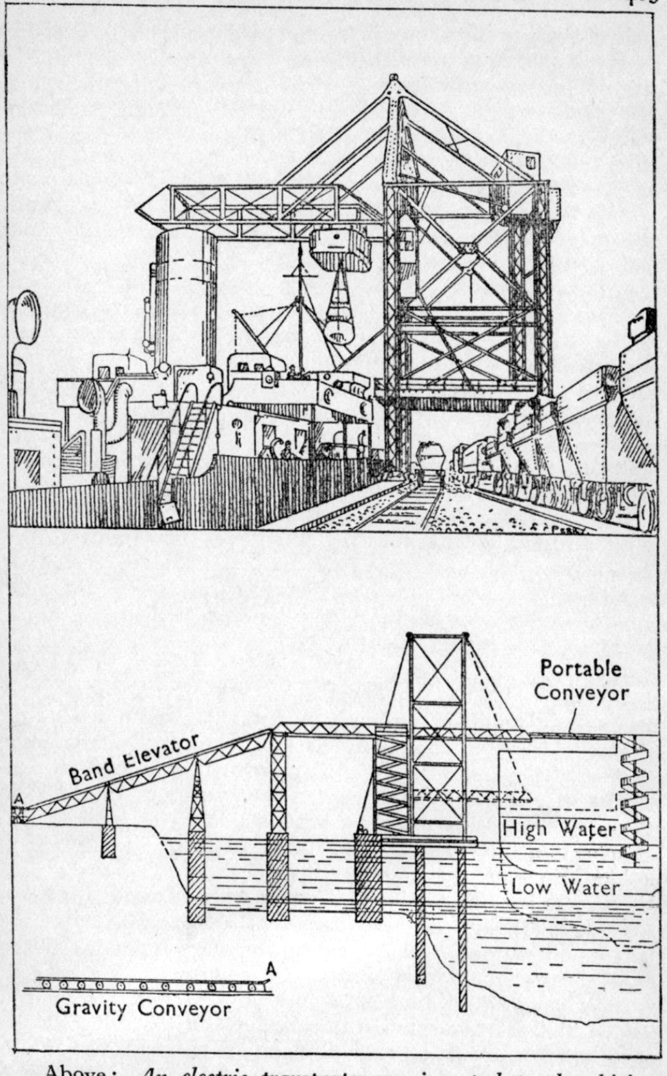


Above: *An electric transporter moving steel to the ship's hold.* Below: *An installation for loading a ship with oil.*

lowered, as well as rotated. Thus they can work very close together, and it is possible for six or eight cranes to work on a vessel at the same time, which gives a very rapid rate of loading and discharging. The most up-to-date cranes are driven by electricity, although steam and hydraulic power are still in common use. Various appliances are fitted to them—sling chains for slinging round ordinary goods, such as iron or steel bars, etc., crates or platforms for bagged or case goods, grabs for coal or iron ore, hooks for barrels, and nets for motor cars, luggage, or unwieldly packages.

Special apparatus is in use for different classes of bulk cargoes. For loading coal there are coal hoists, on which ten or twenty ton wagons are lifted sixty or seventy feet into the air, tipped up on to a slant, and an end door opened, so that the coal is dropped down a shute into the hold of the vessel. Alternatively, an endless belt can be employed from a silo or elevator in which there are several hundred tons of coal, the belt conveying the coal over the hold and then dropping it in. The railway trucks containing the coal can also be run over a shute on a raised railway track, the bottom doors in the trucks being opened, so that the coal falls down the shute into the hold. In some up-to-date ports the coal is dropped on to a revolving platform in the hold, which sprays it into the hold and ensures that it is evenly distributed without the need of trimming or levelling.

### A SELF-CONTAINED METHOD OF LOADING AND UNLOADING

A METHOD still in common use is for the vessel to load or discharge the cargo with her own gear, consisting of a boom or derrick attached to the mast or derrick post, which runs a wire down to the cargo and swings it out over the side of the vessel. Power for these is supplied by electric or steam winches on the vessels, and these derricks are in effect cranes fitted on the ship itself, instead of acting from the shore. As a rule, a vessel's derricks will lift about three to five tons, although in some cases they are specially fitted to lift a hundred tons or more, and so can deal with cargo which is too heavy for shore appliances. It is usual to employ the vessel's derricks for timber cargoes, as these are frequently loaded into vessels anchored in a harbour or bay, or at small ports where there are no suitable shore cranes available. This method of dealing with cargo is also used at certain harbours where it is impossible for the ship to approach close to the shore, so that the cargo has to be brought out to the ship in small craft or lighters.

For discharging coal or iron ore, and such-like cargoes, baskets are sometimes necessary at more primitive places, with a constant stream of labourers carrying them to and from the ship. For the most part, however, grabs are used for lifting large quantities at a time, in some cases as much as ten tons, and working in all the holds at the same time, so that cargoes of several thousands of tons are dealt with in a few hours at really efficient ports. For rapid grab discharge, vessels with large open holds and wide hatches are necessary; hence the tendency to build modern coal and ore carriers with as much hatch space and as little deck space as possible.

A grain cargo is usually loaded by gravity from large silos or elevators, from which the grain is poured into the vessel's holds. At modern ports it is discharged by suction plant, a long tube being lowered into the hold and the grain being sucked up through it into the elevator or mill, at the rate sometimes of several thousand tons a day. The tendency with all modern cargo handling is to reduce the actual handling to a minimum, and to use machinery of one sort or another to the greatest possible extent, but this is only possible at ports where there is a constant flow of traffic to keep these expensive appliances regularly employed. At the majority of ports and harbours throughout the world the methods of loading and discharging are still comparatively primitive.

The rate of loading and discharging is of great importance to a shipowner, as the more quickly he can deal with each cargo, the more likely he is to be able to run at a profit. For this reason the modern tendency is for cargo to be concentrated as much as possible at quick loading and discharging ports, and for smaller, slower ports to find it increasingly difficult to compete.

## HOW CARGO IS STOWED AND TRIMMED

THE question of stowage of cargo also enters into the rapidity of loading and discharging, as good stowage can enable the cargo to be handled more quickly and easily, while poor stowage is not only likely to affect the stability of the ship, but may also cause the cargo to shift on passage and either damage the ship or get damaged itself.

In the case of coal and grain, where the vessel will take her full deadweight with her holds full, the cargo is liable to shift if there is any space left, and for this reason it is necessary to see that it is carefully levelled off as it is loaded; in the case of grain, shifting boards are fitted into the holds to prevent the cargo from moving about. With such cargoes good trimming means that extra cargo can be carried, as the best use is made of all available space, and this extra cargo may make all the difference between a profit and a loss on the voyage.

With cargoes such as iron ore and iron or steel, where a vessel will carry her full deadweight without the holds being full, stowage is not of such great importance; nevertheless, it is necessary to see that it is effected in such a way that the vessel will be on a even keel when she sails, and also that there is no possibility of the cargo shifting on the voyage.

In the case of timber, where the vessel will probably not carry her full deadweight, and where a high deck load is carried, raising the centre of gravity of the vessel and so affecting her stability, it is very necessary to see that the best possible use is made of the under-deck space by fitting the planks and boards as closely together as possible, so that the centre of gravity is as low as it can be. Where the centre of gravity is raised high, the vessel is said to be "blown up" and to become "tender." It frequently happens that she does not take as much cargo as expected for this reason. Moreover, she may develop a list before sailing or on passage, which becomes dangerous, and means that some of the cargo has to be discharged or jettisoned, with loss to all concerned.

It is with general cargo on liners that stowage becomes of great importance. In the first place, it is necessary to ensure that valuable damageable goods are stowed in such a way that there is no possibility of other cargo coming into contact with them, or crushing them; and in the second place, where the cargo is being loaded at two or more ports, or is going to discharge at two or more ports, it is vital that the cargo should be loaded and stowed in such a way that cargo for one port can be dealt with easily and expeditiously without interfering in any way with cargo for another port. For this reason it is usual to have two or more decks on such vessels, so that cargo both light and heavy for the first port of discharge can be loaded on the top deck, and cargo for the second port of discharge on the bottom of the ship. This is absolutely necessary in cases where the ship may have to load iron and steel or other deadweight cargo for the first port of discharge, and cases or bales of goods or other light and damageable material for the second port of discharge, as it would be impossible to load the iron and steel on top of the other cargo, particularly as such a liner may be frequently carrying as much as ten thousand tons.

## SAFEGUARDS PROVIDED BY THE STOWAGE PLAN

FIG. 1 is an example of stowage of a vessel which loads at two ports for discharge at two other ports. The loading stevedores make out a stowage plan, showing where all the various lots are stowed, and this is then sent to the discharging stevedores, who are thus able to identify all the

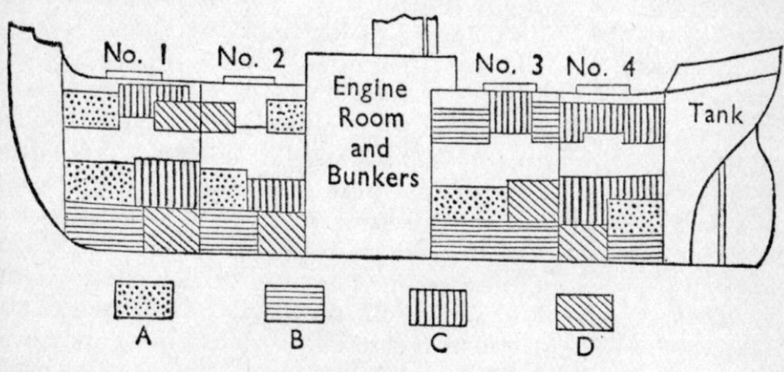


1. HOW CARGO IS STOWED

*Two-deck vessel, with light cargo arranged on the upper deck and heavy cargo down below.*

*A. Goods from 1st loading port to 1st discharging port.*
*B. Goods from 1st loading port to 2nd discharging port.*
*C. Goods from 2nd loading port to 1st discharging port.*
*D. Goods from 2nd loading port to 2nd discharging port.*

different lots and make their discharging arrangements accordingly. As an additional safeguard it is also customary for all parcels shipped in the regular liners to be marked in some way or other, and these marks are also shown on the bills of lading for the goods and on the stowage plan, so that the possibility of error or mixture in the case of a vessel carrying a hundred or more different parcels is reduced to a minimum.

The stowage is done by experienced stevedores, and is supervised by the ship's officers, who are well experienced in dealing with all kinds of cargoes, and who are more concerned with the stability and trim of the vessel than with the particular cargo she has to carry.

### THE SERVICES PROVIDED BY A PORT

At all ports continual improvements are being made to enable ships and cargoes to be dealt with as easily and as cheaply as possible. Ports which fall behind in this race for improvement and up-to-date methods soon find that their traffic decreases, and that some neighbouring competitor is capturing their business. Among the main considerations is the depth of water available and the easy navigation of the entrance to the port and of the port itself. Regular pilotage services are maintained with pilots always on the look-out for vessels in good weather and bad, to steer them safely into port, and, within the precincts of the port, dock pilots are also provided to move the vessels with the minimum of risk from one berth to another. In enclosed waters the navigation of a large vessel moving at a slow speed always requires expert handling, and the extra expense of employing men well versed in special local conditions is usually well worth while.

At all ports where there is a regular trade, tugs are always in constant attendance to assist with the steering of large vessels at slow speeds and also to move ships which may not have steam up to move under their own power while in port. These tugs are, as a rule, very powerful, so that the largest ships can be towed with ease, and they provide an additional element of safety when dealing with vessels that may be easily damaged and that can do a lot of damage to quays or other tonnage if they go adrift.

Most modern ports also provide facilities for dredging and diving. Wherever there is an entrance channel to a port, or a tidal river that may be subject to silting, continual dredging is necessary to keep the channel at the stipulated depth, and also to ensure that all berths or quays are able to deal with vessels drawing up to the maximum allowed, without the risk of grounding or scraping the bottom. Even in enclosed docks considerable silting is going on the whole time, and regular dredging is necessary to maintain the water depth of the port.

Diving is a service that is also very necessary, for by this means vessels that have been damaged can be examined below the water-line to see if the damage necessitates immediate repair, and wharves and quays can be regularly inspected to ensure that the strength of the structure is maintained and that no under-water flaws develop.

In cases where the port is tidal it is necessary, as a rule, to build an enclosed space of water, known as a dock, to which vessels get access through large entrance locks, capable of dealing in many cases with ships up to a thousand feet long and a hundred feet wide. These locks are enclosed by large entrance gates, which open in turn to let the vessel through, and the amount of water required to lift vessels of ten thousand to twenty thousand tons up to the inside dock level from the outside water level can be pumped into the locks in a matter of a few minutes. The docks keep a constant water level, and once inside, a vessel remains always afloat irrespective of the level of the tide outside. Wherever there is any range of tide of more than a few feet, docks are necessary if a large quantity of shipping is to be dealt with, as, although in many cases there are wharves where vessels lie aground when the tide is out, this is unsatisfactory where large ships are concerned, and is likely to cause damage to the bottom of the vessel by the continual grounding as the tide goes out.

## WHAT HAPPENS TO THE SHIP IN DRY DOCK

DRY docks are constructed on the same principle as entrance locks to a dock, except that there is a gate at one end only. This gate is opened to let the vessel in when the level of water in the dry dock and outside is the same, and is closed when the vessel is safely inside. The water in the dry dock is gradually pumped out, while the vessel is allowed to settle on large blocks at the bottom of the dry dock, and is supported at the sides by props or stays. When the dry dock is empty of water it is possible to walk all round the vessel, as well as underneath, and she can thus be inspected and repaired as required, without difficulty.

In some cases these dry docks are floating ones, with tanks on them that are filled with water until the dry dock sinks below the bottom of the vessel, and the vessel is then moved over it. The water is pumped out of the tanks and the dry dock rises in the water, lifting the vessel with it until it is clear of the water. By means of these dry docks any repairs that may be required can be effected quickly and easily, so that the ship is not long delayed from her business of earning freight on the cargoes she carries.

In order to deal with all kinds of cargo the various ports

and docks provide large transit warehouses of the most modern kind, where cargo can be stored and sorted both before and after shipment. These warehouses are fitted with overhead cranes and movable trolleys, so that the goods of all sorts and sizes can be easily moved about and stored to await shipment or inland forwarding. In some cases these warehouses have special cooling and refrigerating plant for dealing with such goods as fruit and frozen meat, and every up-to-date appliance is fitted for facilitating the cheap and expeditious handling of whatever cargo may be offered for warehousing.

Elevators for the storage of grain, weighing machines for weighing up to a hundred tons or more, sidings for accommodating thousands of trucks of cargo, special cranes and loading and discharging gear of all sorts (whether electric, steam, or hydraulic), timber floats for timber imports or exports, cattle lairs for importing, selling, and killing cattle or other live-stock, are only a few of the diverse facilities that are provided in a modern port for the transport needs of the district it serves.

A modern port or dock is a very large consumer of power, which frequently is generated by the port authority. Where entrance locks are required, a terrific power is necessary to open or close the lock-gates and to fill or empty the lock; while if many coal hoists and cranes are working at the same time, the hoists lifting up to twenty-ton wagons of coal and the cranes dealing with loads of three to five tons at a time, it will be appreciated that power generation for all these services is not the least of the requirements of the port authority. In most modern cases electricity is the force that is decided upon, as it is the most speedy in action and also can be most easily and accurately controlled, but hydraulic and steam power are still in constant use at ports throughout the world, and will probably continue to be so for many years.

### WORKING OUT THE VOYAGE ESTIMATES

In considering what cargoes or rates to take and what not to take, the shipowner works out what is known as a voyage estimate. In the case of the liner companies this is not really necessary, as they have to maintain their services in any case, and it is from the results of the service that the decision has to be taken whether it is worth continuing or not. Whether a new service should be started or not can be worked out to a certain extent by voyage estimates, but this is not the only basis; a new service very often has to be started without immediate prospect of profit, and is based more on estimates of what traffic can be attracted by a regular service than on any estimate of rates and quantities at the time of commencement.

With tramp vessels, however, the voyage estimate is most important. The tramp can go wherever the most remunerative business offers, and it is for the owner to decide which is likely to be his most profitable trade. The work of making out competitive voyage estimates for all sorts of alternative voyages or cargoes that may be offering is a task that can never fail to interest, and one on which much of the successful running of ships depends.

## HOW FREIGHT IS CALCULATED

THE rate of freight is, of course, the most important thing to consider, and has to be estimated against the probable costs to see what margin of profit there is likely to be left. It is necessary to calculate the quantity of the particular cargo the vessel is likely to lift, particularly in the case of cargoes of which the vessel will not lift her full deadweight. A rough example of a handy way of voyage-estimating is given below :

| | | | |
|---|---|---|---|
| Cost at loading port . | £100 | FREIGHT : 3200 tons at 7s. per ton . | £1120 |
| Cost at discharging port . . . | 175 | | |
| TIME : 20 days at £20 per day . . | 400 | | |
| BUNKERS : 9 days at sea at 20 tons per day ; 11 days in port at 5 tons per day= 235 tons at 15s. . | 176 | | |
| BROKERAGES : £1120 at 5 per cent. . | 56 | | |
| TOTAL . . | £907 | PROFIT : 20 days at £10, 13s. per day . | £213 |

Of the items listed here the cost at the loading port includes dock dues, agency fees, pilotages, tugs if required, the vessel's share of the cost of loading, etc. The cost at the discharging port includes the same dues and fees, and also the ship's share of the cost of discharge, unless this is definitely fixed in the charter at, say, sixpence, or a shilling, or one franc per ton, in which case it can be made a separate charge in the same way as the brokerages.

The cost per day is the total cost of wages, insurance,

interest on capital, depreciation, stores, superintendence, etc. Every shipowner has a figure for the cost per day for each ship, worked out by the accounts department on the basis of the actual experience of the ship. The time allowed includes all time taken in loading and discharging, as well as the actual voyage, from the time of commencement of loading to the time of commencement of loading the next cargo, including the ballast voyage to another port after the discharging, if this is necessary. Very often time is saved over the time allowed by charter, and in some cases the shipowner has to pay dispatch for this, so that in saving time he does not save money; sometimes dispatch is not payable, in which case the shipowner gets the full advantage of the time saved. He must, however, reckon in his voyage estimate on the full charter time being used, so as to be prepared for the worst.

The consumption of the vessel both at sea and in port will be known to the shipowner, so that he merely has to reckon the price he pays for the bunkers, including the cost of loading and trimming, if he has to pay for these in addition to the price.

### VOYAGES IN BALLAST SHOULD BE AVOIDED

In working out possible future voyages, the shipowner tries as much as possible to get round voyages, so that long ballast shifts between one cargo and the next can be avoided. If one cargo can be discharged and the next one loaded in the same port, great economy can be effected, and this influences him in considering what business to take. For this reason the Plate round, out with coal and home with grain, is a favourite one with large vessels; if, for instance, they go to the Mediterranean with a coal cargo, they may have to proceed in ballast to South America or India for their next cargo, and ballast trips are not only expensive but more dangerous than voyages with cargo, and should be avoided wherever possible.

Another consideration is the cost of bunkers at various places. If a coal-burning vessel can get bunkers in South Wales at fifteen shillings per ton, sufficient to get her back to South Wales or Newcastle, then she can afford to take a lower rate of freight than if she has to take bunkers at a port like Gibraltar, for instance, where the cost may be ten shillings to fifteen shillings a ton more. Sometimes it is possible to work out a voyage on a triangular basis, as, for instance, coal from South Wales to the Mediterranean, salt from the Red

Sea to India, and generals from India back to Europe. Frequently a vessel is sent out without any definite programme in view, and may be away for a year or more, carrying cargoes wherever the most remunerative freights offer, until finally she works her way home again.

### WHAT A SHIPBROKER DOES

NOT the least important part in the sea carriage of goods is played by the ship's agents, shipbrokers, and forwarding agents. A shipowner cannot follow his ship round and make all the necessary arrangements for her at each port she visits. He must get agents to do this work for him. In the first place, there is the shipbroker, who does the work of arranging cargoes, and also of ship's agency. When an owner with a vessel going to South Wales, for instance, wants a cargo of coal outwards from South Wales, he gets in touch with a shipbroker, who finds all the suitable cargoes on the market and telegraphs them to the owner, as usually there is no time to waste. The owner decides which of these he prefers, and authorises the shipbroker to arrange the cargo at a certain rate of freight. For this service the broker gets his fee of usually one-third of 5 per cent. of the freight paid, though sometimes a little more.

When the vessel comes along, the broker, to whom the owner usually also entrusts the vessel's agency, makes all the necessary arrangements, such as advising the dock company that she is coming in, arranging a berth for her, advising the charterers of the position, and ensuring that the cargo will be ready to start loading immediately. He also probably advises the pilots to be on the look-out for her, if she is likely to require a pilot, and arranges for tugs if necessary, or for dry-docking if this should be required before loading is commenced. He sees the captain on arrival, and finds what bunkers are required, and makes sure that everything is done in accordance with the terms of the charter party. He reports the vessel at the Customs, and eventually clears her outwards to whichever port she is going to. If the captain requires it, he assists him at the Board of Trade Offices with signing on or paying off officers or crew, signs the bill of lading on behalf of the captain when the cargo has been loaded, and in every way acts as if he were the owner, on behalf of the owner. He also pays all the necessary accounts for dock dues, pilots, tugs, loading, or discharging, and advances money to the captain that may be needed for paying crew's wages or buying stores or provisions, afterwards charging all these amounts to the owners in his final disbursement account, and including his agency fee at the scale laid down by the Shipbrokers' Institute.

## THE DUTIES OF THE SHIP'S AGENT

THE work of the ship's agent is much the same as that of the shipbroker, except that he does not fix the cargo in the first place, but acts solely as the agent of the owner at his particular port. In Great Britain he is usually also a shipbroker, which gives the owner the protection of his being a member of the professional institute. The ship's agent, besides making all the necessary arrangements for the vessel at the port, also collects her cargo together in the case of a general cargo vessel, and loads and stows it, or discharges it, and forwards to the inland destination, acting as a cargo agent as well as a ship's agent.

A forwarding agent is a cargo agent alone, and has nothing to do with the work of the vessel, except that he provides the cargo for her, or takes it from her, and forwards inland. He acts on behalf of merchants or shippers, secures the bill of lading for them on loading, or delivers it to the ship to get the goods on discharge, and pays the charges for delivering to f.o.b. or receiving c.i.f. As a rule, general cargo liners have their own offices at their main ports of call, and so do not require ship's agents, but forwarding agents are still necessary to look after the interests of the shippers or receivers of the goods.

## HOW GOODS GO THROUGH THE CUSTOMS

CUSTOMS work is a very important part of the work of shipbrokers, ship's agents, and forwarding agents. Besides reporting the vessel and her cargo inwards and outwards at the Customs Office, special duty papers have to be filled in, and duty has to be paid in cash, or by a bank draft or guaranteed cheque before the goods can be released for forwarding. When a vessel comes in with a hundred or more bills of lading, each requiring separate papers and calculations of duty, it will be seen that the amount of work required by the agent is very considerable. The vessel's stores, and any articles she takes out of bond, such as tobacco, for instance, on which payment of excise duties is thus avoided, also have to be declared on special forms at the Customs.

## THE CARRIAGE OF GOODS BY RAIL

INLAND transport by rail, road, and canal, while not so diverse as sea transport, nevertheless probably deals with a considerably larger quantity of traffic. In nearly every case it forms the final link in the chain of transport by effecting delivery to the individual consumer. The large amounts shown by the railway traffic receipts that are published weekly in the newspapers give some idea of the enormous quantity of goods handled every day by the railway companies. These weekly receipts also form a very valuable indication of business activity as a whole, and thus of the general prosperity of the country.

In Great Britain railway transport is divided among four main large companies, and, as it is important to prevent duplication of railway lines, government control is necessary; small railway companies cannot start as and where they will, as is possible with sea transport. Railway rates are all scheduled and controlled, goods being divided into twenty-one different classes, and standard rates based on distance being in force for each class. It is, therefore, possible for any merchant, by the use of a classification book and a distance table, to find out the rate for any class of goods in quantities varying from one hundredweight to hundreds of tons. Thus the everyday quoting for cargoes, which is the regular business of shipping companies, enters very little into the daily work of a railway company.

Each of the four large companies covers its own particular area, with a small amount of overlapping in certain districts, and this monopolistic position necessitates parliamentary control in the interests of the traders of the country. All parts of the country are covered with a close network of lines, and each small village has its station where goods and passengers are dealt with by regular services. In addition, each dock or port has miles of railway sidings, and most large works also have their sidings where trucks can be put in and loaded or discharged by the works themselves. These stations and sidings form the "railheads."

### "LINER" AND "TRAMP" ON THE RAILWAYS

THE railway companies, like the shipping companies, run what can be called both regular liner serviccs and tramp services. Apart from the passenger trains, there is also a regular time-table of goods services. Small lots of valuable goods, the value of which justifies the payment of the higher rates entailed, can be sent by the passenger services, but by far the greater quantity of the goods traffic is dealt with by the separate goods services. Between all the large centres fast and regular goods trains are put on wherever the quantity and regularity of traffic makes them worth while, and these can be likened to the shipping liners. In addition, lots of all sizes can be sent in one truck or hundreds of trucks from any station or siding to any other station or siding on the whole national system, either by attaching them to one or more of the regular goods trains, and so working them in the required direction, or by putting on a special train, as is done in the case of train lots.

It will be realised that both full and empty trucks are being worked hither and thither over the system in all directions and at all times in a way that demands almost a miracle of organisation and control in order to ensure an efficient and speedy service. Where there is a regular two-way traffic the organisation is not so difficult, but in many cases there is a large volume of traffic in one direction only, and the trucks have to be worked back to the place of departure. They may get loads to intermediate places, or a load to a third place from which there is cargo to the original point of loading, or they may have to go in ballast the whole way back. There is, of course, heavy extra cost if each truck does not do the largest possible percentage of load mileage, and runs too great a proportion of ballast miles, just as in the case of a vessel carrying cargoes by sea.

### HOW THE RAILWAY SERVES THE SHIPS

THE full business of railway management can best be seen at the large ports of the country. Cargoes of all sorts, which have to be split up for numerous destinations, are constantly arriving; one week there may be very few arrivals of vessels, while the next week thousands of trucks may have to be worked towards the port, either with or without load, so that each vessel will be provided with sufficient trucks to enable her to discharge at full speed. The railway in this way is acting as a continual feeder for vessels loading, and a continual distributor for the cargoes being discharged.

The shipping company advises the port or dock authority

that the vessel is due, and also appoints a stevedore to do the discharging. The dock authority or the stevedore advises the railway company of the quantity of cargo to be dealt with, and its nature, particularly if it is a mixed general cargo, so that the necessary trucks can be provided. These are duly shunted alongside the vessel, and after discharge are consigned and marked for their requisite destination. The consignment notes are handed to the railway company, and from them the goods are forwarded to their destination; the consignee is advised of their arrival, or they are shunted into the appropriate siding, if they have been consigned to siding. In cases where the goods are required to be delivered to domicile by the railway company, they are taken by cart or motor lorry to the stated address, in exchange for a signature which can be produced to the consignor as proof of delivery.

### FIXING THE RAILWAY RATES

A RAILWAY company is a common carrier, and is compelled to accept all traffic that is offered to it, on the terms being accepted as reasonable for the particular class of goods by the Railway Rates Tribunal. This tribunal is a body set up by parliamentary authority to act in a judical capacity between the railway companies and the traders, and decide on fair rates and conditions for the carriage of goods of all kinds.

There is a general railway classification of goods comprising twenty-one classes, with a separate class for coal and coke, for which very special rates have to be given. Class 1, the lowest, contains such material as iron ore, which is of low value per ton and passes in large quantities; the highest is class 21, containing such valuable material as gold, which only passes in small quantities, and such damageable goods as glass globes, which take up a great deal of room in proportion to their weight.

The rates vary from 1s. 8d. per ton for the minimum mileage of six miles in class 1, to £7, 4s. 4d. per ton for two hundred miles in class 21, and, of course, it rises proportionately higher for greater distances. These rates and classes are for the ordinary standard rates, but wherever a regular quantity of traffic is found to pass to or from a particular point, then a special rate up to 40 per cent. or even more below the standard rate is given. There are now an enormous number of these special rates. In addition, other special rates can be given applicable to special conditions; for example, a rate based on a percentage of the purchase price of all the goods which one large firm forwards by rail from and to all destinations. In this way the railway companies are assured of securing all the traffic from the consignors with whom such arrangements are made, and an enormous amount of clerical work is saved to both the consigners and the railway company.

### THE RAILWAY'S FACILITIES FOR STORING GOODS

JUST as the railway companies act as feeders and distributors for the shipping services, so they have to have their own feeders and distributors to provide services for their traffic. At most large stations there are warehouses where goods can be stored cheaply and safely until they are actually required, and in some cases these warehouses are specially adapted for particular uses, such as the storage of fruits or meats, by being cooled or refrigerated. The basic object is to ensure that goods of all kinds can be dealt with easily, and with the minimum of handling. Where particular firms require it, they can be supplied with private railhead depots of their own, so that their goods can be stored and delivered as required, either by their own staff or by the railway company's staff.

Collection and delivery of goods at a particular station is carried out partly by means of horse-drawn carts, partly with motor lorries, and goods of all sorts and sizes are regularly dealt with in this way. In some cases a central station for a district is taken as the railhead distributing centre, serving an area of perhaps thirty miles radius, and all goods for that district are dealt with *via* that station.

Saving is effected by having auxiliary road delivery from such a centre. In the first place, merchants forwarding to that area can bulk their consignments for the one station, and so get a lower railway rate for a larger quantity ; in the second place, a through truck load to a railhead station usually means a quicker transit than is possible with small individual consignments ; special trains, or trucks with only part loads, do not have to be sent along branch lines to stations which, in any case, only have a small quantity of goods traffic. The bulk loading to the central station also, as a rule, means less handling, and so less risk of loss or damage. The station is fitted with all the most modern appliances for handling and dealing with goods, such as cranes to lift all ordinary weights, and weighing machines to weigh up to as much as twenty tons.

## TYPES OF GOODS THAT REQUIRE SPECIAL TRUCKS

JUST as there are many types of ships for dealing with different classes of goods, so there are a great many different types of railway wagons. The ordinary truck is the open type "common user," which carries goods of all sorts up to either ten or twelve tons, and can be sheeted with a tarpaulin if required. For more special classes of goods there are vans completely protected from the weather, refrigerated vans for chilled meat, etc., ventilated vans for fruit, etc., special cattle trucks, special load trucks for goods up to fifty or sixty feet, and specially constructed trucks for carrying heavy materials, such as machinery, up to a hundred tons or more.

A modern development is the container. This is a large box, which is carted to the merchant's premises to be loaded, is then fitted on to a flat wagon and conveyed to destination, and is finally carted to the consignee's premises to be unloaded. Thus railway collection and delivery service is provided with the minimum of handling and risk, since the merchant can himself lock the goods in the container and send the key to the consignee. An additional advantage is that the consigning merchant can himself pack the goods into the container, and, as he is probably an expert in packing his particular class of goods, this gives further safeguards against damage.

## CO-ORDINATION OF CONTROL IS THE BASIS OF RAILWAY TRANSPORT

IN the efficient management of a railway company co-ordination of control is of the greatest importance. While the local man can probably judge the local needs better than anyone in the central office, central control is the only means to ensure, for instance, that the trucks over the system as a whole are being so moved about and distributed that the largest possible proportion of load miles to ballast miles is being secured.

Each station has its goods manager, each district its district goods manager, and the whole is co-ordinated under the general goods manager of the system. In this way local needs and district needs are adequately provided for, and at the same time the policy and general organisation of the whole group is effectively centralised. Railway transport is probably the most efficient form of transport that exists, and performs the vital service of delivering goods of all sorts to the final consumer, whether they come from a nearby factory or from overseas.

## TRANSPORT BY ROAD, AIR, AND SEA

ROAD transport is a comparatively modern development, and has become a formidable competitor to the railways. When the roads all over the country were gradually made better and better, and large motor vehicles to carry ten or twenty tons at a speed of twenty miles an hour became an economical proposition, a new mode of transport came into being which could vie with the speed and cheapness of the railways.

Road transport to-day has many advantages over rail transport. In the first place, the modern network of roads all over the country provides a ready-made track to even the smallest places, with the added facility of having this track available from door to door of almost every house and factory in the country.

Again, as a result of this track from door to door, goods can be loaded up at one place and delivered at another without any handling in between. In the ordinary course of events, when goods are collected by the railway companies, they have to be taken to the station, unloaded from the cart or lorry, loaded into the truck, conveyed to destination station, and there again unloaded from the truck, and put on to the lorry to be transported to the consignee's premises. This naturally greatly increases the risk of damage, loss, or pilferage, particularly with the more valuable classes of goods, which are the most paying classes from a transport point of view. It is largely to combat this advantage of road transport that the railway companies have inaugurated the containers which have already been mentioned.

Thirdly, road transport can quote whatever rates it likes for any class of goods, instead of being bound by Act of Parliament and the Railway Rates Tribunal, and is also able to refuse goods, if they prove unremunerative, which the railway companies, as common carriers, are unable to do. In this way it can avoid large quantities of one-way traffic, which might entail having to work the vehicles back " in ballast " at heavy cost. In fact, it has the great advantage of being able, when deciding whether to take or refuse any traffic, to act in accordance with its own needs of the moment, instead of being bound to act at all times in accordance with the needs of the community.

## ROADS ARE MAINTAINED AT PUBLIC COST

FINALLY, the chief advantage of road transport over the railways is that the roads provide a track which is made and kept in order largely at public cost. The continued upkeep of the line entails enormous cost for a railway company, and there are, in addition, heavy interest charges on the original purchase price of the land. Moreover, the whole expense of keeping the fabric of bridges in repair is thrown upon the railway companies, regardless of the fact that it may be the users of the roads over the bridges who reap all the advantage. It is true that road transport vehicles have to contribute to the cost of keeping the roads in repair by means of their annual taxation, which has recently been largely increased, but this provides only a small proportion of the upkeep cost of the track they are able to use.

As a result of all these advantages road transport has increased to a very large extent. The procedure is much the same as with the shipping companies as regards quoting rates and catering for traffic. Regular " liner " services are run, in the same way as by the shipping and railway companies, on which merchants can rely from day to day, whether sufficient traffic offers for a full load or not. There are also " tramp " services, to take special lots in any direction, and for this special rates are quoted as required. Lists of rates, dividing goods into about four or six classes, are frequently published in connection with the regular services, and merchants can rely on these in the same way as on the railway rates, although, of course, they do not cover all destinations and all goods in the same comprehensive way as the railway rates. Rates are given for a particular traffic, which is then picked up and taken to destination sometimes on a consignment note, sometimes with only a letter of instructions, and delivered there to the consignee.

## COMPETITION BETWEEN ROAD AND RAIL BENEFITS THE MERCHANT

IN order to compete with this road transport competition, and also to provide more efficient " feeder " services for their rail services, the railway companies have started a road transport section of their own. The chief features of the system of having a central railhead have already been discussed, but it must be remembered further that the railway companies are able to quote what rates they like for their road services, and so can compete more effectively on the question of rate in special cases. This continual competition between rail and road is of great advantage to merchants, as it means that rates are kept as low as possible, and that continual improvements are being effected by both rail and road to enable goods to be transported more speedily, more safely, and more cheaply.

### THE CANAL: CAUSES OF ITS DECLINE

For fifty years before the building of our main railway lines both raw materials and finished goods were carried by an intricate network of canals. With the coming of the railways many canals were doomed, for, in spite of comparative cheapness, canal transport is rather slow. Yet the owners of the canals put up a very poor fight against their new competitors; they took little trouble to improve their waterways and services. Naturally their trade suffered.

As a result, an Act of Parliament was passed at the petition of the canal companies, which compelled companies seeking to lay down new railway lines to purchase the interest of the canal shareholders in the areas concerned. Naturally the railways used their ownership to raise canal rates and generally to foster railway traffic at the expense of canal traffic. In 1875, however, railways were debarred from acquiring control of a canal; since 1888 they have not been allowed to purchase even an interest in them.

One reason for the decline of the canal system is therefore clear. But there is another. The great canal systems on the Continent are partly based on the use of broad, navigable rivers, like the Rhine, the Scheldt, and the Seine, which themselves form connections across the Continent, and can easily be linked by canals with industrial centres. Our own rivers are narrower and shallower, which means a greater expense on locks.

To-day there are in this country about 1,200 miles of independent canals and some 900 miles of canals managed by railways. In spite of the decline of the canals, some of the most important are highly prosperous. For instance, the Manchester Ship Canal has made Manchester into a port, and the volume of traffic it carries is again rising rapidly.

The future of the canals has been widely debated: but apart from short stretches of canal, taking vessels of deep draught and linking an inland manufacturing centre with the sea, their future in this country is small.

### THE SAFEST METHOD FOR VALUABLES

At the opposite extreme to inland waterways comes the air. Inland waterways can carry heavy loads in large quantities at a very cheap rate; aeroplanes are limited both in the space available and the weight that can be lifted, and the cost is, in comparison, considerable. There are, however, two advantages, which make the transport by air an economic method for two main classes of goods. First of all, there is an element of safety which is to be found nowhere else. If goods travel by ship, road, or train they must of necessity pass through many hands. There are a variety of loaders and unloaders and others who are constantly in contact with the goods, and the goods may have to be left standing about in warehouses and the like for some time. Thus the danger of pilfering and the chance of goods getting mislaid is greater. On the other hand, they can be taken by air more or less direct to their destination, and are out of reach most of the time. For this reason air transport is practically adapted to the carriage of small articles of great value, bullion and jewellery and the like, which are easy to pilfer unless closely guarded, and which will justify the extra expense.

Secondly, air is by far the most rapid form of transport. It is not only that the aeroplane is capable of a speed greater than a ship, train, lorry, or barge can hope to attain, but all the intermediate causes of delay are eliminated. Instead of having to go by a roundabout route according to where there is sea to sail on, or of wasting time by being transferred from ship to land carrier, goods can go direct from one point to another without any break in the journey. When, therefore, speed is so vital that the extra cost is worth while, the aeroplane is the ideal vehicle. An example of this is perishable produce, especially cut flowers, which must reach the market, perhaps a distant market, in as fresh a condition as possible.

### COASTAL SHIPPING: A CHEAP SERVICE FOR HEAVY TRANSPORT

Coastal shipping does not differ essentially from ordinary overseas shipping, but it is dealt with here, in conjunction with rail, road, canals and rivers, because it is competitive with these services in the traffic with which it deals. An idea of its importance in this country can be seen from the figures of the Port of London authority. In the course of a year about fifteen million tons of cargo are carried coastwise in and out of the Port of London alone, which means about fifty thousand tons per working day throughout the year.

The great advantage that coastal shipping has over both rail and road is that of cheapness; wherever cheapness is of more importance than speed of delivery, when both the dispatching point and the place of delivery are within easy reach of a seaport, then the coastal vessel becomes a very serious competitor for the business. Things that are moved in large quantities, and are not of sufficient value to permit high transport charges, go by the coastal route wherever possible. Even on the question of speed the coastal vessel is not to-day very far behind. Goods consigned by rail from South Wales to London, for instance, will, as a rule, take about two days to get to their destination, whereas by a coastal vessel they can be transported from door to door in three or four days at the most.

### COASTAL SHIPS TRAVEL TO A TIME-TABLE

The regular liners trading round the coasts do not cater much for passengers, and it is on goods of all sorts that they chiefly rely. They have a regular time-table of arrival and departure at all their specified ports, and adhere to this with almost unfailing regularity. All classes of goods are dealt with, and, as case and bag goods form a large part of the cargoes, the regular liners are usually vessels with two or more decks. The various lots can thus be stowed in such a way that all parcels can be handled at intermediate ports without disturbing cargo for later ports; at the same time, heavy deadweight goods can be loaded on the bottom of the ship and all lighter damageable goods in a 'tween deck space.

The stowage of such vessels is a real work of art, as, if they are going regularly to six ports, and loading and discharging cargo at each one to or from each of the other five, it will be seen that a carefully thought out plan is necessary to load cargo in port A for port B, while at the same time discharging cargo from port C, without interfering with or over-loading material from or to ports D and E. By rail or road small separate lots can be dealt with in separate vehicles, but by coastal vessel this is not possible to the same extent. As a rule, the lots arranged for shipment by merchants or forwarding agents at the various ports are shipped on a bill of lading, in the same way as with overseas shipping, but sometimes a consignment note is sufficient, as in the case of rail or road transport.

The chief handicaps of such a method of transport are, first, the relatively large amount of handling of the goods that is unavoidable, and, secondly, that coastal vessels require much more " feeding " by subsidiary transport services than either rail or road. For this reason the cost of dispatch and delivery for goods outside quite a small area becomes prohibitive, owing to the high cost of the " feeding " and handling services.

### THE COASTAL TRAMP CATERS FOR HEAVY MATERIALS

THE tramps that convey traffic of all sorts round the coasts are run on practically the same lines, as a general rule, as the ordinary overseas tramps. The vessel is chartered for a cargo, and a bill of lading is made out when the cargo has been loaded, and has to be presented before the cargo can be delivered. There are large quantities of bulk cargoes of all sorts regularly being shipped by coastal tramp ; coal, iron and steel, tinplates, sand, road-stone, etc., are a few of the more usual. Whenever a shipper has a sufficient quantity to make up a cargo he gets quotations from rail, road, and coastal vessel ; and if the coastal route is the cheapest, and there is no special need for speed, then a vessel is chartered, and the shipment is effected.

The propulsion of coastal vessels is still effected largely by steam and coal, although the motor engine, using crude oil, is finding greatly increasing favour. With coastal vessels draft and length are vitally important factors. Many of the ports to which the vessels have to trade are small and shallow, and the larger quantity a vessel can take on a given draft, the greater is her chance of being able to run at a profit. Motor engines are, therefore, finding increasing favour for coastal work ; they are lighter and take up less space than steam engines, while the bunkers are also of less space and weight. A high funnel can be dispensed with, and this is of great benefit in trading to rivers where there are bridges with low head-room, which steamers, unless they have hinged funnels, cannot get under.

### FROM SHIPPER TO CUSTOMER : THE JOURNEY DESCRIBED

IN order to show how general cargo is transported by sea and inland transport from one point to another, let us consider an example of some cases of glassware being sent from Belgium to Birmingham.

The shipper, having secured a price f.o.b. a continental port, probably Antwerp, approaches a shipping company with sailings from Antwerp to a port convenient for Midland traffic, such as London, Hull, or Newport, and asks them to quote him a through rate from f.o.b. Antwerp to Birmingham delivered domicile. The shipping company look up the railway rate, which may be one of the hundreds of special rates in existence for all classes of goods, or an ordinary standard rate. From Newport to Birmingham, for instance, the special glassware rate, including delivery, is 35s. 10d. per ton, as against the standard rate of 48s. 5d. for class 18 in which this material is included. The shipping company also considers the costs of loading from f.o.b. at Antwerp, and of discharging at Newport, the class of material, particularly the space it will occupy, the risk of damage, and the time taken to load and discharge it, and quotes a through rate accordingly.

The shipper accepts the rate of the line which suits him best for speed or cheapness, and books space with the shipping company for a certain date, advising them at the same time the name of the suppliers in Belgium and the point of delivery in Birmingham. The shipping company's Antwerp agent then approaches the suppliers, giving the dates of the sailings, and asking them for which date they can supply, also advising them to which berth in Antwerp the goods must be forwarded. On receiving their reply the necessary space is reserved in the ship, and the goods are ordered forward by the ship's agents for the specified date. The suppliers load them up and forward by rail to Antwerp, giving the railway company instructions to deliver to the order of the shipping company at their particular loading berth, and the goods duly arrive alongside.

In the meantime it is necessary for the shipper to take out a marine insurance policy on the goods, either through the shipping company or with his own insurance agents. When the vessel arrives the glassware is loaded to f.o.b. by the suppliers' agents, and the shipping company receives it on board and stows it safely and carefully in the ship. As it is in cases and easily damaged, it is loaded on top of all other cargo, or in a 'tween deck space. The vessel sails, for example, to Newport, and the mate's receipt, which has been given for the goods, goes to the shipping company's office in Antwerp, where the bill of lading is made out and handed to the shippers.

A copy of the bill of lading is kept for reference purposes, and another copy is sent to the vessel's agents at the port of discharge, together with a stowage plan, showing where all the various parcels are stowed in the ship. The original bill of lading is sent to the buyer of the goods, either direct or through a bank, and he pays for the goods on receipt of the bill of lading.

The shipping company at the discharging port, on receipt of their copy of the bill, informs the shipper that the goods are on board, and asks for the necessary Customs papers, advising the amount of sea freight that has to be added to the f.o.b. price in calculating the dutiable value, and requiring a bank draft or guaranteed cheque for the amount of duty payable. If delivery instructions have not been previously given, these should also be sent to the shipping company immediately the vessel arrives.

## WHAT HAPPENS WHEN THE GOODS ARRIVE

On arrival the cases are discharged into a railway truck alongside, tallied carefully as they leave the ship, and sheeted, if they are likely to be damaged by rain. The Customs forms, duly filled in, together with the money for payment of the duty, are taken to the Customs office, where they are examined and checked, and sent to the Customs officer at the docks. He checks them with the goods, and with case goods usually asks for one or more cases to be opened for examination, and then gives the necessary release to the railway company that the goods may be forwarded.

In the meantime the shipping company hands the railway company a consignment note, giving a description of the goods, the number of the truck, the weight and number of the goods, where they are to be consigned to, and whether the consignor or the consignee is responsible for the railway rate. In some cases the shipper will have sent the bill of lading direct to the shipping company, in which case the railway company is instructed to deliver to the stated address immediately on arrival at destination, getting a signature for the number and weight delivered. Frequently, however, the bill of lading is not to hand in time, or has to be sent to a third party, to whom the goods have been sold ; in that case the railway company will receive instructions to deliver the goods only in exchange for the original bill of lading, which then has to be sent to the shipping company.

If the goods arrive all in good order the transaction is completed by the payment of the through rate to the shipping company. If, however, the goods arrive in a damaged condition, or short of the correct number, the consignee endorses his signature to the railway company to this effect, and a complaint is made to the shipping company. Steps are taken to see where the damage or shortage occurred, whether during the sea transit or after delivery to the railway company, and the shipping company or the railway company deals with the claim accordingly. If the damage or loss is found to be due to bad weather during the vessel's voyage, or to risks which are not covered by the shipping company according to the terms of the bill of lading, or by the railway company according to the terms of the consignment note, then a claim is made on the insurance policy which has been taken out to cover the goods in transit.

## WHAT TO READ NEXT ON TRANSPORT

Those who are interested in the various branches of transport will find many good books to read. The whole subject is treated in the standard text, *Industrial Traffic Management*, by George B. Lissendon. *Shipping and Shipbroking*, by MacMurray and Cree, is a large and thorough work on all shipping questions, and ranks as a standard authority. Interesting accounts of particular branches of shipping work are contained in *Shipbuilding and the Shipbuilding Industry*, by J. Mitchell; and *Cargo Handling at Ports* and *Port Administration and Operation*, both by Brysson Cunningham. *Railways*, by W. F. Wood and Sir Josiah Stamp, is a comprehensive but admirable lucid description of the work of rail transport. Somewhat smaller in compass is *Practical Railway Operating*, by T. Bernard Hare. *Canals and Inland Waterways*, by George Cadbury and S. P. Dobbs, can be thoroughly recommended for that branch of the subject.

# RISKS THE BUSINESS MAN WILL MEET

*by A. B. L. MURISON, M.A.(Cantab), A.C.A.*

In business, as in private life, there are risks of every kind. Certain obvious risks, such as fire or burglary, suggest themselves at once, but there are many others which are less commonplace. Again, some risks are common to almost every business, while others apply only to businesses of a special class.

Fortunately, most business risks are comparatively remote, but that does not lessen the loss they involve when they do occur. It is only too easy to indulge in a false sense of security and think: "That couldn't possibly happen to *me*!", but all prudent men and women will catalogue most carefully every possible risk which the business they own or control may be running, and consider how best they can prevent each risk materialising, or minimise and provide against its effects.

With this purpose in view, it will be convenient to classify business risks for discussion under two main headings. First, there are controllable risks to which a business is exposed primarily as a result of mismanagement, neglect, or inefficiency. Risks of this kind are largely under the control of the manager of the business, and with care and foresight, can, in the main, be prevented. Secondly, there are uncontrollable risks, which can only be attributed, when they occur, to pure misfortune. The most that can be done is to lessen, as far as possible, the chances that they will occur, and the losses involved when they do occur.

## LOSSES CAUSED THROUGH CARELESS STAFF

The first to be considered under the head of risks which are controllable are those which arise from dishonesty, and to a lesser degree from incompetence in the staff of a business. These are perhaps the most common, and therefore the most dangerous of all the risks to which a business is exposed, and their importance should never be underestimated. They can be prevented to some extent by care in selecting staff and by vigorous supervision of every one employed. Almost equally common are the various kinds of risk which result from the negligence of staff, such as loss of or injury to the property of the business, including injury to other employees. So far as the latter is concerned, this is now governed by the Workmen's Compensation Acts, and will be dealt with under the next heading.

Loss of or damage to the property of the business through negligence may arise in various ways, but chiefly in connection with the transport of cash or goods. Taking cash first, it is inevitable in many businesses that large sums of cash have to be carried at regular intervals from the business premises to the bank or *vice versa.* While it is unlikely that the cash will be mislaid on the way, if in the hands of a trustworthy employee, the motor bandit has made it only too plain that even in well-policed, civilised cities it may easily be stolen.

A simple precaution which will go some way towards minimising this risk is to ensure that the the money is always accompanied by at least two persons. Another precaution which might be more widely adopted is that used by bank messengers, who have their satchels chained to their persons. Although this may sound cumbersome and unsightly, it is a very efficient safeguard against sudden attack.

Many people favour the carrying of firearms as a protection while travelling with large sums in cash. The use of firearms is fortunately less prevalent in this country than in most countries abroad. The habit is to be discouraged, as a widespread use of them by the defenders inevitably leads to an equally widespread use of them by the attackers, with consequences which need not be stressed. In addition, a defender who has successfully employed a firearm in resisting attack may well find himself faced with a charge of manslaughter, though in normal circumstances, he will almost certainly be acquitted.

To some extent the same considerations apply to transport of goods. In the case of goods, however, the total possible loss is usually smaller, and negligence and carelessness correspondingly greater. Perhaps the commonest cause of losses of this kind is the leaving of vans and lorries unattended. Petty pilferage may occur, or the loaded vehicle be driven away by the thieves and later abandoned—empty. To prevent this, employers should enforce a strict rule that their goods vehicles should *never*, as far as is humanly possible, be left unattended. Where the driver of the vehicle has to leave it in order to deliver goods, another employee should, if possible, accompany him on his rounds. For this purpose a boy is usually quite sufficient.

Pilferage also takes place with some frequency during loading and unloading of vehicles. A dishonest driver may remove goods from the warehouse other than those which he has orders to deliver, and dispose of them himself. The best precaution against this is an efficient and trustworthy gatekeeper, who will check the contents of all vehicles leaving the warehouse with copies of the delivery notes supplied to him independently by the accounts department. In some cases, where practicable, every vehicle entering or leaving the warehouse yard is weighed on each occasion.

### ACCIDENTS THAT THREATEN THE PROFITS

IN connection with motor vehicles a very common cause of possible loss to a business in these days arises from accidents due to negligence on the part of a driver of a motor vehicle belonging to the business. In a lesser degree accidents may also occur in connection with other machinery used in the business. So far as damage to the property of the business is concerned, the total loss which may be in-involved is limited, but in addition an employer will nearly always be liable under the Workmen's Compensation Acts for any injury which the employee may do to himself in the course of his employment. This applies, therefore, to accidents of every kind, whether motor vehicles or other machinery in use in the business is involved or not. The liability thus thrown on the employer is so heavy that the only reasonable, and indeed essential provision that can be made to meet it is insurance.

An almost equally serious risk which an employer has to run is the liability imposed on him by law for injury to third parties caused by the negligence of his employees. In the case of drivers of motor vehicles, insurance against this risk has wisely been made compulsory by Act of Parliament. In other cases the risk varies with the type of business carried on, and is of less alarmingly frequent occurrence, but heavy damages are often awarded by juries against employers for injuries caused by their employees.

This type of risk, though classified as "controllable," is, as will be realised, in practice exceedingly difficult to control.

It is, for instance, not easy to prevent house-painters dropping pots of paint on passers-by, to take a simple case. All that can be done is to keep a careful watch on the type of workmen engaged, verifying that they have been adequately trained for their jobs. It is also most important to ensure that they are well supervised by an efficient foreman.

Apart from the risk of loss which any business is subject to through the dishonesty, incompetence, or negligence of its employees, very similar risks are run through the unsuitability, inefficiency or inadequacy of its premises. One of the objects of having premises is that of protection from risks, and the owner of any business should make it his first duty to see that his premises are carrying out their function of protection as efficiently as they can be made to do. For example, the first kind of protection afforded by premises is probably that against the weather. This is normally more a question of comfort than of risk, but valuable stock or machinery may easily be ruined by want of a little attention to the roof. All buildings occupied by the business should be inspected regularly, and arrangements made for necessary repairs to be done as soon as possible. It is foolish to wait until defects call attention to themselves.

### HOW TO DEFEAT THE BURGLAR

THE second and more important protection afforded by premises is that against burglars and other unauthorised intruders. The degree of protection necessary in this case naturally varies with the type of business and the type of premises—in fact, it depends upon what there is to protect. It ranges from the plain, locked door and fastened window of a small office, to the elaborately guarded vaults of the Bank of England. Considering first an office; usually this will contain only the company's books (which, though they require the most careful protection, are not of intrinsic value and are rarely likely to be stolen), and a comparatively small sum in cash. In this case stout doors, which should not contain glass panels, and good modern locks, together with securely fastened windows (barred, if considered necessary where the office is near ground level), will usually be sufficient as an outer protection.

As an inner protection locked desks are practically useless, and wherever possible, safes should be employed. Where there is nothing of any great value a fairly modern safe of simple design should suffice. But where large sums of money in cash or bearer bonds, etc., are kept in the office it is essential to have a really first-class safe. Such a safe should be as recent a model as possible, and made by a thoroughly reliable firm. More risk is run in such circumstances by using old-fashioned and out-of-date safes than most business men realise. Many such safes afford practically no protection against the devices employed by the scientific burglar of the present day. The question of type of safe can usually be left to the skilled advice of the suppliers in each particular case. Safes built into the wall are more satisfactory as a rule than those which are not fixed—in any case, the latter should be too heavy to be moved by less than three men, and then only with difficulty. The best form of lock is probably one of the " combination " type.

The installation of " night safes " by most banks in recent years has proved a great boon to many businesses. Where considerable sums of cash are collected, as is often the case, after the banks have closed, the money need no longer be left on the premises overnight, but can be deposited at the bank in the night safe, where it will be in complete security. The night safe is in form a large letter-box with a spring flap which ensures that nothing can be fished out.

An additional protection against burglary is the burglar alarm. There are many different types of these, but they practically all have two features in common : they are operated electrically, and when started they ring a loud bell. Many suffer, however, from a serious disadvantage, as, though admirable in theory, in practice the bell is rather too frequently liable to start by accident in the middle of the night, and nobody can stop it till the staff arrive the following morning. Improvements, however, have now made the better models practically foolproof, and they are worthy of serious consideration by business men who desire additional safeguards against burglary.

An interesting recent development of the burglar alarm is the light operated type. A beam of light falls on a selenium cell forming part of the electric circuit operating the alarm. If the beam of light is interrupted by somebody crossing it, a current is automatically induced in the electric circuit and the alarm is operated. This type of alarm has been employed to protect valuable objects in museums and exhibitions to which the general public have had free access, a use to which it is particularly suited.

### ANTICIPATING THE "SMASH-AND-GRAB" RAIDER

THE question of burglar alarms brings us to the case of the shop, where they are more often used than in offices. A shop is much more difficult to protect against burglary than an office, as it must be almost entirely fronted with glass. On the other hand, except in a shop such as a furrier's or a jeweller's, there is nothing of great value to be stolen, and the fact that the shop as a rule faces openly on to a public highway is usually sufficient to deter the ordinary burglar. But where valuable stock is displayed in the window the prevalence of " smash-and-grab " raids shows that some additional protection is necessary.

The first and obvious precaution is to remove all valuables from the window each night and store them in a safe. This ensures reasonable safety at night, but does not help so far as the daytime is concerned. The usual protection employed then is a strong metal " grille," fixed firmly behind the window. This provides almost complete safety, but has the disadvantage of partially obscuring from the public view the valuables displayed. A few types of reinforced and unbreakable glass, which get over this difficulty, are now on the market, and they will probably eventually come into general use.

Another very common cause of loss to which a department store lays itself open is petty pilfering from the counters by customers during busy periods. The only satisfactory protection against this is to have a sufficient number of plain-clothes " house " detectives, and to prosecute every offender without exception as a deterrent to others.

The third class of premises liable to burglary is the warehouse. The degree of protection necessary depends upon the kind of goods stored. If bulky and weighty and of comparatively small value, stout doors and windows may be sufficient. Otherwise the most satisfactory safeguard is to employ a reliable night-watchman. If this is done a point not to be overlooked is that he should be in a position to give the alarm easily if suddenly attacked. Night-watchmen are also often employed in jewellers' shops, and they are always a valuable, though expensive, additional protection.

In conclusion it may be pointed out that the strength of a

building's armour against burglary lies in protecting its weakest points. The back-door should be as strong and as securely fastened as the front. Trap-doors to the roof should not be overlooked, and even the roof itself should not be forgotten, as cases are not infrequent in which a burglar forces an entry through the ceiling.

### BUILDINGS FULL OF HIDDEN DANGERS

BESIDES the increased risk of burglary owing to defects in buildings, there is another type of risk which may arise where the defect is of such a nature that it may result in an accident involving injury either to employees or to third parties, for which the occupier of the premises will normally be liable. The commonest defects are rickety and badly lighted staircases and insecure trap-doors. Rarer but more serious defects may exist in the brickwork or stonework itself. Projecting portions of the buildings may become detached and fall without warning on persons in a street or yard below. Walls, or whole buildings, as has actually happened in one or two instances, may collapse completely, with possible appalling consequences and certainly with considerable loss to the owners.

In nearly all cases, even where the defect is not apparent, accidents which are due to a building being allowed to get into a dangerous state can be prevented by having rigorous inspections of the building made at regular intervals by expert architects or builders, and by carrying out their recommendations immediately. Unfortunately, many employers regard this an unnecessary expense, but the expense is nothing to that of the possible consequences of neglect to take such precautions.

Risk of injury is perhaps even more common where there are defects in plant, machinery, or equipment than when there are defects in buildings. Almost every machine is a potential source of danger if there is a defect in it—some more so than others. The kind of risk run depends entirely upon the nature of the machine, and as it would be impossible to consider in a short article the risks attaching to every particular machine, a discussion of one or two of the commoner types of plant and equipment must suffice. Generally speaking, however, the maxim of regular inspection applies with equal force to all machines, and foremen should be given strict orders to see that every machine receives the maintenance and attention necessary, whether it is in use or not.

In addition, where safeguards for the workers using the machine are recommended by its makers, these should always be adopted, and the employer should satisfy himself from time to time that they are actually being employed.

Boilers of all kinds are a very common source of danger, as there is always the risk that they will explode. Careful attention to the safety gauge will usually avert an accident of this kind, but as an additional precaution boilers should be housed separately if possible, in order to minimise the consequences of an explosion. At any rate, a strong wall should cut off the boilers from the working part of the factory.

Another very common item of equipment—found more frequently in offices and shops than in factories—is the lift, and this is also a potential source of accident. Modern lifts are, however, almost invariably fitted with some form of safety device which renders the worst kinds of lift accidents practically impossible, and even the cages used in collieries are considerably safer now than they were twenty years ago. Nevertheless it would be unwise not to take advantage of the service of regular inspection which is offered by most lift manufacturers at a very small fee.

It may be convenient to mention here, before leaving the subject of defects in premises and equipment, that the risks to which employees are exposed under this heading have been considerably minimised by legislation embodied in the Factories Act. Under this Act certain standards of safety and well-being for workers have been set up, varying according to the circumstances of different trades, and government inspectors have a right of entry to business premises to ensure that these standards are being maintained.

### THE BAD DEBT THAT COULD BE AVOIDED

BEFORE concluding the consideration of controllable risks there may be mentioned a rather different class of risk which must be regarded as coming under this head, and which may be conveniently termed Management Risks. Bad management can, of course, expose a business to every conceivable kind of risk, but there are one or two kinds of risk in particular which even the most prudent business men must be prepared to run, and which deserve a brief special mention.

The first of these is the risk of incurring bad debts. In the case of ordinary trading debts, this is a normal incident of business dealing, and provided the bad debts do not exceed a certain small percentage varying with the type of trade carried on, they must be accepted as inevitable. Where, however, breach of contract is involved, the consequences may be much more serious, and the loss indirectly greater than is estimated at first sight. The law certainly provides the means to a remedy in these cases, whether great or small, but if the debtor or breaker of the contract has no money with which to make good the loss he has caused, recourse to the Courts will provide only an empty consolation.

The only way of protecting oneself against this kind of loss is to exercise caution—but with restraint, for excess of caution would result ultimately in no business being carried on at all. Traders should be very reluctant to give credit or enter into contracts with persons whose references are in any way unsatisfactory, and every fresh business transaction, even with persons already known, should be considered on its merits. Agencies exist for supplying traders with confidential information as to the financial status of prospective customers or clients, and full use should be made of them where it seems advisable to do so.

The second risk is that of deterioration of stocks. This risk applies, of course, only to businesses which deal in perishable or easily damaged products. In such cases, however, undue exposure to sunlight or damp, or even the storing together of products which contaminate one another by proximity, may involve a business in loss. Scientific assistance in determining the nature of the risks which may be run should be obtained, and the necessary steps taken to prevent any tendency to deteriorate.

## RISKS WHICH CANNOT BE CONTROLLED

UNCONTROLLABLE risks are rather more diverse in nature than those discussed so far, but roughly they may be summarised under four headings: fire, catastrophes caused by nature, strikes, and Government acts.

The first of these is fire, and the risk of fire and the means of its prevention and control are almost a complete science in themselves. The risk of fire is common and constant to all businesses, and the damage it may cause is always incalculable. It is true that it is some three hundred years since a fire which started in a little baker's shop resulted in the destruction of the whole of London, but even now no business man should underestimate the possible consequences of fire.

Fortunately the science of prevention and control of fire, which has been studied from the earliest times, has now reached the pitch almost of perfection, and although serious fires continue to occur, both the risk of fire and the losses caused by fire are progressively diminishing. The establishment of highly efficient fire brigades in the towns of all civilised countries has done much to bring this about, but the trader should always regard the fire brigade as his second line of defence, and establish, on the spot, as many reasonable safeguards against fire as possible.

First, he should consider the safety of his employees by ensuring that his buildings are easily evacuated in more than one direction within a few seconds of the sounding of the fire-alarm. A plan for the evacuation should be worked out and executed by the employees in the form of fire-drill at regular intervals, so that there is no confusion or panic if a fire occurs. A few picked employees should be detailed for special training in the handling of the fire-fighting appliances which are available.

### MARSHALLING THE ENEMIES OF FIRE

DEVICES for the protection of buildings against fire are of many kinds. The use of fireproof material in the construction of buildings is expensive, but of proved effectiveness. A little will go a long way if carefully distributed so as to isolate, as far as possible, the most likely sources of fire from the rest of the building. It should always be used in the construction of safes and strong-rooms, but in the case of safes it should be remembered that the heat of a serious fire may become so intense that the contents of the safe will be irreparably damaged, even though protected from actual contact with the flames. Where it is possible, therefore, to remove objects of value to a place of safety when the fire breaks out, this should be done.

A nearby source of water for the use of hoses, in addition to the ordinary water supply within the building (which it may be impossible to use if the fire rapidly reaches considerable proportions), is another aid to the suppression of fires which should not be forgotten. Within the building itself it is often the practice to have hoses already attached to hydrants so that they can be brought into operation in a few seconds. They should be placed in strategic positions, so that every part of the building is within range of one hose or another. Fire-buckets are also not to be despised, as they are extremely useful in disposing of a small outbreak before it has time to gain a greater hold.

Water should never be used in attempting to put out fires in which petrol or oil is involved. The burning petrol or oil will only float on the water, and, instead of being put out, the fire will be spread in all directions. For fires of this type, sand is the simplest extinguishing method. Where, therefore, there is any danger of a petrol or oil fire breaking out, boxes of sand with scoops should be placed within easy reach. Even in the ordinary case of fire, sand is useful for small outbreaks, and it has the advantage that it does not cause so much damage to books, stock, and furniture as water does. More damage is often caused in a fire by the water used in putting it out than by the actual fire itself.

Sand is, however, rather a clumsy remedy, and the liquid supplied in most patent fire-extinguishers is of such a nature that it may be used on petrol and oil fires with the same effectiveness as on fires of other kinds. Unlike water it does not allow fires of this kind to spread, and owing to certain chemical properties it is of greater efficiency than water in extinguishing fires of all kinds. These patent fire-extinguishers vary in external design, but are mostly constructed on the same principle. They usually consist of a portable cylinder containing the special liquid under a high pressure. By unscrewing a nozzle a powerful jet of the liquid is obtained which can be directed on the seat of the fire. Their qualities of portability and quickness in use, and the special chemical qualities of the liquid they contain, give them a distinct advantage over simpler fire-fighting appliances.

A more elaborate and expensive safeguard against fire is the automatic sprinkler. This consists of a series of water pipes suspended from the ceilings, and in the pipes there are sprinkler jets every two or three feet. If the temperature of the room exceeds a certain pre-determined level, which could only be reached if the room were on fire, the jets automatically come into action, and streams of water descend on the burning room.

One final word in connection with fire-fighting appliances and safeguards : their effectiveness in time of need depends entirely upon their being kept always in perfect order. To ensure this, no business man should neglect to have them inspected and tested at regular intervals by experts. This is a simple and obvious precaution to take, but it is surprising how often it is neglected.

### WHEN NATURE PLAYS TRICKS ON THE BUSINESS MAN

FLOODS, earthquakes, and violent storms need only be mentioned to indicate the magnitude of the risk they involve. The steps, if any, which can be taken to minimise the risk depend entirely upon local circumstances. Some classes of Nature's disturbances, however, can be guarded against, and it should be hardly necessary to mention that every building ought to have a lightning conductor. Apart from this all one can do is make sure that one's buildings are kept in a fit state of repair and have no inherent weakness which might render them specially liable to damage by natural phenomena.

Nor should it be overlooked that Nature can often play tricks in many small ways, and upset the most elaborately careful calculations Torrential rain for the whole of "sale" week may mean a very heavy loss, while a cold summer may render a large stock of thin dresses, underclothes, beach pyjamas, and the like absolutely unsaleable. In such cases the business man can, to some extent, guard himself by prudence, but for the most part he has to trust to luck and to his insurance policy—his best form of prudence.

Strikes of workers may affect the business man directly or indirectly, and they almost invariably result in loss to both employers and employees. So far as strikes of one's own workers are concerned, they may generally be avoided by treating one's employees as well as is humanly possible. This can only partially prevent the possibility of strikes, however, as all serious strikes result from orders by the employees' Trade Union, which must be obeyed irrespective of the personality of the particular employer. Nevertheless if every employer would do the best he possibly could for his employees, it is not going too far to say that the strike menace would largely disappear.

Strikes in raw material or transport industries may also affect a business indirectly with equal seriousness, and over this class of strike, a trader has even less control. All that can be done is to consider the possibility of alternative trans-

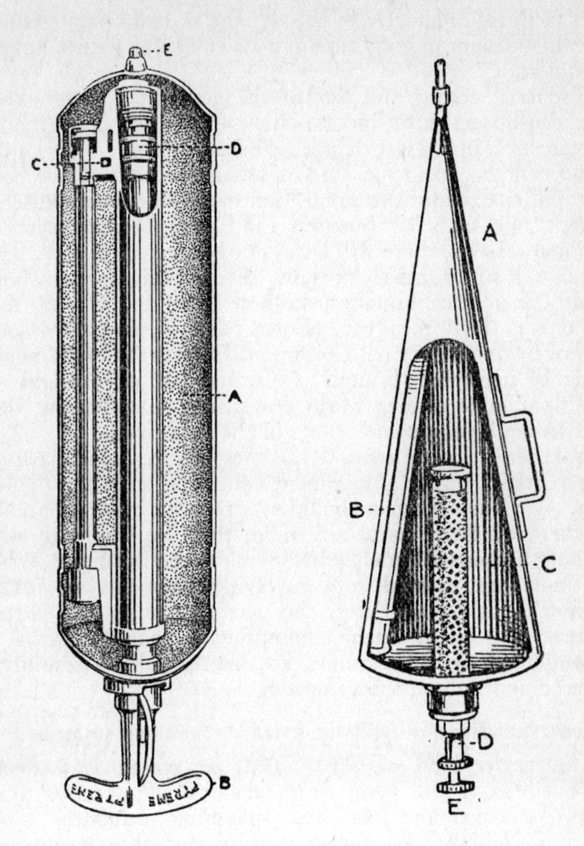


TWO WELL-KNOWN FIRE EXTINGUISHERS

Left: *The "Pyrene" Tetrachloride Extinguisher. The handle B is worked with a pumping action, the liquid being sucked in from the container A to the inner tube D through the ball valve C and ejected through the nozzle E.*

Right: *The "Minimax" Acid-Alkali Extinguisher. An alkaline solution in the hollow cone A is acted upon by acid released by the plunger D which breaks a glass container inside the metal cage C, and the pressure generated ejects the fluid through the narrow tube B.*

port facilities or sources of supply, and to make arrangements to employ them in good time if a strike of this nature appears imminent.

Foremost among the acts of the governing power which may cause loss to businesses is the imposition of tariffs and quotas, and, in a lesser degree, of excise duties. This subject is too controversial to go into in detail, but it should be borne in mind that while the imposition of tariffs and quotas may benefit one class of business, and may be necessary for national reasons, there will always be another class of business which will suffer loss as a result. Every business man should study the political situation, both at home and abroad, in so far as it is likely to affect his own business, and the association of business men with common interests to defend should never be neglected through apathy and lack of foresight. A combination is always more powerful in making its views heard than a lone voice crying in the wilderness.

Another source of possible loss to a business which is at any rate partially under government control is currency fluctuation. No business man should ever take the risk of gambling in currency fluctuation, any more than he would think of backing horses with money belonging to the business. Where contracts are entered into involving payments in foreign currencies at future dates, the necessary supply of foreign currency to meet such commitments should always be "bought forward" at once, so that the entire liability is covered and limited from the start.

## GOVERNMENT ACTIVITIES THAT JEOPARDISE BUSINESS

A DIFFERENT kind of Government act which may affect a business is the compulsory removal of premises under local road-widening or town-planning schemes. Compensation is, however, always paid for such interference, and is usually on an adequate scale. When the question of compensation is being discussed, however, the availability of suitable alternative sites should be borne in mind ; also the possibility that a road-widening scheme may change a busy shopping centre into a deserted speedway has to be remembered.

War must probably be classed as an executive act : the effects on business are too apparent for any business man to need much reminder of them. Though a certain class of business man may be able to make vast fortunes out of wars, the large majority stand only to lose—in some cases everything they have. There is no remedy for war except a steady desire for peace, which temporary hysterical enthusiasms or panics should never be allowed to swamp. Riots are similar in their effects to war, on a much smaller scale, and are, of course, usually local affairs. A strong police force is, as a rule, sufficient to give adequate protection against this risk.

In conclusion, there is a secondary consequence of almost all the risks which have been discussed here, which, though of the utmost importance, is nevertheless overlooked by otherwise prudent business men. Loss of profit consequent upon the occurrence of an accident may be much more serious than the loss involved by the accident itself. A fire, a boiler explosion, or the collapse of the premises means that, in part at least, business cannot be carried on until the damage is repaired. Alternative arrangements can sometimes be made, but these are seldom entirely satisfactory. The best protection against a loss of this kind, as, indeed, against all business risks, is a carefully framed policy of insurance.

## SUGGESTIONS FOR FURTHER READING

THERE is very little specialised literature on the subject of business risks, but readers desiring further information will find certain aspects of the subject considered at greater length in various general books, such as *Modern Office Management*, by Simpson (Pitman), and *Commercial Management*, by Cunliffe L. Bolling (Pitman). *Insurance of Profits*, by A. G. Macken (Pitman), deals in a thorough and lucid manner with the question of loss of profits. Further particulars of the latest fire protection appliances and burglar alarms, etc., can always be obtained from the manufacturers of these articles.

# INSURANCE: THE BASIS OF ALL BUSINESS SECURITY

*by KENNETH McILROY*

BUSINESS is still essentially romantic, but much of its colour and adventure has been taken from it by insurance—by the ease with which it is possible to become indemnified against the consequences of loss. No longer is the merchant's fortune at the mercy of gale or pirate; these and other such violent perils are covered by policies of insurance, leaving only the subtler business risks to keep us wakeful—strikes, famines, fluctuations in exchange and commodity values, rumours of war—and even these are frequently insured against by business men. Insurance has become an element of business; without it no vehicle of transport on sea or land is allowed to move, nothing is built, and no wheel turns. No man of wisdom attempts to make economies in his insurances.

Insurance transactions are conducted upon principles which, upon examination, prove simple and almost self-evident, yet they are constantly being invoked, and we must never lose sight of them. The first of these principles is good faith. There must be the utmost good faith and frankness between the assured and underwriter; the whole truth must be told about the subject of the insurance (known as the insured interest) and all circumstances surrounding it, in order that the underwriter may know the extent of his risk and how much he should charge for the insurance of it. The withholding of any relevant information is a most serious matter, because it gives the underwriter legal grounds upon which to declare the contract void.

It is essential that the insured shall have an actual interest in the subject of the insurance; either he must own part or whole of it or he must be in such a position that injury to it would affect him adversely. For instance, a man may legally take out a policy which will pay him an amount in the event of the death of his business partner, it being understood that the death of his partner would be to the assured's financial detriment. It would not be legal, however, for a man to insure the Albert Memorial against the risks of riot and civil commotions unless that man has an actual interest in the edifice and would suffer material loss in the event of any injury to it—unless, in fact, he had an insurable interest in it.

Furthermore, in the event of some mishap to the insured property, it is an essential principle that the owner (the assured) shall act as though uninsured, and make every effort to preserve his property. He must take such steps to this end as he considers prudent, and, should his property be touched by peril, he must do everything in his power to minimise the loss and to save what is left. In a word, he must act as a prudent uninsured person would do.

### SHIPOWNERS WHO SOMETIMES BENEFIT BY "LOSS"

A POLICY of insurance is a contract of indemnity, and is not a contract by which the assured should be able to make a profit; it is intended merely to make good his actual loss. Nevertheless, the practice in different forms of insurance varies on this point, and a policy-holder is sometimes considerably benefited by the loss or destruction of his property. Such a position is frequently encountered in the insurance of ships, the valuations of which have been previously admitted and agreed between the parties.

From this principle of indemnity follows naturally what is termed "subrogation." This means that, in the event of an assured person being indemnified by an underwriter, his rights as to recovery from a possible third party pass automatically to the underwriter. Let us suppose that a vessel has been sunk in collison with another and that underwriters have paid a total loss, then the owner's possible rights to recover from the owner of the other steamer belong to the underwriters, and they may make what efforts they wish to recoup themselves for their loss.

The policy is an enforceable stamped document signed, not by both parties, but only by the underwriters. In it are set out clearly and accurately the names of the policy-holder and underwriters, a description and value of the insured property, the risk or risks covered, the period or duration for which the insurance is effective, and all conditions relevant to the contract. There is, however, a preliminary document known in marine insurance as a "slip," and non-marine insurance as a "proposal form," and the accurate completion of these documents is of the utmost importance, because it is from the information contained in them that the policy is eventually prepared. When the insurance has been arranged, a "cover note" is frequently issued by the underwriters and held by the insured person pending the preparation of the actual policy.

### HOW LLOYD'S GUARDS ITS REPUTATION

IN this country the bulk of marine insurance is underwritten at Lloyd's, and of non-marine business with the Tariff and Non-Tariff Companies. Nevertheless, there is considerable overlapping: Lloyd's undertake non-marine business on an immense scale, and many of the "Companies" are associated with Lloyd's in the marine market. Lloyd's is a society of underwriters formed into groups for the purpose of conducting business, and it is the practice for one member to act as agent for his group. The Society has for centuries been justly famed for generous and fair business methods, and is sufficiently jealous of its honourable name to make membership a privilege difficult to attain. Candidates for membership are balloted for by the Committee of Lloyd's, who scrutinise their qualities with the greatest care.

In addition to paying a large deposit, each underwriting member must annually provide proof of his ability to meet his liabilities, as he is legally liable in respect of his insurance engagements up to the whole extent of his financial resources. It is interesting to know that although members of the Society are not responsible for the consequences of an individual member's default, they accept the responsibility and make good the deficit.

The activities at Lloyd's are not confined by any means to insurance, for a great part of the measures to protect and save shipping and the lives of those at sea has been sponsored and organised by the Society. They have also made themselves responsible for the rapid collection and publication of shipping news so necessary to the maritime community.

Most insurance companies underwrite marine business at Lloyd's in association with members of the Society, but the greater part of their business consists of non-marine risks —fire, accident, life, etc. The companies are broadly of two types: Tariff and Non-Tariff—the former being members of an association of insurance companies bound by agreement among themselves to accept business only at rates previously agreed. Non-Tariff companies, on the other hand, are free to accept risks at any rate they choose.

Non-marine insurances may be arranged either direct with an insurance company or through the medium of an agent or broker—whether a Lloyd's broker or not. It is, however, the custom to approach Lloyd's marine underwriters through the medium of a Lloyd's broker, whether for the purpose of obtaining quotations and arranging insurances, or of making and collecting claims. The broker does, in fact, conduct business between the two principals who remain invisible to each other, and it is often erroneously concluded from this that he is the agent of both. Actually, although responsible to the underwriters for the premium, he is the agent of the assured.

The Lloyd's broker must at all times render service to his client to the best of his ability, but he must never permit this duty to his client to be so dominant in his mind as to allow himself to strive to gain advantages from underwriters for his client by other than fair means : the principles of insurance apply to him as well as to the assured and to the underwriter.

## INSURANCE THAT COVERS HAZARDS AT SEA

THE majority of marine insurance policies in this country are arranged on the basis of clauses drawn up by the Institute of London underwriters ; these are known shortly as the " Institute " Clauses. The perils against which the shipowner commonly wishes to be indemnified by policies of insurance are covered by the scope of the " Institute Time Clauses—Hulls." These clauses are popularly known as " All Risks " clauses ; and although there are many modified forms of this insurance giving the owner cover for less premium, no ship is considered fully insured except on the basis of Institute Time Clauses—Hulls.

The principal peril against which the owner may be indemnified by these clauses is total loss. This does not necessarily mean the ship's complete destruction : should she be so damaged or in such a position that to make her fit for sea again would cost more than the insured value of the vessel, underwriters agree to treat the claim as though the vessel were a total loss.

## WHEN DAMAGE IS DONE TO SAVE A SHIP

THE clauses also cover damage or loss of a partial character. When the damage or loss is incurred voluntarily on an occasion when the vessel and cargo is in peril, it is termed *General Average.* Also " general average expenses " are those which are incurred for the benefit of the whole venture, *i.e.* ship, cargo, and/or freight at a time of peril.

There are many types of general average acts, but three are most commonly encountered, namely, jettison, machinery damaged in working a vessel off a dangerous strand, and port of refuge expenses. Jettison is the deliberate casting overboard of cargo with the object of making the vessel more seaworthy, but the jettison of deck cargo is not admitted in general average unless carried in accordance with the custom of the particular trade in which the ship is engaged. The general average loss or damage may be incurred solely by the ship or by the cargo and freight. Let us suppose that the whole of the general average damage is to the ship. Because the sacrifice was made for the good of the whole venture, it is only reasonable that the owners of the ship—and eventually the underwriters on the ship—should receive contributions from the freight and cargo towards making good the damage. Each interest—ship, cargo, and freight—contributes according to its value at the place where the venture ends. It is essential to apply to any act which seems to be a general average act two tests, namely : " Was the whole venture in peril ? " and " Was the sacrifice deliberate ? " The answer to these questions should be in the affirmative in order to constitute the act General Average.

*Particular Average* is the term applied to a partial damage or loss sustained accidentally from a peril insured against. The damage or loss is made good by the party receiving it, and not by all parties as in general average. Particular average is only payable by underwriters (under Institute Time Clauses—Hulls) should it amount to more than 3 per cent. of the insured value. But should the vessel be stranded, sunk, on fire, or in collision, the " franchise " of 3 per cent. does not apply.

Owners have the option of calculating their 3 per cent. franchise on the whole insurance valuation of the steamer, or upon the separate valuations for hull and for machinery which are arrived at and agreed by underwriters and owners at the inception of the insurance. By way of example, let us suppose that a ship is valued for insurance at £10,000, and that of this amount the hull is given (at the inception of the insurance) a value of £6,000, and the machinery a value of £4,000—known as the "separate values." The 3 per cent. franchise on the whole valuation is therefore £300, and on the separate valuations it is £180 and £120 on hull and machinery respectively. The ship has encountered heavy weather, which has resulted in extensive straining and damage to the machinery which would cost £2,000 to repair, but the damage to the hull itself is slight and could be repaired for £150. The cost of repairing the machinery damage is well "above franchise," and is therefore recoverable in full from the underwriters, but the hull damage is less than franchise.

As has been pointed out, an owner may, if he wishes, calculate his 3 per cent. franchise on the whole valuation of the steamer, and the example before us illustrates the advantages of this option. Even though the hull damage (£150) is less than the hull franchise (£180), it is recoverable if the owner exercises this option by adding the cost of repairs to the hull to the cost of repairs to the machinery. These amounts together total £2,150—a figure well above the 3 per cent. franchise on the whole valuation (£300); thus the whole amount of the repairs is recoverable from the underwriters.

Of late years franchise seems to have become less popular among some underwriters; they prefer, perhaps rightly, that there shall be no franchise in the policy, and that owners instead shall become their own underwriters for a certain amount. Thus an increasing number of vessels are nowadays insured "excess of £— each Particular Average accident, Institute Time Clauses," or "Owners bearing the first £— of each and every claim, excluding total loss." It is believed that the change tends to the benefit of both underwriters and owners.

As an example demonstrating the essential differences between particular and general average, we could take the instance of a vessel having become stranded in a perilous position. The damage sustained by the vessel as a result of the impact or series of impacts is particular average; the considerable damage to machinery which is probably incurred as a consequence of efforts made to "work" the vessel off the strand and thus save her from further damage is general average.

## INSURING AGAINST THE COST OF RESCUE

If help is rendered to a vessel in peril which results in her being brought to a safer position, the " salvors " are entitled to remuneration, which is called " salvage," for their services, even though no contract has been signed. In these days, it is true, a document known as Lloyd's Salvage Agreement is in common use ; it is signed by the master of the ship upon which salvage attempts are to be made, and is a contract which provides that, should the salvage efforts be successful, the salvors would be paid such reward as would be determined by some third party, or by subsequent agreement between salvors and salved. It says much for the recognised integrity of the underwriting community that Lloyd's Salvage Agreement is invariably accepted by salvors, whether British or foreign.

Whereas salvage is assistance given voluntarily by a third party, expense may further be incurred by reason of the owner himself, or his agents, taking such measures as are practicable in order to avert or minimise the loss. This expense is termed " sue and labour " charges. It is notable that these charges can be claimed from underwriters under the Institute Time Clauses even if they have already paid, or eventually pay, a total loss on the vessel. Further, the 3 per cent. franchise does not apply to the damage which, for the sake of example, has been minimised by the owner's or his agents' efforts.

When a vessel does damage to another in collision, three-fourths of her liability (if to blame) to the other vessel is covered by the " Running Down Clause " which is Institute Time Clause No. 1. The remaining one-quarter is covered by a complementary insurance usually underwritten by one of the Protecting & Indemnity Associations.

## FILLING UP THE GAPS IN A LLOYD'S POLICY

It will be noticed that certain risks are specifically excluded by the Institute Time Clauses, and there are other risks of which no mention is made in a Lloyd's policy and which are therefore uncovered. This is where the Protecting & Indemnity Associations come in. The cover which they offer dovetails with Institute Time Clauses and really fills up the gaps left in the Lloyd's policy. So we find that the one-fourth of the shipowner's collision liability, which is expressly excluded from Clause 1 of Institute Time Clauses, is covered by the Protecting & Indemnity Associations. The Associations also cover the risks excluded in Clause 2, namely, damage to dock, jetties, cranes, and other fixed objects, and the liability of the shipowner for loss of life or personal injury, including liability under the Workman's Compensation Act towards his own crew.

Similarly the risks of which no mention is made in Lloyd's policy are covered by the Associations. Among them are the following interesting examples: quarantine expenses, including provisions and wages; expenses incurred in landing an injured or sick man; the repatriation of stowaways; repatriation of sick or injured members of the crew, and payment of their hospital expenses; the cost of sending out officers in place of those sick or injured; the cargo's proportion of general average when otherwise not recoverable by the owners; shipowner's liability in respect of cargo; war risks; deviation (or change of voyage).

Steamers are usually insured by "Time" policies for twelve months, although shorter periods may be covered if required. Formerly most vessels—particularly those expected to be on one passage for long periods—were insured voyage by voyage, and there is still a considerable amount of business effected on this basis, particularly amongst large sailing craft. The risks covered are of course fundamentally the same as those covered by Institute Time Clauses—Hulls, but in a voyage policy there is an "implied warranty" of seaworthiness, which means that the seaworthy condition of the vessel is understood as between owners and underwriters: if the vessel puts to sea in an unseaworthy state, the underwriters are not liable for subsequent losses, even though the owners were not aware of the vessel's unseaworthiness.

There is, in fact, a form of policy suitable for every type of marine risk and for every class of insurable interest. There are policies framed to cover the hulls of the vessels during building operations, launching and trial trips, and it is, of course, the ship-builders who have most need of this form of insurance. There is also the port risk policy which covers the vessel while she is lying up in port.

Cargoes, again, are insured voyage by voyage and cargo policies have clauses very much their own. Indeed, nearly every type of cargo has its own particular set of clauses covering the risks peculiar to its nature. For example: coal clauses, timber federation clauses, institute corn trade clauses, and institute dangerous drugs clauses. However, many cargoes do not need such special treatment as this, and will be insured either fully by the "Institute Cargo Clauses (with average)," or partially by the "Institute Clauses (free of particular average)." Actually there is very little difference in the extent of cover offered by these two forms of policy, and in practice it will be found that the only serious loss or damage for which the owner is indemnified by the "With Average" Clauses and not by the "Free of Particular Average" Clauses is that of heavy weather.

### THE METHOD OF INSURING A SHIP

In such a brief explanation of marine insurance there are necessarily points to which no reference has yet been made, but it may be possible to remedy this to some extent by giving an illustrative example of the placing of a steamer's insurance from the moment that a new owner purchases her.

Messrs. Hopeful & Jones have purchased the s.s. *Swallow*, of 2,000 gross registered tonnage; built in 1922. They paid £11,000 for her, but to raise the money were forced to appeal to a Bank for assistance. In this they were successful, for the Bank, having obtained an expert opinion upon the vessel's potentiality as a money-maker and a report upon the intending owners themselves, agreed to advance half the purchase price—and thus became mortgagees. This is of importance, because experienced mortgagees are apt to insist upon full insurance, a luxury which many hard-pressed shipowners deny themselves. There is nothing for it, therefore, but to seek the advice of a firm of Lloyd's Insurance Brokers, and eventually to instruct them to approach underwriters in the marine insurance market for quotations for full insurance.

Now let us turn to the insurance brokers, the angle from which they look on this particular problem and the advice they give their clients. The insurance brokers first make inquiries as to the vessel's position and movements, because it is most important to cover her from the moment she changes hands and becomes the property of Messrs. Hopeful & Jones. They are told that the s.s. *Swallow* is due to arrive on the following Saturday in London, where she will commence discharging on the following Monday morning and will probably be turned over to her new owners during the middle part of the week, and it is their intention to keep her there for overhaul for a couple of weeks at least.

The insurance brokers therefore advise that a port risk insurance be taken out for thirty days to cover the vessel while laid up in London; Messrs. Hopeful & Jones agree to this suggestion, and the insurance brokers place the insurance with underwriters at Lloyd's at 1s. per cent. on a valuation of £16,000, the insurance to attach automatically from the handing over of the steamer. The insurance brokers are very pleased to realise that they have perhaps three weeks in which to arrange the twelve months "Time" policies, because they know that the ship has been singularly unfortunate in the matter of damage, and is not the sort of risk to bring a happy light into underwriters' eyes. They wait, therefore, until a suitable moment arrives, and then approach underwriters with the ill-favoured *Swallow* escorted by a fleet of modern vessels which it is their duty and pleasure to insure also. They hope by this expedient to persuade the underwriters, in their joy at being offered such good risks, to look as favourably even upon the *Swallow*. The underwriters, probably quite unimpressed, quote a rate of £11 per cent. on a valuation of £16,000. They offer full Institute Time Clauses and Institute Warranties.

## RULES THAT ARE MADE FOR INSURING SHIPS

Now there are two points arising out of this which need explanation. First, the values: A shipowner is legally liable in a case of collision up to £8 per gross ton of his vessel; the *Swallow* is 2,000 gross tonnage, and the collision liability therefore is £16,000. It follows that the vessel must have a valuation of at least £16,000 to be fully covered as far as collision is concerned. Underwriters themselves are as insistent that the value shall not be too low, because a low value produces a correspondingly low franchise; further, the lower the valuation a vessel has, the more easily she can become a "constructive" total loss.

Secondly, it is necessary to explain the *Institute Warranties.* These are clauses limiting the ship's sphere of operations. There are certain areas of sea and coast considered by underwriters to be so dangerous to shipping that they are placed "out of bounds" for the whole or part of the year. One type of cargo also—Indian Coal—is banned between 1st March and 30th June. These exclusions have to be rigorously obeyed by the shipowner if he is to remain covered, and breaches of them—when permitted by underwriters—usually call for the payment of additional premium.

Messrs. Hopeful & Jones receive their brokers' news without enthusiasm, confronting them with evidence that Messrs. Smith & Robinson insure their s.s. *Sparrow*, which is approximately the same age and size as the *Swallow*, at eight guineas per cent. Patiently and with courtesy their brokers explain that the *Sparrow* has an insurance valuation of £24,000 and therefore pays a larger premium. They point out the advantages of a low valuation—from the point of view of franchise and constructive total loss—and eventually convince their clients that the terms quoted to them are reasonable. They are therefore instructed to proceed with the placing of the insurance on hull and machinery, and also of the subsidiary lines on Freight, Disbursements, and Premiums Reducing. These last three interests require explanation.

Shipowners usually insure their freight for a period of twelve months—not the total freight they expect to earn in a year, but the greatest amount of freight likely to be at risk at any one time. It should be noted that freight is usually insured not only against the risk of total loss, but also against general and particular average, salvage, sue and labour, etc. An appropriate set of clauses (Institute Time Clauses—Freight) are in general use for this purpose.

An insurance on "disbursements" is frequently arranged against the risk of Total Loss only—merely with the object of providing a greater recovery in the event of the vessel being lost. "Excesses" are also frequently insured, in cases where the sound value of the vessel is greater than the value insured. Such a state of affairs would mean that claims under the collision clause, for general average, for salvage, and for sue and labour might not be wholly recoverable under the policies. The "Excesses" insurance is designed to remedy this. By the provision of the Institute Time Clauses—Hulls, the amount which may be insured on interests other than hull (*i.e.* freight, disbursements, etc.) is limited.

Insurance on "Premiums Reducing" covers a contingency which is a corollary of Total Loss. It should be remembered that premium is not returnable in such an event, and accordingly shipowners are permitted to insure their premiums against the risk of total loss. The amount recoverable under the Premiums policy is reduced by one-twelfth monthly.

Our broker friends, after consultation with their clients, decide that £2,400 shall be covered on freight against "All Risks"; that, as the owners are already sufficiently covered in the event of total loss, disbursements need not be insured at all; and that the actual amount of premium to be paid shall be covered. One other point is determined before the operations actually commence—that of separate values for hull and machinery. As previously stated, it is upon these "separate values" that the 3 per cent. Particular Average franchise may be calculated. The brokers suggestion of £11,000 on hull and £5,000 on machinery is accepted by Messrs. Hopeful & Jones, and the stage is set.

The underwriters who have quoted 11 per cent. are again approached by the brokers with a "slip" on which the details of the insurance are stated. The underwriters express their willingness to lead the insurance by taking a "line" of £1,000; this line is placed on the slip and initialed. Other underwriters in turn are then approached; some refuse, but others accept the risk at this rate, and the insurance is eventually placed and ready to operate for twelve months from any time desired by the owners.

Cover notes setting out the terms of the hull and machinery, freight all risks and "premiums reducing" are sent to the owners with a request for early information as to the time and date of the vessel's sailing. It is suggested by the brokers that, if the owners have not already done so, they should apply for membership to a Protecting and Indemnity Association. Academically, this is not a point which really concerns an insurance broker, but the brokers are aware of the inexperience of Messrs. Hopeful & Jones as shipowners, and they remind them that, although the port risk insurance under which the vessel is now covered includes protection and indemnity risks, the protecting and indemnity risk should be covered separately by the Association of which they are to become members, as soon as the port risk insurance becomes ineffective.

### HOW THE PREMIUM IS PAID

In due time the brokers are warned that the vessel is about to sail to the North-East Coast where she will load her first cargo under her new ownership; she sails—whereupon the underwriters are advised of the time and date, and a set of debit notes and copy policies are prepared by the brokers and forwarded to the owners. In connection with these debit notes, it should be noted that, unless otherwise stated, a discount of 10 per cent. is allowed, no matter whether the premium is paid in one sum or by instalments. The insurance brokers' commission (or brokerage) is based upon the gross figure—that is to say, before the deduction of discount.

The premium, of course, is payable to the brokers who arrange the business, and they in turn are responsible to the underwriters for the premium, less their brokerage. Messrs. Hopeful & Jones, after consultation with fellow-shipowners, decide to pay by instalments, and ask their brokers whether such a method is acceptable to them. It is acceptable, and the brokers suggest a cash payment of one-fourth of the premium, plus their whole 5 per cent. brokerage, the balance to be paid by bills on the third, sixth, and ninth month of the insurance.

About this time, Messrs. Hopeful & Jones's bankers, who are also the mortgagees, let it be known that the proceeds from all claims collected by the brokers shall be paid to them. Each bank has its form of undertaking to be signed by the insurance brokers, and frequently by the owners as well, but it is understood by the Bank that the brokers, as they are being paid by instalments, have a lien in respect of their premium on any amounts they may collect in claims. This right of the brokers is recognised by the Bank and admitted in their letter of undertaking, and the owners themselves sign a document which is held by the brokers as an admission of their lien.

In the event of the owners defaulting in their payment of premium, it is therefore legally within the power of the brokers to recoup themselves for loss of premium by deducting the amount from any claim under the policy which they may be collecting; the balance, of course, if any, must be paid to the Bank. Lastly, the policies themselves are prepared, examined, and passed by Lloyd's Signing Bureau and, if necessary, forwarded to the owners for endorsement. Should the policies be in the joint names of the owners and bank, it will be necessary for the Bank also to endorse the documents. They are then returned to the brokers, who retain them.

## HOW CLAIMS ARE MADE

THE Institute Time Clauses demand that underwriters shall be informed as soon as possible of any loss or damage which may result in a claim on their policies. If a damaged vessel is abroad, the information should be given immediately to the nearest Lloyd's agent. Lloyd's agents are appointed by Lloyd's in all parts of the world, and it is their duty to keep Lloyd's advised of all movements of shipping in their respective areas and of any casualties. In the event of damage or loss, a Lloyd's agent will, if necessary, appoint surveyors on the underwriters' behalf, and will act generally in the underwriters' interests.

It is also a provision of Institute Time Clauses that underwriters are entitled to decide the port to which a damaged vessel shall proceed for docking or repairs; they may also veto any proposal to employ a repairing firm or a place of repair, and they further have the right to require the owners to ask for tenders from various repairing firms. Let us suppose that the s.s. *Swallow* is already in trouble and is now in a British port awaiting tenders for the repair work; the Salvage Association (a claims organisation associated with Lloyd's) or some surveyors appointed by Lloyd's have made an examination of the damage in company with Messrs. Hopeful & Jones's own marine superintendent. Between them they ascertain what damage is actually the result of perils insured against.

The tenders come in, are examined, and the work is given to a local repairer, who in due course presents his accounts to the owner for settlement. These accounts, together with the log books covering the period during which the damage or loss was sustained, and the "protest" by the Master, are handed to an average adjuster. Average adjusters are experts employed by the owners, but their fees are recoverable from underwriters; the duty of the average adjuster is to draw up the general claim in accordance with law and to be impartial as between his clients and their underwriters. The average adjustment, with such of the supporting documents as may be considered necessary, is presented to underwriters *via* the brokers, and the brokers follow its progress with the utmost care, explaining, persuading, and, if necessary, arguing their clients' case.

The *Swallow's* claim after perusal by underwriters, and the claims bureau at Lloyd's is paid, and a remittance, less 1 per cent. collecting commission which the broker retains, is forwarded to the mortgagees on the vessel in accordance with the undertaking given to them at the inception of the insurance.

Messrs. Hopeful & Jones draw cheques on their Bank with which to pay the repairers, average adjusters, and other claimants concerned with the affair. It should be noted, however, that frequently repairers of vessels require an undertaking that their account shall be paid direct by the brokers, and the presence or absence of this practice provides a commentary on the financial state of British shipping.

Returns of premium may be claimed from underwriters at rates stated in the policies for completed periods of thirty days during which the vessel is laid up, whether under repair or not. These returns of premiums may be claimed from underwriters at the expiry of the policies and on the safe arrival of the vessel.

## FIRE INSURANCE: FREQUENT SUBJECT OF CONTENTION

THE basis of insurance is indemnity, and in the practice of fire insurance in particular one is constantly reminded of this. In some other forms of insurance it is possible to make a just claim for more than the actual loss, but the ordinary fire insurance policy contrives to make this impossible, and there is in consequence a lot of misunderstanding between very many insured persons and their insurance companies, manifesting itself frequently in bursts of indignant protests from the former. There must be thousands of disgruntled persons who have complained at one time or another that they were not "put in the same position as they were before the fire." Nevertheless, it is reasonably safe to say that the attitude of most of these unfortunate people is the wrong one.

Most of these complaints arise as the result of the working of the "Average Clause," and many of the others may be traced to the fact that, in the event of damage or loss to insured property, the Insurance Company is bound to pay only the cost of replacing the damaged property, less an allowance for wear and tear. It might be as well to examine these two rather uncomfortable and contentious points.

The Average Clause has a name redolent of marine insurance, but it is nevertheless of fire insurance origin. It says in effect that a claim shall be paid in the proportion that the insured value of the property bears to its real value, and it is a warning against under-insurance. As an example of its application, let us assume property insured for only £1,000, but really worth £3,000; the insurers of this dangerously under-insured property are liable for only one-third of any claim if the Average Clause appears in the policy.

In foreign fire insurance, the average clause plays a much greater part than in this country, but English companies are employing it more and more. It is a very reasonable clause, because it tends to bring about a reduction in rating, to encourage full insurance, and, above all, to impress on the property owner the necessity of having his property accurately valued before insurance. There are objections to it, but nevertheless it is generally considered that its wider employment would be a blessing.

### THE MISTAKE OF UNDER-INSURING PROPERTY

An examination of the basis of valuation follows logically upon these considerations. Generally speaking, property should be insured for the amount which would have to be spent on replacing it; it is not safe to insure second-hand property for the price paid for it, because the property may be old and of first-class construction and might, in expensive days, cost much more to replace than to buy in the first instance. Let us refer again to the property insured for £1,000 but really worth £3,000.

As has been said, if the policy contains the average clause, then underwriters are liable for only one-third of any loss or damage. If, however, there is no average clause in the policy, the owner of the property may recover damage or loss up to the amount of the insured value—but no more; his insurance would therefore merely be a cover for partial damage up to £1,000, and unless he is satisfied that his property is so constructed and protected that a fire could not destroy more than one-third of it, then he should revise his insurance without delay.

But revision of the valuation to a figure which represents the cost of replacement by exactly similar property is not sufficient to give every property owner complete indemnity. There is always the deduction made for wear and tear, or depreciation. Furthermore, it is necessary to bear in mind the possible loss of profits. A factory owner, as a result of fire and explosion destroying an important part of his machinery, is compelled temporarily to close down his factory; a considerable part of the anticipated profit of that year is lost, and yet his "standing charges" have still to be paid (wages to permanent staff, advertising expenses, rates, taxes, insurance premiums, rent, etc.).

On condition that his fire risk is covered, he may also effect a Loss of Profits policy. The amount insured is arrived at by adding together the net profits and the standing charges for the last twelve months. Let us suppose that these total £3,000 or three-twentieths of last year's "turnover" (£20,000). Now, in consequence of this fire and explosion, his annual turnover decreases by £10,000. He is entitled to claim three-twentieths of this shortage (£1,500) under his Loss of Profits policy. Thus, the insured is indemnified for a loss not taken into account by the ordinary fire policy.

There are other forms of Loss of Profits insurances, designed to suit the peculiar circumstances of certain businesses, but the form described is the one encountered most frequently. The period of indemnity need not come to an end at the expiry of the Profits policy but is effective for a pre-stated period, usually twelve months from the date of the fire.

### DEFECTS IN BUILDING THAT RAISE THE PREMIUMS

THE risks of fire and explosion vary to an enormous extent, but the fire insurance world has classified them as a result of years of experience. Nearly every type of insurable property has been given a basic or "normal rate" for the insurance of its fire risk, to or from which additions and deductions may be made in arriving at the eventual rate to be quoted by the insurers. A certain factory, for example, may be of a type which calls for a basic rate of 3s. per cent.; but, on survey by the prospective insurers, the rate may quite likely be increased to, say, 7s. 6d. per cent. by successive additions of small amounts as each hazardous feature of the factory comes to light.

These features are known as "common hazards" and are queerly diverse in character. The construction; the method of lighting; the method of heating; the source and type of power used; the height of the buildings, in addition to the basic rate being made for each storey above the first; the cubic capacity of the building are some of them. On the other hand, he forms of fire-fighting appliances are very naturally taken into consideration in determining the eventual rate, and deductions are made in proportion to their number and the efficacy they are believed to possess.

It is a usual condition of fire insurance that the insurers

be advised of loss or damage as soon as is practicable, and that the claim be made within thirty days of the fire. Insurers are entitled to every consideration in this respect, for there is much that they may do by way of minimising the loss and collecting evidence. Delay in giving information prejudices the insurers' chances. It may well prejudice the insured's also. Moreover, it is in every case incumbent on the insured to provide proof of his loss.

## INSURANCE AGAINST THE RISKS OF THE ROAD

So far it has been possible to avoid mention of the many Acts of Parliament affecting the subject of insurance, but the Road Traffic Act, 1930, so intimately concerns motor vehicle insurance that something must be said about it. From the 1st January, 1931, it became law that users of motor vehicles were to be insured against third party risks by an authorised insurer within the meaning of the Act. The third party risks which must be covered under the Act are those of death or bodily injury to any person arising out of the use of the insured vehicle.

Third party risks, however, as understood by the insurance world, comprise risks of damage to property, as well as of death and bodily injury to persons, and the Act is frequently criticized on this point ; it was designed to protect aggrieved and innocent parties against the acts of persons so irresponsible as to be without insurance, yet it left property owners unprotected.

The Road Traffic Act, 1930, also provides that a policy is of no effect until the holder of it is possessed of a " certificate of insurance " containing particulars of the conditions subject to which the policy is issued. A certificate of insurance usually contains the following details : index mark and registration number of the vehicle insured ; the name of the policy-holder ; the period during which the certificate of insurance is effective ; a statement as to the persons or classes of persons entitled to drive ; a statement as to limitations of the vehicle's use ; a signed declaration by a responsible representative of the insurance company to the effect that the certificate is issued in accordance with the provisions of Part Two of the Road Traffic Act, 1930. Furthermore, as a safeguard against persons driving an uninsured vehicle, a certificate of insurance must be produced on application for a motor licence.

### THREE WAYS OF INSURING A MOTOR CAR

It is perhaps convenient to examine private motor car insurance, as the insurance of commercial vehicles and motor cycles does not vary sufficiently to warrant being treated separately. A vehicle in road use may be insured in one of three ways: first, against the risks designated by the Road Traffic Act; secondly, against full third party risks; and thirdly, "Comprehensively." As regards the first, or Road Traffic Act cover as it is called, it has already been pointed out that this is in respect of death or bodily injury to persons.

Full Third Party insurance cover includes not only the risks comprised in the Road Traffic Act cover, but also the Insured's legal liability for damage to the *property* of Third Parties, and is effective whether the insured is driving his own car or any car other than a hired one. It also covers any person driving the insured car with the insured's permission. The risks of fire and theft are occasionally included at a small additional premium in a Third Party policy although they are not, of course, Third Party risks.

A "comprehensive" form of policy covers full third party risks (and therefore, of course, conforms with the requirements of the Road Traffic Act) and in addition covers the cost of repairing accidental damage to the insured's car or its accidental total loss. It is a condition of most Insurance Companies' policies that, although repairs to a damaged car may be commenced immediately, particulars of the occurrence, together with a detailed estimate by the repairer of what the damage is likely to cost, shall be forwarded to the Insurance Company without delay.

Other risks generally included in a comprehensive cover are such things as fire damage to the car and to any of its contents incidental to motoring; fire damage to the garage containing the insured car (up to £100); proportional refund of cost of licence in the event of the car being stolen or burnt; theft; personal accident to the insured or his wife; medical expenses up to an agreed sum; sea transit within stated limits; continental travel with stated limits upon payment of an additional premium; and free legal defence of proceedings against the insured or his paid driver in respect of alleged motoring offences in the United Kingdom.

Some insurance companies offer an " agreed value " which is paid in full in the event of the total loss of the car, but others adhere firmly to the principle of indemnity by offering to replace the destroyed car or pay to the insured the market value. When determining the rate to be charged, the purpose for which the car is to be used, and the occupation of the insured, are factors taken into consideration, but the principal factors are horse-power and value. Nevertheless, many non-tariff companies offer special rates of insurance on certain well-known makes of cars, not on the basis of horse-power and value, but on the model.

Additional premiums are charged to cover fully accidents to the owner and passengers, and legal liability to the chauffeur. On the other hand, deductions are made from the premium if the insured car is warranted driven by the owner only, or by some named driver only, or if two or more cars are insured under the same policy. Allowances, too, are made in the premium if the insured agrees to bear an " excess " by which he becomes his own underwriter for a stated amount of each claim. For example, if he agrees to bear the first £10 of each claim, he may expect to benefit by a deduction in his premium of as much as 25 per cent.

### YEARLY REWARDS FOR NOT MAKING A CLAIM

If no claim is made during a year of insurance, a rebate known as a " No Claim Bonus " is allowed off the renewal premium. This rebate is capable of increase year by year, insurance companies adopting differing limits beyond which their bonuses can be increased no further. The tariff companies allow 10 per cent. bonus in the event of no claim being made in the first year, and this may rise to, and remain at, 15 per cent. in the years following. Non-tariff companies give bonuses capable of being increased year by year to as much as 25 per cent. of the premium, and even larger bonuses are obtainable from a few companies.

The giving of a generous no claim bonus may be rightly regarded by the car-owner as a reward for careful driving, but the insurance companies look at it from a different view point: it is their aim to have on their books as many good and careful drivers as they can attract by their offer of large no claim bonuses. Further, it is realised that a car-owner earning a large bonus will be reluctant to prejudice it by making a small claim which would put him, as it were, " back at the beginning." It is worth noting that a no claim bonus is not necessarily lost as the result of a transfer of the insurance to another company; but, in the event of a car insurance earning a larger bonus than the maximum bonus offered by the new company, there will naturally be a loss of part of the bonus.

Agreements of various sorts exist between motor insurance companies with the object of simplifying settlement of claims, and of making recourse to law as infrequent as possible. Some companies have "halving" agreements between themselves whereby the total of the repair bills consequent upon a collision between two cars is divided equally between the two insurance companies concerned. A better known form of agreement between insurance companies is the Knock-for-Knock Agreement, under which each company concerned pays for the damage received by its own car irrespective of the question of liability for the collision. An insured motor car owner may be the victim of a collision for which he was without blame, but his insurance company will pay for his damage (if he is comprehensively insured) without taking any steps to recover from the guilty party, if a Knock-for-Knock Agreement exists between the insurance companies.

## THE EMPLOYER'S LIABILITY FOR HIS WORKMEN

THE legal liability of an employer to pay compensation to employees is defined by the Workman's Compensation Act of 1925–31, the Employers' Liability Act, 1880, the Fatal Accidents Act, 1846, and Common Law. The result is to render an employer legally liable to pay compensation to an employee disabled in the course of his employment, and to pay compensation to dependents of an employee who loses his life as a result of an accident or specified disease arising out of, or in course of, his employment. The compensation payable to the dependents of an employee who is the victim of a fatal accident or of a specified disease having fatal consequences, varies from medical and burial expenses with a maximum expenditure of £15, to a payment not exceeding £600, according to the number and circumstances of his dependents, if any.

The amount of compensation payable weekly to a man either totally incapacitated or partially incapacitated depends upon his average weekly wage. If the accident is a direct consequence of the employee's own serious and wilful misconduct, compensation will be payable only if the injuries prove fatal or result in permanent disablement. When it becomes obvious that injury is of a permanent nature, resort is usually made to a lump sum settlement.

## PREMIUMS BASED ON THE WAGES BILL

THE legal liability thus imposed upon employers may be covered by insurance at premiums which are based on the estimated amount of wages likely to be paid during the period of insurance. At the expiry of the policy a declaration is made by the employer showing the exact amount in wages paid during the year of insurance, and the premium is then adjusted either in the employer's favour or in favour of the underwriters, according to whether the original estimate was greater or smaller than the actual wages expended.

The rate of premium itself is arrived at by an examination of the nature of the hazards to which the employees are exposed. A factor which has, of course, a great influence on the rate is the past " claims experience " of the individual risk upon which the prospective insurers are quoting.

Advice of a claim or of an injury likely to result in a claim must be promptly given to the insurers. A claim form is completed by the employer and, with medical certificate, is examined by the insurers who, on being satisfied that the claim is in order, authorise weekly compensation to be paid at the scale rate by the employer, who is eventually reimbursed by his insurers.

## PERSONAL INSURANCE THAT PROTECTS AGAINST ADVERSITY

LIFE assurance of a personal nature is of great interest to the individual, but a knowledge of it is not often necessary for the conduct of a business. It is " Group " Life Assurance which a business man needs to understand. There are, however, certain features of life assurance which may be dealt with, in order that the more important subject of group life may be seen in its proper perspective.

Personal life assurance is variously regarded as a provision for dependents, a means of saving, and an investment. While a simple form of endowment policy combines these three virtues, circumstances can be so diverse in character that many other types of policy have had, of necessity, to be evolved.

In the case of an endowment policy premiums are payable annually (sometimes at shorter intervals) to secure a payment of a capital sum at the end of a fixed number of years, or at death if this should occur during the term of years. Policies of this sort may be issued with or without "profits." As a simple example of endowment life assurance we take the case of a young married man who desires to make provision for his wife and young family in the event of his death; at the same time he realises that life assurance is perhaps the best method of almost compulsory and yet benevolent saving, and that should he survive the term of years he will benefit considerably as a result of his thrift. He is nearly thirty-five and, on application to an insurance company, finds that for an annual payment of approximately £100 he will receive £1,000 at the end of ten years, to which profits will be added amounting to approximately £200. Should he die before the expiry of this ten-year term, the sum of £1,000, with such profits as have accumulated, will be paid to his dependents (assuming that he has so directed), and the obligation to continue paying the annual premiums will cease.

A *Whole Life Assurance* policy is looked upon principally as a means of providing for dependents, not as a means of saving money. The assured pays at regular intervals, usually annually, premiums which secure to his dependents, or any persons he may wish to benefit, a capital sum which is payable to them at his death. Policies of this sort may be had with or without profits.

It is also possible to have a policy on the lives of two or more persons, *Joint Life Assurance* as it is called, and the capital sum is paid at the first death. "Last Survivor" policies, as the name implies, pay on the death of the last of those assured.

Another form of policy is *Education Assurance* which makes provision for the payment of agreed sums when a child reaches certain ages (usually the ages of 14, 15, 16 and 17), in return for annual premiums. It is a convenient method of making sure that a child's education will not be prejudiced by the untimely death of a parent. Children's endowment policies are also in common use for this purpose. Somewhat similar policies can be taken out to relieve an estate from the serious burden of death duties. These are called *Estate Duty Assurance.*

If it is desired to secure payment at death only if it occurs within a fixed number of years, this can be effected by a *Term Assurance* policy. At a higher premium, the assured has the option of converting the policy into whole life or endowment, without medical examination or evidence of health. Insurance companies, however, do not often permit the conversion during the last few years of the term.

Another method of making provision for dependents, or for oneself, which is not really a form of insurance at all, is an *Annuity*. This is simply a pension obtained by a cash payment (or cash instalments) to a life insurance company, which contracts to begin disbursing a pension when the assured reaches a previously agreed age. It is possible to arrange an annuity in such a way that the premiums are returnable if the commencing age is not reached.

## SCHEMES FOR MITIGATING THE FEAR OF OLD AGE

There are many forms of group life schemes, but all of them are designed and brought into use with the object of banishing from the minds of employees, the apprehension which increases as a man grows older. The spectre of unemployment and sickness is to some extent kept out of sight by the operation of the existing National Insurance schemes, but there is no national scheme except the meagre old age pension to deal with retiring or disabled employees, and it is the plain duty of an employer to provide for these by Group Life Assurance.

The benefits which may be secured by one or more of the many schemes in operation include the payment of a sum of money at an agreed retiring age, or at death if it occurs first. Some schemes provide for the payment of this sum in the event of total disablement; others, for the payment of the capital sum (at the option of the employee) in the form of a pension. Most, if not all schemes, allow certain advantageous options to the employee who leaves the services of his employer.

In determining the rates of premium to be charged on any particular risk, an Insurance Company will examine the class of work done by different categories of the employees in the firm, the risk of accident, and the mental and physical strain to which they may be subjected. Companies usually require a "group" to be 100 strong, and it is understood that each group is to receive the same benefits and pay the same scale of premiums. It is sometimes advantageous to divide employees into different groups according to the nature of their work, and to vary the benefits applying to each group. Some firms adopt insurance schemes whereby the benefits obtainable by an employee increase with his service with the firm.

Assuming that the risk has been examined in detail and accepted by the Insurance Company, it is usual for a complete schedule of employees to be supplied to the Insurance Company, and the premium is then calculated for the first year on the ages of the employees. If, for example, there are fifteen employees aged 47, then the premium on them would be calculated by multiplying the scale rate for a man of this age by 15. The premium, of course, varies from year to year, and, although the age of each employee is increased at each renewal by one year, the aggregate increase is counteracted by retirement and death. A feature of group life assurance is that most companies dispense with medical examination of employees; after a little thought such a procedure will be seen to be equitable.

The contract of assurance is stated in one policy, although certificates of insurance are frequently issued to each employee. Premiums may be paid either wholly by the employer, or by employer and employee in agreed proportions, and it may interest potential users of these schemes to know that full benefits are obtainable for a very few pence per week.

Although each Company underwriting this form of assurance has its own carefully prepared scheme, an employer may have his own ideas on the subject; in this event he would have no difficulty in obtaining quotations from Insurance Companies on the basis of any suggested scheme of his own.

## HOW TO INSURE AGAINST FRAUD BY THE STAFF

EMPLOYERS may be indemnified by insurance from the risks of embezzlement and fraud on the part of their employees; this is known as "fidelity guarantee" insurance, and is frequently adopted as a precautionary measure in cases where new and untried employees are given positions of trust. Frequently the arrangement of a fidelity bond by the employee himself is made a condition precedent to the offering of a position of trust. However, it is not always considered desirable—or in the best of taste—to impose such a condition on an employee unless the practice is recognised in the firm as a general one applying to all persons employed in positions of trust. For this reason, the " collective " policy is becoming more in vogue, embracing, as it does, all employees falling within certain categories, or, alternatively, the whole staff.

Underwriters take into account a number of obvious factors in determining the premium to be paid for an individual fidelity bond; for example, the largest amount of money to be handled by the employee, the nature of responsibility of his position, his length of service, his past record, his financial position, commitments, and the number and status of his dependents. The rate of premium is usually quite small, and is charged upon the value of the bond. " Collective " policies are naturally " rated " much more favourably from the employer's point of view than policies on individuals, and for this reason, as well as for that mentioned previously, should be considered more desirable than a series of individual fidelity bonds on certain employees. To single out as subjects for fidelity bonds those servants of whom an employer is not sure is a poor exercise in psychology.

## A GUIDE TO FURTHER READING

THOSE who are interested in the subject of insurance will find a host of books dealing with it. The legal aspect of insurance is covered by Chalmers' *Marine Insurance Act, 1906* (Butterworth), and the works of Welford and Otter-Barry on *Accident Assurance* and *Fire Insurance* (Butterworth). More general discussion is contained in Victor Dover's *Handbook to Marine Insurance*; Arnold E. Geilinger's *Motor Vehicle Insurance*; *The Dictionary of Fire Insurance*, issued by the New Era Publishing Co.; and *The Lectures on the Principles and Practice of Insurance*, delivered to Lloyd's Students' Society, and printed by the Corporation of Lloyds. The indispensable works for the practitioner are *The Fire and Marine Insurance Year-Book*, published by Stone & Cox Ltd., and *Lloyd's Calendar*.

# HOW BUSINESS RECORDS ARE KEPT

*by K. W. GRAHAM*

THE great aim and object behind all records and statistics is to save somebody's time. Take any form of record you like and you will find that motive for its existence. The financial columns of the daily paper are a statistical record. If the Editor forgot it one day it would mean that a good many people would have to waste time in finding out by some other means what they wanted to know. Close of Play scores are also statistical records. Think of the time it would take to collect that information for ourselves! The balance sheet of a company is a statistical record, and is always presented in the same way because people have come to expect that information in that way; they can scrutinise it easily and so it saves their time.

This should always be borne in mind when any form of statistical record is prepared. Is it going to save somebody's time? Is it going to save the time of the person for whom it is prepared? Is it presented in the form that shows most information with the least expenditure of time? If "yes" is the answer to all these questions, then it is a good piece of work.

### HOW STATISTICS CAN DELUDE THE UNWARY

VERY nearly the most useful knowledge in statistics is a knowledge of the pitfalls into which an over-zealous statistician can fall. These pitfalls are many and deeply dug, and, in spite of many warnings, people just forget about them and nobody is more surprised than they when they fall into the pit which they themselves have dug. It is just one of the branches of knowledge which people for some unaccountable reason do not apply. Professors of pure statistics say that one should never set out to prove anything by statistics. They say that one should study the figures and allow them to prove what they will. That is all very fine in academic circles, but in business it is impossible to wait for things like that. We have to spur statistics for all they are worth, in order to make them show all they can and as quickly as they can.

It is just because we have to spur them on that we have to be very careful that they do not lead us astray. The sort of thing that is liable to happen when figures are collected and used thoughtlessly is this. Somebody, wanting to create an impression, or merely for the sake of being a nuisance, looks round for something to make a fuss about. He sees a table of figures :

TENNIS RACQUETS.

*Production Plans*, 1935.

| | |
|---|---|
| 25s. . . | 12,000 |
| 30s. . . | 6,000 |
| 35s. . . | 8,500 |
| 40s. . . | 12,000 |

*Fig.* 1.

He wonders if the figures have been arrived at scientifically and proceeds to find out the sales for the previous year. He adds those figures to the table and it now looks like this :

TENNIS RACQUETS.

| | *Production Plans*, 1935. | *Sales*, 1934. |
|---|---|---|
| 25s. . . | 12,000 | 10,000 |
| 30s. . . | 6,000 | 5,000 |
| 35s. . . | 8,500 | 7,000 |
| 40s. . . | 12,000 | 12,000 |

*Fig.* 2.

He looks at these figures and makes a remarkable discovery, as he fondly hoped he would. He sees that the estimated production figures are apparently based on a percentage increase estimate of about 20 per cent. in the case of the 25s., 30s., and 35s. racquets, but that no increase is allowed for in the case of the 40s. racquets. What he should now do is to find out if there is any particular reason for this. But no ; he does not stop to think or ask : he does a set of highly dynamic but very foolish things, and looks the bigger fool when somebody gently tells him that the sales of the 40s. racquets were very unusually high that year and were caused by the Maharajah of Tiffinwallah buying a huge consignment of 3,000 racquets because he wanted to introduce the game into his State as an alternate form of amusement to the practice of trying to assassinate him. Therefore no increase on this unusually high figure could be expected.

This is, of course, a highly improbable and extreme case, as all good demonstration cases must be. But the point is that figures alone can be very misleading, and circumstances can and do play a very important part. The moral is that all figures at all times should be treated with the deepest suspicion and that conclusions should never be drawn until every circumstance has been taken into consideration as far as possible. If this is not done there is a risk that the figures may be quite valueless, and merely a waste of time.

### TWO SINS AND HOW TO AVOID THEM

ANOTHER great pitfall is the danger of showing a busy man statistics which are of no interest to him, though they may be of great interest to other people. In fact, there are sins of commission as well as sins of omission—the sin of omitting essential information which has a bearing on the case, and the sin of putting in stuff that nobody wants. These two sins can be avoided by carefully studying the facts, taking care that all the facts are being studied, and only taking into consideration the facts that matter.

After making sure that the figures can be relied on, the next pitfall to avoid is that of obscurity. As statistics are made to save somebody's time, it follows that the information they contain must be set out in the form that can be most easily and quickly understood. Information of the highest value may be brushed aside just because it is presented in too complicated a form. Even the highest officials are human and therefore will be lazy if encouraged sufficiently by showing them information that is needlessly buried in a mass of figures.

## TELLING THE STORY BY INDEX AND CHART

THE first thing to do after deciding what information is to be shown, is to decide how to show it. One of the golden rules is never to show information in the form of a list if a table will do instead. In some cases, particularly when there are only a few figures to be shown, a list is the only way and the right way. Fig. 1, for instance, is but a list and a very short list. But supposing you had to show sales of tennis racquets not only at each price, but at each weight at each price, you could put the information down like this :

25s.—12 oz. . . . 8
12½ oz. . . . 10
13 oz. . . . 18
13½ oz. . . . 20
14 oz. . . . 2
30s.—12 oz. . . . 5
12½ oz. . . . 6
13 oz. . . . 14
13½ oz. . . . 8
14 oz. . . . 3
40s.—12 oz. . . . 5
12½ oz. . . . 5
13 oz. . . . 11
13½ oz. . . . 15
14 oz. . . . 3
50s.—12 oz. . . . 2
12½ oz. . . . 2
13 oz. . . . 7
13½ oz. . . . 25
14 oz. . . . 1

*Fig*. 3.

Or you could put it down like this :

| Price. | Weights. | | | | |
|---|---|---|---|---|---|
| | 12. | 12½. | 13. | 13½. | 14. |
| 25s. . . | 8 | 10 | 18 | 20 | 2 |
| 30s. . . | 5 | 6 | 14 | 8 | 3 |
| 40s. . . | 5 | 5 | 11 | 15 | 3 |
| 50s. . . | 2 | 2 | 7 | 25 | 1 |

*Fig*. 4.

The table is obviously the better way, and the more figures you have, the more essential it is to tabulate them. This may seem an obvious truth, but it is in actual practice in the hurry of the day that the simplest truths are forgotten. People will not stop to think because they imagine they have got no time even for thought, but what a lot of time quite a little thought would save.

Supposing you were told to get out the sales of these tennis racquets under these headings, and the only way for you to do it was to go through dozens of invoices all thrown together in no sort of order in a drawer. If you did not stop to think at all, it is conceivable that you might make a list of invoices as you came across them and then tabulate the results from that list. But if you tabulate straight away you will be able to save one operation. This can be done by making out a blank table, with the prices ready written down the side and the weights along the top. Then you can go through the invoices, or whatever the documents may be, in any order, placing dots in the correct columns to indicate sales—one dot representing one sale. When you have finished, your table would look like this :

| Price. | Weight. | | | | |
|---|---|---|---|---|---|
| | 12. | 12½. | 13. | 13½. | 14. |
| 25s. . . | ◆◆<br>◆◆<br>◆◆<br>◆<br>◆ | ◆◆<br>◆◆<br>◆◆<br>◆◆<br>◆◆ | ◆◆◆◆<br>◆◆◆◆<br>◆◆◆◆<br>◆◆◆<br>◆◆◆ | ◆◆◆◆<br>◆◆◆◆<br>◆◆◆◆<br>◆◆◆◆<br>◆◆◆◆ | ◆<br>◆ |
| 30s. . . | ◆<br>◆<br>◆<br>◆<br>◆ | ◆◆<br>◆<br>◆<br>◆<br>◆ | ◆◆◆<br>◆◆◆<br>◆◆◆<br>◆◆◆<br>◆◆ | ◆◆<br>◆◆<br>◆◆<br>◆<br>◆ | ◆<br>◆<br>◆ |
| 40s. . . | ◆<br>◆<br>◆<br>◆<br>◆ | ◆<br>◆<br>◆<br>◆<br>◆ | ◆◆◆<br>◆◆<br>◆◆<br>◆◆<br>◆◆ | ◆◆◆<br>◆◆◆<br>◆◆◆<br>◆◆◆<br>◆◆◆ | ◆<br>◆<br>◆ |
| 50s. . . | ◆<br>◆ | ◆<br>◆ | ◆◆<br>◆◆<br>◆<br>◆<br>◆ | ◆◆◆◆◆<br>◆◆◆◆◆<br>◆◆◆◆◆<br>◆◆◆◆◆<br>◆◆◆◆◆ | ◆ |

*Fig.* 5.

You will notice that in some ways this is a better table than Fig. 4, because it shows graphically where the sales bulk and the eye is at once drawn to the best combinations of price and weight. And it saves time, because it enables you to tabulate in one operation without making any lists and without having to sort the information into groups. This is just the sort of thing that people read about in the quiet seclusion of their homes and forget completely in the rush of actual practice. And yet what a lot of time these things can save.

### EXPANDING THE TABLE TO COVER NEW FACTORS

FIG. 4 shows the way to set out information when there are two factors—in this case price and weight. What happens when there are three or more factors ? The first thing that we must resign ourselves to is the fact that on paper we have only two dimensions to play with, and that, although we can make beautifully clear tables using two dimensions, we cannot use three dimensions to show three factors. We've got to think of the best way of using two dimensions. And, furthermore, we shall have to realise that the more factors we have to show, the less clearly shall we be able to show them.

Suppose in our table we have to introduce another factor, say, the size of handle in which there are three sizes, A, B, and C. We can show the information by splitting the price lines like this :

<table>
<tr><td colspan="2"></td><td>12</td><td>12½</td><td>13</td><td>13½</td></tr>
<tr><td rowspan="3">25s.</td><td>A</td><td></td><td></td><td></td><td></td></tr>
<tr><td>B</td><td></td><td></td><td></td><td></td></tr>
<tr><td>C</td><td></td><td></td><td></td><td></td></tr>
</table>

*Fig.* 6.

Or we can show it by splitting the weight columns like this :

<table>
<tr><td rowspan="2"></td><td colspan="3">12.</td><td colspan="3">12½.</td><td colspan="3">13.</td></tr>
<tr><td>A</td><td>B</td><td>C</td><td>A</td><td>B</td><td>C</td><td>A</td><td>B</td><td>C</td></tr>
<tr><td>25s.</td><td></td><td></td><td></td><td></td><td></td><td></td><td></td><td></td><td></td></tr>
<tr><td>30s.</td><td></td><td></td><td></td><td></td><td></td><td></td><td></td><td></td><td></td></tr>
</table>

*Fig.* 7.

Or we can have separate tables for each size of handle. The choice will be guided by the most important total. If we want to know the total number of racquets *sold at a price* more than the total sold at a weight or in each size of handle, we shall show it in the form of Fig. 7. If we want to know the total number of racquets sold in each weight more than the others, we shall show it in the form of Fig. 6.

## HOW TO COLLECT INFORMATION

THE tables we have been looking at so far have really been summaries. In order to make them we should have had first of all to collect the information, and the collection of information is almost a subject in itself. It is fairly easy when the number of items or groups is small, as in the examples given so far. But when the items become very large it is worth while installing a system merely to record the first details. It must be noted, however, that the first recording should also summarise as well, so far as this is possible—because it saves time.

Suppose the general manager of our tennis racquet manufacturing firm wants full and up-to-date daily details of sales of his racquets in price, weight, and size of handle, made by all his agents. The way to do it is a card-index system. Why on a card? Why not in a book? There are many reasons. Cards can be sorted into any order you like. If the information overflows one card, you can insert another. If a dealer ceases to be a dealer through death or dishonesty, his card can be extracted and thrown away. You can take out the cards you want for reference and leave the others behind to be worked on, thus not holding up the work of recording the information.

It is true you can also do this in the case of a loose-leaf book. But if the leaves are to have a lot of handling, their life will not be a long one. Moreover, the leaves of a book do not lend themselves to the manipulation, by machinery or otherwise, that is possible in the case of cards. Cards can be filed in a variety of ways so that a little bit of each card is in view, and you can write an indication of the nature of the card on the visible part so that the cards can each be found quickly. If cards are filed vertically, the visible index is made by having a small tag on the top of the card. The cards are filed in such a way that each tag is a little to one side of the tag on the cards next to it, and so each tag is made visible, and one tag does not obscure another.

This is not a very good way of doing things except when the number of cards is few. A better way is to have your

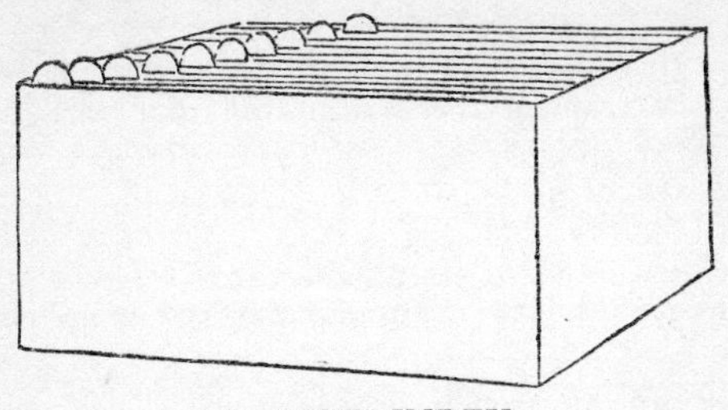

8. CARD INDEX

*A system suitable for a small number of cards.*

cards in cabinets made specially for the purpose. These cabinets contain trays and the trays contain pockets into which the cards are fitted. The pockets overlap in such a way that a strip at the bottom of each card is left exposed to view.

In the illustration you will see that each card has a visible strip, equal in length to the length of the card, and a considerable amount of information can be written on this slip. By looking down the visible strips you can see the essentials of the information on the card, and when you have found anything that particularly interests you, you refer to the card itself, by turning back the cards on top of it, in order to get further particulars.

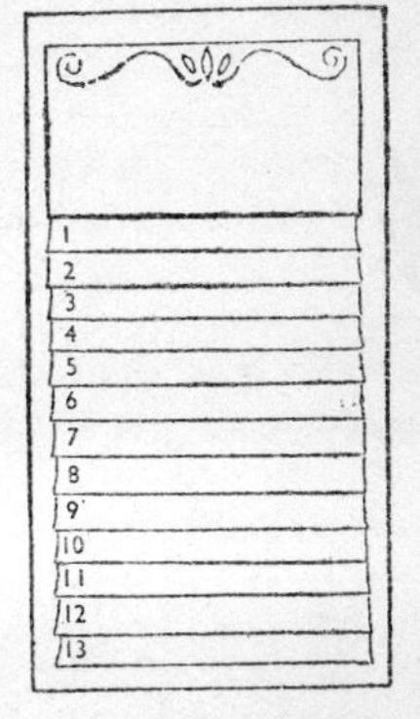


9. CARD INDEX

These special arrangements are made for the main purpose of indexing the information contained in the cards, and this means that particular cards or groups of cards can be more easily found. This is sometimes done by having cards with numbered perforations round the edges.

Now suppose you wanted these cards kept so that all cards recording information on tennis racquets of the same price were to be found in a bunch together, but at the same time you wanted to arrange that you could find all the cards that referred to the same weight. You would do this by assigning one particular hole in the card to each weight—the weight would be given a number and the hole would bear the same number on every card. Then on each card on which information about that particular weight was recorded you would clip away the edge of the card round that particular hole. Suppose 12 oz. was weight No. 4, then on every card that referred to racquets of that weight you would clip away the edge from hole No. 4 (Fig. 10).

When you wanted to see all the cards referring to weight No. 4, you would take a thin rod like the homely knitting-

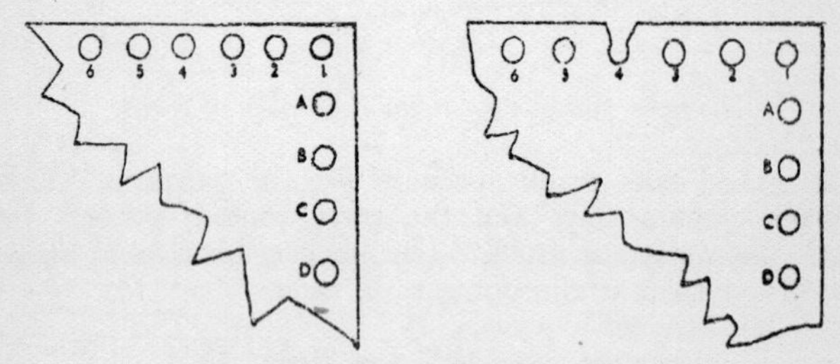


10. A SELECTIVE CARD INDEX

*The diagram shows the arrangement of holes, with one broken to allow a group-selection of the cards by means of a thin rod.*

needle and push it through hole No. 4 in the batch of cards. You would then lift the cards up a little by the rod and shake them. Those cards which had hole No. 4 intact would, of course, remain on the rod, while those cards on which hole No. 4 had been clipped away would fall out, because there would be nothing to hold the card.

### A "THERMOMETER" THAT TELLS THE TEMPERATURE OF SALES

THE design of the cards in any card-index system needs a lot of thought in order to get the best possible form. The circumstances in each particular case are the only guide, and each case must be judged on its own merits. This leaves plenty of scope for ingenuity and a great deal of fun can be had from designing weird rulings for special occasions. For instance, suppose you had to record sales and stock of an article that sold very fast and was therefore coming in hard all the time and going out equally quickly. At any one time the latest information on the card might read something like this : Stock 1,264. Sales for the last five days 12, 7, 13, 15, 4, and so on daily. The problem is: Should you order some more or have you a sufficient number of weeks' supply in stock ?

The card as it is does not show that, and it would not show it unless the weekly sales or the monthly sales were totalled—a long job if there were many cards like it. Even when totalled, a certain amount of calculation would be necessary to find the number of weeks' supply in stock. Now suppose you had a card ruled as shown.

When stock comes in you draw a line down the "thermometer" column against the graduations which show the quantity. When stock is sold another line is drawn in the adjacent column, and this line is marked off at the end of the week. Then the difference in the length of the lines will give the size of the stock in hand, and it is an easy matter to match by eye the length of this difference against the past sales and to see how many weeks' supply it represents.

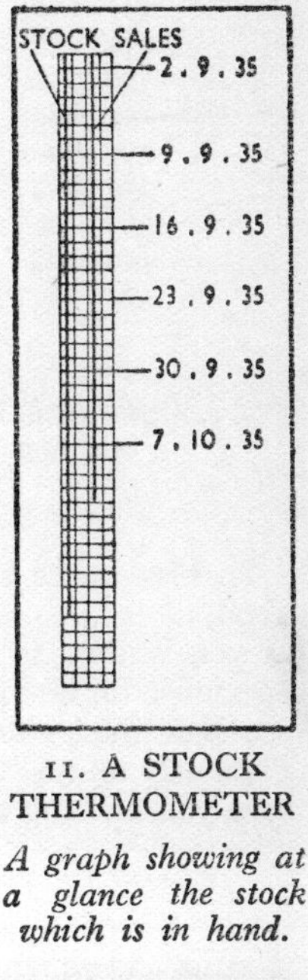

11. A STOCK THERMOMETER

*A graph showing at a glance the stock which is in hand.*

## SOME USEFUL WAYS OF SHOWING FACTS

THE use of averages is another way of saving time. It is plainly quicker to say that a cricketer's average is 63·8 for a certain period than to recite the totals of all his innings during that period. The difficulty is that averages of this sort are sometimes of little use in business. Suppose you had a multiple shoe store with a hundred branches. If you wanted information of the sort of trade each branch was doing—high class, medium, or low—a hundred tables would have to be made like Fig. 12, showing the sales at each price of the range in each branch. But what a job to look at a hundred tables of that kind and to extract that information from them! How could time be saved and useful information also given? What you want to do is to express the important features of each table in a single number if possible, and the way to do it is to find an average for each case.

SALES OF SHOES.

| Price | Pairs | Quartile |
|---|---|---|
| 8s. 11d. | 300 | |
| 9s. 11d. | 2,200 | |
| 12s. 11d. | 1,600 | —1st Quartile. |
| 15s. 11d. | 1,000 | |
| D—19s. 11d. | 800 | —2nd Quartile (Median). |
| B—25s. 9d. | 200 | |
| A—29s. 6d. | 3,500 | —3rd Quartile. |
| 35s. 9d. | 500 | |
| C—39s. 6d. | 600 | |
| 45s. 9d. | 200 | |
| 49s. 6d. | 100 | —Top Quartile. |
| | 11,000 | |

*The quartiles show how the numbers of pairs of shoes can be divided into four equal parts covering four price ranges.*

*Fig.* 12.

In Fig. 12 the average number of shoes sold at one price is 1000, *i.e.* 11,000 divided by 11. But is that very interesting? If you wanted to sell equal quantities at each price and not specialise on one price, then you could look at each table and see how the prices differed from the average. But there is obviously no real benefit to be gained by that, and it certainly tells you nothing about the level of trade.

#### MEANS OF DISCOVERING THE "FASHIONABLE" PRICE

BUT fortunately there are other kinds of average besides this one which is called the arithmetic mean. First, there is the *Mode*. The mode is "the measure that most frequently occurs." In Fig. 12 more shoes were sold at 29s. 6d. than at any other price; 29s. 6d. (A) is therefore the mode—the price which is, as it were, *à la mode*. This is an interesting and useful figure. Instead of looking at 100 tables, you need only look at one table of 100 modes, and it would tell you the most popular price at each branch, which would be some sort of measure of the class of trade you would be doing there. The mode of your Bond Street salon would perhaps be

49s. 6d., and the mode of your Mile End junk shop would be 8s. 11d.

Another kind of average is the *Median*, " the measure of the middle item." This can be rather confusing, as the question arises " The middle of what ? " In Fig. 12 one can find at least three " middle " items. If you take the prices in the order of their own magnitude, then the middle price, as it is a series of eleven prices, is the sixth price, and this is found to be 25s. 9d. (B). If you take the prices in the order of the magnitude of the sales at each price, then 39s. 6d. is the middle price (C). If you take the price such that the total number of shoes sold above that price is equal to the total number of shoes sold below that price, then that is a middle price from another point of view. In this case 5,100 shoes were sold above 19s. 11d. and an equal number were sold below 19s. 11d. (D).

Again this is a thing which depends on particular circumstances. In this particular case it would probably be most useful to take the middle price of the sales as a total, *i.e.* 19s. 11d. But in almost every case there is scope for a great saving of time and also for finding out things which have never before been realised because they have not been made apparent by simple tables.

If information is wanted on how the sales tend to distribute themselves over the price range, it can be obtained by the use of quartiles. In Fig. 12 the total sales are 11,000. A quarter of this is 2,750. The sales at the two lowest prices together total 2,500, while the three lowest add up to 4,100. Therefore the point which is a quarter of the way up the sales scale lies within the group at 12s. 11d. This price is then the first or bottom quartile. Half-way up is 5,500, and this lies in the group at 19s. 11d. Three-quarters of the way up the sales scale is 8,250, and this lies in the 29s. 6d. group, which is the third quartile.

In order to compare the position of the quartiles in actual prices, it is a good thing to draw a line against the prices, or to bracket them, showing the range of the quartile; this can be very useful indeed where you have a large number of tables to look at in showing where sales bulk. For instance, in Fig. 12 the top quartile is spread over four prices, while the middle two quartiles cover only two prices each.

Averages of all kinds have very useful properties which

amply repay a trial, but they are things which people read about and then just don't apply.

### HOW TO MAKE GRAPHS AND CHARTS

GRAPHS and charts are great time savers is used properly. It is very difficult to see from long columns of figures just how each series rises and falls, and how those fluctuations compare with fluctuations in other series of figures. But one can see at a glance the rise and fall of a line plotted on paper, and it is easy to compare the curves of several lines. As it is sound policy to talk about a number of useful things in the order in which they are most liable to be neglected, logarithmic or ratio charts must undoubtedly be put first.

Most people who plot statistics on squared paper have only heard of the ordinary squared paper—they have not realised that there is such a thing as logarithmically ruled paper. Yet for business purposes it is probably logarithmic paper which is the more useful. The people who have heard of it have probably been frightened away by the imposing name—doubtless thinking that only eminent mathematicians with shocks of hair and bulging foreheads can ever hope to use such complicated aids to success. They are quite wrong. It is, of course, interesting to know the fundamental reasons for everything, but no mathematical knowledge at all is required to make and use logarithmic graphs, and the word logarithmic need have no terrors—in fact, it can merely be used for impressing people and lending an air of distinction to the office, after which it can be quietly forgotten.

A logarithmic chart is shown in Fig. 15. If you are of a timid nature you will probably be horrified to see that the horizontal lines are not drawn with equal spaces between them. The reason for this apparently strange proceeding is really quite simple. Suppose we take a piece of " ordinary " or arithmetically ruled paper and we take ten horizontal lines and give them values of one to ten as in Fig. 13.

If we then draw a line plotting an increase of one unit for each distance along the base line, we get a line, as shown in Fig. 13 from X to Y. This line records an equal rise for each unit. That is to say, the rise from 5 to 6 is represented on the chart by the same vertical distance as the rise from 2 to 3.

Now the percentage rise of 2 to 3 is 50 per cent., *i.e.* a rise of one on two. But the percentage rise of 5 to 6 is only 20 per

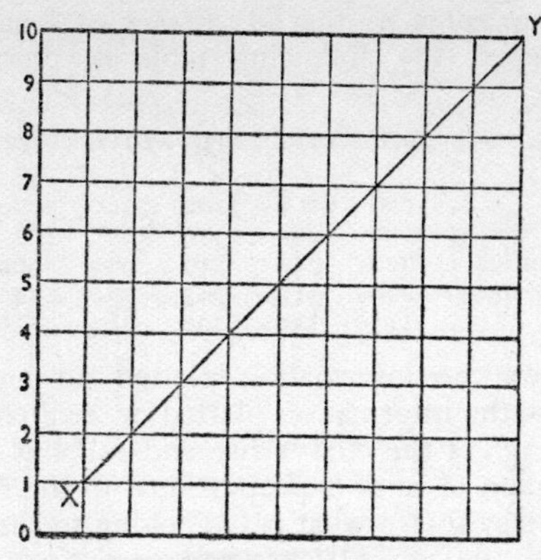


*Fig.* 13

cent., *i.e.* one on five. Yet these different percentage rises are shown by the *same* rise in the chart. So that if you want to show *percentage* increases or decreases, arithmetic paper is no good to you at all. Instead you have to use paper ruled in such a way that increases or decreases of the same amount *per cent.* are represented by equal vertical distances on the paper. Paper which is so ruled is called logarithmic paper.

### AN ANSWER TO THOSE WHO SHUN EVERYTHING NEW

PEOPLE are so very frightened of new things that they will go to great pains to think up reasons why they should not adopt them. It is really a form of laziness. If they spent less time in being obstructive, and used that time to acquire an understanding of new things, it would be a grand thing for themselves and everybody concerned. These people will ask at this juncture why percentage and ratio results need be shown at all? The answer is that heads of firms often ask such questions as: What percentage increase has department A made compared with department B? What percentage of our sales is now done in territory C? Is the proportion of our stocks to our sales going up or down? How is the percentage of advertising to total costs varying? In short, there are quite as many questions asked about percentage variation as there are about actual variation. Even at the very end of all our labours, the profit we make is handed out to the shareholders in dividends of so much *per cent.*

To illustrate some of the advantages of logarithmic over arithmetic paper, the following table is plotted on both kinds:

| | 1928. | 1929. | 1930. | 1931. | 1932. | 1933. | 1934. |
|---|---|---|---|---|---|---|---|
| | £ | £ | £ | £ | £ | £ | £ |
| Sales . . . | 5000 | 6000 | 7200 | 7300 | 7000 | 6000 | 8000 |
| Total Costs . . | 1000 | 1200 | 1300 | 1800 | 1620 | 1700 | 1900 |
| Travellers' Salaries . | 620 | 740 | 740 | 900 | 900 | 840 | 1200 |
| Travellers' Expenses. | 260 | 315 | 345 | 750 | 540 | 700 | 440 |
| Advertising . . | 115 | 150 | 200 | 160 | 150 | 150 | 250 |

Fig. 15 shows the information plotted on log paper and Fig. 14 shows the information plotted on ordinary arithmetic paper. In Fig. 14 the curves rise and fall but do not show if the fluctuation of sales is proportional to the fluctuation of costs. It is easy to see what is happening to the big figures, but the small ones are obscure and deceptive. Fig. 14, for instance, offers no obvious reason for the marked increase in sales for 1934.

Fig. 15 shows things very differently. It brings out the variations in the curves and shows the smaller details in their right proportion to the larger ones. The increase in sales is seen to follow a sharp increase in advertising costs. It also gives a true picture of the percentage of each item of the costs to the total costs and to the total sales.

One of the lesser beauties of this type of chart is the fact that the actual percentage figures can be measured off by using a suitable scale. This scale can be made simply by cutting off a strip of the same paper used for the chart itself. If you want to find out what percentage one value is of another, you place the top of the scale, as in the illustration, against the higher value, and read off the percentage of the lower value on the strip. Thus the illustration shows that the total cost of selling was 20 per cent. of the sales in 1931 and that advertising was responsible for about 2·5 per cent. of this.

The *increase* that one value represents on a lower value is measured by putting the *lower* end of the strip on the lower value and reading off the percentage of the higher value on the strip. The *decrease* that one value represents on a higher value is measured by placing the *top* end of the strip against the higher value and reading off the percentage on the strip against the lower value.

## FOUR THINGS A LOG CHART DOES WELL

To sum up some of the uses of log paper (1) Equal percentage increases or decreases are shown by equal rises or falls of the curves. (2) The actual proportion of any value to any other value can be measured off by using a suitable scale. (3) Both very small and very large numbers can be plotted on the *same* scale on the *same* sheet of paper, and yet give clear results. (4) Actual *amounts* can still be read off the scale. It must be remembered, however, that log paper must *not* be used when *amount* is the only thing that matters and *percentage* is of no value.

If the foregoing inspires anybody to use log paper for the first time, the first difficulty he will find is that of buying the actual paper. It is amazing how few people sell it. A good selection of log paper is kept by Messrs. Wightman Mountain Ltd., Artillery House, Artillery Row, Westminster, S.W.1, and by Messrs. W. F. Stanley & Co. Ltd., 286 High Holborn, London, W.C.1. The second difficulty will be the actual plotting of the lines. You will see that the scale has no zero. The reason is a mathematical one and need not concern us now. The bottom line is always 10 or a multiple or sub-multiple of 10, such as 100, 10,000, ·1 or ·01.

In Fig. 15 the bottom line is 100. The next horizontal line is 110, the next 120, and so on by ten's up to 500. Here the lines are getting so close together that the printer thought it would be a good idea to leave out every alternate line and so they now go on by 20's,—500, 520, 540 and so on by 20's to 1,000. Here it looks as if the whole thing became desperate and started afresh at the beginning again, but really it goes straight on. What has happened is that the lines have been getting too close together again and the printer has left out some more lines. The lines carry on by 100's now, 1,100, 1,200, 1,300, etc. When plotting figures people are apt to get caught out at the points where the printer leaves out some more lines, that is to say at the 5 and 10 lines when the space of the line alters.

When choosing paper you will be asked how many "cycles" you want. A cycle is 1–10 or 10–100, in fact from the bottom to where it looks as if it were all starting again. The number of cycles you want on your paper depends on the range between the highest and the lowest numbers you have

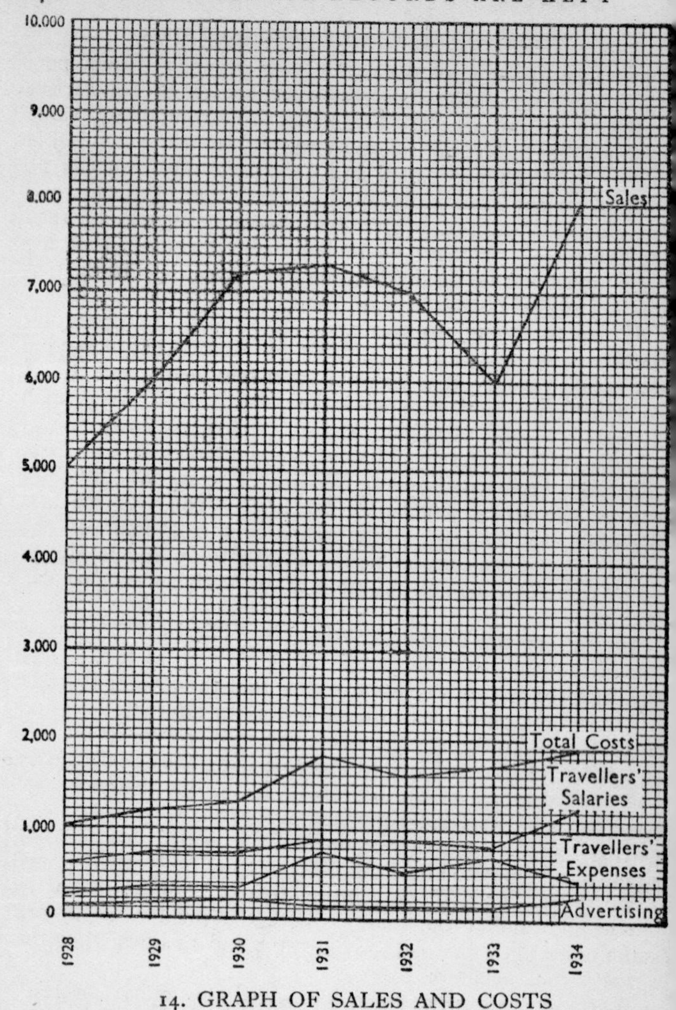


14. GRAPH OF SALES AND COSTS

*Here ordinary graph paper is used, sales and costs are plotted in pounds sterling vertically, and the years are plotted horizontally. This type of graph indicates the relative amounts of the various items plotted, but the scale does not permit of an adequate representation of variations in the smaller sums.*

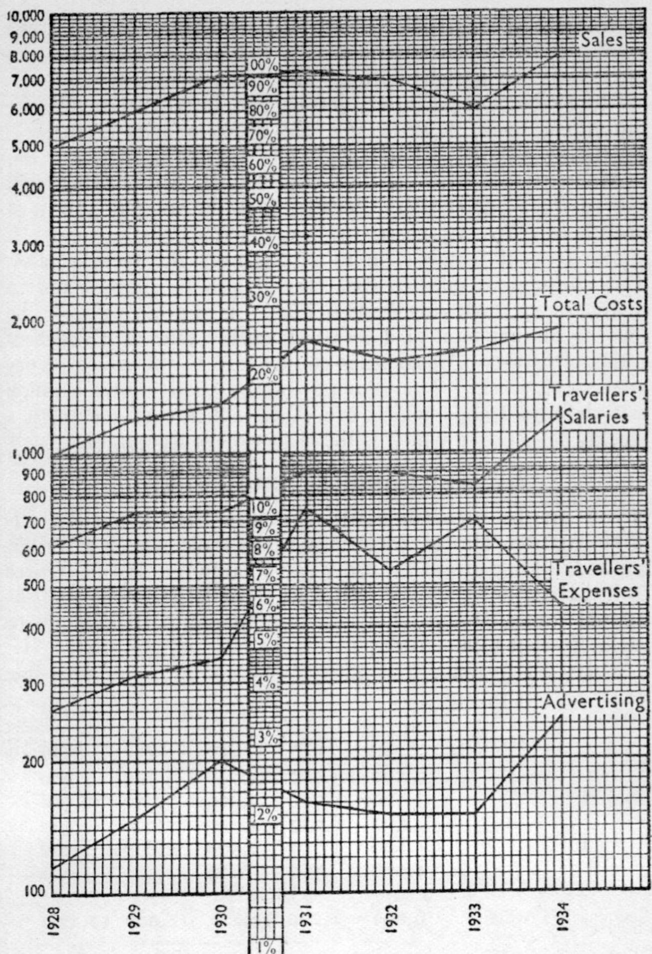


15. LOGARITHMIC GRAPH CORRESPONDING TO FIG. 14

*On this paper the variations in large and small sums are shown equally well, whilst equal percentage increases and decreases are shown by equal rises and falls of the curves. The strip marked in percentages is being used to show all other items as percentages of the sales in 1931.* [*W. F. Stanley & Co. Ltd.*

to record. Three-cycle paper, that which makes two fresh starts, is the most commonly used and gives a range of 1 to 10,000, or a range of multiples of these two figures.

More about logarithmic graphs can be found in W. G. Sutcliffe's book, *Statistics for the Business Man* (Harper & Brothers).

Many people who use line charts quite freely fail to get the best use out of them, because they do not plot the most useful figures. In cases of sales charts, for instance, it shows lack of imagination to plot merely the weekly sales. The cumulative sales to date should also be plotted and in many cases a " Moving Annual Total " is of great value. The moving annual total of a series of weekly sales is a series of totals of fifty-two weeks sales counted up to the end of every successive week. The moving annual total shows gradual but definite trends which are often difficult to see from a weekly sales curve which is liable to violent fluctuation.

### FIGURES PICTURED BY THE BAR GRAPH

BAR graphs save some time because they can show information almost pictorially, but their scope is rather limited. They are of no use when a large number of figures is involved, but they are useful to show large totals, such as annual totals, and to show the component parts that go to make up that total.

Take, for instance, the sales of five commodities over five years set out in Fig. 16 :

| Commodity. | 1930. | 1931. | 1932. | 1933. | 1934. |
|---|---|---|---|---|---|
| A . . | 1,500 | 3,300 | 3,700 | 3,500 | 3,500 |
| B . . | 1,500 | 1,700 | 2,000 | 3,000 | 2,500 |
| C . . | 1,200 | 1,500 | 2,000 | 2,000 | 2,500 |
| D . . | 800 | 1,000 | 1,500 | 2,000 | 1,500 |
| E . . | 1,000 | 500 | 800 | 1,500 | 2,000 |
| Totals . | 6,000 | 8,000 | 10,000 | 12,000 | 12,000 |

*Fig.* 16.

These sales are far more clearly demonstrated by the bar graph in Fig. 17.

A " pie-chart " is sometimes used to demonstrate this type of information, but is not a very good way of doing it. First it takes a long time to make, as the quantities concerned have to be reduced to degrees in a circle ; and secondly it is not easy for the eye to measure differences in the area of circles or the arcs of their sectors.

In practice, bar charts can be very useful as they lend themselves sometimes to ingenious methods of daily adjustment. For instance perhaps, somebody wants to know daily the daily sales and stocks of a number of items, and how the

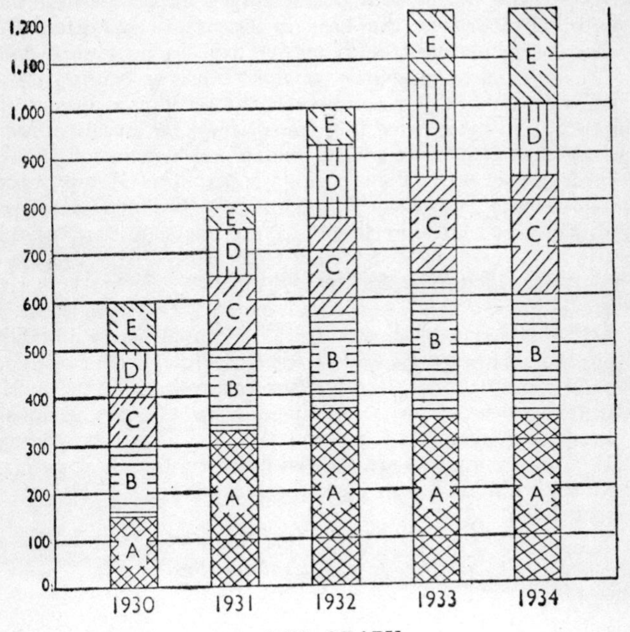


17. BAR GRAPH.

stocks in hand compare with the sales. He can have hung up in his office a large square of board with graduations ruled on it to indicate quantities of sales and stocks. Placed round this board, vertically, would be bands of ribbon, part of each band being coloured and the rest white. The bars of colour on the bands form bar graphs which register against the scale on the board, and the height of these bars can be adjusted in a few seconds by pulling the band of ribbon round one way or the other.

## A GUIDE TO FURTHER READING

It is not possible to discuss in a short section all the methods by which important business records can be kept, but sufficient has been said, perhaps, to indicate the wide range of possibilities afforded by statistics. The first necessity for those who wish to pursue the subject further is to get a sound knowledge of the basic principles of statistics. A brilliantly simple yet comprehensive exposition of these will be found in *An Introduction to the Theory of Statistics*, by G. Udney Yule (C. Griffin & Co.), the recognised master of the subject in his generation. *Statistics for the Business Man*, by W. G. Sutcliffe, is a lucid and practical account of the general aspect of statistics, and *Statistics in Theory and Practice*, by L. R. Conner (Pitman), and *Budgetary Control of Distribution*, by Grisell (Hamilton), are also sound and useful books. More specialised accounts of card indexing are contained in *Filing Systems*, by Edward A. Cope (Pitman); *Indexing and Filing*, by Hudders (Ronald Press); and *Modern Office Machinery*, by Foster (Gee). Graphs are admirably discussed in *Charts and their Use in Purchasing*, by L. H. D. Acland (International Management Institute). These books and many others can be obtained from the Management Library, 23 Bloomsbury Square, W.C.1. This is a lending library, and the books are allowed out for a month at a time. As most technical books are rather expensive, this library is a great boon.

# BUSINESS AS A CAREER

*by J. E. BRUTON, B.Sc. (Hons. Econ. Lond.), Principal, Upper Hornsey Road, L.C.C. Commercial Institute*

A NEW type of business man is rapidly evolving. It used to be a commonplace that the cleverest children at school entered the Civil Service or became professional men—doctors, solicitors, barristers, accountants, teachers—and that the less brilliant entered the business world. That is not now true. Modern large-scale organisation implies staffing schemes comparable to those of large Government Departments, and the successful applicant must depend more upon his own personal qualities and less upon " knowing someone " in authority. Even should recommendation gain him a post, ability alone will enable him to retain it. The ideal man for business is one whose educational qualifications give him the respect of his colleagues and who, in addition, possesses a forceful but pleasing personality, abundance of tact and good humour, and an up-to-date mind, ever on the alert for methods of improving the technique of his business. His character and reputation must be beyond reproach, for a good name in business is a valuable asset.

In the multitudinous organisations that collectively make up the business world it is not difficult to make out at least four distinct grades amongst those employed. The lowest grade comprises messengers, telephone attendants, and office-boys, who perform work requiring little or no training and no responsibility. In the next grade are to be found those performing routine work demanding special knowledge or skill but little or no initiative and responsibility ; these are typists, book-keepers, correspondence clerks. The third grade is made up of those who have the responsibility for special departments—assistant managers, sales managers, accountants, production controllers, staff managers, buyers, travellers. In the highest grade are those responsible for the activities of the concern as a whole—managing directors, company secretaries, general managers, chief accountants, area managers.

These appointments may also be classified from the point

of view of the activities of the business. There are three distinct groups. There is the factory group, which undertakes all activities connected with the purchase of raw material, manufacturing and productive processes, works management, and research work. Here are to be found engineers, technical experts, works managers, staff managers, costs and works accountants. Another group is the sales group, which undertakes marketing, forwarding, advertising, and publicity. The most important men in this group are salesmen, brokers, sales-managers, travelling representatives, and publicity managers. Finally comes the financial and executive group which undertakes secretarial, accounting, and financial activities. This is the group which contains the three most important men in the business, the managing-director or general manager, the chief secretary and the chief accountant.

## FROM SCHOOL TO JOB: STARTING AT THE BOTTOM

The particular stage at which a newcomer enters business is determined largely by the type of school he has attended. The elementary school boy usually enters the first grade. Just before leaving school he and his parents are invited to attend an After-Care Conference consisting of the head teacher, representatives of the Employment Exchange, the heads of local technical and commercial educational institutions, and secretaries of social organisations. The boy's school record and his natural abilities are discussed, he is advised as to his future work and education, and his name is placed on the "live" register of the local Employment Exchange. The majority of elementary school "leavers" obtain their first posts in this way, or by their own personal approach to a local employer. It is very important for a boy to obtain a post while actually at school, so that there is not a gap between leaving school and entering the business world. It will be seen that these boys start in business at an early age and with a definite handicap as regards their educational equipment. They start in the lowest grade, but if they make use of all the opportunities for continuing their education, they have every prospect of passing into the second grade and even the third grade, for they have one great advantage—they will eventually have gone through every section of the work.

### THE BOY WHO BEGAN HIS TRAINING AT SCHOOL

THE Central School boy starts in a much better position. He has the advantage of possessing a knowledge of French, Book-keeping, Shorthand, Typing, and Business Economics, and so naturally fits into the second grade. In fact, he is a serious rival to the secondary school boy who has not specialised at school and who therefore comes into business less well-equipped commercially. On the other hand, he is not so well placed for passing professional examinations, for the secondary school boy has usually passed the Matriculation examination, which exempts him from the first examination of all professional examining bodies. Boys attending Central Schools are placed in business either direct by the head teacher or by a special department of the Ministry of Labour.

Boys attending Secondary Schools are assisted by the joint efforts of the Incorporated Association of Head Masters and Headmistresses of Public Secondary Schools and of the Ministry of Labour. In addition to the actual placing of scholars, these bodies issue very cheap pamphlets in a *Choice of Careers* series. Each pamphlet deals with a separate vocation and explains very clearly the nature of the employment, its possibilities, the way to enter it, its educational requirements, and the particular organisations to which to apply in the first instance. These pamphlets cost but a few pence, and are invaluable. They may be obtained at H.M. Stationery Office, Kingsway. Many of the large public schools have careers officers whose special duties are to watch the boy through the school, to get a personal knowledge of him, to compile data of his record at school, and to assist him to enter that civil or military career best suited for him. These officers frequently keep in touch with their old boys, who in turn, assist in placing their successors.

### THE UNIVERSITY MAN IN BUSINESS

THE University student leaves at about the age of twenty-two, and he has behind him the assistance of the University Appointments Board. This board, which varies slightly at each University, interviews those graduates needing help, and does a great deal to place students in appointments at home and abroad. The type of business man with small academic qualifications is disappearing, and with him goes the unreasonable antipathy to the university man in business. The graduate enters business at a much later age than the other applicants, and his training tends to make him more fitted for responsibility than for routine work. In the professions, and in certain specialised industries, degrees and diplomas are absolutely necessary, but in general business houses, a university qualification is not regarded as essential. The possession of a degree of Bachelor of Science (Economics) or Bachelor of Commerce is proof certain that the holder has enjoyed a sound theoretical training in the chief branches of modern business, and that he has, in addition, a trained mind.

In many business houses, notably on the railways, graduates are allowed to pass right through to the higher grades without having to submit to the ordinary requirements. Such graduates are regarded as being in training, and during that period they receive a nominal salary only, but promotion afterwards is usually very rapid, and there is no upper limit to their advancement. A university training is of little value if the graduate does not possess also a good personality, and an adaptability which enables him to use his opportunities to the greatest advantage. Personality without education will often take a man farther than education without personality, but personality with education may take a man anywhere.

## GETTING A JOB AND "GETTING ON"

THE day a young man starts out on his first job is a red-letter day for him. Happy is he who strikes lucky in securing a post which he likes, and which offers scope for advancement to a position of responsibility and trust. Waiting lists are in most cases long, and application should be made a long time (in some cases years) before the post is actually required. Those wishing to enter Banks should, for instance, see the local managers at an early date. Although the majority of posts are filled through school organisations, a large number of firms still use the medium of advertisements. The most widely used papers for this purpose are the national and the trade journals, which are to be seen displayed daily in the corridors of public libraries.

The applicant should exercise great care in answering advertisements, or he will never be called up for an interview. He should write the letter in his own handwriting, on good paper, and in good style, and he should enclose a stamped addressed envelope for reply. There must be no mistakes in spelling, and no grammatical errors. The letter must be simple and short, and there must be no boasting in it. The most effective type is one which begins: "I wish to apply for the post advertised in to-day's *Daily Echo*. The statement I enclose gives full particulars of my educational experience and of my references. Will you please grant me an interview at your early convenience?" References are always needed, and the school reference is all important. The applicant must arrive at the interview in time, and attend to his personal appearance. He should look neat and behave naturally. He must avoid being pert or argumentative—on the other hand there is no need to be humble. He will create the best impression if he answers up smartly, and does not make the fatal mistake of pretending to be what he knows he is not.

### PREPARING TO ADVANCE: SPARE-TIME STUDENTS' CLASSES

Just as those in the employment of professional men should aim at obtaining the highest qualifications in that profession, so too those in business should aim at getting the fullest acquaintance with the organisation of the whole business as well as that of their own section. The influence of supervisors and managers is of the greatest importance in securing promotion. The beginner should study them, and try to be regarded as dependable and capable. Some at any rate of his spare time should be devoted to increasing his knowledge. Fortunately for those who enter business before getting expert qualifications, there are ample facilities for study in spare time. In London and in the great provincial towns there are private business colleges, such as Pitman's, Clark's, and Gregg's, which offer sound commercial training at reasonable fees. Education authorities provide Polytechnics where almost every subject needed in industry and commerce is taught. Some of these Polytechnics are "recognised" training centres for particular industries. The fees are exceptionally low, and full courses in most subjects can be obtained for roughly £2 to £3 per session.

There are also the highly organised Technical and Commercial Evening Institutes which offer evening tuition in all technical subjects, and also in Book-keeping, Accountancy, Shorthand, Typewriting, Languages, Banking, Law, Economics, Insurance, Shipping, Salesmanship, Advertising,

Surveying—to mention but a few. The fees at Junior Institutes are only 4s. for a complete course, and at the Senior Institutes 12s. to 18s. per session for six hours' tuition per week. The staff engaged at these Institutes are all practical business experts with university qualifications and diplomas. Some Institutes specialise in Banking, some in Insurance, some in Stock Exchange, others in Law. Those who are not fortunate enough to be able to attend day classes will have little difficulty in finding somewhere an evening class which will give them the best possible tuition in the subject they require. Full particulars of London Institutes may be obtained from the Education Officer, County Hall, S.E.1., or from the Principal of any of the Institutes. Students of Commercial Institutes have the advantage of a scheme for placing them in positions in the commercial world. This scheme has been drafted by representatives of the London County Council and of the Ministry of Labour, and has proved very successful.

## WOMAN'S PLACE IN THE BUSINESS WORLD

WOMEN are found now everywhere in business, and the questions already discussed apply to them as well as to men. Women are very suitable for the teaching, medical, and nursing professions, for social and welfare work, for secretarial and administrative posts in the Civil Service, for the catering trades, and as housekeepers and matrons of Institutions. In business also there is great scope for women's services. In factories and shops they may become supervisors, departmental managers, head saleswomen, and staff managers. There is also a mass of work on the clerical side of a business for which their neatness makes them peculiarly fitted—dealing with correspondence, keeping record files up to date, and the like. Above all, there are a large number of secretarial posts. Girls usually make good secretaries, and secretaries, on account of their close contact with the heads of the business, and the wide knowledge of the business they get through this contact, often make speedy advancement.

### THE BUSINESS GIRL'S EQUIPMENT: SHORTHAND

A YOUNG woman entering business cannot do better, in order to qualify herself for a job, than study typewriting and shorthand, subjects which are absolutely necessary for all business girls who wish to obtain secretarial positions. The best way of acquiring a knowledge of shorthand is obviously to attend a good class taught by a good teacher. In fact, for some it is the only way. Others, however, may with success teach themselves the art of sound-writing. They should obtain a guide such as *Pitman's Shorthand Manual* and work very carefully through it. A really earnest student will master the theory in about two or three months. The study itself consists of the mastery of consonants, vowels, diphthongs, position writing, phraseology, circles and loops, initial and final hooks, compound consonants, halving and doubling principles, and grammalogues.

The young person teaching herself should note that the shorthand outlines represent the blended consonant and vowel sound of each word. Shorthand has an "alphabet of sounds." The forms used are stroke consonants, and the signs for showing vowels and diphthongs. Writing "in position" (above, on or through the line) indicates the first vowel. Devices of circles, loops, hooks, and varying lengths of strokes allow forms to be written closer than would be the case without them. Abbreviations and contractions are special forms for common words which make them easier to write than they would otherwise be. Phrasing is a method of joining together special forms into easily written and easily read "phrase outlines."

Shorthand is an art rather than a science. She who would teach herself should press into her service all friends and relatives willing to dictate to her. After she has learnt a definite portion she should ask a friend to dictate to her, so that from the very first start, and each day throughout her study, she is writing from sound. Continual repetition, continual writing drill from dictation, continual copying of shorthand, continual checking, and continual painstaking will bring the enthusiast success. But shorthand is a means and not an end. The end is the transcription. It is not possible to take too much pains in getting shorthand outlines clear and accurate, for otherwise much of the transcript will depend upon guessing. Shorthand writers should also have a thorough acquaintance with commercial and professional terms. Above all, style is very important in correspondence, for it has been truly said that a firm's reputation rests largely on the style of its correspondence.

## WHAT IS EXPECTED OF THE TYPIST

EVERY woman in business should also be able to type. All modern commercial schools have a large range of machines of all kinds on which students are taught by the "touch" method. Those unable to attend such schools may become proficient typists if they obtain a good Typist's Manual and if they practice in the correct manner. They should place covers over the keyboard so as to make it impossible to look at their fingers. Correct fingering is of very great importance. Without it speed is impossible. The "one finger" typist can never develop the highest speed. This method of practice will be slow and irksome at first, but the time spent well repays her who carries it out conscientiously. An expert typist should be able to type every kind of letter and commercial document, and should aim at producing typewritten matter that is flawless and arranged in the most effective and pleasing manner.

The study of English is not generally regarded as a commercial subject, but a good command of English, both written and spoken is perhaps not less important than a good knowledge of typing and of shorthand.

The shorthand-typist must turn out a final product in good English, without spelling or grammatical mistakes, and to eliminate the latter she may have to edit what has in fact been dictated to her. The spoken word is not always grammatical, but what is written should be. She should remember, not only that badly written letters create a bad impression on customers, but also that her own advancement depends on the knowledge and efficiency she shows in doing these things. Nothing betrays an uneducated person more clearly than slipshod English. A director will be favourably impressed by a secretary who tactfully and of her own initiative, without pestering him about it, edits what he has dictated and saves him from falling into a mistake which may be only grammatical, or may be something more serious. Nevertheless, such corrections must be tactful in the extreme and will in every case depend on the temperament of the employer.

## BOOKS THAT HELP IN THE CHOICE OF CAREERS

IT is impossible here to give in any detail the different openings in the various branches of commerce. Those desirous of obtaining detailed information should consult books written to give this information. Young men will find *Careers for our Sons* (A. & C. Black) a mine of information on every appointment at home and abroad, while young women will find equally useful to them the companion volume, *Careers for our Daughters* (A. & C. Black), and *Careers and Vocational Training*, issued by the Central Bureau for Women and Students' Careers Association. His Majesty's Stationery Office publish many books giving similar information, such as the *Choice of Career* Series already referred to.

A very useful and interesting book is published by the Telephone Development Association, entitled *Your Future Job : How to Choose It and Keep It.* The various chapters are written by Dr. G. H. Miles, Sir Francis Goodenough, Sir Woodman Burbridge, B. Seebohm Rowntree, and W. W. Wakefield. There is also a section by Lord Wakefield taken from his invaluable work, *On Leaving School* (Hodder & Stoughton).

# INDEX AND PRONOUNCING GLOSSARY

*by L. M. MONT-CLAR and C. H. KNOWLES, B.Sc.*

HOW TO USE THIS INDEX.—In order to facilitate immediate reference to the principal entry on a particular subject, the page number for this entry is set in italics, thus: *258*. Subsidiary references to the subject which occur elsewhere in the book are indicated by numerals in roman type, thus: 387. References to illustrations are indicated by numerals in roman type surrounded by square brackets, thus: [156]. Cross references given in the index refer only to the index pages.

THE PRONOUNCING GLOSSARY.—Where the pronunciation of proper names and technical terms is not immediately understood from the spelling, or where the spelling may be misleading, a separate pronunciation is given after the first index entry. In simple cases a hint may be considered sufficient; in all doubtful cases a complete phonetic re-spelling is given. The word is broken into syllables as it is spoken, and an accent mark (′) follows the syllable on which the stress is placed. The notation used for the phonetic re-spelling is as follows:

| | | | | | |
|---|---|---|---|---|---|
| ā | m*a*te | ė | th*e*re | th | *th*in |
| ē | m*e*te | å | f*a*ther | TH | *th*ine |
| ī | m*i*te | ẹ | h*e*r | zh | lei*s*ure |
| ō | m*o*te | aw | *aw*l | ch | *ch*ur*ch* |
| ū | m*u*te | oi | *oi*l | g | *g*et |
| ōō | b*oo*t | ow | *ow*l | j | *j*am |

The French nasalised *n* is denoted by italicising the vowel and the nasal concerned, thus: *un*, b*on*, v*in*.